DAVID O. MCKAY LIBRARY
D1180136
DEPOSITORY ITEM
JAN 7 2003
WITHDRAWN
NOV 2 9 2023
PROPERTY OF:
DAVID O. McKAY LIBRARY
DAVID O. McKAY LIBRARY
BYU-IDAHO
REXBURG ID 83460-0405

The Yemens
country studies

Foreign Area Studies
The American University
Edited by
Richard F. Nyrop
Research completed
June 1985

On the cover: Man in popular dress wearing the *jambiyya* (dagger)

Second Edition, 1986; First Printing, 1986

Copyright © 1986 United States Government as represented by the Secretary of the Army. All rights reserved.

Library of Congress Cataloging in Publication Data

The Yemens : country studies.

(DA pam ; 550–183)
Rev. ed. of: Area handbook for the Yemens / coauthors, Richard F. Nyrop . . . [et al.]. 1977.
"Research completed June 1985."
Bibliography: p.
Includes index.
1. Yemen. 2. Yemen (People's Democratic Republic) I. Nyrop, Richard F. II. American University (Washington, D.C.) Foreign Area Studies. III. Area handbook for the Yemens. IV. Series.

DS247.Y4Y46 1985 953'.32 86–1164

Headquarters, Department of the Army
DA Pam 550-183

For sale by the Superintendent of Documents, U.S. Government Printing Office
Washington, D.C. 20402

Foreword

This volume is one of a continuing series of books prepared by Foreign Area Studies, The American University, under the Country Studies/Area Handbook Program. The last page of this book provides a listing of other published studies. Each book in the series deals with a particular foreign country, describing and analyzing its economic, national security, political, and social systems and institutions and examining the interrelationships of those systems and institutions and the ways that they are shaped by cultural factors. Each study is written by a multidisciplinary team of social scientists. The authors seek to provide a basic insight and understanding of the society under observation, striving for a dynamic rather than a static portrayal of it. The study focuses on historical antecedents and on the cultural, political, and socioeconomic characteristics that contribute to cohesion and cleavage within the society. Particular attention is given to the origins and traditions of the people who make up the society, their dominant beliefs and values, their community of interests and the issues on which they are divided, the nature and extent of their involvement with the national institutions, and their attitudes toward each other and toward the social system and political order within which they live.

The contents of the book represent the views, opinions, and findings of Foreign Area Studies and should not be construed as an official Department of the Army position, policy, or decision, unless so designated by other official documentation. The authors have sought to adhere to accepted standards of scholarly objectivity. Such corrections, additions, and suggestions for factual or other changes that readers may have will be welcomed for use in future new editions.

The Director
Foreign Area Studies
The American University
5010 Wisconsin Ave., NW
Washington, D.C. 20016

Acknowledgments

The authors are indebted to numerous individuals in various agencies of the United States government and international and private organizations in Washington, D.C., who gave of their time, research materials, and special knowledge on Yemeni and Arabian affairs to provide data and perspective. The authors are particularly grateful to Dr. Jon Mandaville, president of the American Institute for Yemeni Studies, Dr. John Kennedy, Dr. Dina Dahbany-Miraglia, Dr. Jon Swanson, and Dr. J.E. Peterson, who provided inestimable bibliographic advice and shared their firsthand experiences. In addition, the staff of the Checchi Company was also very helpful. None of the individuals is responsible for the work of the authors, however.

The authors also wish to express their appreciation to members of the Foreign Area Studies staff who contributed to the preparation of the book. These included Denise Ryan and Dorothy M. Lohmann, who edited the manuscript; Harriett R. Blood and Gustavo Adolfo Mendoza, who prepared the maps, charts, and other graphics; and Gilda V. Nimer and Lynn W. Dorn, who provided valuable bibliographic and library assistance. The cover art and illustrations were prepared by Mr. Mendoza. The authors appreciate as well the contributions of Ernest A. Will, publications manager; Eloise W. Brandt and Wayne W. Olsen, administrative assistants; and Rachel Johnson, who prepared the index. The inclusion of photographs was made possible by the generosity of various public and private organizations.

Contents

List of Figures

Preface

Although in the mid-1980s the governments of the two Yemens ostensibly remained committed to eventual unification of the two countries, few observers expected this to occur in the foreseeable future, if ever. The People's Democratic Republic of Yemen (South Yemen) was more closely aligned with the Soviet Union than any other Arab state, and the structure and organization of its government and the Yemen Socialist Party—the sole political party—resembled the Soviet model. The authoritarian regime of the Yemen Arab Republic (North Yemen) relied heavily on the Soviet Union as a source of military equipment and training, but it retained close, albeit frequently strained, relations with the rigorously anticommunist monarchy in Saudi Arabia.

The Yemens: Country Studies replaces the *Area Handbook for the Yemens* published in 1977. Like its predecessor, the present book is an attempt to treat in a compact and objective manner the dominant historical, social, economic, political, and national security aspects of the contemporary societies. Sources of information included scholarly books, journals, and monographs; official reports and documents of government and international organizations; foreign and domestic newspapers and periodicals; and interviews with individuals having special competence in the affairs of the two countries and of the region. The economic and other data available were not always in agreement and were often estimates or approximations.

Brief comments on some of the more valuable sources for further reading appear at the conclusion of each chapter; the bibliography is located in the back of the book. A brief chronology of important events appears in Table A. Measurements are generally given in the metric system; a conversion table is provided to assist those who are unfamiliar with the system (see table 1, Appendix). English usage generally adheres to *Webster's Ninth New Collegiate Dictionary*.

The transliteration of Arabic words and phrases posed a problem. For many of the words—such as Muhammad, Muslim, hadith, and shaykh—the authors followed a modified version of the system adopted by the United States

Board on Geographic Names and the Permanent Committee on Geographic Names for British Official Use, known as the BGN/PCGN system; the modification entails the omission of diacritical markings and hyphens. In numerous instances, however, the names of persons or places are so well known by another spelling that to have used the BGN/PCGN system might have caused confusion. For example, the reader will find Mecca rather than Makkah, Mocha rather than Al Mukha, Hodeida rather than Al Hudaydah, Aden rather than 'Adan, Socotra rather than Suqutra, and Gamal Abdul Nasser rather than Jamal Abd an Nasir.

Arab names are frequently confusing to the Western reader, but they should be viewed as a genealogical chart. For example, the name of the ruler who was deposed at the establishment of North Yemen—Imam Badr—was formally known as Imam al Mansur Billah Muhammad al Badr ibn (or bin) Ahmad Hamid al Din. *Imam al Mansur Billah* were his honorific titles, *ibn* (or *bin*) *Ahmad* indicated that he was a son of Ahmad, and *Hamid al Din* was the family name. (The word *bint* means daughter of, and the word *bani* means sons of, hence tribe or clan. A Yemeni woman rarely takes her husband's name; women's names, like men's, usually include the father's name and possibly the name of the family, clan, or tribe.)

Many names—such as Rahman, Rahim, Azim, and 96 others—are designations of the attributes of God and are common names for males among peninsular Arabs and Muslims everywhere. The names sometimes stand alone and sometimes have modifiers. For example, a popular name is Abd al Rahman (sometimes transliterated as Abdul Rahman or Abdurrahman); *Abd al* means servant or slave of, and *Rahman* means merciful; the name therefore literally means servant or slave of the Merciful (God). The name *Muhammad*, the Prophet or Messenger of God, is probably the most widely used name for males in the world.

*Table A. Chronology of Important Events**

Date	Event
1000 B.C.-A.D. 575	South Arabian kingdoms of Saba, Qataban, Maain, Hadhramaut, and Ausan flourish.
500 B.C.	Construction of great dam at Marib
Late 200s A.D.	Himyarite rule in Saba unites South Arabia under one ruler
Late 300s	Occupation of South Arabia by Ethiopia for 40 years
575	Sassanid emperor Chosros I sends troops requested by dissidents to conquer Sabaean kingdom
628	Iranian satrap in Yemen embraces Islam
661-750	Yemen under Umayyad governors
750-822	Yemen under Abbasid governors
822-1037	Banu Ziyad dynasty rules most of Yemen; instability through most of ninth and tenth centuries because of conflict with Zaydis, Ismailis, and small Yufirid state
Late 800s	Al Hadi ilal Haqq Yahya, founder of Zaydi imamate in Yemen, is invited to mediate among northern tribes
1037-1138	Sulayhid rule in Yemen; in about 1063 Ali al Sulayhi reunites former Himyarite kingdom under indigenous ruler
1138-73	Yemen is ruled by Mahdid Dynasty (indigenous Sunni family)
1173-1232	Saladin's brother takes Yemen in 1173; Ayyubid governors rule until 1232
1232-1446	Rule by Rasulid Dynasty (Sunni)
1446-1517	Rule by indigenous Tafirid Dynasty
1515	Yemen attacked by Mamluks of Egypt
1517-1636	Ottomans rule Yemen (east and southeastern parts) until nationalist uprising under Zaydi imams forces them to abandon South Arabia.
1618	British begin to establish trading center in Mocha
1658	Zaudi Imam Muayyad Muhammad reunites old Himyarite kingdom as far east as Dhofar, the last time all of Yemen under one rule
1731	Lahij and Aden become independent from the Zaydi imams, and areas to the east begin to accept British "protection"
1798	Napoleon overthrows Mamluks of Egypt; British occupy Perim Island
1818	Muhammad Ali, viceroy of Egypt, intervenes in Yemen at the command of the Ottomans
1839	British seize Aden
1840	Ottomans force Muhammad Ali to leave Yemen
1849	Ottomans force Zaydi imam to become their vassal
1857	British occupy Lahij
1873	Ottoman forces in Yemen begin to encroach on areas of British influence

Table A. Continued.

Date	Event
1886	British sign formal protection treaty with Hadhramauti sultan
1891	Beginning of national uprising against Ottoman rule led by Zaydi imam
1911	Treaty of Daan concluded between Imam Yahya and Ottomans
1918	Ottoman forces withdraw from Yemen following their defeat in World War I
1918-54	Thirty-one major treaties of protection and 90 conventions signed between the British and local ruling families
1925	Imam Yahya seizes Hodeida from the Idrisi amirs
1934	Treaty of Sanaa between the British and Imam Yahya; Treaty of Taif between Imam Yahya and King Abd al Aziz of Saudi Arabia
1937	Government of India Act gives Aden status of crown colony
1940s	Opposition group against imam, the Free Yemenis, formed in Aden
1947	Aden Colony Amendment Order creates legislative council in Aden composed of local patriarchs
1948	Imam Yahya assassinated; power seized briefly by group including Free Yemenis; Ahmad becomes imam
Mid-1950s	Local groups opposed to British rule emerge in Aden: South Arabian League, Trade Union Congress (and affiliated People's Socialist Party), and the National Liberation Front
1954	British construct oil refinery in Aden
1955	Minor tax rebellion becomes coup attempt by army chief of staff in Yemen
1956	Jiddah Pact signed in April by Imam Ahmad, President Nasser of Egypt, and King Saud of Saudi Arabia; strikes in Aden throughout year
1957	Increasing number of border incidents early in year between Yemen and area under British authority
1959	New Aden constitution (January); Federation of Arab Amirates of the South created by British (February)
1960	Strikes continue in Aden
1962	Imam Ahmad dies in his sleep (September 19); Under British pressure, Aden Council agrees to join federation (September 26); Military coup in Sanaa (September 26-27); Yemen Arab Republic (North Yemen) established; eight-year civil war begins

Table A. Continued.

Date	Event
1963	On October 14 the NLF declares its determination to lead armed struggle against British rule
1964	Nasser makes first visit to Sanaa and draws up new constitution (April); Nasser and King Faisal of Saudi Arabia meet in Alexandria, but agreement reached not implemented (September)
1965	British suspend Aden constitution and impose direct rule (September); Faisal and Nasser meet in Jiddah and reach agreement on cease-fire, which was not implemented (August); Representatives of republicans and royalists meet at Harad; no agreement reached, conference adjourns, civil war continues (November-December)
1966	British white paper announces intention to withdraw all forces by 1968 and not to sign defense treaty with the Federation of South Arabia (February)
1967	Israel defeats Egypt, Jordan, and Syria in June 1967 War; Last Egyptian troops leave North Yemen (October); Abdallah al Sallal government deposed and replaced by Republican Council under Abd al Rahman al Iryani (November); British withdraw from Aden and NLF takes over, establishing People's Republic of Southern Yemen (South Yemen) (November); Royalist forces begin siege of Sanaa (December)
1968	Royalist siege of Sanaa ends without success (February); North Yemeni army and national guard units clash in Hodeida (March); Fourth Congress of NLF in South Yemen; left gains upper hand; army and police clash with supporters of new NLF program (March); Leftists of NLF oust old leaders; new leadership of "Corrective Revolution" takes form of presidium under Chairman Salim Rubay Ali (June); North Yemeni army and national guard units clash in Sanaa (August)
1970	Jiddah peace conference produces agreement on end to civil war (March); Royalists added to cabinet as part of reconciliation in North Yemen (May); South Yemen changes name to People's Democratic Republic of Yemen (December); Permanent constitution agreed on in North Yemen (December)

Table A. Continued.

Date	Event
1972	South Yemeni National Front (NF) dissolves high command, replacing it with a central committee and political bureau; NF assumes control of communication media (March); Heads of state of two Yemens agree to end conflict (October); Heads of state of two Yemens meet in Tripoli, agree to unify two nations (November)
1974	North Yemen head of state Iryani deposed in military coup, Ibrahim al Hamdi becoming chairman of Military Command Council (June)
1975	In South Yemen the NF joins two smaller parties in United Political Organization under Abd al Fatah Ismail, causing disagreement with Salim Rubay Ali (October)
1976	Opposition group, National Democratic Front (NDF), forms in North Yemen (March)
1977	North Yemen head of state Hamdi assassinated in Sanaa one day before scheduled departure for meeting with South Yemen leaders; Ahmad al Ghashmi takes over (October)
1978	People's Constituent Assembly established in North Yemen (February); Ghashmi named president of republic (May); Ghashmi killed in his office by bomb in briefcase allegedly carried by messenger from South Yemen president, Salim Rubay Ali, who two days later loses power struggle and is executed in Aden; Ali Abdallah Salih becomes president in North Yemen; Ismail takes power in South Yemen (June)
1979	Border clashes between two Yemens escalate into war; mediation by members of League of Arab States results in cease-fire and an agreement to implement 1972 unity accord
1980	Ismail loses power struggle to Ali Nasir Muhammad al Hasani, who becomes chairman of the presidium and secretary-general of the party and who remains prime minister (April)

*Dates before the eighteenth century should be treated as informed estimates.

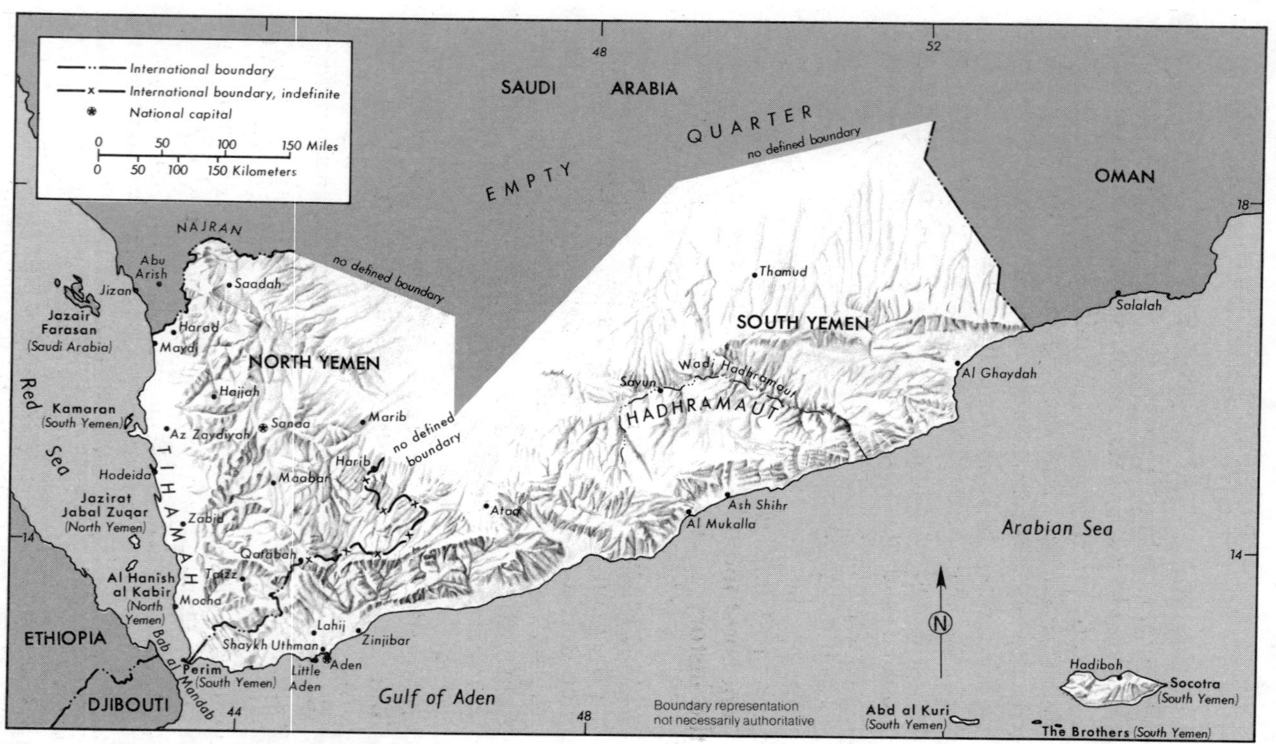

Figure 1. The Yemens, 1985

Introduction

IN ANCIENT TIMES that part of the Arabian Peninsula now occupied by the two Yemens was known as Arabia Felix—happy or prosperous Arabia. It was the source of frankincense and myrrh—gum resins that were highly valued by the civilizations of the eastern Mediterranean Basin—and it was erroneously believed to be the source of spices, silks, precious stones, and a variety of exotic items from South and Southeast Asia that were brought to the commercial and trading centers of the Levant by South Arab merchants. The kingdom of Saba—the biblical Sheba—was but one of several kingdoms that flourished in the area during the first millennium B.C. (see South Arabia in Pre-Islamic Times, ch. 1).

The most important cultural, political, and social event in the history of the Yemens was the coming of Islam. By A.D. 630—only a few years after the Prophet Muhammad began to preach and the same year that he returned to Mecca in triumph—many Yemenis had professed their adherence to Islam, and by the end of the ninth century Islam was the faith of the overwhelming majority. The adoption of Islam did not resolve the problems of tribal autonomy and conflict, however, and in fact may have added to the ancient factionalism of the society, which remained socially and politically significant in the late twentieth century. In the mid-1980s most citizens of the People's Democratic Republic of Yemen (South Yemen) were Sunni Muslims of the Shafii school (see The Shafiis, ch. 1). An estimated 50 percent of the residents of the Yemen Arab Republic (North Yemen) were also Shafii, but the remainder were Shia; most of the Shia were Zaydis, but a few score thousand were Ismailis (see The Ismailis; The Zaydis, ch. 1).

During the late eighth and early ninth centuries, many Zaydis fled the area that became Iraq to the east coast of Africa and the highlands of present-day North Yemen. Within a relatively short period most of the highland tribes either became Zaydis or accepted the suzerainty of the Zaydi imams (see Glossary), who established what became known as the Rassid Dynasty. Although the area was eventually conquered by and became part of the Ottoman Empire, the various imams retained considerable internal autonomy (see Early Islamic Rule in Yemen; Foreign Domination and the Beginnings of Yemeni Nationalism, ch. 1). The last imam—Muhammad al Badr, who was overthrown in 1962—was recognized as the 111th of the Rassid Dynasty to hold the title.

Whereas Ottoman control was sporadic and only occasionally of lasting importance, British rule in what became South Yemen was absolute in some places and important everywhere. British imperial needs had prompted an early interest in the region. The opening of the Suez Canal in 1869 made it essential—from the standpoint of British India and the British presence in the Persian Gulf and East Africa—that the Red Sea, the Bab al Mandab, and the Arabian Sea either be directly controlled by the British or be subject to British influence (see fig. 1). In 1839 the British captured and began to develop the small port of Aden. By 1937, when Aden became a crown colony under the direct rule of the British Colonial Office pursuant to the provisions of the Government of India Act of 1935, Aden had become one of the busiest ports in the world and was a vital link in Britain's global defense strategy.

In the hinterland the British sought with varying success to impose indirect rule, a device that was widely used in British India and in some of Britain's African possessions. In essence, indirect rule meant that the British ruled through scores of local chiefs—variously known as sultans, amirs, or shaykhs and frequently fixed in place by the British in contravention of centuries-old custom—pursuant to individual treaties or analogous agreements. The treaties assigned control over external relations, and therefore over relations among the small states, to the British and left the local rulers with substantial internal autonomy (see Background to Postindependence Politics, ch. 3). The British eventually sought to integrate the states into protectorates and later still into a federation. During the early 1960s, however, the British lost control of the situation to warring factions in the independence movement. By November 1967, when the British left and an independent government was formed, one of the factions—the National Liberation Front (NLF) of South Yemen—had crushed its adversaries and had provoked the exodus of perhaps one-fourth of the population to North Yemen as political refugees (see The Final Year of the British in Aden, ch. 1).

In 1985 North Yemen was governed by leaders who remained heavily dependent upon the support of the country's military forces. Ali Abdallah Salih, a senior army officer, secured power in 1978 after the violent death of the incumbent chief of state, who himself had come to power following the assassination of his predecessor in 1977 (see Political Developments, 1967-78, ch. 2). Salih assumed the office of president of North Yemen, and in 1983 the 159-member People's Constituent Assembly (PCA), an appointed body, elected him for a second five-year term (see Political Institutions, ch. 2). By late 1985 Salih had ruled longer than any of his republican forerunners and had achieved some, albeit far from total, success in extending government control throughout the country. Although there was no elected parliament in late 1985, despite promises that one would be established, Salih sought popular support through the medium of the People's General Congress (PGC); this body, established in 1982 as an instrument of political mobilization and education, had 1,000 members, of whom 700 were popularly elected.

The tribes in the Northern Highlands retained the will and the capacity to resist central government domination, in part because of continued subventions from Saudi Arabia and in part because tribal warriors possessed large supplies of arms and ammunition (see Social Class and Tribe; The Northern Tribes in the mid-1980s, ch. 2). Although Salih did not head a military dictatorship, senior army officers constituted the most powerful interest group; they and the nation's civilian leaders favored the implementation of relatively moderate, fairly conventional domestic and foreign policy goals that were in the mainstream of Arab nationalism.

In sharp contrast to their counterparts in North Yemen, the South Yemeni leaders remained ideologically committed to radical Marxist-Leninist revolution at home and abroad. The Yemen Socialist Party (YSP)—the successor to the NLF and the only legal party—and the government were structured on the Soviet model, although some institutions reflected Cuban experience and influence (see The Yemen Socialist Party, ch. 3).

At the conclusion of the Third Congress of the YSP on October 16, 1985, Ali Nasir Muhammad al Hasani, secretary general of the YSP Central Committee and chairman of the Supreme People's Council Presidium, informed the congress of the results of the Central Committee election of the members of the Political Bureau (Politboro). It is often difficult in the South Yemeni context to distinguish "moderates" from "hardliners" because such little known issues as personality conflicts or loyalties and internal power struggles may be of greater significance than ideological disputes. Nevertheless, foreign observers tended to view eight of the 15 members of the Politboro, of which Ali Nasir was the senior, as potential opponents of Ali Nasir. Abd al Fattah Ismail, who in March had returned from several years in Moscow, was assumed to be in opposition to Ali Nasir, as were Ali Abd al Razzaq Ba Dhib and his brother Abu Bakr Abd al Razzaq Ba Dhib.

The information available to Western observers in the mid-1980s remained sketchy and at times contradictory, but it seemed clear that thousands of officials and technicians from the Soviet Union, the German Democratic Republic (East Germany), and Cuba were serving in numerous South Yemeni government ministries and organizations. International organizations, such as Amnesty International, were generally agreed that the YSP had imposed upon the society a repressive, tyrannical regime that reacted ruthlessly toward dissidents and deviationists. It nevertheless was clear that the Marxist-Leninist rulers had achieved impressive success in expanding educational and health services. At independence in 1967, for example, adult literacy was about 15 percent; by 1985 the government claimed that about 53 percent of all adults were literate, and although the claim may have been somewhat inflated, the nation's educational achievements were no doubt considerable. In contrast, North Yemen's accomplishments were far less impressive. The literacy rate at the time of the creation of the republic in 1962 is not known, but it was very low. By the mid-1980s an estimated 85 percent of the adult population remained illiterate, and some estimates of female illiteracy ran as high as 98 percent.

According to the World Bank (see Glossary), in the 1980s the two Yemens were among the economically least developed countries in the world. In 1983 North Yemen possessed a gross national product (GNP) of about US$4.2 billion—US$510 on a per capita basis, as calculated by the World Bank. The GNP of South Yemen in 1982 was estimated at US$950 million—US$470 on a per capita basis. Both economies remained heavily dependent on foreign aid and on remittances from citizens working abroad, mostly in Saudi Arabia and the smaller states of the Arabian Peninsula. In the early 1980s an estimated 1 million North Yemenis working abroad sent home about US$1.2 billion annually—over one-fourth of the GNP—thereby contributing significantly to the society's disposable income, investments, and growth of imports (see Labor Force; Balance of Payments, ch. 2). In the early 1980s an estimated 100,000 South Yemenis working abroad remitted home about US$467 million—about 50 percent of the nation's GNP—and therefore critically important to the economy (see Balance of Payments, ch. 3). As a result of the worldwide decline in the demand and prices for petroleum products in the 1980s, the economies of the oil-exporting states of the peninsula contracted considerably, and the number of Yemenis working abroad and the amount of money that they sent home presumably declined correspondingly. Confirming data were not available in mid-1985, however.

In the mid-1980s, however, North Yemen discovered oil and showed promise of joining the ranks of the oil exporters, although on a very small scale, according to preliminary evidence. In 1984 the Yemen Hunt Oil Company—consisting of firms from North Yemen, the United States, and the Republic of Korea (South Korea)—announced that it had located commercially exploitable oil fields about 70 kilometers from Marib. North Yemeni officials asserted that production would be between 100,000 and 200,000 barrels per day (bpd) and could reach 300,000 bpd (roughly 14 million tons a year). Additional drilling was under way in 1985 in an effort to determine the extent of the fields, and definitive estimates of the recoverable reserves of oil and gas probably will not be available until late 1985 or 1986. If no additional fields are discovered, the Marib reserves will remain small by world standards, but they will be of major significance to the North Yemeni economy (see Industry, ch. 2). In August 1985 the government created the Ministry of Petroleum and Mineral Resources to manage all aspects of its new oil industry.

Whereas the North Yemeni economy possessed at least the possibility of expansion and improvement as a result of the oil discovery, the South Yemeni outlook was grim. The preindependence economy had been characterized by subsistence agriculture—including limited fishing in one of the richest offshore fishing grounds in the world—and the bustling, prosperous port of Aden. In 1966 about 6,000 ships called at Aden for bunkering and supplies, thereby making a major contribution to the economy. After the Suez Canal was damaged and closed during the June 1967 War between Israel and Egypt, Jordan, and Syria, Aden's port traffic fell sharply, declining to about 1,200 ships in 1974 and to only about 2,360 in 1982.

By 1982 the government's budget deficit was about 41 percent of the GNP, significantly higher than the seriously high North Yemen budget deficit, which reached 28 percent of GNP. Despite—or perhaps because of—government efforts, agriculture continued to provide employment for about 44 percent of the work force but contributed only 12 percent of the gross domestic product (GDP), and food imports accounted for 40 percent of GDP. To finance the huge import bills and the various development efforts, South Yemen depended on foreign loans and credits. In the early 1980s the Soviet Union contributed about 40 percent of all loans and grants, China and East European states about 20 percent, and Arab states and international lending institutions such as the International Monetary Fund (IMF—see Glossary), the remainder. By 1984 South Yemen's external debt exceeded US$1 billion, most of it owed to the Soviet Union and the latter's allies in Eastern Europe. Loans and grants slowed significantly during the early 1980s, and should the loans and grants continue to decrease, the government and the YSP would be forced to abandon various development projects and to impose unpopular austerity measures (see Role of Government, ch. 3).

South Yemen's heavy and increasing economic dependence on the Soviet Union and its close relations with such radical states as Ethiopia and Libya provoked apprehension among the moderate Arab states and some Western powers. The Soviet Union's close relationship with South Yemen included access to military facilities in Aden and elsewhere on the mainland and on the islands of Socotra and Perim. Perim is located in the Bab al Mandab, the strait between the Red Sea—and hence the Suez Canal and the Gulf of Aqaba, the latter being of greater importance to Jordan and Israel—and the Gulf of Aden and the Indian Ocean. The prospect of possible Soviet control of the strategic island remained a matter of concern to South Yemen's neighbors,

Western shipping nations, and the Western and Third World nations that were opposed to Soviet expansion.

During the 1970s and 1980s, relations between the two Yemens vacillated between armed confrontation and effusive professions of Yemeni brotherhood. In the 1979-82 period, the Aden government supported the leftist National Democratic Front (NDF) in its attempts to overthrow the government in Sanaa. This effort failed for both military and political reasons, and in the mid-1980s the leadership in both states affirmed the goal of eventual Yemeni unity. Top officials conferred with each other on a regular basis and in 1982 a joint constitutional commission approved a draft constitution for the projected "Yemeni Republic." This document designated Sanaa as the capital of the new state, Islam as the state religion, and Islamic principles as the basis for its ideology. The combined population—in 1985 an estimated 6 million in North Yemen and 2.1 million in South Yemen—would rival that of Saudi Arabia and presumably would make the new state a major power on the Arabian Peninsula. Even if a common political ideology were achieved, however, which seemed unlikely, a merger of two governments, two military forces, and two civil service establishments would inevitably result in the loss or diminution of status and power for numerous individuals and interest groups in each country. Unification continued to be identified as a laudable goal, but few Yemenis and even fewer foreign observers expected it to occur for many years, if ever.

October 21, 1985 Richard F. Nyrop

During the afternoon of January 13, 1986, the YSP Politburo announced that it had thwarted a coup attempt earlier in the day. According to the announcement, which was broadcast over the government's radio station, a special Politburo committee had tried, convicted, and executed four individuals for their "conspiratorial activities" in connection with the coup attempt. Among those reportedly executed were Ismail and Brigadier General Ali Ahmad Nasir al Bishi (popularly known as Ali Antar), a former defense minister and until February 1985 the first deputy chairman of the Council of Ministers. Shortly after the broadcast the radio station lost its signal, public telecommunication links with the outside world were broken, and the Aden airport was closed.

Earlier in the day the prime minister, Haydar Abu Bakr al Attas, had arrived in New Delhi on the first stage of official visits to India and China. On or about January 15 he and his entourage—which included the foreign minister, Abd al Aziz al Dali—proceeded to Moscow. During the next several days Soviet officials gave every public indication of being uninformed about events in South Yemen and unable to impose a cease fire.

Between January 15 and 23 some 4,000 to 5,500 foreigners—one-half to two-thirds of them Soviets or East Europeans—were evacuated from Aden and other coastal cities. Among the evacuees were diplomats and other trained observers who described unusually fierce fighting in and around Aden betweeen loyalist and rebel forces. According to these reports, large areas of the city had been burned and devastated and an estimated 9,000 to 11,000 people had been killed. A senior diplomat stated that four or more groups that were united only in their opposition to President Ali Nasir were receiving help from rural areas, and the diplomat opined that tribal and personal rivalries, not ideological or doctrinal disputes, were the major causes of the bitter warfare.

On January 25—a few days before this book was delivered to the printer—Prime Minister Attas flew from Moscow to Aden, where the 49-year old civil engineer was greeted by the surviving members of the YSP Central Committee as the interim chief of state; on leaving Moscow he had received a Soviet pledge of support. A YSP spokesperson stated that Ali Nasir had masterminded "a criminal bloody plot to physically liquidate the party's collective leadership and establish a terrorist dictatorial regime." Among those reported dead were Ali Antar, his successor as defense minister Brigadier General Salih Muslih Qasim, and an estimated 50 other YSP officials. As of January 28 the Western press had not yet commented on the fate or whereabouts of Ismail, whose return from Moscow in March 1985 may well have set in train the renewal of intraparty disputes that erupted in violence and strife. And in Sanaa, North Yemen, diplomatic sources speculated that the civil war was not yet over, noting reports that Ali Nasir had returned to his home in Abyan and was rallying loyal soldiers and tribesmen for an attack on Aden (see fig. 12).

January 28, 1986 Richard F. Nyrop

Chapter 1. Historical Setting

Sailing dhow

THE YEMEN ARAB REPUBLIC (NORTH YEMEN) AND THE PEOPLE'S DEMOCRATIC REPUBLIC OF YEMEN (SOUTH YEMEN) have more in common than merely a name. Although ruled as a single unit only rarely—most recently in the seventeenth century—they share a common history at least until the eighteenth century. Even after the coming of British control in the southern and eastern parts of the region, strong links existed between events in the two parts of South Arabia that eventually became North Yemen and South Yemen. They entered the twentieth century under foreign rule, by the Ottomans in the north and the British in the south and east. The contemporary states were born in violence and have been marked, in different ways, by the legacy of their rich history. Although subject to many of the historical trends that influenced the rest of the Arabian Peninsula—including the ancient trade routes, the coming of Islam, and the problems of modernization—Yemeni history has been different from that of the rest of the peninsula.

In pre-Islamic times the area that encompasses both present-day states was called Arabia Felix—happy or prosperous Arabia—by the foreigners envious of such riches as frankincense, myrrh, pearls, silks, and spices, which they thought came from the area known to the Arabs as Al Yaman. In the centuries before the coming of Islam, this area was ruled by a number of indigenous dynasties in several different kingdoms. One of the major early kingdoms was ruled in succession by Jewish, Christian and, finally, Muslim kings.

Several important patterns established in ancient times and during the early centuries of Islamic rule have left their mark on politics, religion, and social life. The persistence of tribal autonomy has been a major factor in modern politics. The isolation of some areas has also led to divergent rates and paths of political and social development. This was accentuated by foreign rule and has affected twentieth-century politics in both Yemens. Even the coming of Islam did not bring tribal autonomy and conflict to an end. In fact, Islam took several forms in Yemen and thus only added to the factionalism.

In what became North Yemen the inaccessible highlands were held by fierce Zaydi tribes that were rarely subject to any foreign domination and accepted some measure of control by the Zaydi imams only under duress. The Sunni tribes of the Tihamah—the coastal plain along the Red Sea—did come under foreign rule from time to time and developed a more advanced commercial life, while losing tribal cohesiveness. Although the Ottomans controlled the lowlands of what became North Yemen and had nominal authority in the Zaydi highlands, Ottoman rule only briefly encroached on the areas the British controlled, the lands that in 1967 became South Yemen. Within this nation as well there were independent tribal areas only loosely administered by Britain. These hinterland areas developed quite differently from the booming port of Aden, which was under direct British rule. Yemeni experiences with foreign rule throughout history were not happy, and the foreign rulers did not prosper—facts that have been insufficiently understood in the twentieth century by states that have sought to influence the course of events in either of the two Yemens.

The citizens of both countries are very aware of their own history, and even their remotest past is preserved in folk traditions. In the late twentieth century, when there existed enough enmities to satisfy even the most ardent factionalist, Yemenis continued to draw from traditions over two millennia old to add further divisiveness to a society that one author describes as remarkable for its "genius for chaos."

It is always necessary to be careful when referring to one of two countries that have very similar names. In the case of the two Yemens, this difficulty has been compounded by historical ambiguity and name changes. When it became independent after World War I, the nation that is now informally known as North Yemen did not formally declare its independence and was simply referred to as Yemen. In 1962 the officers who took over in Sanaa renamed the country the Yemen Arab Republic; this new government (hence the new name) was widely—though not universally—recognized. The nation that is now informally known as South Yemen was referred to by its British rulers first as Aden Protectorate and the Hadrawmawt, became Aden Colony and the Protectorate, then Aden Colony and the semiautonomous Federation of Arab Amirates of the South, then (when Aden joined the federation in 1963) the Federation of South Arabia. Upon independence it was declared the People's Republic of South Yemen. In December 1970 the name was changed to the People's Democratic Republic of Yemen.

For clarity, when referring to either of these two countries in the twentieth century, up to 1967 Yemen will be used in this book to mean North Yemen, and the areas under British rule will be referred to by their individual names (Aden, the Eastern Protectorate, Lahij, etc.). After 1967 the common conventions of North Yemen and South Yemen will be used.

South Arabia in Pre-Islamic Times

In the mid-1980s, investigations of pre-Islamic Arabia were still in an early stage, but archaeologists were already certain that only two of the four geographic and environmental zones of South Arabia were settled in ancient times. The narrow coastal plain along the Red Sea and the Gulf of Aden seems always to have been inhospitable to human habitation. Likewise, the Rub al Khali (Empty Quarter), where present-day Saudia Arabia and the Yemens meet, seems not to have supported a settled population in ancient times (see fig. 1). The two zones in the middle (the mountain ranges that run parallel to the Red Sea coast and then turn eastward along the Gulf of Aden, and the high plateau and valleys that lie between the mountains and the Empty Quarter) contain numerous sites of ancient habitation.

As archaeologist Gus W. Van Beek notes, prehistoric peoples occupied parts of South Arabia during the period equivalent to the Lower Paleolithic era in Europe. Artifacts of what may be the equivalent of the Middle Stone Age have been found at numerous sites in the Wadi Hadhramaut, as have some artifacts associated with the Upper Paleolithic period. Artifacts found in the Empty Quarter and the Wadi Hadramaut indicate that the Neolithic inhabitants were primarily hunters and gatherers, unlike Neolithic peoples farther north. Carbon dating of tools found in the area indicates that the Neolithic period lasted as late as 3000 B.C. in this region.

The first three known Arabian civilizations were coastal settlements. The oldest evidence of civilization in north-

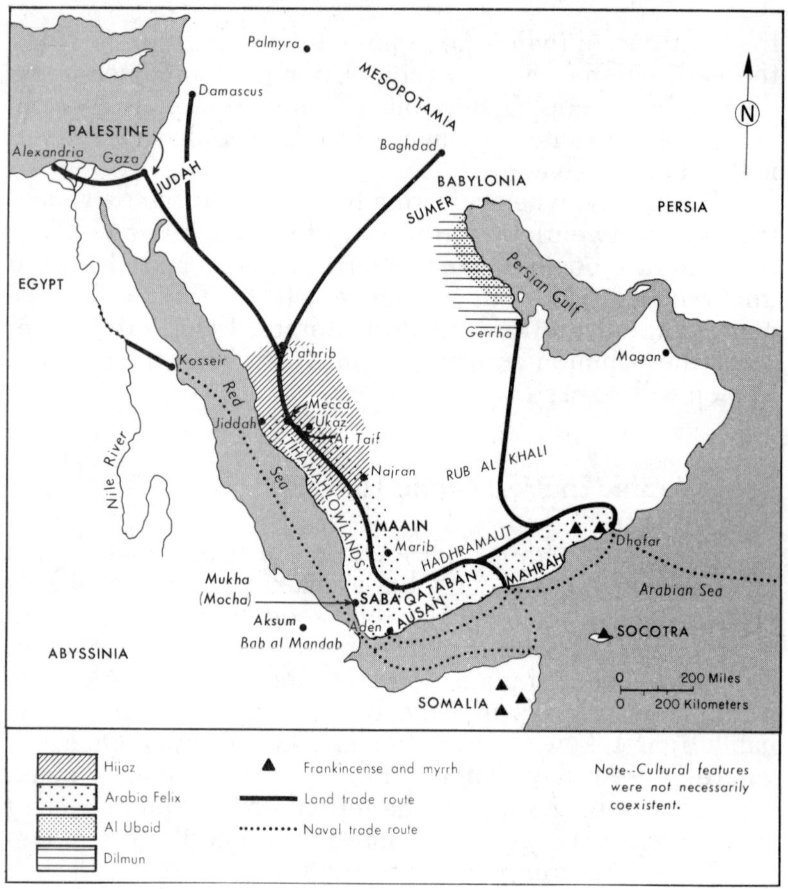

Figure 2. Ancient Arabia

ern Arabia consists of artifacts found 90 kilometers north of Dhahran on the coast of the Persian Gulf. Dated to 5000 B.C., they are identical with those of the Al Ubaid culture of Mesopotamia, the first people to cultivate and settle the Fertile Crescent—the valley of the Tigris and Euphrates, a crescent arching from present-day Kuwait to modern Israel—and the ancestors of the Sumerians, one of the first people to develop a high culture.

From about 4000 to 2000 B.C. the Dilmun civilization dominated about 400 kilometers of the eastern coast of Arabia from present-day Kuwait to Bahrain and extended 90 kilometers into the interior to the oasis of Hufuf in Saudi

Arabia. At its zenith in 2000 B.C., Dilmun controlled the route to the Indies and was the trading link between the civilizations of the Indus Valley and Mesopotamia.

Arabia was only sparsely peopled in the interior. Until about 3000 B.C. inland Arabia was sufficiently verdant to support both cereal agriculturists and herding peoples in the north and hunting and gathering societies in the south. As climatic conditions changed and the desert slowly encroached on land that had formerly supported both animal and human life, the inhabitants were faced with three choices: to cling to the inland oases, to move to the coasts, or to leave Arabia entirely. Those who made the third choice and migrated to the north, northeast, and southwest are the only ones who left a historical record in this millennium.

Sometime in the third millennium peoples of Mesopotamia and Egypt discovered that the area of southern Arabia possessed two unique and desirable aromatic gum resins, which were grown only in Dhofar and its colonies of Somalia and Socotra (see fig. 2). Frankincense, an essential element in certain Jewish and other religious rituals, was burned as an offering to the gods. It was used lavishly in cremation services and in Egypt for embalming. Pliny the Elder noted that at the funeral of Nero's wife an entire year's harvest was burned. Frankincense also has healing properties; it was used as an antidote to poisons and to stop hemorrhages. Myrrh was the foundation of many cosmetics and perfumes and was also used medicinally in poultices and ointments to relieve inflammation and heal wounds. With so many uses and in such short supply, these resins were as precious as gold in the centuries preceding the beginning of the Christian era.

For almost two millennia foreigners dominated and controlled this trade until descendants of Arabian migrants, attracted by the products of southern Arabia, returned from the area that is present-day eastern Jordan and southern Iraq to their ancestral homeland. These migrants from the Fertile Crescent had benefited from the diaspora of their ancestors into Mesopotamia. They were familiar with the institutions of urban life and brought with them irrigation techniques, metallurgical and ceramic skills, an alphabetic script, a complex religion, and a developed art. They arrived in two waves: one before 1400 B.C. and one about 1200 B.C.

Five kingdoms flourished in South Arabia during the first millennium B.C. Saba (Sheba) with its capital at Marib, Qataban with its capital at Timna, and Hadhramaut with its capital at Shawba were the earliest of the three kingdoms. Maain with its capital at Qarnaw, and Ausan in the mountains between Qataban and Aden, appeared somewhat later, around the middle of the first millennium B.C. Each kingdom enjoyed periods of prosperity and predominance. Historians and archaeologists have differed on the periods of dominance of each of these kingdoms but, in general, the ascendancy of the western kingdoms (Saba, Qataban, and Maain) was successive, while Hadramaut, to the east, had periods of importance at the same time as some of the western kingdoms.

Although thousands of monument inscriptions in the graceful, symmetrical script of the ancient language of southern Arabia are available to scholars, most consist of personal names. As Van Beek suggests, scholars know the names of most of the rulers in southern Arabia from the first millennium B.C. until the sixth century A.D., but few inscriptions provide any insight into the history of the region.

It is known that these five kingdoms possessed a common culture, and the fact that the ancient towns of the region were unfortified suggests that they enjoyed comparative peace, perhaps because of their isolation from the less tranquil areas to the north: Egypt, Israel, Assyria, Babylonia, Persia, and Greece. The southern region was the only area of the peninsula that was agriculturally self-sufficient. The people imported mostly luxury items for their own use, seldom foodstuffs. This was possible because they capitalized on the potential of their area by using an ingenious irrigation system. Van Beek notes that the "system was not based on the exploitation of perennial rivers, as in Mesopotamia and Egypt, but instead capitalized on the runoff water from the region's infrequent rains . . . the dams of southern Arabia never retained water in a reservoir system but served only to deflect the runoff from the occasional rains into irrigation canals."

The largest and most famous dam was constructed around 500 B.C. near Marib. It provided irrigation for some 1,600 hectares, which agricultural experts suggest could have supported a population of about 300,000. Sections of its 600-meter face, canals, and sluices can still be seen. Traces of stone sluices, canals, and dams have been found in all the arable valleys of the inland side of the South Arabian watershed.

A huge and complex commercial network comprising both land and sea routes was established by the people of southern Arabia. In addition to their own exports they became the middlemen for trade from India and the Horn of Africa. Customers of the Arabian market assumed that all the goods were products of Arabia, hence the designation of the area by ancient writers as Arabia Felix. Among the items of trade were pearls from the Persian Gulf; spices, textiles, and swords from India; Chinese silk, slaves, monkeys, and ivory; and Ethiopian gold and ostrich feathers.

The Indian Ocean trade was carried to Arabia by ships and from Aden was transported largely overland to the markets of the western Mediterranean, Mesopotamia, and Egypt. Navigation on the northern part of the Red Sea was dangerous because of monsoon winds; therefore, goods for Egypt were usually transported halfway by sea and then transferred to overland caravans. Caravan cities, colonies of southern Arabia, developed along these trade routes and became the nuclei for the important cities of the Hijaz in the medieval period. The use of the camel as a carrier and the development of such caravan cities as Mecca, Yathrib (present-day Medina), Palmyra, and Petra formed a part of the legacy of the southern Arabs to the north that eventually enabled the north to succeed to mercantile supremacy. Because demand for South Arabian products grew, prices rose, trade routes increased, and the transportation of goods became organized under stricter control. Increased trade was possible because of more effective use of the camel, which had originally been domesticated by the southern Arabs as a dairy animal.

The Sabaeans, a desert tribe to the north, were the first southern Arabs to control the inland trade route. More accustomed than some of the southern and more strictly commercial tribes to the intricacies of tribal politics, the Sabaeans established a confederation of tribes, each under a local chieftain who was responsible for frankincense production and transport in his area. The Sabaeans developed an elaborate political and administrative system; their capital, originally east of Sanaa, was later moved to Marib, an area with natural defenses.

In the first period of Sabaean dominance in South Arabia, toward the end of the fifth century B.C., a federation was formed under Sabaean rule that included most areas of South Arabia. Robert Stookey, a specialist on Yemeni affairs, notes that the Ptolemaic explorer, Anixicrates, sent by Alexander the Great in 322 B.C. to explore the Arabian Peninsula, found complete Sabaean domination of South Arabia and made no mention of any other state in the area.

By the third century B.C. this unity had disappeared as the kingdoms of Hadhramaut, Qataban, and Maain reasserted themselves. The geographer Eratosthenes, writing in the third century B.C., described four equal and prosperous kingdoms. Monument inscriptions from this period of Sabaean decline refer with increasing frequency to the Hamdan tribal federation—the Hashid and Bakil tribes. These tribes figured prominently in Yemeni politics well into the twentieth century.

Two developments in the first century of the Christian era were to prove damaging to the trade that had made southern Arabia prosper. Various scholars have noted that during the reign of Emperor Claudius (A.D. 41–54) a Roman ship by chance was blown from the Yemeni coast all the way to Ceylon (present-day Sri Lanka). The Romans learned in this way that many of the goods they had imported from Arabia came, in fact, from lands to the east. When, in the following generation, a Roman discovered the pattern of the monsoon winds, Roman ships began to sail directly to India and the east, bypassing the South Arabian ports that had thrived as a result of this trade.

Roman encroachment on the trade routes coincided with the rise of the kingdom of Aksum (or Axum) in Ethiopia and with a long period of warfare in South Arabia. Although these events probably were involved in the ultimate decline of Arabia Felix, their effect did not become clear for more than a century. South Arabia continued to enjoy prosperity until at least the beginning of the fourth century A.D. Indeed, it was only at the end of the third century A.D. and the assumption of power in Saba by the Himyarite tribe that South Arabia was unified for the first time under one ruler. Alleged descent from this ancient dynasty was one of the genealogical claims of the twentieth-century rulers of North Yemen to legitimate authority in all of Yemen.

Several events of the fourth century, combined with what had happened in the previous 200 years to Yemeni trade routes and tranquillity in South Arabia as a whole, helped bring to an end the independent Himyarite kingdom of Saba. The proclamation of Christianity as the religion of the Roman Empire by Constantine in 323 was the death knell of South Arabia's frankincense market. The small demand for church ceremonies and medicine did not compensate for the vast quantities no longer consumed in funerary rites, now officially banned. Only four years after Constantine's proclamation, Ethiopia began to be converted to Christianity. Ethiopia occupied South Arabia for some 40 years. Although the Himyarites were able to throw off Ethiopian rule before the end of the fourth century, Stookey suggests that foreign occupation may have had at least two important effects on the subsequent political development of South Arabia. The success of the Ethiopian invasion damaged the credibility of the many tribal gods who had failed in their duty to ensure victory in battle and to safeguard the community, and the occupation by the newly Christianized Ethiopians may have "encouraged the innovative idea that the coercive propagation of particular forms of worship is an appropriate function of the state."

The first monotheists in Yemen were almost certainly Jews, who (according to the ancient traditions of Yemeni Jews) entered the area before the destruction of the First Temple in the sixth century B.C. or, as some scholars suggest, after the destruction of Jerusalem by Titus in A.D. 70. In any case, the first Christian missionaries to Yemen in the fourth century found well-established Jewish communities within the predominantly polytheist environment. Although Christian legend suggests that the Apostle Thomas visited Yemen on his way to India, it is likely that the first Christian missionary was sent by the patriarch Theophilus in the years 341–46. Christianity arrived in Yemen during the Ethiopian occupation, but not because of it.

In the latter half of the fourth century a prince of the deposed Himyarite Dynasty liberated the kingdom of Saba from Ethiopian domination. He is said to have been a monotheist of some sort, and there is some certainty that his son was a Jew. It was under the Jewish Himyarite kings that the kingdom of Saba, during its last 100 years, reached its greatest territorial extent, including even Najd (in present-day Saudi Arabia). These kings also exerted mighty efforts to repair flood damage to the great dam at Marib. The effects of diminished trade, however, as well as the loss of frankincense revenues and the rise of the Byzantines and the Iranian Sassanids, threatened the independence of the Sabaean kingdom. The last of the Jewish kings of Saba, Yusuf Ashaar Dhu Nuwas, was famous for his zealous efforts to propagate the faith. Legends, as well as Christian and Muslim writings, tell of his campaign against the Christian community of Najran, where he demanded that the inhabitants renounce their faith or die. It is reported that the majority refused apostasy, and 20,000 were cast into pits of burning oil. According to Stookey, the "survivors spread news of the atrocity as far as Byzantium, which countenanced massacres of Christians only by other Christians of the established sect, and was horrified. The emperor urged the king of Aksum to intervene against Dhu Nuwas." Under the leadership of Emperor Caleb, the Ethiopians reoccupied Yemen in 525, although another revolt 10 years later removed the Ethiopians and left the area under only the nominal authority of Aksum.

This time the new ruler of the declining kingdom, Abraha, was a militant Christian who ruled until the Sassanid emperor Chosros I sent a force requested by dissident Himyarites in 575 to bring the Sabaean kingdom to an end. Before its demise, however, Abraha made the last efforts to repair the dam at Marib and was even reported to have taken a military force mounted on elephants to attack the polytheist shrines at Mecca.

The year of Abraha's famous attack on Mecca was a major turning point in the history of southern Arabia. Called in Arab tradition the "Year of the Elephant" because of Abraha's unsuccessful foray north into Arabia, two other important events are said to have occurred that year. The great dam at Marib collapsed for the last time, forcing those who depended upon it to migrate elsewhere. The third event, held by Arab tradition to have occurred in 570, ushered in the greatest change in the history of Arabia and the major turning point in Yemeni history—the birth at Mecca of the Prophet Muhammad. Even before the end of the half-century of Iranian occupation, Yemen came under Islamic rule when the Iranian satrap, Badhan, embraced Islam in 628.

The pattern of tribal divisiveness and the strongly polarized geographic and religious allegiances that characterized Yemen through the 1960s were already established in its pre-Islamic period. The ancient oligarchic kingdoms, intent only on securing wealth, had never attempted to organize or control the region further than was necessary to protect commercial interests. With each succeeding rule the tribes were granted more local autonomy, circumscribed only when their accustomed anarchy threatened the ruling power. The Islamization of the area, which would occur in the seventh century, instead of creating a larger association of allegiance produced further factionalism without erasing the old animosities. A tradition already existed among southern Arab tribes to call upon a respected outsider as an arbiter in tribal disputes. This concept would play a major role in religion and politics in Yemen and became even more deeply rooted after the coming of Islam, when those called upon to settle such disputes were descendants of the Prophet.

Among the genealogical claims of the imams (see Glossary) of Yemen was one that they often asserted as an argument for their legitimacy to rule over all of southern Arabia—that they were descendants of the Himyarite kings. As a symbol of the claim, the imams continued into the 1960s to sprinkle red powder on their signatures and ciphers (*ahmar*, meaning red, is an element in the word *Himyar*). Other customs remain from this remote period: the Grand Council of Maain, a meeting of the Banu (see Glossary) Maain, has continued to meet for over a millennium; in North Yemen the Banu Saba and Banu Hamdan, descendants of the enemies of the Himyar, still exist in considerable numbers and remain aware of the ancient rivalry; and in Aden an important nationalist family named Luqman traces itself to Luqman ibn (see Glossary) Ali, the king reputed to have built the Marib Dam.

In addition to the factions that arose out of religious and political affiliations, the southern Arabs entered the Islamic period with a sense of an ethnic distinction between themselves and all other Arabs to explain the differences of language, custom, and physiognomy. Popular belief held and still holds that although all Arabs are descended from a common ancestor, Sham ibn Nuh (Shem, son of Noah), the "pure" or southern Arab (Qahtani) is descended from Qahtan ibn Abir (Joktan ben Eber), or Hud, as he is often called, whereas the northern Arab (Adnani) is descended from Ismail (Ishmael) through Adnan. Other Arab nationals, particularly those of tribal societies, know or think they know to which group they belong but are little concerned about it, but this split is a matter of importance to Yemenis, and many twentieth-century feuds can be traced back to it. The imams of Yemen claimed Qahtani descent as a consequence of their alleged descent from the Himyar, although they were in fact Adnanis if, as they did, they also claimed to be descendants of the Prophet Muhammad through his grandson Hassan. Author Manfred Wenner points out that both claims are possible as a result of intermarriage.

Islam

Tenets

In A.D. 610 Muhammad (later known as the Prophet), a merchant belonging to the Hashimite branch of the ruling Quraysh tribe in the Arabian town of Mecca, began to preach the first of a series of revelations granted him by God through the angel Gabriel. A fervent monotheist, Muhammad denounced the polytheism of his fellow Meccans. Because, however, the town's economy was based in large part on the thriving pilgrimage business to a shrine called the Kaabah and numerous polytheist religious sites located there, this vigorous and continuing censure eventually earned him the bitter enmity of the town's leaders. On September 24, 622, he and a group of followers were invited to the town of Yathrib, which came to be known as Medina (from Madinah al Nabi—the Prophet's City) because it became the center of his activities. The move, or hijra (see Glossary), known in the West as the Hegira, marks the beginning of the Islamic era and of Islam as a force on the stage of history; the Muslim calendar, based on a 354-day year, begins in 622. In Medina Muhammad continued to preach, eventually defeated his detractors in battle, and consolidated both the temporal and the spiritual leadership of all Arabia in his person. He entered Mecca in triumph in 630 and returned there to make the pilgrimage shortly before his death in 632.

After Muhammad's death his followers compiled those of his words regarded as coming directly and literally from God as the Quran, the holy scripture of Islam; others of his sayings and teachings and the precedents of his personal behavior, recalled by those who had known him during his lifetime, became the hadith. Together they form the Sunna, a comprehensive guide to the spiritual, ethical, and social life of the orthodox Muslim.

The Shafiis of the Yemens, as Sunni Muslims, adhere to the tenets of the Sunna (see The Shafiis, this ch.). The Shias, however, differ in some respects (see The Zaydis; The Ismailis, this ch.). The *shahada* (literally, testimony or creed) succinctly states the central belief of Islam: "There is no god but God (Allah), and Muhammad is his Prophet." This simple profession of faith is repeated on many ritual occasions, and recital in full and unquestioning sincerity designates one a Muslim. The God preached by Muhammad was not one previously unknown to his countrymen, for *Allah* is Arabic for *God* and is not a particular name. Rather than introducing a new deity, Muhammad denied the existence of the many minor tribal gods and spirits worshiped before his ministry and declared the omnipotence of the unique creator. God exists on a plane of power and sanctity above any other being; to associate anything with him in any visual symbol is a sin. Events in the world flow ineluctably from his will; to resist it is both futile and sinful.

Islam means submission (to God), and he who submits is a Muslim. Muhammad is the "seal of the prophets"; his revelation is said to complete for all time the series of biblical revelations received by the Jews and the Christians. God is believed to have remained one and the same throughout time, but humans had strayed from his true teachings until set aright by Muhammad. True monotheists who preceded Islam are known in Quranic tradition as *hanifs*; prophets and sages of the biblical traditions, such as Abraham, Moses, and Jesus (known in Arabic as Ibrahim, Musa, and Isa), are recognized as inspired vehicles of God's will. Islam, however, reveres as sacred only the message, rejecting Christianity's deification of the messenger. It accepts the concepts of guardian angels, the Day of Judgment (last day), general resurrection, heaven and hell, and eternal life of the soul.

The duties of the Muslim form the five pillars of the faith. These are the recitation of the creed (*shahada*), daily prayer (*salat*), almsgiving (*zakat*), fasting (*sawm*), and pilgrimage (*haj*). The believer is to pray in a prescribed manner after purification through ritual ablutions each day at dawn, midday, midafternoon, sunset, and nightfall. Prescribed body movements, including genuflections and prostrations, accompany the prayers, which the worshiper recites while facing toward Mecca. Whenever possible, men pray in congregation at the mosque under a prayer leader and on Fridays are obliged to do so. The Friday noon prayers provide the occasion for weekly sermons by religious leaders. Women may also attend public worship at the mosque, where they are segregated from the men, although most frequently those who pray do so at home. A special functionary, the *muadhdhin*, intones a call to prayer to the entire community at the appropriate hour; those out of earshot determine the proper time from the sun. Daily prayer consists of specified glorifications of God. Prayers seeking aid or guidance in personal difficulties must be offered separately.

In the early days of Islam, the authorities imposed *zakat* as a tax on personal property proportionate to one's wealth; this was distributed to the mosques and to the needy. In addition, freewill gifts (*sadaka*) were made. Although it has become a private matter in most Islamic lands, *zakat* remained a public duty for the believer in Yemen until 1962. The government collected *zakat* in the form of a tax. Furthermore, many properties contributed by pious individuals to support religious and charitable activities or institutions have traditionally been administered as inalienable religious foundations (waqfs). Such endowments support various charitable activities.

The ninth month of the Muslim calendar is Ramadan, a period of obligatory fasting in commemoration of Muhammad's receipt of God's revelation, the Quran. Throughout the month all but the sick, the weak, soldiers on duty, menstruating, pregnant, or lactating women, travelers on necessary journeys, and young children are enjoined from eating, drinking, smoking, and sexual intercourse during daylight hours. Those adults excused are obliged to endure an equivalent fast at their earliest opportunity. In many places in the Muslim world a festive meal breaks the daily fast and inaugurates a night of feasting and celebration. The pious well-to-do usually do little or no work during this period, and some businesses close for all or part of the day. Because the months of the lunar calendar revolve through the solar year, Ramadan falls at various seasons in different years. Though a considerable test of discipline at any time of year, a fast that falls in summertime imposes severe hardships on those who must do physical work or travel in the desert. Frayed tempers and poor work performances are annual concomitants of the fast.

Finally, all Muslims at least once in their lifetime should if possible make the *haj* to the holy city of Mecca to participate in special rites held there during the twelfth month of the lunar calendar. Those who have completed the *haj* merit the honorific *haji*. The Prophet instituted the requirement, modifying pre-Islamic custom to emphasize sites associated with Allah and Abraham, founder of monotheism and father of the northern Arabs through his son Ismail. In Islamic belief Abraham offered to sacrifice Ismail, son of the servant woman Hagar, rather than Isaac, son of Sarah, as described in the Bible.

The permanent struggle for the triumph of the word of God both within oneself and between people, the jihad, represents an additional general duty of all Muslims, construed by some as the sixth pillar. In addition to specific duties, Islam imposes a code of ethical conduct encouraging generosity, fairness, honesty, and respect and forbidding adultery, gambling, usury, and the consumption of carrion, blood, pork, and alcohol.

A Muslim stands in a personal relationship to God; there is neither intermediary nor clergy in orthodox Islam. Those who lead prayers, preach sermons, and interpret the law do so by virtue of their superior knowledge and scholarship rather than because of any special powers or prerogatives conferred by ordination.

Early Development

During his lifetime Muhammad held both spiritual and temporal leadership of the Muslim community; he established the concept of Islam as a total and all-encompassing way of life for humanity and society. Islam teaches that Allah revealed to Muhammad the immutable principles governing decent behavior, and it is therefore incumbent upon the individual to live in the manner prescribed by revealed law and upon the community to perfect human society on earth according to the holy injunctions. Islam traditionally recognized no distinction between religion and state. Religious and secular life merged, as did religious and secular law.

Islam recognizes that the Prophet Muhammad was the last of the line of prophets that includes Abraham, Moses, Jesus, and others from the Jewish and Christian traditions. The Prophet, however, was also the spiritual and secular leader of the Muslim community (*umma*). After Muhammad's death it was necessary to select a successor to administer the *umma* and to lead prayers and decide questions on which the Quran was not explicit. The Prophet neither designated his successor nor decreed how a successor should be chosen, and as a result there was some difficulty in agreeing upon a new leader. Some members of the *umma* felt that Muhammad's successor should be a close blood relative of the Prophet, i.e., Ali, who was a member of the Hashimite line, the Prophet's father's brother's son, and the husband of Fatima, Muhammad's sole surviving daughter. Other Muslims believed such kinship was not a necessary prerequisite and held that the caliph (from *khalifa*—successor) should be chosen by the community. A split in the ideally egalitarian and harmonious *umma* developed over this issue; the rift would in time enlarge and generate the two major divisions of Islam: Shia, from Shiat Ali—the party of Ali—and Sunni, from men of the Sunna and Jamaa, i.e., those who favored a leader chosen by the community.

Some of the reasons for the divisiveness were political. Aisha, Muhammad's favorite living wife, was the opponent of both Fatima, Muhammad's daughter by a different wife, and Ali. Aisha supported the election of her father, Abu Bakr (also one of the Prophet's earliest followers and closest friends), to succeed her late husband. She and her allies won the political battle, and Abu Bakr was chosen caliph by the consensus of the leaders of the *umma*. S. Husain M. Jafri, an Islamic scholar, contends that the as yet minor rupture in the *umma* antedated Islam and had its roots in the north-south religious, political, and tribal differences within the Arabian Peninsula—the Adnani and Qahtani. Abu Bakr was apparently quite popular, and Ali and his supporters recognized Abu Bakr's legitimacy. Historical events after Abu Bakr's death tended to solidify the Sunni-Shia political and ideological differences.

Umar, who succeeded in 634, and Uthman, who took power in 646, enjoyed the recognition of the entire community. Dissatisfaction with the rule of Uthman began to mount in various parts of the Islamic empire, however. For example, the codification of the Quran, which took place under Uthman, hurt the interests of the professional Quran reciters. Some, such as those at Al Kufah in what is present-day Iraq, refused to go along with this reform. Others accused Uthman of nepotism. Although himself an early Muslim, Uthman came from the Banu Umayyah lineage of the Quraysh, who had been Muhammad's main detractors in Mecca and had resisted him for a long time. The appointment of many members of this house to official posts naturally caused resentment among those who had claims based on earlier loyalty. Still others objected to corruption in financial arrangements under Uthman's caliphate.

Ali, with his frustrated claim to the caliphate, became a perfect focus for dissatisfaction. In 656 disgruntled soldiers killed Uthman. After the ensuing five years of civil war, known to most Muslims as *fitnah* (the time of trials), the caliphate finally devolved on Ali. Aisha, continuing her earlier rivalry, objected, demanding that Uthman's killing be avenged and his killers punished by the Hashimites.

The killers insisted that Uthman, by ruling unjustly, had relinquished his right to be caliph and deserved to die. Ali, whose political position depended on their action and their support, was forced to side with them. From his capital at Al Kuhaf he refused to reprimand the killers.

At this point Muawiyah, the governor of Syria and a member of the Banu Umayyah, refused to recognize Ali's authority and called for revenge for his murdered kinsman, Uthman. Ali attacked, but the Battle of Siffin was inconclusive. Muawiyah's soldiers advanced with copies of the Quran on their spears, thus calling symbolically for God to decide or for the question to be submitted to arbitration. Ali agreed to this settlement, and each side selected an arbitrator. Some of Ali's supporters rejected the notion that the caliph, the Prophet's successor and head of the community, should submit to the authority of others. By so doing, they reasoned, he effectively relinquished his authority as caliph. They further argued that the question of Uthman's right to rule had been settled by war. When Ali insisted on his course, the group seceded and came to be known as the Kharajites; they withdrew to Haura, near Al Kufah, and chose their own leader.

The arbitration went against Ali in 658. He refused to accept the decision but did not renounce the principle of arbitration. At this point the Kharajites became convinced that personal interest, not principle, motivated Ali. His support dwindled, and he tried unsuccessfully to attack Syria. Muawiyah gained in battle, and in 661 a Kharajite murdered Ali.

His death ended the last of the so-called four orthodox caliphates and the period when the entire community of Islam recognized a single head. Muawiyah then proclaimed himself caliph from Damascus. The Shiat Ali, however, refused to recognize Muawiyah or the Umayyad line. They withdrew, and in the great schism of Islam proclaimed Hassan, Ali's son, the caliph. Hassan, however, eventually relinquished his claim in favor of Muawiyah and went to live in Medina, supported by wealth apparently supplied by Muawiyah.

The breach between supporters of the Alid (an adjective derived from Ali) claims and Sunnis was by this time too wide to be repaired by Hassan's actions. In 680 Yazid I, Muawiyah's son, succeeded to the caliphate with the support of his father, who was still alive. Ali's younger son, Husayn, refused to recognize the succession and revolted at Al Kufah. He was unable to gain widespread support, however, and was killed along with a small band of soldiers at Karbala in Iraq in 680. To the Shia, Husayn became a martyred hero, a tragic reminder of the lost glories of the Alid line, and the repository of the Prophet's family's special right to the caliphate. The political victor of this second period of *fitnah* was Marwar of the Umayyad line, but Husayn's death aroused increased interest among his supporters, enhanced by feelings of guilt and remorse and a desire for revenge.

The Shias founded their objections to the Umayyad and later non-Shia caliphs on a notion that members of the house of Muhammad, through Ali, were the most appropriate successors to his positions both as political leader and, more important, as prayer leader. Many believed that Ali, as a close associate, early had a special insight into the Prophet's teachings and habits. In addition, many felt that he deserved the post because of his personal merits and because they believed that the Prophet had expressed a wish that Ali succeed him. In time these views became transformed for many Shias into an almost mystical reverence for the spiritual superiority of Ali's line. Some Shias also believe that Muhammad had left a written will naming Ali his successor but that this was destroyed by Ali's enemies, who then usurped leadership.

Because the correct selection of the imam was the crucial issue over which the Shias departed from the main body of Sunni Islam, the choice of later successors also became a matter of conflict. Disagreements over which of several pretenders had the truer claim to the mystical power of Ali precipitated further schisms (see The Zaydis; The Ismailis, this ch.).

The early political rivalry remained active as well. Shiism eventually gained numerical dominance in Bahrain, Iran, and Iraq, as well as in North Yemen. Shias are also numerous in Syria and are found in varying numbers in most present-day Muslim countries.

The early Islamic polity was intensely expansionist, motivated both by dedication to the new religion and by economic and social factors. Conquering armies and migrating tribes expanded from Arabia, spreading Islam by military triumph and by suasion. By the end of Islam's first century, Islamic armies had reached far into North Africa and eastward and northward into Asia. The Prophet is reported to have sent Ali on a mission to Yemen, and Ali is credited with converting a large number of Yemenis. Muhammad also is said to have sent Muadh to convert the Yemenis. In local belief this ministry resulted in the construction of the mosque at Al Janad in North Yemen, said to be the first built outside the Hijaz, Muhammad's native region.

Muhammad enjoined the Muslim community to convert polytheists, but he also recognized the special status of the People of the Book, Jews and Christians, whose revealed scriptures he considered perversions of God's true word but nevertheless in some sense contributory to Islam. These peoples, approaching but not yet having achieved the perfection of Islam, were spared the choice offered the polytheists—conversion or death. Jews and Christians in Muslim territories could live according to their own religious law and in their own communities if they accepted the position of dhimmis, or tolerated subject peoples. This status entailed recognition of Muslim authority, special taxes, prohibition of proselytism among Muslims, and certain restrictions on social, economic, and political rights. The Zaydi imams and the city of Aden were said to have been particularly hospitable to Jews, whose communities in South Arabia antedated Islam, although Jews suffered political, economic, and social discrimination in keeping with Islamic law. Sizable communities of Jewish artisans and farmers lived in Yemen until they migrated to Israel in the 1949–50 period, although a good deal of migration to Palestine occurred before 1948. As of 1971 a small Jewish community consisting, according to various estimates, of 2,000 to 9,000 people continued to reside in the Saadah area.

The first centuries of Islam saw the Muslim community grow from a small and despised cult to a powerful empire ruling vast domains. They also saw the evolution of sharia, a comprehensive system of religious law to regulate life within the community. Derived from the Quran and the hadith by various systems of reasoning, four schools of religious law—the Hanafi, Shafii, Maliki, and Hanbali—are generally recognized; each Sunni Muslim theoretically acknowledges the authority of one of them.

With the passage of centuries Islam gradually absorbed influences from sources other than the prophetic revelation. Pre-Islamic practices reappeared; people in the Arabian Peninsula resumed venerating trees and stones, although they maintained their identification with the Muslim community. Various holy men, especially those who claimed descent from the Prophet, achieved reputations for exceptional spiritual or magical powers. Pre-Islamic beliefs in the inheritance of special spiritual powers in certain family lines blended smoothly into popular Islam. Stories of miracles circulated, and people began visiting those individuals or their graves to seek cures, fulfillment of wishes, or other favors. Tombs of holy men maintained by the holy lineages of their descendants remain important in the Yemens, especially in Shafii communities. In many cases the tomb of a holy man became the focus of a *hawtah*, or holy place of sanctuary. As in the essentially similar Haram of Mecca, founded by the Prophet, violence is forbidden within the sacred precincts, and members of possibly hostile tribes can worship together in safety.

In the beginning of the eighth century, bands of mystics, or Sufis (from *suf*, wool, of their rough clothing), sprang up in various countries, claiming to achieve communion with God through various ecstatic means. In most regions, including South Arabia, people fell away from the austere cult preached by Muhammad and adopted practices that made it more personal and emotional. Sufi orders gradually arose among both Sunnis and Shias, their leaders teaching particular mystic ways to God. Sufism gained ac-

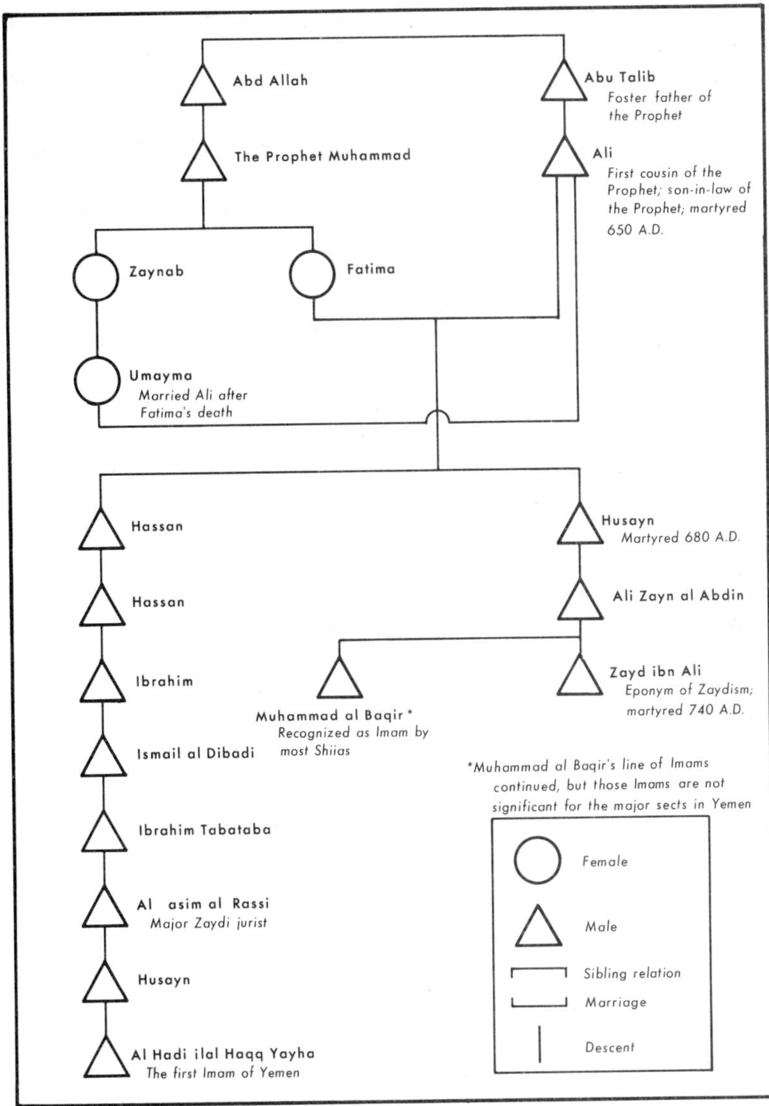

Figure 3. Family History of Muslim Religious Figures Important in Yemen

ceptance in large parts of the Islamic world. Sufism tends to be more widespread among Sunnis, however, because most Shia sects embrace mysticism and encourage emotional responses to God and to Shia martyrs. Thus, members of Shia groups may not feel the need for the additional ecstatic experience provided by Sufism.

Sufi religious life generally centers on orders or brotherhoods that follow a leader, or shaykh, who teaches a mystical discipline known as a *tariqa* (way). Sufism places a great emphasis on a verse from the Quran (7:172) that recounts a long-standing covenant between God and all humans, even, the verse implies, those humans not yet born: God cherishes and sustains humans, while humanity recognizes this and agrees to submit to God's will. Peter Awn, a scholar of Islam, asserts that "the goal of every mystic is to reestablish the living intimacy between the Lord of the worlds [*sic*] and the human soul proclaimed at that moment of the covenant." In order to achieve such an ecstatic state of intimacy and union with God, Sufis have recourse to a variety of methods, including repeated rhythmic movements, bodily gyrations, whirling, dancing, and music. Sufism gained considerable influence in Shafii regions of the Yemens but is generally disapproved of by Zaydis, who, unlike most Shias, reject mysticism.

The Zaydis

In order to explain the Zaydis and their contribution to historical and political developments in Yemen, it is necessary to return to the Sunni-Shia split. As the division between Sunnis and Shias widened, ideological as well as political differences increased both between and within the Sunni and Shia sects. Shias continued to believe that the Alid line had a special claim to leadership of the Muslim community. Sunni caliphs exercised their power largely in the political and military arenas; the imam, leader of Shias, also had military and political authority but acted firstly as a religious leader. Special reverence was attached to the imams because of their kinship with Ali's family and with the Prophet himself. Sunni caliphs, who were not necessarily Alids, did not share this special regard by their followers.

Zayd ibn Ali Zayn al Abdin, grandson of Husayn, great-grandson of Ali, and great-great-grandson of the Prophet, rebelled against the Umayyad caliph as his grandfather had. Zayd asserted his claim to the caliphate as a direct descendant of the Prophet and of Ali. The Kufans (residents of Al Kufah), traditional supporters of the claims of Ali and his family, backed Zayd, but their support was insufficient, and

Zayd was killed at Al Kufah in 740. The followers of Zayd, the Zaydis, continued to assert the claims to the caliphate of Zayd and his descendants. Other Shias did not share the Zaydi position, however; instead, they supported Zayd's brother, Muhammad al Baqir, and his line (see fig. 3).

The early history of the Zaydis is not well known, nor are the religious teachings of Zayd. The succession after Zayd and his son Yahya became a matter of dispute among various Zaydi factions, and many imams were chosen from collateral lines descended from Hassan rather than from Husayn.

Zaydi religious teachings are closer to Sunni than to any other Shia sect, which has led some to refer to them as the "fifth Sunni school" (after the Maliki, Hanafi, Shafii, and Hanbali). Zayd is known to have agreed with the Mutazilite, or rationalist, school of Islamic theology. The Mutazilites have been called the "Protestants of Islam" because they reject any sort of mysticism and believe in the existence of free will, i.e., people determining their actions through their own reason. Mutazilites also adhere to a strict monotheism, eschewing anything that savors of polytheism; they reject the notion, accepted by many Sunnis, that the Quran was never created and was eternally in existence. Such a possibility, they argue, brings the Quran too close to God, its creator, who is the only eternal being. Not surprisingly, Zaydis reject any occult exegesis of the Quran. They are strongly opposed to the mystical content of Sufi beliefs and practices.

Zaydi prayer differs slightly from other sects. Zaydis insert "Come to the good work" in the call to prayer. Unlike many other Muslims, Zaydis pray without moving their hands, keeping their hands at the sides of their bodies during prayer. They do not conclude prayers with "Amen" as do many other sects of Muslims.

Zaydi beliefs disagree with other Shias and with Sunnis on a number of points, but the major area of disagreement is the reason and method for the selection of the imam. Unlike the Sunnis, the Zaydis insist that the leader must come from the lineal descendants of Ali. Unlike most Shias, however, the Zaydis assert that Ali was Muhammad's choice because of his personal merits rather than because of some special inheritance that is automatically passed on to descendants. They reject the idea that the Prophet left a written will naming Ali his successor, believing that the

Prophet designated Ali his successor by description. They accept as legitimate the caliphs preceding Ali. They further support Ali's actions in arbitration and thus support the right and duty to overthrow unjust rulers.

The Zaydis therefore believe that the imam must be chosen from among Ali's descendants, or the Ahl al Bayt (People of the House), according to personal merit. Any male of the Ahl al Bayt is therefore theoretically eligible for the imamate, provided he fulfills 14 qualifications of office. He must be a freeborn male descended from both Ali and Fatima; be sound in mind and senses; have his extremities intact; be known for his justice, piety, generosity, administrative capabilities, and learning in Muslim law; be demonstrably brave; and have paid taxes. Several of these requirements serve purposes beyond the letter of the law. The necessity that extremities be intact, for example, excludes convicted felons who under sharia law would have had an extremity amputated as punishment. The requirement of descent from Fatima excludes Ismailis. The requirement for bravery signifies the ability to defend oneself by force; this excludes children and also negates the possibility of the kind of "hidden" leader favored by some Shias; the imam must be publicly known and ready at all times to act in the defense of the regime. If all required traits do not appear in a single person, however, more than one imam may be chosen, each to carry out specific responsibilities. Zaydis also recognize that, realistically, occasions may arise when there will be no imam, as, for example, when the office is disputed among several contenders. The right to rebel against improper authority has encouraged various pretenders to the imamate to put forward claims, and at many times in history rival imams have arisen to overthrow the ruler.

The imam is elected at a meeting of three groups that represent the community as a whole: the ulama (religious authorities), tribal chiefs, and community leaders. In theory only male members of the Ahl al Bayt can vote for the imam. Because the imam must be elected on his own merits, there is a strong prejudice against designation of the imam by his predecessor. The imam ideally abides by the Quran, sharia, and hadith, and consults with members of his government as well as the people.

Zayd did not accept the notion condoned by some Shias of *taqiyya*, or religious dissimulation. Zaydis believe that their faith must be practiced openly and that the imamate should be filled at all times. During his rule a properly constituted imam is believed to possess infallible judgment in matters of faith, religion, and personal morals and behavior. In matters other than the imamate the Zaydis do not differ greatly from Sunni Muslims. Scholar Eric W. Bethmann quotes a Yemeni scholar as stating, "Politically we follow Zaid ibn Ali, dogmatically we are Mutazilites, and according to rites we follow the school of Abu Hanifa [the Hanifi]."

Obscurity surrounds the early political history of the Zaydi movement. In about 864, however, a Zaydi state under Al Hassan ibn Zayd appeared near the Caspian Sea in Tabiristan, in present-day Iran. This imamate endured until the early twelfth century, when it merged into another group.

In the last decade of the ninth century, Yahya ibn al Hussayn al Qasim al Rassi, known as Al Hadi ilal Haqq (the Guide to the Truth), established a Zaydi imamate in the area that is North Yemen (see fig. 1). Until that time, authorities believe, adherence to Islam among the highland Yemenis, who were nominally subservient to the Sunni caliph, had been largely political, and local cult practices figured importantly in religious life. Al Hadi came on the invitation of the Sharafa tribe of Naham, in keeping with an ancient custom known in Yemen as hijra. Many tribes had been unable to resolve their increasingly disruptive quarrels. As a member of a holy lineage, Al Hadi was eligible to serve as mediator in tribal disputes; a holy man takes up residence with a tribe, thereby providing its members with moral and religious leadership and bestowing honor on them at the same time. Al Hadi's first stay in Yemen was brief because the Sharafa did not easily accept sharia law. But after his departure, tribal dissension erupted once again, and the tribes asked Al Hadi to return, promising to abide by his decisions. When he returned, Al Hadi served as a mediator in disputes between a number of tribes, was accepted by many other tribes, and even reached an understanding with the Christians of Najran.

Al Hadi founded the Zaydi state of Yemen in the last decade of the ninth century and was the first imam of the Rassid Dynasty, named for his grandfather Al Qasim al Rassi, a sixth-generation descendant of Ali and Fatima through Hassan. The Zaydi imamate and the Rassid Dynasty survived a turbulent history into the second half of the twentieth century, even if at various times it controlled only small territories in the highlands. The last imam, Muhammad al Badr, was the 111th of his dynasty to hold the title (see The 1962 Coup d'État in Yemen, this ch.).

Adherence to the Zaydi imamate consisted generally of tribal allegiance to the imam. The bond of each tribal group with the imam was more important than bonds with other fellow believers. Even into modern times some tribes also had hijra arrangements with other holy men of the Ahl al Bayt, who ran, in effect, independent theocracies limited to small areas. Competition with holy men of other persuasions has been constant in Zaydi history. The early years of Zaydi rule, for example, coincided with the advent of a rival Shia sect, the Ismailis, or Carmathians, who resisted the spread of the Zaydis.

The Ismailis

Ismailis numbered between 24,000 and 60,000 in North Yemen in the 1970s but had figured more prominently in the country's history. At various times they had controlled larger sections of the country but in recent years have been concentrated in the remote Jabal Haraz district near Manakhah west of Sanaa. The Ismaili sect, which began as a radical movement in the eighth century, arose from a dispute over the identity of the seventh Shia imam. Unlike the Zaydis, the Ismailis side with the main body of Shias in recognizing Muhammad al Baqir and his successor, Jafar al Sadiq, instead of the Zaydi line.

Jafar al Sadiq first named his eldest son, Ismail, his successor, then changed his mind and named a younger son, Musa al Qasim. Ismail died before his father, however, and thus never had an opportunity to assert his claim. When Jafar died in 765, the imamate devolved on Musa. One group, however, refused to recognize the imamate of Musa and insisted on Ismail and his infant son, Muhammad ibn Ismail, as the true line of successors. There are many different sects of Ismailis with widely differing beliefs.

The Ismailis found in the Yemens are of the Mustalian division (also referred to as the Western branch) because of a schism in 1094, and within that division, of the Sulaymani branch, because of a schism in 1589. The other group resulting from the latter schism, the Daudis, also live in Yemen, although many emigrated to India, where there were already many Daudis because of extensive Yemeni Ismaili missionary activities carried out in India since the tenth century. In the mid-1980s many Ismailis of both the Sulaymani and Daudi branches were still concentrated in the Haraz area of North Yemen.

Ismaili beliefs are complex and syncretic, combining elements from the philosophies of Plotinus, Pythagoras, Aristotle, gnosticism, and the Manichaeans, as well as components of Judaism, Christianity, and Eastern religions. Ismaili tenets are, in fact, unique among Muslims. Mustalian Ismailis differ from other non-Ismaili Muslims in many ways. Ismailis place particular emphasis on *taqiyya*. Their beliefs about the creation of the world are idiosyncratic, as is their historical ecumenism, toleration of religious differences, and religious hierarchy. Furthermore, the secrecy with which they veil their religious beliefs and practices (together with their practice of *taqiyya*) makes it extremely difficult to establish what their actual religious beliefs are. What is clear is that there is a division of theology into exoteric (including the conservative sharia) and esoteric (including the mystical exegesis of the Quran, which leads to *haqiqa*, or the ultimate reality and truth). Their conceptions of the imamate also differ greatly from those of other Muslims. The peculiar features of the Mustalian imamate deserve further attention so as not be be confused with the Zaydi imamate.

In Western (Mustalian) Ismaili belief there is always an imam, but the imam may be hidden or revealed; furthermore, a hidden true imam may designate a follower to assume the identity of a revealed imam in order to test the political waters. After the seventh imam (Muhammad, Ismail's son) there were three hidden imams. The Fatimid caliphs, who ruled much of the Arab world from Cairo, were Ismailis, and Ismailis consider the first of the 14 Fatimid caliphs from Egypt to be their eleventh imam. Together with other Shias, Western Ismailis accord Ali a special place. Unlike other Shias, however, they do not consider him an imam; because they revere him so highly, they place Ali above the status of imam, and, indeed, above the Prophet as well. Unlike Zaydi imams, who are elected, the Mustalian imam is always a son of the previous imam and is always appointed by the imam during his lifetime. Problems arose when the nineteenth imam, Al Amir, was assassinated.

His son, Al Tayyib, was believed to have been hidden by his father, who had presaged political turmoil and feared for his son's life. Al Tayyib was the twenty-first Ismaili imam and was a hidden imam. The imams since that time, Mustalians believe, live in hiding and will go on living and producing offspring in hiding until they become revealed (*zuhuur*) on the day of resurrection.

In addition to special beliefs about the imamate, Mustalians have an idiosyncratic messianic theology. Noted historian Bernard Lewis writes that "frequent references are to be found in Yemenite local [Ismaili] literature to a Himyaritic messiah, to be called Mansur Himyar or Mansur al Yaman." Because the imams are hidden, Yemeni Ismailis are ruled by a *dai*, who historically was the messenger or propagandist of the imam.

Since the seventeenth century every *dai* has belonged to the Makrami family. The recent history and present-day condition of the Ismailis appear as obscure as their earlier periods. Some authorities suggest that in the twentieth century, persecutions occurred under the Zaydis. In 1902 secret Ismaili documents fell into the hands of the Zaydi imam, and their fate is not known. Dai Ali ibn Muhsin died in 1936, but the fate of his successor, Husayn Ahmad—who was taken to Mecca when King Abd al Aziz ibn Abd ar Rahman Al Saud of Saudi Arabia occupied the Najran region—is not known to outsiders.

The Shafiis

In 1985 slightly more than half the citizens of North Yemen and almost all in South Yemen were Sunni Muslims of the Shafii school. The Shafii school follows the teachings of Muhammad ibn Idris al Shafii, a legal scholar who lived from 768 to 820. The founder of the Islamic science of law (*fiqh*), Shafii took a moderate position between the Maliki school, which emphasizes hadith as the source of law, and the Hanafi school, which depends on *qiyas* (reasoning by analogy from earlier cases). Shafii took the revealed word of God as the basis of all law and tightened the requirements of acceptable hadiths. In order to be valid, according to Shafii, a tradition must remount to the Prophet rather than to his companions and must be supported by an unbroken chain of witnesses. He emphasized the Quran as the standard for deciding between contradictory hadiths; the closest Quranic text was to be accepted. Other legal scholars had based legal decisions on reports of the Prophet's sayings or behavior, which were not well documented, or they had used reports pertaining to Muhammad's close associates as well as to Muhammad himself. Shafii also recognized as a valid source of legal interpretations the consensus of the *umma*, which came to mean consensus of the learned community, and he placed this only after the revealed work and properly validated traditions as a source of law. Shafii was extremely factual in his approach to Islamic law, allowing little room for personal opinion or whim; he approached the Quran historically and advocated that a jurist should possess a thorough command of the grammar of the language as it was used at the time of the Prophet.

In the mid-1980s the Shafii area of Yemen was, in Viscount Buckmaster's words, the area "south of a line running, very roughly, east-west and crossing the Sanaa-Taiz road some twenty-five miles south of Sanaa." This division is only approximate. Other sources place the dividing line farther south. In addition, some communities of Zaydis reside in traditionally Shafii areas. Thus, the Shafiis were concentrated in the Tihamah, the foothills, and other areas of the south. Historically, the Shafiis were dominated by the Zaydis. Stookey writes that under the Rasulids (1232–1442) Shafiism became the predominant religion in the parts of Yemen that Shafiis still occupied in the mid-1980s. The incursions of a Zaydi imam (Sharaf al Din) forced the Shafiis to retreat to the Tihamah, however. The imam appointed his son governor of the Shafii southern highlands, and the Shafiis suffered from the rigor of his rule, so much that they aided the invading Ottomans and were subsequently able to return to their full territory. Shafii areas once again fell under Zaydi control when the imams captured the Shafii areas from the Turks in the early seventeenth century.

Shafii prayer differs from Zaydi prayer, although both groups sometimes pray at each other's mosques. Shafiis begin their prayer with their hands at their sides; they then raise their hands to their heads and cross their hands (right over left) in front of their bodies. In general, the major Zaydi-Shafii differences have been historical, political, and matters of ethnicity rather than issues of religious difference.

Early Islamic Rule in Yemen

The governors sent to Yemen under the early caliphs varied in quality over the years. Stookey cites an Arab writer who tells of one of the governors who served in the years of the eighth century. Upon arrival in Yemen, he pointed to his camel and said, "This is my riding camel; if I depart with anything more, I am a thief." It is said that he left Yemen 20 years later carrying with him only his sword, his spear, and his copy of the Quran. The Yemenis were not so fortunate with other governors sent to rule them.

Control by the Abbasid caliphs ended in Yemen in 822 when one of the Arab governors sent to the Tihamah declared an end to control from the Abbasid caliph in Baghdad. Under the rule of the dynasty he founded—the Banu Ziyad, which lasted (nominally at least) for two centuries—the only vestige of authority from Baghdad was Friday prayers still being said in the name of the Abbasid caliph.

Although for a brief time the Banu Ziyad Dynasty established authority over the whole of the former Himyarite kingdom, the end of the ninth and the early tenth centuries were chaotic. Ismaili missionaries sought power in Yemen and fought with the Banu Ziyad as well as with an aspiring noble family of Sanaa, the Yufirids, who were able to push the Banu Ziyad back into the Tihamah and establish their own rule over the eastern and southern parts of Yemen. Meanwhile, the northern tribes between Najran and Sadah quarreled among themselves so bitterly that finally, following an ancient South Arabian tradition, they called upon a distinguished outsider to act as judge between them. This turned out to be a momentous decision, for the arbiter called in by the northerners was Al Hadi ilal Haqq, the founder of the Zaydi imamate. Of all the Yemeni rulers who had and who would in subsequent years come to power in Yemen, only the Zaydi imams would enter the twentieth century claiming an ancient right to rule all of Yemen.

As scholar Robin Bidwell reports, Sanaa changed hands 20 times in the first 12 years of the tenth century, a time when there were no fewer than four relatively independent kingdoms in Yemen. By the beginning of the eleventh century there were vitiated Banu Ziyad and Yufirid states in the south and a Zaydi state in the north, and the Ismailis were still seeking power as an underground movement. The establishment of Fatimid (Ismaili) rule in Cairo in 969 was of great help in this effort, and in 1037 a Yemeni who had become an Ismaili (although he was the son of a prominent Sunni judge) took power and reunited the territories of the former Himyarite state under the suzerainty of the Fatimid caliph in Cairo. The new ruler, Ali al Sulayhi, put down a Zaydi uprising and killed the imam. Despite this, he established a fair administration and refrained from sectarian persecution unless attacked. A major campaign was required to subdue many areas, especially those of his own kinsmen, the truculent Hamdan confederation—the Hashid and Bakil tribesmen of the north.

By about 1063 Ali al Sulayhi had brought all of the former Himyarite kingdom under the control of an indigenous leader for the first time since the demise of the Sabaean kingdom. He was murdered, however, and succeeded in office by his son, who, for reasons that remain obscure (some scholars suggest illness, others an inclination to "merrymaking"), virtually abdicated. He entrusted his kingdom to his wife, Sayyida al Hurra Arwa bint Ahmad al Sulayhi. The queen was his cousin and, as was the custom in the Sulayhi family, had been educated to the same standards as men. Stookey provides a translation of the words of a Yemeni historian who described her as "well-read and herself a fine writer. She was versed in the chronicles, poetry, and history. She knew well how to read between the lines and distinguish between the literal and the true meaning."

Although many areas had risen in rebellion after the death of the king, Queen Arwa decreased the use of the military and sought to establish tribal loyalty through fair administration and by a series of political maneuvers. Her efforts failed, however, and Sulayhid rule disintegrated during her reign. Her death in 1138 brought an end to Fatimid control and the slow decline of the Ismaili population in Yemen.

After a brief period of rule by the indigenous Mahdid clan (a Sunni family claiming Himyarite descent), Saladin, who extinguished Fatimid rule in Cairo and founded the Ayyubid Dynasty, sent his brother in 1173 to take Yemen. With the exception of the Zaydis in the highlands, the Ayyubids were able to exert control over almost all of Yemen.

In 1232 rule in Yemen was taken over by one of the amirs appointed by the Ayyubids, Nur al Din Umar ibn al Rasul, whose remote ancestors were said to have been

Yemenis who left after the collapse of the Marib Dam. Left in charge by the last of the Ayyubid governors, who died shortly after his departure, Nur Al Din took over the existing bureaucracy and established a dynasty that provided over two centuries of Sunni rule over most of the territory of Yemen. The two centuries of this Rasulid Dynasty were years of relative peace and prosperity because of a revival of trade and a lack of interest in Yemen by the major powers of the period. Learning also flourished under the Rasulids. Bidwell reports that in the city of Zabid alone there were 230 "colleges." The Rasulid rulers were known and respected abroad and were in contact with the kingdoms of India, Ceylon, and Ethiopia.

The glories of Rasulid rule were expensive, however, and were based upon heavy taxation. By the middle of the fourteenth century, the Zaydis were raiding Aden and Zabid with impunity. Relying increasingly on Mamluks (officers of European descent who had served the Ayyubids and would themselves take over Egypt) and other mercenaries, Rasulid control had disintegrated by the middle of the fifteenth century. After only a brief period of rule by yet another local dynasty, the Tafirids (who were never able to subdue the rival Zaydis), the Mamluks of Egypt attacked Yemen in 1515, looting and plundering the cities of Zabid and Taizz.

The period of almost 900 years between the coming of Islam and the advent of Ottoman rule in Yemen was one that reinforced many of the existing trends in Yemeni political, social, and religious life. The contentious tribes were in no way subdued by the ephemeral rule of the various foreign and domestic dynasties that exercised control over them from time to time. Tribal customs and independence survived, indeed flourished. The Rasulid era in particular left an important mark on Yemen. As Thomas Gochenour, a scholar of medieval Yemen, suggests, the sectarian divisions in Yemen were well in place by the beginning of the thirteenth century, with the Shafiis in the southern highlands and the Tihamah and only the tribal areas of the northern highlands subject to Zaydi control. Stookey points out that the division between highland Yemen and the coastal plain, which predated the Rasulid era by hundreds of years, was consolidated under the Rasulid Dynasty. Its leaders were content to leave the ungovernable highlands alone and concentrate their efforts in the lowlands, which were not only easier to handle but also more profitable to exploit commercially. The two centuries of Rasulid rule thus underlined contrasting styles of leadership in these two areas, a difference that would be reinforced well into modern times by differences of religion and social structure.

Relative prosperity and political stability (rule passed almost without exception from father to son) reigned in the coastal areas, while in the isolated highlands claims to be imamate were made by men from 10 different clans during the years between the early thirteenth and the early fifteenth centuries. As Stookey further notes, authority in the Zaydi highlands always had to be exerted by force. Tribal rivalries became entangled with the succession to the imamate and were thus reinforced in the mountains while they were subsiding to some extent under the different leadership style of the Rasulids in the coastal zone. The people of the coastal areas became accustomed to rule based on commercial considerations, while in the Zaydi areas religious leadership based on the standards required of Zaydi imams was the rule, even when it was resisted. The division between the Zaydi highlands and the Sunni lowlands was one that affected every government well into the twentieth century.

Foreign Domination and the Beginnings of Yemeni Nationalism

When the Ottoman Turks conquered the Mamluks in Egypt in 1517, they fell heir to areas under nominal Mamluk sovereignty on the Arabian Peninsula, including Yemen. In 1538 the Turks consolidated their hold on the area by capturing the east and southeast coast of the peninsula (see table A, Preface).

Under Admiral Sulayman Pasha they captured and razed Aden and hanged its governor. Taizz was taken in 1545 and Sanaa soon after. A pasha (viceroy) was installed at Sanaa as governor general over the entire southern area, but the brutality of Turkish rule made his hold on the area precarious. Even Turkish expeditionary forces sent in 1569 could not pacify the Zaydi area. In 1590 a Zaydi hero, Al Mansur Billah al Qasim (Qasim the Great), began a unified resistance movement against the Turks. Qasim was 20 years old and the descendant of seven Zaydi imams. A scholarly guerrilla, Qasim pursued his studies while leading the Turks on an elusive chase over the length and breadth of Yemen, establishing cells for the resistance. For the first time—but not the last—Shias and Sunnis were united in a common cause against foreigners.

In 1597 Qasim was elected imam, and by the following year he had 11 provinces allied with him. With the help of Arab agents, Turkish reinforcements broke the initial uprising. By 1608, however, Qasim's tribal support was substantial enough to force the Turks to conclude a 10-year truce. Qasim decided to reside at Sanaa and was the first imam to do so. According to the truce terms, the imam retained control of his provinces, the Turks managed foreign affairs, and there was freedom of movement between Turkish (mostly Shafii) and Zaydi areas.

The first year of the truce marked the initial visit of the British to the area. A ship of the East India Company called at both Mocha and Aden to explore commercial possibilities. The ship's factor, John Jourdain, reached Sanaa and, although the visit in itself was disappointing, he was optimistic about the future. Sir Henry Middleton, encouraged by Jourdain's report, visited in 1610 and was imprisoned for a year. The East India Company, in no way deterred, dispatched three ships the following year, which were well received by the new governor of Mocha. By 1618 the British, buttressed with a *firman* (an official decree) from the Ottoman sultan, had begun to establish a factory (trading center or post) in Mocha, which was an important port for the coffee trade.

In 1629 the Turks surrendered Sanaa to Qasim's son and successor, Muayyad Muhammad, who resumed the struggle against the Ottomans. Viewed in Yemen as corrupt and immoral oppressors, the Turks were undergoing internal political difficulties at home and were at war with Venice. In 1636 they abandoned Yemen. Muayyad managed to reconquer all the territory of the former Himyarite kingdom as far east as Dhofar (in present-day Oman) by 1658. This was the farthest extent of Zaydi authority, the last time that all of what is now the two Yemens was under one rule, and the major basis for the claims of the twentieth-century Zaydi imams to legitimacy in all of South Arabia.

From 1658 on, the Zaydi imams gradually lost control of the outlying areas. Lahij and Aden became independent in 1731, and the areas east of Aden, which eventually came under British "protection," gradually slipped away from Zaydi control.

Rebellion in the far reaches of the area of Zaydi hegemony encouraged rebellion closer to home. In 1763 much of the Tihamah was under the independent control of the sharif (see Glossary) of Abu Arish, who had been placed there as governor by the imam. Mocha was still throughly imamic, in large part because potential inland conquerors assumed that the British and other Europeans who had come there would back the imam. The British, although they had occasional tiffs with local rulers, had no political interest in the area yet; thus they were able to pursue their commercial interests relatively unharassed, and by 1770 they controlled the largest share of the coffee trade.

Until the nineteenth century the Dutch and the British had control of Yemen's foreign trade. The imams were content with the arrangements. In addition to economic benefits for the imam, Europeans were becoming useful in other ways. In 1772, for instance, Imam Abbas was able to quell a rebellion in Sanaa because of the combined aid of the commander of his artillery, a Muslim convert from Scotland, and a French convert, who supervised the imam's embryonic munitions works.

The situation changed abruptly in 1798 when Napoleon overthrew the Mamluk sultans of Egypt, vassals of the Ottomans. The British could not afford to allow the French to destroy their connections with India, so they quickly moved to occupy the island of Perim in the Bab al Mandab in hopes of preventing the French from reaching the Indian Ocean. Scarcity of water compelled them to decamp to Aden, where the sultan of Lahij warmly welcomed them and even offered them Aden. Meanwhile, the imam at Sanaa, Ali al Mansur, ordered his governors to supply all British ships with necessary equipment and permitted the erection of a naval hospital at Mocha.

The Establishment of the British Presence

Yemen continued to be ostensibly under Ottoman rule, but it was rule characterized by benign neglect. For the most part the politically fractured area ruled itself until the interest of the Sublime Porte (the popular term designating the Ottoman government) in Yemen was rekindled by a challenge to its authority from within the peninsula by the

Wahhabi (see Glossary) sect, which under the leadership of the Saud family was busily subduing north and central Arabia. The Wahhabis turned their attention to Yemen in 1803 and, with the help of the sharif of Abu Arish and the powerful Hashid and Bakil tribes, soon captured Hodeida (Al Hudaydah) and attacked the imam at Sanaa. Wahhabi activity in Yemen was finally quenched in 1818 when at the command of the Sublime Porte the Ottoman viceroy of Egypt, Muhammad Ali, sent his brillant and ruthless son, Ibrahim Pasha, to the Tihamah. Ibrahim rid the area of the Wahhabi presence and restored the imam under promise of tribute.

In 1833 Ibrahim took Mocha. The British were not overly concerned because coffee was now available from less troublesome places, but unofficially the British encouraged the Ottomans to reestablish a real presence in Yemen; Muhammad Ali, who had broken away from the Ottomans, appeared more likely than they to threaten a new British interest in the area. Steam navigation also necessitated permanent and secure coaling stations. Several places in the region were being considered when a fortuitous attack on a ship flying the Union Jack provided the excuse for the British capture of Aden.

The Ottomans and the British in Yemen

The British were not the first Europeans to appear in Aden. At the beginning of the sixteenth century Alfonso de Albuquerque sailed with his Portuguese fleet to Aden from Goa and vainly attempted to storm its old fortifications. The Egyptians made a similar attempt a few years later. The Turks were successful in 1538 because they used a ruse to enter the town.

The Adenis virtually gave Aden to the Portuguese in 1551, assuming any European presence to be more beneficent than the Turkish. Less than a year later the Turks recovered Aden and added to its ancient fortifications. Aden, once a flourishing port for local as well as for Greek and Roman trade, had declined to a cluster of impoverished fishing villages, protected from invaders only by the fortifications built in the fourth century. The reason for revived interest in Aden was its ideal location as a bunkering station for European ships on their journeys to South and East Asia. All attempts to establish such a station were blocked by the

Ottomans until they lost interest in the area in the seventeenth century.

When a British ship first anchored at Aden in 1609, the Turks were still in control, but by the end of the eighteenth century the British had made several successful visits to the area. In 1802 Britain signed a treaty of friendship and commerce with the sultan of Lahij, who was nominally in charge of Aden because his pirates used it as their working base. The treaty, signed with Sultan Ahmad ibn Abd al Karim, who had offered Aden to the British in 1799, established peaceful relations until it was abrogated by Ahmad's nephew, Sultan Muhasin, in 1838.

In 1820 Commander Stafford Bettesworth Haines of the British Indian Navy was told by Ahmad's brother that Ahmad would welcome a British agent in Aden from the East India Company in exchange for assistance against hostile tribes. At that time the government of British India had no intention of making such a political commitment. But the situation had changed radically by the 1830s, and no place seemed as satisfactory as Aden for a coal depot; it appeared that the Egyptians would control it unless the British moved in. In January 1837 a ship flying British colors and belonging to an Indian ruler, the nawab of the Carnatic, was wrecked on the coast of Aden. The Adenese promptly plundered it, relieved the survivors of their posessions, and subjected a group of upper-class Indian women to indiginities, nearly carrying them off for sale in the hinterland.

Haines, who was surveying the area, was ordered to return to Bombay. There he was equipped with a sloop of war and ordered to investigate the outrage and purchase Aden if possible. The sultan denied any knowledge of the despoiling of the ship, a denial Haines refused to believe because the ship's property was being sold from the sultan's warehouse. Reparations were arranged and talks begun for the purchase of Aden. A long and prolific correspondence between the sultan and Haines ensued. The sultan was afraid of losing face by selling Aden, but at the same time he thought he might as well make some profit because the Egyptians were certain to seize Aden if the British did not buy it. The main disagreement was that the sultan wished to retain control of his Arab subjects. Finally, after much internal debate within the British Indian government, Aden was taken by force January 19, 1839.

Muhammad Ali attempted to coerce the imam to rid Aden of the British. The imam refused, and Aden became a dependency of British India and Haines its first political agent. When Haines took Aden, the "Eye of Yemen" was an unkempt village of 500 inhabitants. By the end of his administration in 1854 it was a flourishing trading town with 20,000 inhabitants. Haines did not commit the British beyond what was necessary to protect the post. He renegotiated the treaty with the sultan of Lahij in 1839, again in 1843, and finally in 1844. Several key tribes—the Subayhi, Fadli, Aqrabi, Lower Yafi, and Hawshabi—were amenable to making treaties, and these agreements served as a foundation for the eventual British protectorate (See Consolidation of British Control over the Protectorates and Aden, this ch.).

The second half of the nineteenth century was characterized by chaos both in the Aden hinterlands and in the territories under nominal Zaydi rule. When Aden was taken, Muhammad Ali's forces still occupied the Tihamah. After resisting both the British and his former Ottoman overlords for years, by 1840 he was forced to submit once again to some measure of control from the Ottomans. As part of his agreement with them, he was required to withdraw his troops from Arabia, including Yemen. The withdrawal of his forces in 1840 left Yemen in chaos. Emboldened tribal leaders began to reassert their independence, and the imam could not prevent one group from sacking Sanaa. As the troops of Muhammad Ali left Hodeida in April 1840, the sharif of Abu Arish moved in, and during the next 10 years there was a continuing struggle for the Tihamah between the imam and this local ruling family. Unable to control the disorder, the imam sent an envoy to the British in Aden in 1841, 1843, and again in 1848, asking for protection. The British, however, refused to become involved.

The Ottomans in 1849 thought to seize the moment and under Tewfik Pasha expelled the sharif from Hodeida and reinstalled the imam, forcing him to sign a treaty whereby he ruled the highlands as an Ottoman vassal. While attempting to establish a garrison at Sanaa, Tewfik's forces were surprised by enraged Zaydi troops. Tewfik received a fatal wound, and the "traitorous" imam was deposed.

This time the Ottomans remained for 70 years, and the pattern set by Ottoman and British presence in Yemen had lasting effects on Yemeni politics. As Bidwell suggests, it was inevitable that both the Ottomans and the British would try to expand beyond the areas they controlled and that the areas they ruled would develop differently. The dualism of the Shia Zaydis and the Sunni Shafiis had existed for centuries, but by the end of the nineteenth century the Shafiis were themselves divided between the two foreign powers.

In Aden the British were busy occupying islands off the coast, and Perim Island came under British suzerainty in 1857. In 1857 the British also officially occupied the sultanate of Lahij. The opening of the Suez Canal in 1869 quickened the pace of Western and Ottoman political activity in South Arabia. Ahmad Mukhtar Pasha arrived in Sanaa in 1871, determined to pacify the area for the Sublime Porte. The chaos generated by tribal rivalries and Ismaili and Zaydi imams facilitated his task. Imam Muhasin was relegated to a position as a pious figurehead, and Ottoman Ahmad Mukhtar administered the area. With the quiet encouragement of Imam Muhasin, however, a Zaydi mufti, Sayyid Muhammad ibn Yahya, began to gain wide appeal because of his popular sermons. At this time Anglo-Turkish relations began to sour. Ahmad Mukhtar, having secured the main Zaydi towns for the Turks, began to encroach on areas in the British sphere of influence. In 1873 he took the sultan's palace at Lahij, although he soon withdrew on orders from the Sublime Porte when the British dispatched a force from Aden. The British acquisition of Cyprus in 1878 and the British occupation of Egypt in 1882 annoyed the Turks, as did the plethora of treaties being made with the British by shaykhs who feared Turkish aggression.

Turkish unpopularity in Yemen caused the Bakil and Hashid tribal confederations to revolt, and in 1891, when the influential preacher Muhammad ibn Yahya was elected imam, the country flamed into rebellion. Muhammad ibn Yahya became the focus of a great nationalist uprising that even brought the Shafiis of the coastal area under his control.

A new Turkish governor general, Ahmad Feizi Pasha, arrived at Hodeida in 1892 and proceeded to burn his way to Sanaa. Undaunted by threats, the imam refused to negotiate on the grounds that the Ottoman civil code, the

Qanun, which Ahmad Feizi wished to impose, was contradictory to Zaydi religious law. Repressive Turkish governors drove people to support the imam.

The imam decided that his son Yahya should succeed him and, to ensure the support of the Hashid, married Yahya to the sister of the Hashid shaykh. Yahya became imam in 1904 and, like his father, assumed the title originated with Qasim the Great's son Ismail, *al muta wakil ala Allah* (who relies on God). Although selected by his father, which was not according to Zaydi custom, Yahya was fully qualified to be imam and was formally installed according to the traditional procedures. After defeating several rivals, Yahya called for a general revolt and attacked the Turks at Sanaa. The Turks were aided by Dhayami, a powerful shaykh who opposed Yahya because he believed that Zaydi precepts required the holder of the imamate to be genuinely elected and to be over 40 years of age, and victories alternated from side to side.

In 1911 the Ottomans, troubled by the war with the Balkans and the Italian seizure of Libya, concluded a peace agreement with Yahya. The Treaty of Daan granted most of the demands made by the imam and provided for three kinds of administration in the areas of Yemen presumably under Ottoman rule: Yahya was given a free hand in the northern (Zaydi) areas he already controlled, there was an area of shared control, and the third area (the Tihamah) remained under Ottoman administration. The imam was empowered to appoint judges in the Zaydi areas and in all other ways to rule his domains according to the precepts of his faith.

The Treaty of Daan, finally ratified by the Ottomans in 1913, had both positive and negative effects on the future of the Zaydi imamate. On the one hand, as Manfred Wenner points out, it set the precedent for Zaydi claims to rule once the Ottomans left in 1919, and it established the imam's right of appointment and the legitimacy of sharia in the areas of Zaydi control. On the other hand, as Stookey suggests, some aspects of the compromise may have weakened the Zaydi polity. Resistance to Ottoman rule had been shared by Zaydis and Shafiis alike. The abandonment of this unifying nationalism may have suggested that the imam was more concerned about being leader of the Zaydis than of the whole nation. Furthermore, the country thus was divided officially into parts, and the Ottomans sought to under-

Marble columns at Marib

Minaret of mosque in Al Janad

Photos courtesy Embassy of the Yemen Arab Republic

Section of the remains of Marib Dam
Courtesy Thomas Sennett, Aramco World Magazine

Terraced farming
Courtesy World Bank

Traditional dancing during a qat session by North Yemeni men
Courtesy Embassy of the Yemen Arab Republic

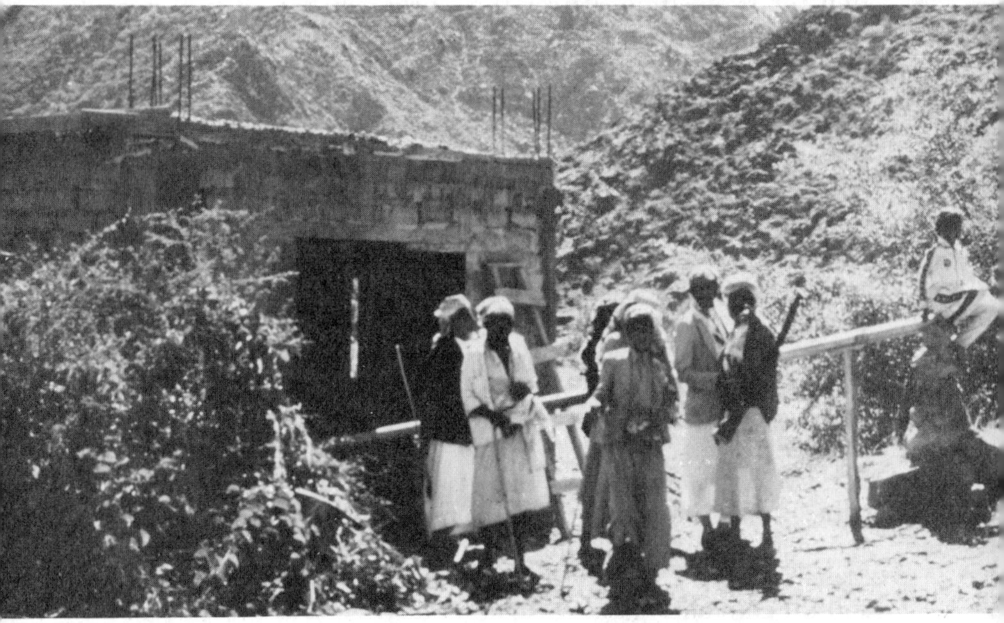

Armed highlanders
Courtesy Chemonics International

line Zaydi-Shafii differences. The distance between the two groups, which is narrow in terms of doctrine and religious practice, grew wider and more politically significant. Stookey also points out that Yahya borrowed from the Ottomans the idea of a professional army and even allowed a number of Turkish officers to remain in service after the departure of the Ottomans after World War I. These officers administered a military academy to produce future professional officers. According to Stookey, "The new element thus established within Yemeni society quite predictably developed interests and orientations distinct from those of other social segments and became an important agent of lasting change in Yemeni politics."

The Turkish presence continued to cause tribes to go to Aden to make alliances of some sort with the British. By 1886 nine tribes, known as the Nine Cantons, had come under British protection, although the relationships were very casually established. In 1886 the British signed a formal treaty of protection with the Hadhramauti Mahrah sultan of Qishn and Socotra, and in 1887 the sultan of Lahij agreed to accept a monthly stipend for British "protection." Although the British had wanted a clear frontier demarcation for some time, it was the Turks who eventually proposed it. Between 1902 and 1904 frontiers were marked that became the defined section of the permanent frontier between present-day North Yemen and South Yemen. The treaty was ratified in 1914 but, after World War I erupted later in the year, the Turks did not permit the frontier to deter them. They occcupied Lahij and part of Aden, which they held until the postwar Treaty of Mudros was concluded in 1918, by which the Turks agreed to withdraw entirely from Arabia. Because the Yemenis remained loyal to the Turks, notwithstanding their hatred of them, the British helped the Idrisi Arabs to capture Asir, in present-day Saudi Arabia, and in 1917 the British took Hodeida, which they ceded to Idrisi in 1921. During the war Britain also acquired Kamaran Island.

Even though Britain had essentially failed some of the tribes under its protection during the war, the new young sultan of Lahij, Fadl ibn Ali, renewed relations with the British in 1918. A total of 31 major treaties of protection and 90 conventions were signed between World War I and 1954.

Independent Yemen

Scholars agree that the rule of the three imams of the twentieth century (Yahya, 1904–48; Ahmad, 1948–62; and Badr, 1962) can be considered as a single period. The course of events during this period was strongly influenced by factors unique to Yemen's religions and history, twentieth-century instrusions that were undermining traditional cultures in many areas of the world, and the conflicting values and goals of the imams.

Several important elements of twentieth-century politics in North Yemen resulted from the unusual institutions and values of Zaydism. The fundamental difference between Zaydis and other sects of Islam—the elective imamate—had a major impact on the course of events. Because any male member of the ruling family or any sayyid family who met certain criteria could hope to become imam, political splits within the royal house and between the ruling Hamid al Din family and the other sayyid families were common (see The Zaydis, this ch.). The two major attempts to topple the Hamid al Din imams up to 1962 prominently involved dissident members of the sayyid class and the Hamid al Din family itself. Attempts by imams Yahya and Ahmad to perpetuate the rule of their family through primogeniture, whether for reasons of stability or ambition, met with serious opposition from the ulama, as well as from the thwarted sayyids and royal brothers, and such an act struck at the heart of Zaydi doctrine. This was especially the case with Badr, the last imam, who did not possess the requisite qualities for election to the imamate. This imposed primogeniture alienated precisely those elements of society on whose support the imams most depended and whom the imams most needed in the face of rising demands for change in the twentieth century.

Morever, because the imams served as the "commander of the faithful" and combined secular and spiritual roles, it was difficult for them to delegate authority. When they did so it was generally to persons they could trust not to rival them for the imamate—either non-sayyids or their own sons. This exacerbated the dissatisfaction of the sayyid class. Worse yet, it made it almost impossible for the imams to administer government affairs efficiently and yet remain accessible to their people in the traditional way.

A third factor related to Zaydism was the desire of the twentieth-century imams to maintain a pure Zaydi rule isolated from the impurities of foreigners—even Arab or Muslim foreigners of a different sect. Yahya carried this policy to an extreme. He never left the Zaydi highlands and never saw the sea from the Yemeni coast. This isolation was shocking to young Yemenis educated abroad and hastened their alienation from imamic rule.

Other important factors in the twentieth century grew out of Yemeni history. The imams believed they were descendants not only of the Prophet through Ali and Fatima but also of the Himyarite rulers of South Arabia.

They claimed the right to rule all of Yemen, including areas held in 1919 by Saudi Arabia (Najran), the Idrisi shaykhs (Asir), and the British (Aden and what would become the Western Protectorate and Eastern Protectorate). The imams also faced the historical truculence and tribal independence of even the traditional Zaydi areas. Even the Hashid and Bakil confederations, known as the "wings of the imamate" for their historial support, did not provide unquestioning loyalty to the imams. Both were allied at one point with the Idrisi shaykhs against the imam, and the end of the Ottoman subsidies to these powerful tribes after World War I resulted in a rash of tribal wars that Yahya also had to suppress.

These two factors—claim to all of historical Yemen and tribal independence—made it necessary for Yahya, and Ahmad after him, to import more and better weapons and to seek military training for Yemeni officers. Ultimately, Yahya was forced to turn to the other Arab states for military training. This made it impossible for him to maintain the isolation of the Zaydi state, and it also accelerated the growth of modernized, dissident elements. The first head of state after the onset of civil war, Colonel Abdallah al Sallal, was in the first batch of young men sent for military training in Iraq in the 1930s. Even with the imported arms and training, the imams were only marginally successful in extending their frontiers and subduing the tribes. The tribal system was far older than the 1,000-year-old Zaydi imamate and outlived it.

Another historical element that constrained imamic rule in the twentieth century was the division within the population between the Zaydis of the highlands and the Shafiis of the plateau and coastal regions. It is important, however, not to view this division as the key factor in the modern politics of North Yemen. Both the British and the

Ottomans overestimated its importance, viewing it as a manifestation of the significant Sunni-Shia split, and underestimated both the level of support for the imams among the Shafiis and the imams' problems in controlling their Zaydi subjects.

While religious and historical factors were helping to create rifts between the imam and his family, his class, and his Shafii subjects, the intrusions of the modern world were fostering dissent among the less traditional elements of society. The imams could not prevent the spread of radio communication, and the transistor played a role in bringing the outside world into the isolated areas of Yemen, just as it did in many other traditional cultures. This made the imams vulnerable to external propaganda—particularly from the powerful transmitters of Radio Cairo. Young Yemenis trained abroad—especially those sent in Yahya's abortive external military training program—returned with new ideas and judged the imams harshly for their old-fashioned ways. Disaffected Yemenis educated abroad played a major role in the downfall of the imamate, and on the occasions when Yahya (and more frequently, Ahmad and Badr) made concessions to the modernists, the traditional elements of society were offended.

When the Turkish forces evacuated Yemen after the Ottoman defeat in World War I, Yahya was left with the growing might of the Saudi rulers to the north, a powerful British position in the south, and incomplete domination of the areas in between. Although he never officially declared independence, the imam set out almost immediately to define his kingdom by extending his rule as far as possible to the north and south.

In 1920 Yahya began to overrun areas under British protection. He then turned his attention to the recapture of areas that formerly had been under Zaydi control. The outbreak of a succession dispute in Asir gave Yahya the opportunity to seize Hodeida from the Idrisi in 1925. Yemeni forces subsequently occupied a number of villages and towns in the Tihamah coastal strip. The following year, however, the Idrisi shaykh was placed under the protection of Abd al Aziz, the newly crowned king of the Hijaz and the future king of Saudi Arabia. Imam Yahya tried to encourage the Idrisi to rebel against Abd al Aziz while challenging the king's control over the Najran area at Yemen's northern border.

It was not until 1930 that Yahya managed to secure firm control of the country. Even the traditionally supportive Hashid and Bakil confederations had to be bought off and subdued by force. One of the few remaining cohesive tribes of the Tihaman—the Zaraniq—rose in rebellion in 1925, going as far as to petition the League of Nations for recognition as an independent state. Yahya's oldest son, Ahmad, subdued them in a brutal campaign that took a year and provided Ahmad with the requisite military credentials to make his succession to the imamate easier. Once the tribes had been subdued, Yahya consolidated his authority by garrisoning potential trouble spots and taking hostages from the tribes.

Government under Yahya was highly personalized. Although a few Turks remained in government service under the imam after 1918 and some sayyids and qadis (see Glossary) performed administrative functions, even the most minute details of administration were usually brought to the imam. Following ancient custom, he sat for two hours a day in a courtyard under an umbrella accepting the petitions of his people. This concentration of power and reluctance to delegate authority were customs that may have satisfied some traditional Yemenis, but they were criticized by others as tyrannical and inefficient. The imam's writ was less potent among the great Zaydi tribes, where the imam tried continually to eradicate tribal and customary law and implant sharia. As Bidwell remarks, "The Hashid, the Bakil and their peers remained as they had always been, allies rather than subjects of the imam." The Shafii areas were ruled by amirs representing the imam: the amirs were often sayyids, but whenever possible they were sons of the imam or qadis (who could not succeed to the imamate, not being descended from Ali and Fatima). Almost all of the officials and soldiers in the Shafii area were Zaydis, and they served as constant reminders of Zaydi domination. The combination of subsidies to powerful tribes, hostages from some tribes, personalized leadership by the imam, and direct control of Shafii areas was harsh and arbitrary by some standards, but it provided a degree of order uncommon in Yemeni history—one that was certainly not possible at that time in the areas of Yemen under direct or indirect British authority.

The British attempted to negotiate with the imam because they had become aware that the demarcation agreements that had been reached between them and the Turks were totally disregarded by Yahya, who considered them merely an arrangement made between two occupying powers and therefore not binding on him. British overtures were rebuffed in 1926. When in 1926 and 1928 Yahya signed treaties of friendship with Italy and the Soviet Union, the British began to use the Royal Air Force against his forces in areas that they viewed as under British authority. Yahya, seeing war with the Saudis in the offing and recognizing the futility of opposing British air power, finally entered into negotiations with the British in 1933. The Treaty of Friendship and Mutual Cooperation, usually called the Treaty of Sanaa, was signed on February 11, 1934.

The treaty remained in effect for 40 years, but disagreements quickly arose that would affect the future course of Anglo-Yemeni relations. Sir Kennedy Trevaskis, a former British high commissioner in Aden, explains the different interpretations of the imam and the British:

> Between the imam's and the British view of the treaty there was a subtle and perilous difference. It arose out of a conflict between their interpretations of the Arabic word *hadud*: "frontier" to the British and "region" to the imam. Thus, while the British believed that the imam had undertaken to accept the status quo on the frontier, the imam thought that the British had agreed to maintain the status quo in the whole region and, consequently, not to move out of Aden. Supposing that the treaty would leave the door open for him to enter the Protectorate at some time within the next forty years, it was understandable that the imam should regard the [British] "forward" policy as a perfidious attempt to slam it in his face.

Once Yahya had subdued both the Zaydi and Shafii areas and had reached agreement with the British on at least temporary demarcation of the frontier between them, he turned his attention to Najran and the northern Tihamah, which had been part of the Himyarite kingdom and had once been ruled by the first Zaydi imam of Yemen. Here he met with the opposition of Abd al Aziz, who had taken Asir under his protection. Saudi efforts to negotiate over Najran and Asir were unsuccessful, and Yahya refused to accept anything less than the whole of Asir. War between the Saudis and the imam resulted in the 1934 Treaty of Taif, in which Yahya was compelled to abandon his claim to Najran and northern Asir but was allowed to retain the port of Hodeida, which had been captured by the Saudis during the brief war.

The Treaty of Taif established excellent formal relations between Yemen and Saudi Arabia that outlasted both Yahya and Abd al Aziz. The irrepressible Yahya, however, held other ideas within the privacy of his own country. Wenner reports that a 1940 Yemeni school textbook divided Yemen into three areas: "independent Yemen; Asir [under Saudi occupation]; and Hadrawmaut and Oman [under British occupation]."

The treaties of Sanaa and Taif, signed within six months of each other, effectively brought an end to Yahya's aspirations to rule all of South Arabia. Troubles frequently developed over interpretations of the agreement with the British, but it was this treaty that set the stage for the existence of two independent nations in the historical area of Yemen. The agreement with Abd al Aziz signaled the end of open conflict between the rulers of Saudi Arabia and Yemen, which was significantly manifested in Saudi support for Imam Badr during the civil war (see Civil War in North Yemen, this ch.).

As Bidwell notes, Yemen was self-supporting during the period before the discovery of oil in the Arabian Peninsula when the other rulers of the region were to a large degree dependent upon British subsidies. Yahya was determined never to depend upon outsiders, and his (and his country's) experience with foreigners did not incline him to trust them at all. Bidwell reports that the imam told one of his confidants that he would rather eat straw than submit to any foreign influence. Yahya believed that India and China had been colonized because they had first given commercial concessions to foreigners, who had used concessions to justify military occupation. He kept Yemen as isolated from foreign contact as was possible in the first half of the twentieth century.

Yahya recognized, however, that he needed military supplies to use against his internal and external enemies. He first turned to the United States, but his 1919 request for recognition was not answered, and a later visit by a United States diplomat produced no lasting results. He turned next to the Italians, with whom in 1926 he concluded his first treaty with any Western nation. The Italians provided weapons, radio links, education, and other facilities in exchange for commercial privileges. The Italians maintained a presence in the country throughout the 1930s with physicians, merchants, and a few diplomats. In 1928 a treaty was signed with the Soviet Union, which tried to become involved in commerce in Yemen but had little success. Treaties signed with the Netherlands (1933) and Belgium (1936) had little practical value, and even the limited relationship with Italy came to an end in 1943. More important were a 1931 treaty with Iraq for military training and a 1936 regional pact with both Iraq and Saudi Arabia directed against Zionism in Palestine, a forerunner of the 1945 pact creating the League of Arab States (Arab League), of which Yemen was a founding member.

Consolidation of British Control Over the Protectorates and Aden

The British worked assiduously during the 1930–50 period to bring the area that is now South Yemen under control. The problems included the changing status of Aden and of the Aden citizen body, the consolidation of the areas most critical to Aden's commerce (the Western Protectorate), and the largely unexplored and anarchic Hadhramaut (the Eastern Protectorate). By 1928 Aden was administered from the Colonial Office in London. The Government of India Act of 1935 gave Aden crown colony status, but the settlement of Aden did not officially become Aden Colony until 1937. (Aden had been in fact the first annexation to the British Empire of Queen Victoria's reign.) Until 1934 the British referred to the "Aden Protectorate and the Hadrawmawt."

In 1937 the term *protectorate* meant in practice what became the nucleus of the Western protectorate (see fig. 4). Groups included in the protectorate were assured that Britain gave to the ruler of each territory and heirs forever the "gracious favour of protection." The rulers were not to sell or cede any of their territories to any foreign power except Britain, were not to enter into any treaties or alliances with any foreign group, and were to notify the British Resident in Aden if any foreigner attempted to intervene in the shaykhs' affairs.

There was actually only one protectorate legally established, but for administrative ease the area was divided into the Eastern Protectorate and the Western Protectorate.

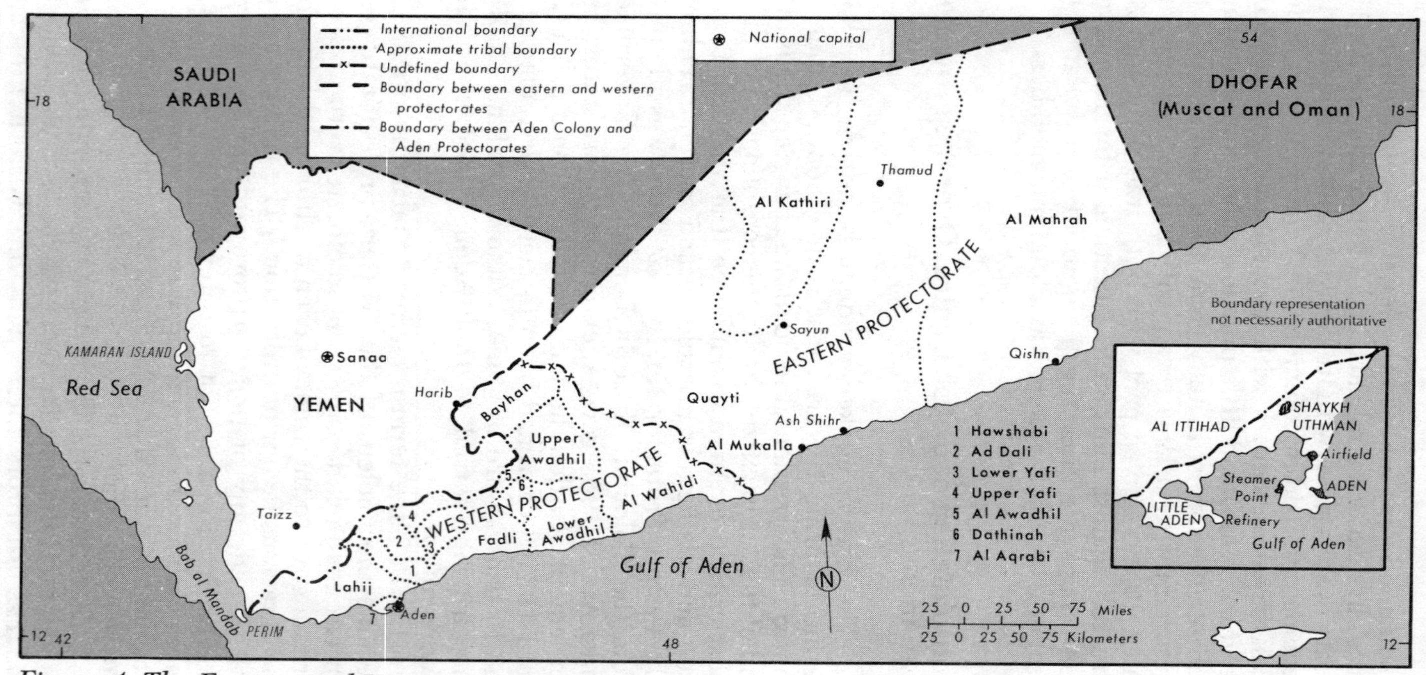

Figure 4. The Eastern and Western Protectorates, 1955

The first concern of the British was to bring order to the Western Protectorate because of its proximity to Aden. In 1928 the British formed a military force, the Aden Protectorate Levies, composed of local tribesmen commanded by British officers. Aden itself had a civil internal security force, the Government Guards, led by British and Arab officers.

By far the most critical area to be brought under control was the Hadhramaut, the area that would encompass the Eastern Protectorate. This area had a social and economic system dissimilar from the states of the Western Protectorate and for centuries had carried on a separate life of its own. The Hadhramaut had a vital economic system compared with the Western Protectorate, of which Trevaskis wrote after his first visit there: "To understand the people who inhabit this cruel land one must know what it is to feel imprisoned, isolated, and hungry. . . . Only so divided and subservient a population could have tolerated such sluggish progress for so long and with such indifference." Notwithstanding the relative closeness of the Western Protectorate to Aden, the area was much more underdeveloped than the Hadhramaut to the east. The first British adviser to the Western Protectorate resorted to wearing a loincloth and conducting his business in a majlis (assembly or gathering).

The Eastern Protectorate comprised some 109,000 square kilometers in the 1930s. Its three most important tribes were the Quayti sultanate of Ash Shihr and Al Mukalla, which had the highest income of all the protectorate states, chiefly from the commerce of Al Mukalla port; the Kathiri, which had at one time controlled the entire Hadhramaut; and the Mahrah sultanate of Qishn and Socotra. The British had first made contact with the Hadhramaut in 1843, when three survivors of the family of the ruler of Al Mukalla fled to Aden to escape murder by a relative who had seized the throne. The government of British India refused to interfere but gave them a small gift of money. In 1851, after the Turks attempted to annex Ash Shihr and Al Mukalla, the sultan offered it to the British, who refused the offer. A later offer in 1869 was also rejected.

British interest in the area quickened when Brigadier W.N. Coghlan, the Resident at Aden, paid an official visit in 1853 and found a flourishing slave trade. By 1863 the British promised to protect the rulers' coastal waters in exchange for the abolition of the slave trade. During this period the British Indian government, overwhelmed by the incessant quarrels of the rulers of the area, asked the ruler of the princely state of Hyderabad in South India to bring pressure on the Quayti because the latter were hereditary *jemadars* (soldier guards) of Hyderabad. In 1888 a protectorate treaty was made with the Quayti, the stronger tribe. On the whole, however, the British were stymied in their attempts to establish order.

In 1933 the British decided that a major effort had to be made to impose order in the Hadhramaut lest the anarchy of the region reinfect the contained Western Protectorate. Harold Ingrams, a British resident adviser, was sent to the Hadhramaut to study the political situation. Ingrams noted, "Altogether I calculated there were about 2,000 separate governments in the Hadhramaut, only two recognized by the British."

These were not "governments" in the British sense. Stookey points out that rule in this area had evolved from the ancient institution of the sacred enclave in which tribal differences could be adjudicated without violence. The families controlling these enclaves often played the role of arbiter, and this privilege devolved upon successive generations. This tradition continued after the coming of Islam, and sayyids often took over this role. The sayyid families exercised influence over the local tribes through a combination of religious and moral suasion, their aristocratic descent, and the wealth they had acquired over the centuries. These families, which the British saw as ruling families in a conventional sense, were often unrelated to their "subjects" and did not have a monopoly on governing functions.

Furthermore, in this system authority did not generally rest with an individual but with the male elders of the family as a group, who named or appointed the chief. Positions of leadership were not passed from father to son but to the candidate selected by the *dawla* (ruling family). Potential dissidents were propitiated with sinecures, positions that the British tried to abolish on grounds of efficiency, with unfortunate results for the solidarity of the *dawlas*.

In this diverse atmosphere Ingrams sought to establish some order. The British government initially rejected Ingrams' suggestions that the British take an active role in pacifying the Hadhramaut, recruit tribal armies under British commanders, and appoint a British adviser to the sultans of the Quayti and Kathiri in hopes of controlling their violent enmity toward each other. In 1936 Ingrams was sent back to advise the rulers on a peace settlement. He was not to make any commitments, and he was not to negotiate with the tribes directly. Ingrams, aware that this line of procedure would net him nothing, proceeded to go from tribe to tribe, encouraging them to accept a three-year truce. By April Ingrams had 1,400 signatures and, when heavy rains fell that month, it was regarded as a good omen, and other tribes flocked to sign.

Ingrams became the first resident adviser to the Eastern Protectorate. As a result of his efforts, elementary public services and a workable administration were established in Quayti territory and other services elsewhere. The advisory treaties gave British officials only limited jurisdiction. To create even a rudimentary administrative system remained impossible in most areas because the British Resident had power only to advise and did not rule directly, and the literate labor force from which to draw local administrators was pitifully small.

In an area where people had been traveling to their fields under cover and where some had for 20 years been afraid to leave their homes, a modicum of peace now prevailed. Drawing on precedents from British India, Ingrams founded two institutions that were quite successful until their termination by the Aden Resident: the Hadrami Beduin Legion, an organization that Ingrams conceived as a combination local police and boy scouts that would spread education, bring medical help, police distant lands, and encourage a sense of trust; and the Aden Protectorate College for the Sons of Chiefs. Opened in 1936, the college had a maximum of 36 boys and an established age limit of 15. It had its own mosque and was staffed entirely by Arab teachers. The shaykhs mistrusted it at first because it bore a remarkable resemblance to the traditional hostage system, whereby imams guaranteed a tribe's submission by taking male children from leading families as hostages and raising them in the palace. The college nevertheless acquired great popularity, and most of the shaykhs were angry at its closure in 1952. The boys from the college eventually held responsible positions.

The principal drawback of "Ingrams' Peace" was that it was antithetical to the tribal system that continually replaced, by election, weak or ineffective rulers. By signing the agreements the British effectively froze those rulers then in power—and their heirs—which was one of the principal causes for the discontent that eventually found an effective outlet in the nationalist organizations forming in Aden Colony.

As several scholars point out, the British misunderstood the situation in the hinterland of Aden. What they imagined were sovereign rulers of well-defined entities were actually families that in some cases were not even related to the inhabitants of the lands they "ruled" but that had been brought in as mediators at some time in the past. Under British protection the role of these ruling houses was expanded beyond their capacity to perform. The British tried to transform ruling houses into the kind of local government that the British thought existed in the first place. Stookey asserts that the efforts by the British to disarm the tribes reduced many tribesmen—now deprived of their traditional role—to the level of common men without status. At the same time, the alien political and administrative forms imported by the British, plus the expansion of trade and communications, created new expectations on social and political levels. Stookey astutely points out that the struggle for independence in Aden and its environs coincided with social revolution at least partially because British rule eroded the old order and transformed the social structure.

Developments in Aden Colony

The development of Aden Colony was in strong contrast to the tribal areas around it. Until it achieved colonial status, Aden had been administered as part of India, and traces of the British-Indian tradition were visible everywhere. Most of the architecture was Bombay Victorian, the local Arabic was adulterated with English and Urdu, and the rulers of the hinterland had treaties similar to those made with India's princes. Aden's currency had been the Indian rupee and was changed in 1951 to the East African shilling. Aden's attractive status as a free port had drawn a polyglot group, most of whom had status as citizens or subjects within the Commonwealth of Nations, which before 1946 was the British Commonwealth of Nations. In 1950 Aden had 90,000 inhabitants living in a 130-square-kilometer area. Aden had a typical colonial administration; two

British agents discharged treaty obligations in the protectorate, and a largely Indian group of junior executives provided most of the bureaucracy. Over all presided the British governor.

The Indians, who were Commonwealth subjects, and a few Arab-Indian families were second in social importance only to the British. Many of the wealthy Adenese families visited India and sent sons to school in Bombay or Karachi. After the Indians and a few upper-class Arab families came the descendants from Turkish or Egyptian armies. Fugitives from the north and immigrants from the protectorate formed a large socially and economically inferior minority, basically comprising peasants who lived together and whose lives were controlled by headmen from their villages.

There was little organized political opinion that was hostile to the British until the mid-1950s. In 1947 the Aden Colony Amendment Order established a legislative council, and a few patriarchs were chosen as representatives of their communities. Anything but critical, they were proud to be part of the official Adenese community. The merchant class formed the first political group, the Aden Association. Primarily, they wished to have more power in the administration of Aden and wished to have all Somalis, Pakistanis, and Indians who had lived there for one or more generations regarded as citizens of Aden and thus receive the franchise.

By the 1950s there were two major anti-British groups: the South Arabian League and the Trades Union Congress (TUC) and its political extension, the People's Socialist Party (PSP). The South Arabian League, although radical in its anti-imperialism, was an elite party led by the ruling family of Lahij and the aristocratic Jifri family. Friendly at first with Egypt and then with Saudi Arabia, the South Arabian League was bypassed in the end and played little or no role in the independence of South Yemen or its post-independence politics.

During the 1950s the TUC and the affiliated PSP, led by Abdallah al Asnaj (an immigrant from Yemen), took the lead in opposition to the British. They were supported by both the Labour government in Britain and by the Egyptian government. Stookey notes that numerous people, including many British in Aden, assumed that the PSP would achieve independence through negotiation with the Labour government, but the PSP was outmaneuvered and defeated in the 1960s by another group, the National Liberation Front (NLF).

All factions working for independence were encouraged by the coup d'état in Egypt that brought Gamal Abdul Nasser and his colleagues to power in 1952. It was not long before the Egyptians were providing tangible support to anti-imperialist and radical groups throughout the Arab world.

The NLF may have begun to organize as early as the mid-1950s. Growing out of the Arab Nationalist Movement—founded in 1954 at the American University of Beirut and including in its early days a diversity of opinion—the NLF did not move into the open until its October 14, 1963, declaration that it would lead the struggle to remove the British by force.

Growing Opposition and the Assassination of Imam Yahya

Underground opposition to the imam had begun as early as the late 1930s in Yemen, and by the mid-1940s major elements of the population were moving into opposition to Yahya's rule. Young Yemenis, particularly the few who had been educated abroad, were shocked at the imam's resistance to modern ways. The Shafiis of the Tihamah were angered by the imam's meddling in commerce and his efforts to monopolize trade. Even the more traditional elements, the ulama and the sayyids of the Zaydi areas, were disaffected. They resented Yahya's efforts, which had begun as early as the late 1920s, to make his eldest son, Ahmad, the next imam by demanding that chiefs and other leaders take oaths of loyalty to him. Although Ahmad was undoubtedly qualified to be imam, being well known as both *mujahid* (warrior) and mujtahid (Islamic scholar), there were other equally qualified candidates available. The concept of primogeniture was repugnant to the ulama because it struck at the heart of Zaydi doctrine and equally so to the sayyids because there were members of that class who also aspired to the imamate, some from families that had provided imams before Yahya's father.

Opposition elements were at first attracted to the imam's son, Ahmad, but after it became clear that he was hardly less autocratic than his father, dissent began to crystallize in Aden, which was beyond the imam's reach. The members of the first major Yemeni opposition group, Al Ahrar al Yeminiyun (Free Yemenis), were members of the mercantile, religious, and intellectual elite, including both Zaydis and Shafiis. Several of the political figures who would play prominent roles on both sides of the civil war were members of the Free Yemenis and associated groups. Free Yemeni efforts at direct change in Yemen failed, and the organization effectively disintegrated in the late 1950s, but from the core of this group came the moderates who brought together the warring factions after eight years of civil war in the 1960s.

In 1946 Yahya tried reconciliation, sending Ahmad to meet with the Free Yemenis in Aden, but this was not successful. In November 1946 one of Yahya's younger sons, Ibrahim, went to Aden and allied himself with the Free Yemeni movement, which had bought a press and had begun its own newspaper, *Sawt al Yaman* (Voice of Yemen), which attacked the system of government in Yemen but carefully refrained from attacking the imamate or Yahya personally at this point.

Eager to show that they were not anti-Islamic despite their opposition to theocratic rule in Yemen, the Free Yemenis developed good relations with the Muslim Brotherhood (Al Ikhwan al Muslimun) in Egypt, whose leaders had met with some Free Yemeni leaders in Cairo. An Algerian member of the Brotherhood traveled extensively in Yemen, working for the goals of the Free Yemenis. Contact was established with influential Yemenis close to the imam, including Sayyid Abdallah al Wazir, a general and an administrator under Yahya who came from a family that had provided many of the Zaydi imams.

The Free Yemenis were hardly revolutionaries. The plans that they finally drew up called for Abdallah to succeed Yahya as imam and for him to follow the traditions of the Prophet. The "Sacred National Pact" that the movement drew up was reformist only to the extent that it called for the establishment of consultative and constituent assemblies independent of the imamate and guaranteed to the towns majority representation in the assemblies to counteract the traditional power of the tribes.

After an abortive coup attempt in January 1948, the conspirators moved again in February. The octogenerian imam was shot as he motored in the countryside, and

Abdallah proclaimed himself imam. Forewarned, Yahya's son, Ahmad, by now 56 years old, marched from Taizz (where he was governor) through Hodeida to Hajjah, the stronghold of the Hamid al Din family, where Ahmad had once been a popular governor. The Hashid and Bakil tribes came to his aid, as did other Zaydi tribes, which were shocked at the murder of the aged imam, their spiritual leader and the hero of the nationalist uprising against the Turks. The tribesmen may also have been perturbed at Abdallah's accession to the imamate when he had, albeit unwillingly, taken an oath to support Ahmad's candidacy.

Ahmad recaptured Sanaa and, furious at the city's acquiescence in the uprising, allowed his Hashid and Bakil troops to sack the capital. Within a month this 1948 coup, the first in the Arab world after World War II, had failed, and Ahmad was firmly installed as imam. The Free Yemenis had set their sights on little more than constitutional reform and a change of personnel at the top. They had succeeded in neither, having no power base within Yemen and having alienated the traditional elements, who shunned those responsible for killing the imam, whatever their own differences with him might have been.

Imam Ahmad, mindful of his father's betrayal at the hands of his people, was even less accessible to his countrymen than Yahya had been but somewhat less mistrustful of foreigners. He moved permanently to Taizz, which—along with his memory of his father's betrayal by many prominent Zaydis—made him somewhat more sympathetic to his Shafii subjects than previous imams. He appointed some to high positions and even led prayers occasionally in the Shafii, rather than the Zaydi, manner. Administration was, as before, concentrated in the hands of the imam, but the facades of ministries were established. Bidwell reports that one minister of agriculture claimed that the whole of his ministry traveled on his donkey. Such details as ammunition, supplies, or even the purchase of a single airline ticket lay in the hands of Ahmad. He was an extraordinary figure—by all accounts physically imposing, a warrior of distinction, and a poet who is said to have freed several of the 1948 plotters because of the excellence of their poetry.

Less xenophobic than his father, Ahmad approved of the importation of foreign machines and allowed more young people to go abroad to study. His treasury was chronically low in funds, and he began early in his reign to seek foreign assistance. He asked for aid from the United States and the Federal Republic of Germany (West Germany), and he accepted Soviet aid for the harbor at Hodeida and assistance from China for a road from Hodeida to Sanaa.

In 1949 frontier troubles resumed, and an agreement made between the imam and the British in October 1950 was satisfactory to neither party. Relations completely deteriorated in 1953 when Ahmad became aware of British plans for the federation of the protectorates. The original formulation was for separate federal areas, one in the east and one in the west, each with a council of rulers and a working committee to which each ruler would nominate three members. Executive and legislative councils would be nominated at first but later would be elected. Both areas would be ruled by the governor of Aden, who would hold the title of high commissioner.

Ahmad was opposed to the plan because he considered the protectorate lands his inasmuch as his family had ruled them in the seventeenth century. If they became federated, they would be much more difficult to reconquer. He also feared the effect on the Shafii population, which was two-thirds of the total population. The Arab League and Egypt supported Ahmad because they felt the new federation would become more completely vassals of the British. From 1954 through mid-1955 Yemen maintained contact with potentially rebellious tribal leaders in the protectorate and supplied them with arms and money. In May 1954 Ahmad, furious at the continuation of federation talks, engineered 25 raids. As journalist and author Tom Little notes, Ahmad seemed to have had more confidence than anyone else in the success of the federation plan, which, in any case, was viewed by the shaykhs of the protectorates as undisguised British rule and rejected.

By the middle of the 1950s most of the surviving conspirators of 1948 had been freed, but the first major uprising against Ahmad did not come from this quarter. In 1955 a spontaneous coup attempt, growing out of a minor tax rebellion and led by the army chief of staff, received the support of the imam's brother, Abdallah. The imam's son, Badr, rushed to his family's stronghold of Hajjah and from there proceeded to Taizz in support of his father. Ahmad was restored to power, and the conspirators, including two of his brothers, were executed.

This was neither a planned movement, as in 1948, nor a move against the imamate as an institution, as would occur in 1962, but merely another attempt to change imams. There were several important results of Ahmad's return to power. He developed renewed confidence in his son, Badr, whose Egyptian education, untraditional life-style, and reformist ideas Ahmad had much mistrusted. From this event as well came Ahmad's mistrust of the army and of many members of the royal family. After the coup attempt of 1955 Ahmad began to move toward ensuring the succession of Badr to the throne. The ulama and the sayyids had been angered when Yahya moved to install Ahmad as his successor in the 1920s, but at least Ahmad had been well qualified for election to the imamate. This was not the case with Badr, who would certainly have been disqualified for his lack of expertise in Islamic law, if not for several other reasons. The legitimacy of the imamate would rest upon Ahmad's impositon of an unqualified successor.

Traditional elements were also dismayed by the extent to which Ahmad had begun to allow foreigners into the country. Reacting to Britain's forward policy in the protectorates and searching for allies as well as foreign aid, Ahmad turned to the Soviet Union, some of the Soviet allies in Eastern Europe, and China—then a Soviet ally. His 1956 trade agreement with the Soviets provided for Soviet equipment, wheat, and rice in exchange for coffee, fruit, and hides. Badr enthusiastically toured Eastern Europe and quickly became a prominent representative of the notions of reform then current in the Arab world. This combination of aid from the communist states and Badr's talk of reform in the Nasserist mold was extremely disquieting to the conservative forces that had traditionally provided the major support of the imamate.

By 1956 Yemen was in the mainstream of the Arab world in its opposition to the British. The Saudis, who had differences with the British, were providing arms to some of the sultans of the protectorate area as well as money to Ahmad for the purchase of arms and equipment in his efforts to dislodge the British from South Arabia.

In April 1956 an unlikely trio met in Jiddah and signed a pact that was to have far-reaching repercussions for Yemen. Imam Ahmad, President Nasser of Egypt, and King Saud signed an agreement that became known as the Jiddah Pact. It included a provision that would later be used by both

Egypt and Saudi Arabia to justify their intervention in the Yemeni civil war. Article II stated:

> The contracting States consider any armed aggression committed against any State thereof or against their forces as an aggression against them. Therefore, and in implementation of the legitimate individual and collective right for the defense of their entity, each of them is bound to hasten to the assistance of the State against whom aggression is committed and to adopt forthwith all measures and to pursue all means at its disposal, including the use of its armed forces, in order to repel aggression and to restore security and peace.

Yemeni scholar Mohammad A. Zabarah suggests that the Jiddah Pact had several goals: to frustrate British plans for the federation of Aden and the protectorate; to offset the British- and United States-sponsored Baghdad Pact (subsequently the Central Treaty Organization—CENTO), which then included both Turkey and Iraq; and to placate reformist and Arab nationalist elements within Yemen (not the least of whom was Badr).

Included in the discussions of the Jiddah Pact were ways to foment unrest in the protectorates, and throughout 1956 efforts were made to destabilize British rule there. The invasion of Egypt by British, French, and Israeli forces in 1956 galvanized support for Egypt in the Arab world. Ahmad allowed over 20,000 Yemenis to volunteer to fight alongside the Egyptians.

Reactions in Aden

In the 1950s Aden grew and changed rapidly. The growth of the port and the British construction of an oil refinery in 1954 had created jobs associated directly with the port and the refinery as well as indirectly in the small industries that grew up to meet the needs of construction, port, and refinery workers. By 1957 Aden was the fourth largest bunkering facility in the world in terms of the number of ships handled. Many of the laborers who flocked to fill the expanding job market came from Yemen and followed their leaders into the unions that were members of the TUC.

Industrial unrest began to become widespread in Aden Colony. Beginning in March 1956 there were 30 strikes involving 6,000 workers in a five-week period. The blocking of the Suez Canal in the late fall of 1956 during the Suez War precipitated further unrest. The harbor was virtually emptied of ships, unemployment was general, and the hostilities of the unemployed focused on the British not only as the rulers of Aden but also as one of the aggressors in the Anglo-French-Israeli invasion of Egypt. Many workers went back to their villages only to return to Aden as nationalist rebels.

In Sanaa the imam began to plan for a major military push against the protectorates. In January 1957 the offensive opened. There were 50 incidents during February. More Soviet shipments had been delivered, including 30 medium tanks, 30 aircraft, antiaircraft guns, troop transports, trucks, and small arms. Pilots, mechanics, and military instructors also arrived. Older weapons were distributed in the protectorate. Ahmad, taking no chances, took one tribesman hostage for every 10 rifles to ensure that the tribes would use the weapons against the British and not against him.

Attitudes toward the concept of federation among the rulers in the protectorates began to change, perhaps because the union of Syria and Egypt in the United Arab Republic (UAR) and the less consequential "union" of Yemen with the UAR had given the concept of federation a better image in the Arab world. The shaykhs may also have feared that if they did not form a federation under British protection they might ultimately come under the rule of the Zaydi imam, who had still not renounced his claims to all of South Arabia.

Although the sultan of Lahij, Ali Abd al Karim, had signed a treaty of "eternal friendship" with the British in 1952, he was opposed to the federation—partly because the state of Bayhan appeared to be taking a leading role but mostly because his adviser, Muhammad Ali Jifri, suggested that in a state independent from the British the sultan could become leader. Privately, the sultan permitted Jifri to make Lahij the base for the subversion planned by the South Arabian League. In April 1958 the Aden government was still attempting to deport Jifri and his two brothers, largely because of a series of recent bombings. That same month the commandant of the Lahij regular forces, Yahya Hursi, deserted to Taizz, taking with him two-thirds of the army (the Government Guards) and the equivalent of British £10,000 from the state treasury.

The British believed that Yahya Hursi's desertion was a part of a conspiracy with the sultan, who they knew was in contact with Imam Ahmad. The British appointed the sultan's cousin, Amir Fadl ibn Ali, acting head of state, and canceled the sultan's appointment to the Council of Electors. The enraged sultan flew to Cairo, where he became a leading propagandist against the British. Nevertheless, Ahmad continued to advance Yemen's claim to the Lahij area. The federation project still seemed Ahmad's greatest fear, and he stopped incursions along the frontier so as not to incite federation plans.

In January 1959 Aden Colony received a new constitution. The franchise, the most important issue to the Adenese nationalists, was not significantly changed, however. The vote was given to anyone born in Aden and to British or British-protected subjects who had lived seven of the previous 10 years in Aden. The council was greeted with little enthusiasm on the part of nationalists in Aden because of the inclusion of non-Yemenis in the electorate, the exclusion of most newly arrived workers from Yemen, and British domination of the whole plan.

In early 1959 the British also responded to the year-old request of six of the protectorate shaykhs for some form of federation. In Februrary 1959 the British created the Federation of Arab Amirates of the South as an autonomous territory under British protection. Executive authority was placed in the hands of a council of ministers under a rotating chairmanship. At the urging of the British, the shaykhs took the ministerial portfolios in the federation in order to give the union a measure of authority in a system where each enjoyed virtual autonomy in his own state. As Stookey notes, this not only increased the shaykhs' identification with the British but also, by keeping them absent from their respective states, "widened the already dangerous distance between the rulers and their subjects."

In September 1959 the foundation stone of the federal capital, Al Ittihad (Union), was laid outside Aden. Lahij joined the federation a month later. This was a positive sign for the success of the federation because it was the largest state of the Western Protectorate, having about one-quarter of its total population. Early in 1960 the Lower Awaliq sultanate, the Dathinah confederation, and the Aqrabi shaykhdom joined, swelling the federation to 10 members.

There were numerous strikes in early 1960, all with political overtones. The Industrial Relations Ordinance was passed in the Legislative Council. Strikes were effectively banned, and prior processes of conciliation were imposed. Strikes were halted for a short time, but essentially the ordinance destroyed the small chance there was of the unions entering into any sort of compromise with the British government. The existing Legislative Council in Aden was scheduled to end in January 1963, and decisions about Aden's merger into the federation would have to be concluded by that time. The many critics of the Aden merger were handicapped because of their inability to unite behind a common front.

Aden was, by this time, very different from the protectorates, not only demographically but also socially and politically. Members of the elite of the colony were worried that in any federation scheme the wealth of Aden would be used to provide the kind of health, education, and other services in the protectorate areas that Aden already possessed and that the political role of the Aden elite would be diluted within a union.

Although the British permitted opponents of Aden's accession to the federation to make their case on a limited basis in the colony during the weeks preceding the vote in the Legislative Council, they put heavy pressure on the council to agree to a union. Although opponents of the merger pointed to the unrepresentative nature of the Legislative Council itself—formed in 1959 on the basis of an election in which 27 percent of an electorate of 21,500 voted out of a population of 180,000—the British view prevailed. By the slim margin of one vote, the Aden Legislative Council agreed on September 26, 1962, that in January Aden would join the federation, which would be called the Federation of South Arabia. The day after the vote, however, a dramatic change occurred in Sanaa that greatly altered the course of events in South Arabia—the coup d'état against the imam that began eight years of civil war in North Yemen.

The 1962 Coup D'État in Yemen

By 1958 it was clear that Imam Ahmad was not in good health and that he was depending more and more heavily on Badr. It was partially as a result of Badr's pro-Egyptian sentiments and partially a shrewd move on the part of the imam that in 1958 Yemen moved another step closer to Egypt, joining Egypt and Syria in a federation called the United Arab States. Different from the UAR, which linked Egypt and Syria in a formal union, the United Arab States had only two practical results. First, a few small Egyptian military and educational missions came to Yemen. More important, the propaganda war carried out by Egypt in the early days of Nasser's radical phase against traditional Arab monarchs spared Ahmad, who was far more conservative than the kings of Iraq and Jordan, who were major targets of Egyptian propaganda. The imam's request to join such a confederation must have taken Nasser by surprise, and it must have been somewhat embarrassing for the leader of the Arab radicals to be thus linked to one of the most traditional monarchs in the region. Nasser, however, could hardly decline Ahmad's request, considering the pan-Arabist sentiment that emanated from Cairo. The relationship with Egypt kept some modern elements of the Yemeni opposition at bay for awhile, but it may also have further alienated the ulama and the tribesmen who already were dismayed at the number of foreigners in the country.

Despite Badr's admiration for, and personal relationship with, Nasser, Ahmad was wary of Egyptian intentions. When in January 1959 antiregime leaflets began to appear, signed by the "Free Officers" (perhaps not yet an organized group but clearly modeled after the "Free Officers" who had taken power in Egypt in 1952), Ahmad took the opportunity to throw out the Egyptian officers who had been training his troops. At this critical juncture and with opposition from traditional elements mounting over the foreign presence, Ahmad fell ill. He left Yemen for medical treatment in Rome, leaving Badr in charge.

The ulama and other traditional elements of Zaydi society were worried; they questioned whether Zaydi prayers were valid in the absence of the imam from Yemen—something that had not happened before. The imam's absence had other implications for the future of the imamate.

Badr took advantage of his interim power to implement several changes that he believed would be greeted with enthusiasm by the reformist factions. Among other things, he recalled the Egyptian officers expelled by his father four months before, established a seven-member representative council, began a reform of the civil service, and started a design for overall development planning. As political scientist J. E. Peterson suggests, these changes brought only halfhearted support from some reformist groups and simply increased the scope of activities of other dissident groups. Some of the Zaydi tribes began to settle old scores, and Badr found it necessary to provide large payments to some of the Hashid and Bakil tribes to buy peace among them. Moreover, he needed their forces to put down urban unrest, which was increasing in Taizz and other cities.

When the imam returned, he was enraged at the changes that had taken place. He undid all of Badr's changes and, in his fury, went beyond the point of wisdom in dealing with the situation. In an attempt to get the Hashid paramount shaykh to return the subsidy he had received from Badr, Ahmad invited the shyakh and his son to visit under a safe-conduct pass in order to discuss the matter. After a violent disagreement with the tribal leaders, Ahmad ordered both of his guests beheaded, an action that betrayed not only normal traditions of hospitality but, more important, the sanctity of the imam's own safe-conduct pass. The impact of this event on the traditional tribal supporters of the imam was great. Several of the Hashid groups never again backed the imamate. Throughout 1960 there were tribal disturbances that the imam was unable to suppress.

In March 1961 Ahmad was shot four times in an assassination attempt. He survived but was weakened, and he reverted to dependence upon his son for administration. The turmoil subsided temporarily after the attack on the imam, and in October 1961 Ahmad publicly called on his people to "follow" Badr, indicating his wish that his son succeed him in the imamate. This step further alienated members of the Zaydi ulama and some of the traditional followers of the imam. The decision was abhorrent to them for three reasons: primogeniture was inconsistent with Zaydi doctrine, Badr was unqualified, and there existed highly qualified candidates favored by the ulama—such as Ahmad's conservative and devout brother Hassan (the country's representative at the United Nations [UN]).

In November 1961 Ahmad abrogated the arrangements with Egypt, perhaps hoping to placate the traditional segments of society. The imam was ruthless and arbitrary, but elegant and articulate; he chose poetry as the vehicle for his new policy, publishing a poem branding Nasser's socialism as anti-Islamic.

Peterson recounts the formal establishment in December 1961 of a group of 15 army lieutenants in Sanaa that called itself the "Free Officers Organization." The goals of the members were similar to those of the Egyptian officers who had toppled King Faruk of Egypt in 1952, i.e., a republican government, a strong army, nationalism, Arab unity, and a nonaligned foreign policy. The young officers had links with the Egyptian government through older officers trained in Egypt, and they hastened to establish ties with other dissident groups and build a relationship with Nasser through the Egyptian chargé d'affaires in Sanaa. Shafii merchants provided key financing for the group. Nasser at this point began to move openly against Ahmad, and in December 1961 tribal leaders from the southern regions of Yemen and from the protectorates were invited to Cairo, where they had several meetings with the National Union (Egypt's sole political organization) in an attempt to secure arms and money for their activities.

The young officers had followed Nasser's example in choosing a senior officer, Colonel Abdallah al Sallal, to be their formal leader. Sallal had been the only one of the first crop of young men sent for training in Iraq in the 1930s to come from a lower-class background. He had been imprisoned for involvement in the 1948 coup attempt and had only been released at the urging of Badr who, according to Zabarah, believed Sallal to be a "well-meaning reformist and liberal thinker." In 1961 Badr made Sallal the commander of his personal guard and promoted him to chief of staff when he became imam after the death of his father.

Ahmad did not live to see the officers' plans come to fruition. He died in his sleep on September 19, 1962, and was succeeded by Badr, who ruled the country for only one week. During that week the dissident officers worked to rally all opposing groups, and to a large extent they were successful. The reformist, pro-Egyptian policies of the new imam were irrevelant to the officers who were resolved to destroy the imamate itself. Many traditional groups—including some of the tribes that had backed the imamate for centuries—had been alienated and did not come to the aid of the beleaguered Badr.

On the night of September 26, 1962, the officers moved. Their bombardment of the palace failed to kill

Badr, but the troops moved into their other planned positions, and by morning the republic had been declared. It was some time before it became known that Badr had survived, and the delay may have removed the incentive for some loyal troops and tribes to move against the republicans. It was not until November that Badr's survival was definitely known. By then it was clear that the lines were drawn between those who supported the military government established after the coup and those who backed the imam, generally referred to as republicans and royalists, respectively. Each side was backed by a nearby Arab nation that had its own ax to grind against the other. Civil war had been set in motion, a war in which Egypt and Saudi Arabia played important roles.

Repercussions of the Yemen Coup in Aden

The reaction in the Colonial Office in London to the Sanaa coup was mixed. There was a strong feeling, however, that Britain should recognize the republicans to counteract Britain's reputation for supporting reactionary governments. Debates on the subject continued through 1962 without resolution. The radical groups in Aden were naturally encouraged by developments in Sanaa but still had not evolved a consistent platform. The PSP and other radical groups were insisting on more civil rights, by which they mostly meant a wider application of the franchise and greater representation of native Adenese; at the same time they were pressing for union with a country—North Yemen—that had virtually no civil rights.

In December 1962 the United States recognized republican Yemen with the proviso that Egypt reduce its commitments there. Sallal, the leader of the new republic, began to broadcast announcements about the formation of the Republic of the Arab Peninsula, a daydream that implied impending revolts in Saudi Arabia, the federation, and the states of the Persian Gulf. The Aden population was receptive to such an idea, and Free Yemenis began returning to Sanaa. Moderate Adenese began to waver.

On November 13, 1962, the federation merger bill passed in the British House of Commons. Strikes and seditious groups were ruthlessly repressed. On January 18, 1963, Aden joined the federation. The governor's title was changed to high commissioner, but he remained the chief executive officer. The Federation of Arab Amirates of the South became the Federation of South Arabia (see fig. 5). That same month a law was passed, aimed particularly at the TUC, that defined as sedition any attempt to claim or incite others to claim that the federation was rightfully part of any other state.

In May 1963 the Federal Supreme Council, the ruling body of the federation, proposed that the goal should be complete independence by 1969, at which time Britain should sign a lease for its base at Aden. There were considerable difficulties about elections between January 1963 and January 1964 because the franchise was still unsettled. The election was postponed.

Important changes were taking place in the NLF. Having operated more or less as cells until October 1963, the NLF publicly declared its determination to lead armed struggle against British rule. The declaration made on October 14, 1963—which was to become the national day in South Yemen after independence—presumably expressed the will of the entire movement, although, as Stookey points out, by 1965 it became clear that a more radical faction of second-level cadres existed within the group. From 1963 on, the NLF made converts from the vitiated PSP and the TUC. The growing radicalism of the NLF also pushed the leadership of the PSP and the unions further to the left and toward advocacy of armed violence to achieve independence from Britain.

The Special Committee on Colonialism at the UN confused the matter further by sending a team to investigate the situation. Refused admission to Aden, the team went to Cairo and Sanaa. In the autumn of 1963 they published a report that alleged repression by the British and called for elections based on universal adult suffrage, self-determination, the release of political prisoners, an end to repressive measures, and the early removal of the British military base. The opposition in Aden was greatly encouraged, and political strikes increased.

In December 1963 Duncan Sandys, the secretary of state for commonwealth relations, summoned the ministers of Aden and the federation to London, but at the Aden airport a grenade fatally wounded the assistant high commissioner, George Henderson, and injured the intended victim—Trevaskis, architect of the federation—and two

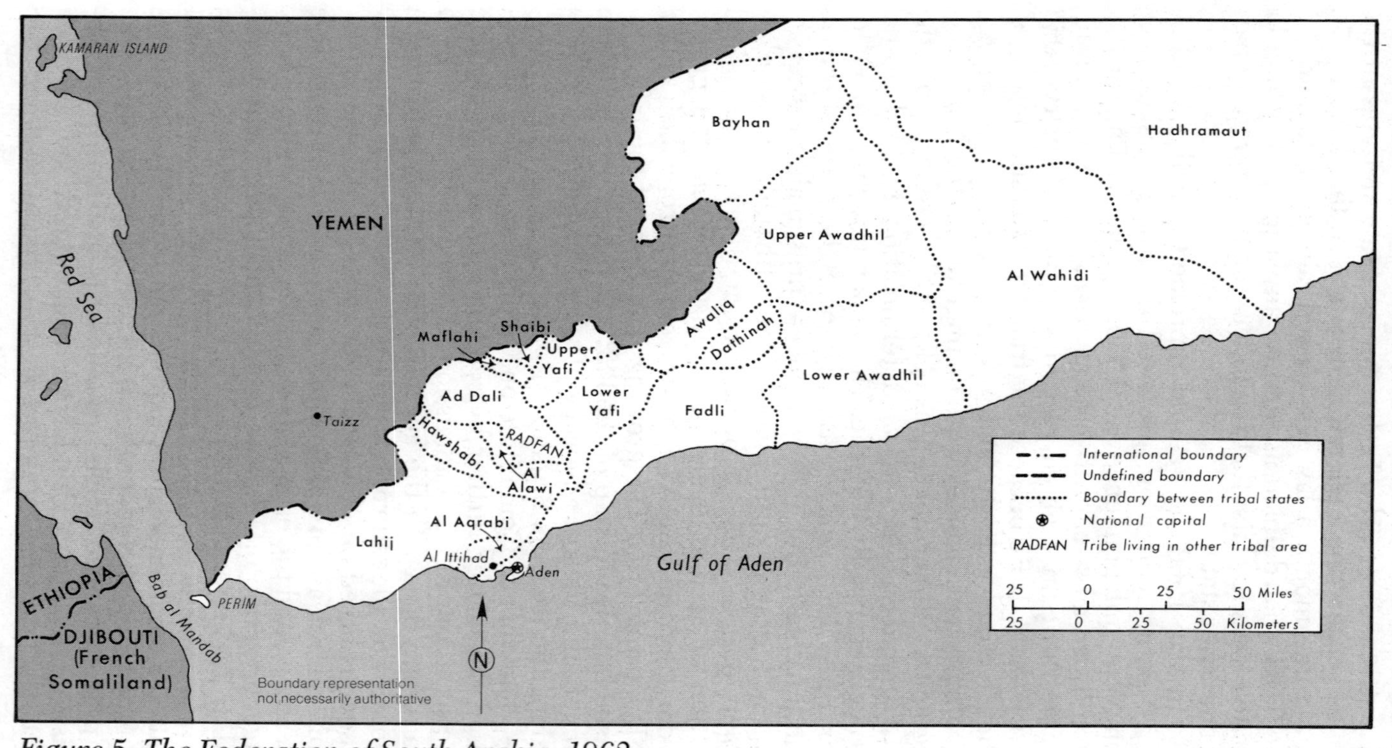

Figure 5. The Federation of South Arabia, 1962

other ministers. Trevaskis declared a state of emergency, deported 280 North Yemenis, and interned 57 members of the PSP and TUC, later released in February. The formerly pro-British government in Aden was very displeased by the state of emergency and by reports that the federal prisoners, who had been removed to the Fadli sultanate, were being tortured.

In 1963 a serious rebellion in Radfan was crushed by the British, and the federation was faced with the additional problem that the Quayti and Kathiri sultans still refused to join; the many attempts during 1963 and 1964 to encourage them to do so had yielded nothing. In June 1964 a constitutional conference was called, composed of self-elected sultans, amirs, and Adenese ministers. By July it was decided that the federation should be reshaped on more democratic lines and that independence should come no later than 1968. At that time a defense agreement would be initiated in which Britain would retain its base.

In October 1964 the Conservative government in Britain fell and was replaced by a Labour government that was unsympathetic to Britain's longtime allies—the shaykhs—and favorable to the emergence of Asnaj of the PSP and the trade unions as future rulers of a unitary state. Trevaskis was recalled to London, and a new high commissioner was appointed who was disliked by all factions in Aden and the federation. Violence in Aden grew, and the NLF began to emerge as a major factor, to the surprise of the new British government, which by now viewed Asnaj and the PSP as relative moderates because they still accepted the notion of negotiations and were no longer closely tied to the Egyptians.

Civil War in North Yemen

The civil war in North Yemen (1962–70) was a complex series of events. It reflected many of the patterns of the country's political history, involved both internal and external forces,was influenced by—and in turn had an impact upon—events in the region as a whole, and left marks that in the mid-1980s remained significant factors in domestic politics.

Most foreigners, especially the Egyptians, were slow to perceive how two major trends during the war were part of the historical pattern of Yemeni politics. Most important was the divisive and opportunistic pattern of tribal politics that had plagued Yemeni monarchs as far back as the Himyarites. Yemenis' traditional xenophobia was also a factor in the civil war. Yemenis have never profited from the long and frequent periods of foreign rule, and if anything can unite Yemenis of different tribes and sects, it is foreign domination. The Egyptians learned this lesson too late, only after many of the republicans—and the tribes allied with them—had been alienated by heavy-handed Egyptian control of the Sallal government.

Both the republican and the royalist factions were marked by internal fragmentation. Additionally, as with most movements that seek to remove an existing government, the republican coalition comprised diverse elements that held together to achieve their common objective but fell apart once that had been achieved. As Stookey points out, the segments of the urban population that supported the revolt against the imamate included both army officers and civilians, and among the civilians were Shafii merchants, young intellectuals, a few industrial laborers, and expatriate dissidents. In the long run the older generation of dissidents proved to be a key element of the republic. Stookey notes that these men, educated along traditional lines, such as Ahmad Muhammad Numan, Abd al Rahman al Iryani, and Qadi Muhammad Mahmud al Zubayri, "were reformers who had become convinced that reform was impossible to achieve under Imam Ahmad's rule." United as all these elements were in opposition to the imamate, "their aspirations were diverse, and in many respects mutually incompatible."

During the week between the death of Ahmad and the coup, the officers tried assiduously to secure the support of key tribal shaykhs of the Zaydi highlands. The weak alliance included only a limited number of tribal leaders, although significantly it split the Hashid and Bakil confederations between the republican and royalist camps. The paramount shaykhs of the Hashid remained in permanent alliance with republican forces because of Ahmad's murder of their shaykh and his son when they had been under his protection. Although most of the tribes of the Zaydi highlands supported the royalists much of the time, a number of shaykhs resorted to the game that had been played in the mountains for thousands of years—they sold the tribe's support to the highest bidder.

The imams had alienated large segments of the politically active population by 1962, but groups like the intellectuals and the Shafii merchants could hardly have overthrown the imamate alone. Because most of the highland Zaydi tribes supported the imam, the conspiracy required the participation of the most crucial element—the military.

Much has been written about the extent of Egyptian participation in the Yemeni civil war and the degree to which the Egyptian government knew of—or even planned—the coup that triggered the conflict. Unquestionably the level of Egyptian involvement was high. The republican forces could not have prevailed without Egyptian troops, and even with Egyptian assistance the republicans were never able to achieve a complete military victory over the royalist forces. Some scholars assume that the Egyptian government played the major role in planning the coup. Others believe that the plotters, fearing Saudi (or perhaps British) assistance to the imam, contacted Egypt with a request for backup support for the coup. Whatever the case, substantial Egyptian military assistance—including troops—arrived within a few days of the coup. Estimates of Egyptian troop strength involved in the civil war vary from about 40,000 to 85,000.

The royalist faction was also fragmented, primarily because of divisions within the royal family. Aid from Saudi Arabia was sought—and provided—almost immediately. Although the Saudis never sent troops to Yemen, they permitted the imam's forces to use Saudi territory, and they provided money and weapons.

Even granting the historical divisiveness of Yemeni politics, the civil war probably would not have lasted as long and certainly would not have been as damaging materially and politically if it had not been for the intervention of Egypt and Saudi Arabia. Both nations invested vast sums of money—and Egypt provided in addition a large expeditionary force—in a war that by the mid-1960s both sincerely wanted to abandon. The coup came at a critical time in inter-Arab politics, however, and inevitably entangled the leading states of the two rival camps in the Arab world. After a string of diplomatic and political successes in the 1950s, Nasser had begun to enter his more radical phase at the beginning of the 1960s. By the end of 1962 he had suffered a serious setback—the angry withdrawal of Syria from the UAR. He was not on good terms with most of the Arab governments and was carrying on a propaganda campaign against the conservative Arab states. The coup was an opportunity to illustrate his continuing commitment to the kinds of changes that became known as Nasserism and to strike a blow against the Saudis and other Arab monarchs. The request of the Free Officers for aid (whenever it was made) must have been irresistible to Nasser, who apparently believed that royalist forces could be defeated quickly and Egyptian troops returned home.

Saudi goals were simpler. One objective was to support the imamate as an institution in the face of a military coup because they were not keen to see successful military takeovers against monarchs become a trend in the region. Most of all they wanted to remove Egyptian troops from the Arabian Peninsula.

Immediately upon taking power in Sanaa the officers installed a Revolutionary Command Council (RCC) of eight members, headed by Sallal. The goals that the RCC proclaimed included the reinstitution of sharia as the law of the land, social justice, the elimination of illiteracy, Arab nationalism and unity, and nonalignment. The first five years of the civil war, 1962 to 1967, were marked in general by Sallal's domination of the republican government and Egypt's domination of Sallal.

By the end of 1962 royalist forces supported by Saudi money had begun to make considerable territorial gains. A broad geographic division emerged with royalists in the north and east and republicans in the west and south.

The Egyptians sought to make material improvements, and health services and educational institutions became more widespread but were severely hampered by the government's instability. These efforts by the Egyptian government were offset by the damage wrought by Egyptian bombing in the royalist-held areas, where sometimes whole villages were razed. Egyptian efforts to subdue dissident areas suffered also from the Egyptian tendency to be too authoritarian with people who barely accepted rule by other Yemenis and who had never been easily controlled by outsiders.

Sallal began to quarrel with his deputy, Abdul Rahman Baydani, a German-educated Shafii economist, who thought the Egyptian occupation was getting out of hand. Baydani flew to Cairo to protest Sallal's techniques and, failing to enlist the support he wished, went to Aden to establish the Yemen Development Board. Sallal deprived him of citizenship in August 1963. A month later Baydani returned to Cairo and was placed under house arrest. The Egyptian government then sent Field Marshal Abdul Hakim Amir and Anwar al Sadat, minister of Yemeni affairs, to Sanaa. They instituted a new government with a presidential council to provide collective rule. Sallal's position was strengthened when he took over the portfolio of minister of foreign affairs, previously held by Baydani.

In January 1964 Sallal increased his power and at the same time inaugurated a constitutional government. He created a nine-man political bureau and a national security council and declared himself chairman of both as well as head of state and commander in chief. In February he appointed an executive council and proposed the formation of a political body patterned after the Egyptian single-party system. He appointed a military board charged with the task of building a strong national army and ordered paper money to be issued to replace the Maria Theresa thaler, which had been in use since the days of the Ottomans. The only project that succeeded was the initiation of paper currency, and leading republicans became very troubled over Sallal's increasingly autocratic methods.

Nasser made his first visit to Sanaa in April 1964 and drew up a new constitution that provided for a president (Sallal), a prime minister (General Hamud al Gayefi), a consultative council, a national defense council, a judiciary, and a municipalities group. Sallal was sent on trips to Cairo, Moscow, and Beijing to gain time for the new institutions to consolidate.

Opinion remained divided in republican quarters about whether Egypt should negotiate with the royalists or push for total victory. The situation was stalemated. The royalists could not vanquish Egyptian troops, but neither could Egypt hold its position in the mountains in the presence of so many fierce tribes accustomed to guerrilla tactics. Reconciliation had been attempted by a number of external sources. In June 1963 Prime Minister Faisal of Saudi Arabia proposed that all outside intervention in Yemen should stop, but he received no reply to this proposal. At about the same time, however, the UN secretary general received messages from Yemen, Saudi Arabia, and Egypt agreeing to end hostilities. In response he sent a team of 200 UN observers under General Carl von Horn to supervise the promised disengagement. The general resigned in September from what he declared was a hopeless task. A January 1964 conference of Arab heads of state agreed that a greater effort should be made to establish peace in the area. Finally in September 1964 Nasser and Faisal met in Alexandria. The meeting was quite amicable, but its effectiveness may be gauged by Faisal's sending a congratulatory message to Badr five days later on "the anniversary of his ascent to the throne."

In retrospect, the only elements within each camp that held promise of any sort of compromise were the moderates. By the mid-1960s these elements began to make their presence felt in both the royalist and the republican factions. Ironically, the most important moderates on the republican side were from the old Free Yemeni group, whose attempt to topple the imam had failed in 1948. In the fall of 1963 the "Third Force" (to signify distance from the extremists of both sides) was established by moderate republicans, including a number of republican tribal leaders. The Hizballah (Party of God) also brought moderate republicans together. The members of these groups generally favored retention of the republic but an end to rule by Sallal and the Egyptians. On the royalist side as well there were stirrings from moderate elements. In the spring of 1964 there was a meeting of some of the ulama, who agreed on the concept of a constitutional imamate.

Royalists and republicans met at Erkowit in Sudan on November 8, 1964, and agreed to arrange a peace conference to take place three weeks later. The meeting, however, never materialized.

Violence in Aden

While negotiations were stymied in Sanaa, the British were busily drawing up plans to defuse the increasingly violent situation in Aden. In early 1965 they tried to persuade the Adenese and other federal ministers to agree on a series of stages whereby South Arabia would become independent in 1968 in the constitutional form of a unitary state to replace the federation. In March 1965 the British summoned a constitutional conference to meet in London. Both Asnaj and the federal government wanted the Eastern Protectorate states that had not joined the federation to take part in the talks. The statement by the Adenese ministers proved too inflammatory for the high commissioner, who banned its publication. The chief minister resigned.

At about the same time, under pressure from Nasser, Asnaj formed the Organization for the Liberation of the Occupied South (OLOS) by amalgamating his own PSP with the South Arabian League and another small group, the Committee for the Liberation of the Occupied South. This last group included many interesting exiles, the two most important being the ex-sultan of Lahij, Ali Abd al Karim, and the ex-sultan of Fadli, Ahmad ibn Abdullah. In an attempt to unify all resistance movements, the South Arabian committee of the Arab League under Asnaj brought the OLOS together with the NLF. The South Arabian Committee included Saudi Arabia, Kuwait, Tunisia, Egypt, and North Yemen. Only North Yemen and Egypt abstained from the committee's recommendation that a political settlement with Britain be attempted that did not demand prior conditions that Britain would refuse to accept. The NLF rejected its decision.

Because the NLF swore to kill any new ministers, it became difficult to replace the various ministers who were daily resigning. Finally the high commissioner chose Abd al Qawi Makawi, a moderate opposition politician, as chief minister of the Aden government. Makawi tried to force a nationalist policy on both the British government and tribal leaders. He had been in power for one month when he dissociated himself from the ban on terrorism and demanded an end to the state of emergency, the release of political prisoners, the restoration of public freedom, self-determination on the basis of adult suffrage, the formation of a provisional government, and negotiations on the military base and independence. He began to work very closely with Asnaj.

The already violent situation deteriorated further. In August 1965 two senior British officials—the superintendent of police and the Speaker of the State Legislative Assembly—were murdered. A curfew was imposed, and the atmosphere became so volatile that the Aden government refused to assist the high commissioner. When Makawi supported a proposal made by two members of the National

Assembly that the British negotiate with the NLF, the British responded by suspending the Aden constitution and imposing direct rule in a vain effort to cope with deteriorating security and the refusal of the ministers to condemn either the rampant terrorism or the NLF.

Stalemate in North Yemen

Gayefi's government in Sanaa had a very short life span. In January 1965 Sallal replaced him with Hassan al Amri, who was made responsible for crushing the moderates who had become too vociferous. Amri formed a tribunal to judge the dissenting moderate ministers. The plan was to consolidate the internal political base for a major military offensive, which was eventually launched at Harib. Egyptian forces were victorious, but the royalists soon recovered. After Amri's failure, Sallal, at Nasser's urging, appointed Ahmad Muhammad Numan, leader of the conciliatory Party of God, prime minister. This was a major change of orientation because Numan was the chief leader of those tried by Amri's primitive tribunal. The first leader of the Party of God, Shaykh Muhammad al Zubayri, had been murdered. Another major party member was Qadi Abd al Rahman al Iryani, who had resigned from Sallal's government the preceding December. Both Iryani and Zubayri had been Sallal's vice presidents.

On April 24, 1965, Numan formed a government and proclaimed its policy to be a return to peace for all of North Yemen. Not surprisingly, Sallal soon was embroiled in conflicts with Numan. Sallal, in his capacity as president, appointed the Supreme Council for the Armed Forces, which became the effective government. The council ordered the arrest of a few of Numan's supporters, and on July 1 Numan resigned and flew to Cairo to state his grievances. A group of moderate republicans, including Iryani and 18 major shaykhs, supported Numan, but their appeal to Nasser for support was unsuccessful.

Nasser agreed to meet King Faisal in Jiddah in August 1965, where they reached an agreement for an immediate cease-fire, the withdrawal of Egyptian troops from Yemen by September 23, and the establishment of an interim government that would hold a plebiscite to determine the constitutional future of Yemen. Amri was returned to power as prime minister, and the various republican factions were brought together in a presidential council that included Numan, Iryani, and Gayefi.

On November 23, 1965, at Harad, 25 representatives each from the royalist and republican sides, plus one representative each for Nasser and Faisal, held a conference. No agreement was reached, and the conference ended on the eve of Ramadan, December 24. They had hoped to elect an interim government, but the republicans insisted that the imam's dynasty be excluded from state positions, and the royalists refused to sanction the holding of a plebiscite while Egyptian troops remained in the country.

The Final Year of the British in Aden

In January 1966 radical dissidents within the NLF suspended the movement's leaders and formed a new "general command," as well as a committee to investigate the old leadership. Stookey reports that the committee included a number of men who became prominent in politics after independence.

The NLF meanwhile had gained strength. Stookey states that by the end of 1965 half of the TUC's 12 most important unions had defected to the NLF, and the process was continuing. Nasser wanted to unite the anti-British forces and to bring them under his influence. To this end he had pushed for a merger of the NLF with Asnaj's enlarged group, OLOS, into a new organization called the Front for the Liberation of South Yemen (FLOSY). Although a merger agreement was signed in the late summer of 1966, the NLF signatories were from the "old," discredited leadership, and the merger was rejected by the more radical cadres that were now in charge of the NLF within the country. The radicals undertook a campaign of violence against FLOSY as well as the British. In December 1966 the two wings of the NLF were reconciled, and the movement began in 1967 to solidify its influence.

Although the Labour government in London was eager to retain the British base in Aden, it was unwilling to do so by propping up an obviously unpopular regime. The British continued to make efforts in 1965 to reach a constitutional solution, but in September 1965 they returned to direct rule of Aden in the face of rising violence. The final admission of British defeat came in a February 2, 1966, white paper, which announced British determination to withdraw all forces by 1968 and made clear that, promises to the shaykhs notwithstanding, there would be no defense treaty with the Federation of South Arabia after the British departure. The shaykhs, whom the British had misperceived from the beginning but whom they had built up into local rulers, were stunned by this announcement and knew that without British protection their future was dim.

Although the British drew up a constitution for the future state, the certainty of British departure encouraged a power struggle among the various nationalists. The government of the Federation of South Arabia virtually ceased to function, and violence increased as the factions fought the British and each other. During March and April there was at least one murder a day. An army mutiny was followed by the collapse of the few federation ministries that were still operating. Unlike the PSP, which had been active primarily in Aden, the NLF had since its inception maintained bases of operation throughout the hinterland. By August 1967 the NLF was in control of most areas, and the federation was in its death throes. Stookey notes that the strength of the NLF had increased with defection of numbers of lower-middle-class Yemenis formerly associated with the army and the police, and this infusion of new supporters was a key factor in the collapse of the federation. The British evacuation, he says, "took the form of a retreat under fire, which coincided with a South Yemeni civil war the outcome of which instituted a profound alteration of the traditional patterns of society, economy and government."

By the end of the summer of 1967 the federation had formally collapsed. Bidwell reports that some members of the British government were pleased that now they would have no obligations remaining behind them upon departure. Faced with a choice between the very radical NLF and the Egyptian-supported FLOSY, which were battling for control of the state-to-be, the British were leery of handing power to a group with strong ties to Nasser, who had undertaken to leave North Yemen in the wake of the June 1967 War between Israel and three Arab states. So the British tacitly supported the NLF, claiming (somewhat disingenuously) that they did not know at the time that it was so radical a group. Even the stalwart sultan of Bayhan, when deposed by NLF forces (some still under nominal British control), did not receive any help from his erstwhile British allies.

Foreign Troops Leave the Yemens

By mid-1966 Sallal had become ill, so Amri was faced with the task of reconciling Egyptian policy with that of the moderates, chiefly represented by the Party of God. Although very sick, Sallal obstructed Amri's efforts and had him and 40 men, including Iryani and Numan, arrested and held in detention in Cairo.

In September Sallal formed a new government in which he served as prime minister and president, and General Abdullah Guzeilan was deputy prime minister and deputy commander in chief. In October 1966 a committee of inquiry was established. Arrests were so frequent that schools, government offices, and barracks were converted to prisons. Egypt began to use napalm and poison gas to quell dissidents.

By 1967 military victory was not in sight for either side. The civil war had virtually destroyed the economy. There were severe food shortages, and prices were inflated by the influx of funds from Egypt and Saudi Arabia. Moderate elements within both camps had become stronger. Many royalists were now willing to accept compromise, and within the republican camp moderate elements had been spurred on by the dismissal of Numan in 1965 and the subsequent imprisonment of republican moderates in Egypt. Sallal's rule, problematic from the beginning, had become unpopular even among devout republicans. The civil war had exacerbated Zaydi-Shafii differences, and the Shafiis mistrusted Sallal because he was, after all, a Zaydi. Zaydis were historically accustomed to aristocratic rule, and even some republicans were uncomfortable with Sallal's humble origins. The major cause of Sallal's downfall, however, was his open dependence upon, and subservience to, the Egyptians, whose high-handedness had become abhorrent to most Yemenis.

Just as the situation in the Arab world had prompted Egyptian and Saudi intervention in North Yemen in the first place, so also did a major event in the region set in motion the events that would end the conflict. The June 1967 War with Israel was a disaster for Nasser. He had been eager to disentangle Egypt from the peninsula for some months before the war, but he must have been particularly despairing as he faced the impending conflict with a large number of his best troops in North Yemen. His losses in the war with Israel undermined his ability to carry on the endless conflict in North Yemen and made it necessary for him to seek financial support from the wealthy Arab oil producers, principally Saudi Arabia. At the August 1967 Khartoum summit of the Arab League, Nasser and Faisal were reconciled, and the major Arab oil producers agreed to provide massive aid to Egypt, Jordan, and Syria. Agreement was reached on Egyptian withdrawal from North Yemen, and this time the agreement was honored.

Egyptian troops left in October 1967. The last British troops were removed on November 29, and at midnight that night the People's Republic of South Yemen was proclaimed. Although the civil war in North Yemen did not end until 1970, by which time both sides were so thoroughly exhausted that neither could score a conclusive victory, all the elements for its resolution were now in play. For the first time in hundreds of years the peoples of South Arabia were independent of foreign rule.

* * *

The ancient kingdoms of the area are described in some detail in Brian Doe's archaeological study, *Southern Arabia*. British expert Robin Bidwell provides a rich historical study in his 1983 book, *The Two Yemens*, which, although deliberately undocumented, provides a wealth of information on both Yemens from ancient to modern times and is most enjoyable reading. A useful scholarly study of twentieth-century North Yemen is Manfred Wenner's *Modern Yemen, 1918–1966*. Robert Stookey's *The Politics of the Yemen Arab Republic*, his *South Yemen: A Marxist Republic in Arabia*, J.E. Peterson's *Yemen: The Search for a Modern State*, and Fred Halliday's *Arabia Without Sultans* are four scholarly works indispensable to an understanding of twentieth-century Yemen. B.R. Pridham's edited volume, *Contemporary Yemen: Politics and Historical Background*, contains a number of helpful articles. *Saudi Arabia: A Country Study* and *Persian Gulf States: Country Studies*, both edited by Richard F. Nyrop, provide information on the other societies of the Arabian Peninsula.

Works by British officials include Harold Ingrams' *The Yemen, Imams, Rulers, and Revolution* and *Arabia and the Isles*; Sir Kennedy Trevaskis' perceptive *Shades of Amber*; and David Ledger's *Shifting Sands: The British in South Arabia.* Other useful books include R.J. Gavin's *Aden under British Rule*, the standard reference on colonial Aden, Tom Little's chronological study of North Yemen up to independence, *South Arabia*, and Yemeni scholar Mohammed A. Zabarah's *Yemen, Tradition vs. Modernity*, which closely examines the fall of the imamate.

Majorie Kelly's edited volume, *Islam: The Religious and Political Life of a World Community*, presents a very good general introduction to Islam; Peter Awn's chapter, "Faith and Practice," is a particularly clear, insightful, and unusually bias-free introduction to Islam by a Westerner. Volume 1 of Marshall Hodgson's *The Venture of Islam* contains a very rewarding discussion of the various schisms that produced the Shia sects as well as material on all other aspects of Muslim history, including an excellent exegesis of Shafii theology. For readers interested in further exploration of the esoteric aspects of Ismaili theology, Henry Corbin's *Cyclical Time and Ismaili Gnosis* is a fascinating, if challenging, starting point. (For further information and complete citations, see Bibliography.)

Chapter 2. North Yemen

One of the numerous, traditional-style mosques in Sanaa, North Yemen

Country Profile

Country

Formal Name: Yemen Arab Republic; Al Jumhuriyah al Arabiyah al Yamaniyah.

Short Forms: North Yemen; Yemen (Sanaa); or YAR.

Term for Citizens: North Yemeni(s); adjectival form—North Yemeni.

Capital: Sanaa.

Flag: Three horizontal bands—red, white, and black; green star in center of white band.

Geography

Size: Approximately 194,250 square kilometers.

Topography: Mountainous interior, coastal plain, and eastern desert (see fig. 1).

Climate: Varies by region; highlands temperate; coastal plain humid, hot, arid.

Boundaries: Mostly defined; some of border with Saudi Arabia and with South Yemen not demarcated.

Society

Population: About 6,058,000 in 1985, although estimates vary.

Education: Free through university to all citizens, although not all students have access to schools. General literacy rate estimated at 15 percent, female literacy as low as 2 percent.

Health: Government clinics but not yet evenly distributed; infectious diseases endemic.

Ethnic Groups: All North Yemenis are Arabs.

Religion: Almost all North Yemenis are Muslims, but are three sects: Shafii Sunnis, Zaydi Shias, and Ismaili Shias. Also remnants of small Jewish community.

Economy

Gross National Product (GNP): US$4.2 billion in 1983—US$510 per capita (World Bank *Atlas* methodology).

Agriculture: Contributed 21 percent of gross domestic product (GDP) in 1983 and employed about 70 percent of work force. Main crops sorghum and millet, minor amounts of other grains, vegetables, fruits, coffee, and qat (main cash crop).

Industry: Accounted for about 9 percent of GDP in 1983. Main industries: building materials, food processing, electric power, metal fabrication, chemicals, and cotton textiles.

Exports: US$10 million in 1982 (excluding reexports). Mostly fish products, cotton, hides, and coffee.

Imports: US$1.5 billion in 1982. Mostly foods, chemicals, petroleum products, and machinery and transportation equipment.

Exchange Rate: YR5.86 per United States dollar (December 1984).

Railroads: None.

Roads: About 3,093 kilometers, of which 2,086 paved in 1983.

Ports: Hodeida main port; two minor ports.

Government and Politics

Government: President, chosen by 159-member People's Constituent Assembly, Ali Abdallah Salih in mid-1985; assumed power on July 18, 1978. After assassination of predecessor, Salih reelected by Assembly for second term on May 22, 1983. Appointed assembly members ratified government measures. Transition to elected legislature promised but not accomplished by mid-1985. In October 1982 Salih convened People's General Congress as instrument of political mobilization; 700 of 1,000 members popularly elected. Judiciary formally independent and based on sharia (Islamic law). Country divided into 11 governorates. Below governorates, four levels of local government: *qada* (district); *nahiyya* (township); *uzla* (a group of villages); and individual villages.

Politics: Political parties illegal, but People's General Congress intended to function as mass political party. Zaydi tribal leaders, or shaykhs, in north of country politically powerful and largely independent of central government. Zaydi-Shafii differences of declining importance, but Shafii support for leftist National Democratic Front (NDF), supported by South Yemen, significant. NDF inactive in mid-1980s, however.

Foreign Relations: Nonaligned foreign policy. Relations with Saudi Arabia and South Yemen most important. Unification talks with South Yemen continuing in mid-1980s; frequent consultations between presidents and ministers of two countries.

National Security

Armed Forces: Total strength in 1985 about 36,500; army—35,000; air force—1,000—1,500; navy—550.

Paramilitary Forces: Tribal levies at least 20,000.

Military Service: Although three-year conscription provided for by law in 1985 all personnel volunteers.

Estimated Defense Expenditure: YR2.4 billion (US$526.9 million) in 1982.

Foreign Military Aid: Soviet Union, United States, Saudi Arabia.

Equipment: Most infantry weapons, military vehicles, tanks, aircraft, and patrol boats Soviet-made; some artillery, antiaircraft guns, and combat aircraft United States-made.

Police: Strength around 13,000; included uniformed police and nonuniformed civilians in Ministry of Interior.

IN THE MID-1980s the Yemen Arab Republic (North Yemen) had attained a measure of political stability under President Ali Abdallah Salih. Salih, who had come to power in July 1978 following the assassination of his predecessor, had experienced some success in building bases of support throughout the country. Politics remained, however, a grim game of survival in an often violent environment. Attempted coups d'état were frequent, and the regime's preoccupation with self-preservation left it with limited time or resources to devote to developing strong political institutions. Genuine national unity remained an elusive goal. Although an observer's comment in early 1984 that individuals could find asylum from governmental authority no more than 20 kilometers outside the capital may have been exaggerated, Zaydi tribes in the northern part of the country remained strong, and tribal leaders could effectively block central government initiatives. In the southern part of the country, the National Democratic Front, an insurgency movement that has been periodically backed by the People's Democratic Republic of Yemen (South Yemen), was largely inactive in the mid-1980s, but it retained the potential to threaten the Salih regime should North Yemen's relations with South Yemen deteriorate.

Although in the mid-1980s the country remained one of the least developed in the world, it had made significant advances since the early 1960s. The substantial remittances by citizens working abroad—most of them in Saudi Arabia—had been a major factor in the growth of the economy, but the continuing contraction of the world's oil economy had already slowed remittances from abroad, and observers anticipated little improvement throughout the 1980s. In 1984 oil was discovered in the Marib governorate and should contribute to economic expansion. Should the oil fields prove to be extensive, the country's socioeconomic situation would change in significant and unpredictable ways.

North Yemen's history accounts for its isolation from the world until 1962, but its geography and climate help to explain the partial isolation of its regions from one another. In this fragmented physical environment, North Yemenis living in different ecological zones adapted to their environment and developed distinctive cultural traits. Certain historical trends—such as the introduction of Islam, the isolationist policies of the imams, the overthrow of the imamate, and the development of large-scale labor migration—have affected all of North Yemen, but in the mid-1980s many regional traits endured. Geographical boundaries such as mountains never entirely prevented contact between peoples residing in different geographical regions, but historical factors led to certain religious-ethnic groups locating in certain regions, and geographic and ecological factors tended to preserve regional differences.

Geographic and Demographic Setting

The Physical Environment

North Yemen occupies approximately 194,250 square kilometers and borders the Red Sea on the west, South Yemen on the south and southeast, and Saudi Arabia on the north and northeast (see fig. 1). Much of the country's border has been the subject of dispute and conflict since the time of independence from the Ottomans in 1918. Yemen's claim to the Asir area along the Red Sea north of contemporary North Yemen led to open fighting on several occasions, notably in November 1933 (see Independent Yemen, ch. 1). The dispute was finally settled in 1934 when Yemen and Saudi Arabia concluded a treaty of friendship whereby the Asir area was incorporated into Saudi Arabia. Since 1934 the northern border with Saudi Arabia, which follows a mountain ridge for approximately 322 kilometers inland from the Red Sea to a point east of the city of Najran, has been demarcated. The Saudi-Yemeni border running southeast from that point, however, was still undefined in mid-1985. Scholars note that North Yemen's boundaries are political rather than geographic because the geographic structure of North Yemen is contiguous with South Yemen and Saudi Arabia.

Swiss population geographer Hans Steffen divides North Yemen into three geographic zones: the western, eastern, and southern escarpments (or regions). The western escarpment includes the Western Highlands, which are over 1,500 meters, the western midlands (500-1,500 meters), and the Tihamah. The Tihamah is a nearly 419 kilometers-long coastal plain—narrow, hot, humid, semidesert, and almost waterless. It extends the entire seacoast from Maydi on the northern frontier with Saudi Arabia to the Bab al Mandab at the country's southern limits and occupies approximately 10 percent of the country's land area. Its location close to the Horn of Africa has historically facilitated contact between the Tihamah and the African continent so that the culture of the Tihamah contains many elements reminiscent of nearby African groups. Seven major wadis (episodically flowing rivers) flow westward from their sources in the central-western slopes of the interior highlands and permit limited agricultural activity. Hodeida, the country's major port, is located in the Tihamah.

The eastern escarpment consists of the highlands, which have an altitude of more than 1,500 meters; the midlands, with an elevation of 1,000 to 1,500 meters; and the lowlands, whose altitude is less than 1,000 meters. Steffen further divides the western escarpment into the Northern Highlands, extending south from the northern border to Jabal Harf and including Saadah's plains, the Kitaf region, and the Barat massif; the Central Highlands, including the area of the main watershed in the west to the area between Dhamar and Ridaa to the east and Naqil Sumarah to the south and including many "intramountainous plains," such as the basin of Sanaa (North Yemen's capital), the basin of Dhamar, and the basin of Yarim. The east-exposed reaches of the Khawlan massif from the altitude of 1,500 meters to 3,510 meters form the Eastern Highlands. The Eastern Midlands are below 1,500 meters and include several major oases, such as Marib. The Eastern Midlands end with the easternmost portion of North Yemen—Rub al Khali, the arid, deserted Empty Quarter—which is included in the Eastern Lowlands and which stretches across Saudi Arabia. The southern escarpment includes the Southern Highlands (over 1,500 meters) and the Southern Midlands (under 1,500 meters). The highlands, especially the Northern and Central Highlands, are quite rugged, and transportation is often difficult between settlements.

These geographical divisions roughly correspond to cultural variation. The Northern Highlands are populated largely by Zaydi tribal people, whereas most Shafiis reside in the southern escarpment and the Tihamah (see The

Zaydis; The Shafiis, ch. 1). The largely Shafii beduin inhabit the eastern regions of the country.

Wadis supply drainage during the rainy seasons and enable residents in some of the more arid sections of the country to farm. South and east of Dhamar and Ibb (both in the southern escarpment), deep and narrow wadis—the Bana and Tuban—flow into the Gulf of Aden and are associated with very steep gradients. Another system of wadis in the Central Highlands flows to the Red Sea; these and some minor wadis descend steep grades to the Tihamah. Yet another system of wadis drains into the Empty Quarter.

Climatic differences, too, contribute to the creation of markedly different ecological zones. Elevation influences climatic variation, as does location on the east, west, or southern escarpments. North Yemen lies in the path of monsoon winds that bring rain to the country from May to September. In the interior foothills, highlands, and plateaus there are two major periods of rainfall brought by winds from the southeast and southwest: one from March to May and the other from July to September. The amount of rainfall varies considerably with the altitude, but in general precipitation becomes heavier as one moves north to south; the Western Highlands from Ibb northward experience less intense rainfall than the area south of Ibb. The western-exposed highlands also tend to receive particularly heavy rainfall. As much as 89 centimeters of rain fall yearly in the highest regions, permitting agriculture without irrigation, and 38 to 51 centimeters in the lower foothills. The amount of precipitation sharply decreases on the eastern sides of the Western Highland massifs, the Central Highlands, and the eastern escarpment.

The highlands enjoy a temperate summer with an average high of 21°C and a cool, dry winter with the temperature occasionally dropping below 4°C. The climate of the Tihamah is tropical; temperatures occasionally rise over 54°C, and humidity ranges from 50 to 70 percent. An annual average of 13 centimeters of rain falls in irregular and heavy torrents. There is little variation in the mean monthly temperature. Dew formation, a result of the high humidity, is common, and because there is so little rain, dew is important to agriculture in the Tihamah. Occasional winds of high velocity, usually from the southwest and northwest, produce sandstorms and soil erosion.

Geologically, the country is quite interesting; complex metamorphic rock consisting mostly of mica schists, gneisses, quartzites, and marbles is intruded by massive granite and basaltlike dikes. This complex is overlaid by Jurassic beds and tertiary rocks consisting of Cretaceous sandstones, volcanic tuffs, basalts, and andesites. The interior plateaus and the Tihamah evidence alluvial formations. In the Tertiary period the Red Sea and the Gulf of Aden opened up as the Arabian Peninsula separated from Ethiopia. The country's mountainous interior was formed as a result of block faulting along a north-south axis parallel to the Red Sea and along an east-west axis parallel to the Gulf of Aden. The central mountain range created by the uplift begins in the vicinity of Taizz. Average elevation in the interior ranges between 2,134 and 3,048 meters, and the highest peak, Nabi Shuayb, located near Sanaa, reaches over 3,760 meters. The country continues to have some volcanic activity, as evidenced by the presence of hot springs and fumaroles.

As might be expected from its geological structure, North Yemen has experienced numerous earthquakes of varying magnitude. The earliest recorded earthquake was in A.D. 742 in the "desert of Saba." In 1983 Viscount Buckmaster, a specialist on the Yemens, estimated that there had been about 25 earthquakes in North Yemen since the eighth century. In January 1941 North Yemen experienced an earthquake that left 1,200 people dead and destroyed an estimated 1,400 dwellings. But as of 1985 the severest earthquake of the twentieth century, registering 5.7 on the Richter scale, occurred on December 13, 1982. The epicenter was about 80 kilometers south of Sanaa in Dhamar Province (see fig. 6). The results of the earthquake were disastrous; estimates range from 1,900 to 3,000 people killed and perhaps more than 400,000 people left homeless. Observers reported that 11 villages were totally destroyed and possibly more than 1,066 settlements were affected. The total cost of reconstruction was estimated by the North Yemeni government in 1985 to be YR2,868 million (for value of the Yemeni rial—see Glossary). Yet the earthquake, like so many other components of North Yemen's natural and social environments, was a regional phenomenon, and the effects, while grievous, were concentrated in only one area of the country.

Population

The actual number of inhabitants of North Yemen was a point of some controversy in 1985. In February 1975 the Central Planning Organization (CPO) of North Yemen conducted a census and subsequently commissioned a Swiss firm to conduct an aerial photographic survey in order to evaluate the reliability of the census data. In 1981 North Yemen conducted another survey, but domestic and foreign demographers generally agreed that the results were highly unreliable. North Yemen participated in the World Fertility Survey in 1979, and demographers accept many of the results, which were published in 1983, as valid. Nevertheless, using the results of the 1975 census, the Swiss aerial photo survey, and the 1979 World Fertility Survey, demographers arrived at very different estimations of the population, depending upon which demographic hypotheses and tests they used. The United States Bureau of the Census estimated the population in North Yemen on the night of the census in 1975 to have been 4,705,336, of which 2,462,534 were female and 2,242,802 were male. In an unpublished report the bureau projected the resident population of North Yemen to be 6,058,000 in 1985, based on an average annual growth rate of 2.8 percent and 9,621,000 in the year 2000. The CPO planned another census for 1986, which was to be carried out with the assistance of the United States Bureau of the Census.

The average annual growth rate was also a matter of some dispute in 1985, estimated growth ranging from 2.7 percent (Population Reference Bureau) to 3 percent (World Bank—see Glossary). The CPO found it difficult to estimate birth and death rates because North Yemen does not have a history of registration of vital statistics. The Population Reference Bureau, an organization based in Washington, D.C., in April 1984 estimated the crude birth rate (number of births per year per 1,000 people) to be 48 and the crude death rate (number of deaths per year per 1,000 people) to be 21. The World Fertility Survey of 1979 estimated the crude birth rate to be 53 for the 1975-79 period.

The age structure conforms to that expected for a population with high birth and death rates. The 1975 census showed that 35.7 percent of the population were children less than 10 years old, and the 1979 World Fertility Survey indicated that almost 50 percent of North Yemenis were younger than 15 years. Estimates for life expectancy at

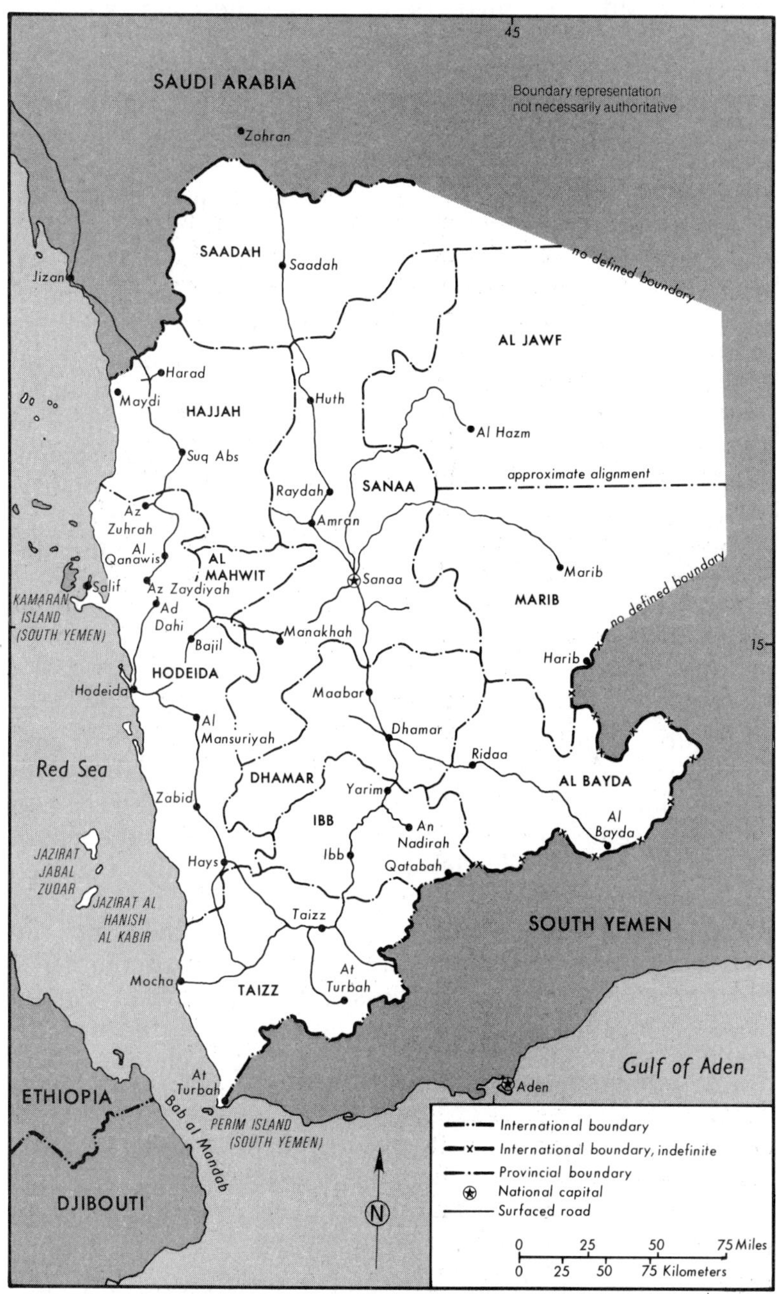

Figure 6. North Yemen: Provinces, Major Cities, and Major Roads, 1984

birth also differed; furthermore, given the country's great regional variation, estimates varied depending on the region of the country. The United States Bureau of the Census figures for the average life expectancy from birth in 1985 were 42 years in the western portion, which includes the Tihamah, and 45 years in the southern region. The Population Reference Bureau calculated the average life expectancy at birth to be 43 years. These figures were low compared with the rest of the world and reflected, in part, the high infant mortality rate. In 1979 the infant mortality rate was between 165 and 170 per 1,000 live births. By contrast the United States, which had a relatively high infant mortality rate for a developed country, showed an infant mortality rate of 10.9 per 1,000 live-born children in 1984. As was the case for other aspects of North Yemen, there were large regional differences in child mortality. Children born in the southern region had a higher chance of surviving infancy than those born in the more mountainous north; the 1979 mortality rates for the first 15 years of life were 210 per 1,000 live-born children in the south and 302 per 1,000 in the north.

The high birth rate may be partially explained by the high infant mortality rate; parents must have more offspring to ensure living children to care for them in their old age. In addition, because both sons and daughters labored in family fields, because sons could also be sent abroad to work and remit money home to their families, and because daughters brought bride-price into the family, children have been perceived as economic assets. The high rate of marriage and low rates of childlessness also illuminate the reasons for the high birth rate. The results of the 1979 fertility survey showed that less than 2 percent of women aged 45 to 49, i.e., those who could be expected to have reached their completed family size, were childless. The number of children born to these older women during their reproductive lives averaged seven live births, but almost one-third had nine or more live births, 46 percent had five to eight live births, and 22 percent had fewer than five live births. If these figures are correct, North Yemen experienced a very high birth rate, indeed. The government initiated a family planning program associated with health centers in the early 1980s; by 1985 methods of regulating fertility were available not only from clinics but also from private pharmacies located even in remote villages. Available methods included oral contraceptives, intrauterine devices, condoms, injectable contraceptives, and vasectomy.

The wholesale emigration of a large proportion of the male adult work force constituted a crucial factor in the population structure of North Yemen, as well as in the country's economic and social structure (see Emigration, this ch.). Men usually emigrated temporarily to Saudi Arabia, where they were employed as unskilled or semiskilled workers. Various sources estimated the male migration rate in the mid-1980s to be from 30 to 50 percent of the total male labor force of North Yemen (see Labor Force, this ch.). In 1975 the CPO estimated that 1,234,000 citizens were temporarily out of the country, while British demographers J.S. Birks, C.A. Sinclair, and J.A. Socknat put the number of Yemeni migrants working abroad in 1975 at 263,100. The Swiss air photo team estimated that 331,649 Yemenis were abroad at the time of the 1975 census, and James Allman and Allan Hill, demographic scholars, estimated 348,000 emigrants. No more recent figures were available in 1985. In the mid-1980s there were differing opinions, but no data, on the effect of mass male migration on North Yemen's fertility rate.

In 1977 Ethiopians began immigrating to North Yemen as a result of the political turmoil and severe drought in their own country. One report alleged that in 1985 an estimated 1,742 refugees lived in Al Khaukha refugee camp in the Tihamah.

Education and Health

The status of education and health in North Yemen exhibited regional differences in 1985, but the generally poor state of the health and educational systems was countrywide because of the isolationist policies of the imams (see Glossary). After the overthrow of Muhammad al Badr in 1962, the newly formed republican government faced the task of autochthonously creating modern health and educational systems. Before 1962 boys were sent abroad for education or received their education in Yemen's traditional Quranic schools. Almost all schools taught religion exclusively before 1962, and the level of education provided was poor. In the 1980s most teachers were Egyptian, and those North Yemenis in the teaching profession tended to come from the traditional social classes that had specialized in Quranic learning. Although North Yemen has made great progress since 1962, in 1985 much remained to be done. There were 3,711 primary schools, 324 preparatory schools (similar to American junior high schools), and 94 secondary schools. A majority of the population remained illiterate in 1985, and most girls' parents opted not to send their daughters to school. Estimates of female illiteracy ran as high as 98 percent.

North Yemen in the mid-1980s was beset by a plethora of serious infectious diseases. Some diseases occurred countrywide, but the distribution of most was regional. Many health problems were both caused and exacerbated by the general lack of safe drinking water throughout the country. Even the piped-in water supply in Sanaa was not considered safely potable in 1984.

By 1985 no full epidemiological survey had been conducted; similarly, only sketchy data on causes of morbidity and mortality were available. From scattered health studies and CPO statistics it was apparent, however, that leading health problems included gastroenteritis, malaria (particularly in the Tihamah and low foothills), amebiasis, schistosomiasis (infection by the parasitic schistosome, a fluke spread by contact with water infested by the schistosome's freshwater snail hosts), typhoid, tuberculosis, paratyphoid, trachoma (a chronic bacterial eye infection resulting in blindness if untreated), helminthiasis (worm infestation), and malnutrition. Infectious hepatitis commonly affected both native and foreign residents.

The incidence of poliomyelitis in the 1980s was alarmingly high. In a survey conducted in 1980 and in 1981, analyst M. M. Hajar and others estimated the incidence of polio in the general population to be 18.6 per 100,000, resulting in a figure of 5,000 children between the ages of five and 13 lamed as a result of the disease. The gravity of these polio rates appears more clearly when compared with the incidence of poliomyelitis during the 1945-54 polio epidemic in the United States; the *endemic* polio rates for North Yemen in the 1980s resemble the *epidemic* rates for the United States.

In 1982 estimations of schistosomiasis infestation placed the number affected at 1 million, almost one-fifth of the population. The incidence of this debilitating and sometimes fatal disease exhibited regional variation; the highest rates of infection and the severest infections were found in

Taizz and Ibb provinces. The higher incidence was owing to the topography, which provided many places favorable to the breeding of snails; high human population density; and water development projects which, in the process of providing more irrigation canals, also supplied an ideal breeding ground for schistosome-carrying snails.

Rates of malnutrition for the 1980s were not available, but the trend toward bottle-feeding rather than breast-feeding appeared to be increasing the incidence of malnourished infants because mothers unwittingly prepared infant formula incorrectly. One study, published in 1984, reported that among mothers attending a child health center in Sanaa, bottle-feeding was "widely but not universally practiced." It was impossible in 1985 to assess accurately how many mothers bottle-fed their infants among nonclinic-attenders in Sanaa or among mothers elsewhere in the country. Cynthia Myntti, a medical anthropologist, conducted intensive research on breast-feeding in rural North Yemen. In the three villages that she studied, Myntti found that mothers breast-fed their infants for an average of 14 months. She comments that mothers are reducing the duration of breast-feeding, and she presents reasons for women's decreasing reliance on nursing and increasing resort to bottle-feeding. These include women's perception that bottle-feeding is more modern, as well as rationalizations based on folk body concepts. As a result of all of the endemic diseases, it was not surprising that North Yemen had high infant and child mortality rates.

In the 1980s many people did not have easy access to cosmopolitan health care and often treated their illnesses at home or sought the aid of traditional medical practitioners. According to Myntti's description of Yemeni folk curing in 1979, traditional healers might be female or male but in either case were usually sayyids (see Glossary). "Sayyid women who are healers earn their income by burning [against fear and chronic pains], massaging [against rheumatism and infertility], and writing holy amulets and cures. Their charges are minimal." Another anthropologist, Najwa Adra, confirmed the sayyid occupation of healer, but she added that other social classes engaged in professional healing and might use techniques, such as cupping and bloodletting, that differed from sayyid specialties. Families also resorted to herbal home remedies. In addition, many women believed that some illnesses might be caused by possession by jinn which required holding a *zar*, a women's ritual to placate the offended/offending jinn. The *zar* is also found in the Horn of Africa and in other parts of the Middle East, such as Egypt and Sudan.

The settlement patterns of much of the country severely hampered government efforts to deliver health care to rural areas. About 90 percent of the population resided in rural areas in the early 1980s, while 78 percent of the population lived in settlements of fewer than 500 people, making it difficult to set up clinics and deliver health care to such small and widely dispersed communities.

The University of Sanaa trained medical personnel, including physicians, but in 1985 most physicians and nurses practicing in North Yemen were foreign. For the year 1982 the CPO reported 920 physicians, 30 hospitals, 150 health centers, and 221 rural health centers. The distribution of medical personnel was not even, however, because in North Yemen, as in the rest of the world where physicians choose their own practice areas, most physicians settled in urban centers.

Qat

Qat (incorrectly spelled—and defined—as *kat* or *khat* in most English-language dictionaries) is North Yemen's primary cash crop. John G. Kennedy and his colleagues, authors of several studies of qat in North Yemen, state that qat as "a member of the celestraceae family, *Catha edulis*, has a straight and slender bole with a light green, almost whitish bark. The elliptical serrated leaves are generally from 5 to 10 centimeters long and 1 to 4 centimeters wide. It has small white flowers with 5 petals and stamens in auxiliary cymes 1 to 8 centimeters long." It is rarely exported, however, because of its perishability; qat becomes unusable within 24 to 36 hours after it is picked. Almost all men and many women chew qat leaves for their mood-altering effect. Qat aficionados report an initial feeling of excitement and elation that commences about an hour or less after the beginning of chewing and lasts for two or more hours. The animation is succeeded by a dreamy, contemplative mood that lasts an hour or more.

Qat chewing usually occurs in afternoon group sessions segregated by gender. Typically the male guest arrives at the host's house after the main meal at about 2:00 P.M. and remains until evening prayers at about 7:00 P.M. Guests usually bring their own qat, which they purchase fresh in the market between 11:00 A.M. and 1:00 P.M. Guests are seated in a special room, the *mufraj*, which is built into traditional houses to be used for the purpose of entertaining guests and chewing qat. Guests are seated in order of status, with members of low-status groups and poor members of higher status groups seated nearest the door. The *mufraj* is supplied with cushions around the walls upon which guests lean, thermoses of cool water because qat chewing induces thirst, and water pipes that the guests use for smoking.

Qat chewers select the leaves carefully. The masticated leaves are held in a bolus in the inside of the cheek and are removed at the end of the qat session. After the drug takes effect men talk animatedly, and many local political decisions are made in qat sessions. Men hold intimate talks or philosophical discussions and on occasion may dance with the *jambiyyas* (daggers). The guests' liveliness is succeeded by silence or quiet conversation, and they eventually depart quietly.

Rural women's qat chewing is less formalized and often less frequent than that of men or urban women. In the early 1980s in the Central Highlands only sayyid and Akhdam (people of African origin) women chewed qat, for tribal women considered qat chewing enervating and inimical to work. Urban women chew qat in the *tafrita*, an afternoon tea and qat session. Women drink water, tea, and soft drinks and smoke the water pipe as well as chew qat in these gatherings. They often perform traditional Yemeni dances in couples or in triads. Dancing reportedly remains more important in women's qat chewing sessions than in men's get-togethers.

The effects of qat on the individual and on the economy have long been a matter of contention. In this debate anthropologists have frequently taken the side of the qat chewers, owing perhaps to anthropologists' enjoyment of participant observation. Critics of qat aver that farmers grow qat instead of coffee because qat is more profitable, may be grown on the same land as coffee or on more marginal land, and requires less water. Qat, this argument contends, is responsible for the decline in domestic coffee production and a concomitant decrease in foreign currency earned through exports. The argument has been demonstrated to be specious, however, because coffee production declined well before soaring qat prices owing to the availability of cheaper sources of coffee on the world market. British anthropologist Shelagh Weir has argued that qat production was actually beneficial to the economy because it sustained banana production (qat leaves were formerly marketed wrapped in banana stems, but by the 1980s qat was usually marketed in plastic wrappings) and saved terraces from the potential ruin and neglect that has been the fate of much terraced land because qat served as a "holding action" for grain production. Many scholars, however, have disagreed with Weir's contentions and have expressed concern that production of qat was replacing food production in the 1980s, as well as draining family income that would be better spent on food.

Qat is also reputed to cause deleterious effects on the chewer's health. A detailed study conducted in Yemen in the mid-1970s found that few negative side effects could be attributed to qat chewing. The researchers concluded that qat-related symptoms include gastrointestinal problems, insomnia, acute gastritis, and liver and urinary problems in women. Some reliable participant observers added male impotence to the list of negative effects of qat. Many symptoms increase with increasing qat use. Qat is nonaddictive, however; Yemeni workers in Saudi Arabia, where qat is banned on the grounds that its use runs counter to the spirit of Islam, experience no withdrawal symptoms.

Emigration

Throughout North Yemen's different regions in the 1980s, men continued to leave home to seek work in other countries, usually on a temporary basis. Although migrants tended to come more from some geographical locations than others, by 1980 probably every area of the country had contributed migrants to the international labor pool. Effects of foreign currency sent home as remittances to relatives reverberated throughout the society, producing social and economic changes. The importance of labor migration to understanding North Yemen, especially in the 1970s and 1980s, cannot be overemphasized.

North Yemen has a long history of emigration dating from pre-Islamic times when Yemenis traveled to nearby areas of the African continent. After the advent of Islam, Yemenis joined the Muslim armies, settling as far away as

North Africa and Spain. Ismaili Yemenis had been sending their sons to India for religious education before the nineteenth century. While in India the Ismaili boys learned the mercantile livelihood of their Indian coreligionists and became extremely successful traders, serving as a model to other Ismaili Yemenis and to non-Ismailis as well (see The Ismailis, ch. 1). British colonization of Aden and their exploitation of its natural harbor as a port provided Yemenis with an opportunity for remunerative employment with British-connected enterprises. North Yemenis migrated to Aden to take advantage of the opportunity and to avoid serving in the imam's army. Aden was not Britain's only colony, however, and in the 1840s and 1850s the British imported Asian Indians to do the work of Yemeni laborers. At this time Yemenis also emigrated for work to the port of Djibouti. From Aden and Djibouti they emigrated to Vietnam, Singapore, India, Indonesia, Madagascar, Kenya, Tanzania, Ethiopia, Sudan, Chad, Western Europe, and the United States. In the mid-1980s numerous Yemenis still remained in many of these countries. The United States boasted enclaves of Yemenis in Dearborn and Detroit, Michigan; Lackawanna, Buffalo, and Brooklyn, New York; and Modesto and San Francisco, California. Some of the migrants settled permanently, but most were temporary migrants planning to return home with their savings.

Ever since the 1973-74 oil boom, most North Yemeni labor migration was directed to Saudi Arabia. Migrants tended to return home for visits every six months to two years, and many spent the entire month of Ramadan each year at home. Women almost never accompanied their male relatives and spouses because the object of emigration was to accrue as much wealth as possible to take back home and thereby raise the migrant's standard of living. To this end, a vast majority of migrants were willing to tolerate poor living conditions rather than pay high Saudi rent for a dwelling suitable for their families. Women virtually never traveled to work abroad.

Anthropologists who are expert in Yemeni migration, such as Jon Swanson, Cynthia Myntti, and Tomas Gerholm, describe different migration patterns for different areas of the country. Yet universal effects existed, including diminished cultivation of agricultural land because of labor shortages and consequent decreased agricultural output; general labor shortages within North Yemen and concomitant soaring wages; inflation caused by massive amounts of foreign currency infused into the economy in the form of migrant remittances; greatly increased importation of foodstuffs and consumer goods; changes in traditional diet toward more highly processed, imported foods; skyrocketing demand for qat; vastly higher bride-prices; increasing access to power and material goods by younger men who contributed the bulk of the migrant population; demand for new consumer goods and investment opportunities; and an increased work burden on women and children (see Profile of the Economy, this ch.). In 1976 many Yemeni Highway Authority laborers were children between the ages of 11 and 15.

Nader Fergany, a planning expert in Kuwait, suggests that the necessity of children's participation in the labor force has undermined North Yemen's attempts at raising the level of education in the country because working children do not have time for school. In some areas, emigration resulted in the creation of new social classes based on wealth instead of, or in addition to, birth. Reports also detailed the destruction of terraced fields that are the product of generations of arduous agricultural toil, owing to the shortage of labor necessary to maintain this terraced cultivation that has characterized much of Yemen for centuries (see Agriculture, this ch.). In the presence of large-scale male labor migration, women usually gain in authority. This has apparently not been the case in North Yemen; men tended to send remittances home to male relatives rather than to wives. Even when money was sent to wives, the husband's male relative whom he had appointed guardian of his wife in his absence made the major decisions as to how the money would be spent (see Gender Roles, this ch.).

The decision for a man to migrate was seldom made by individual choice; the entire extended family participated in the decision and benefited from remittances. In the 1980s anthropologists reported that North Yemenis perceived a shortage of investment opportunities for migrants' cash. Migrants often spent their remittances on marriage, establishing small businesses, buying trucks or taxis, buying generators and/or pumps, improving or erecting a home, buying land, purchasing imported consumer goods, and occasionally providing for their sons' education.

Migrants often employed an agent (*wakil mughtaribin*) to act as a broker between conditions in urban North Yemen, the migrant's village, and Saudi Arabia. Swanson observed that the agent usually lived in urban North Yemen but maintained intense and intimate contact with his clients' villages, acting as the migrants' banker, distributing gifts the migrant had sent home, tending to the migrants' business interests, and facilitating the process of migration. Swanson reported that the *wakil*'s role not uncommonly engendered ambivalence on the part of the migrants because the *wakil* was usually a fellow villager who had made good and no longer needed to leave home and family for the wretched living conditions of the emigrant. The effect on labor migration of diminishing oil production in the Persian Gulf states and the discovery of oil within the country was unclear in 1985.

Dialect

The continued relative isolation of North Yemen's ecological and cultural regions was manifested in the 1980s by differences in dialect. All North Yemenis speak Arabic, but urban centers speak their own dialects; a North Yemeni is able to trace a Sanawi (resident of Sanaa) speaker's origin to Sanaa, for example. Differences between North and South dialects roughly correspond to Zaydi-Shafii areas. For example, the Arabic letter *qaf* is pronounced as *Q* by northerners and as *G* by southerners. Scholars report that this difference in dialect has endured for centuries.

Architecture

Most travelers to North Yemen have regarded its traditional architecture with a mixture of astonishment and awe. Building styles and materials not only vary by region but also express historical and cultural differences. Residents of the Tihamah often construct their houses of wood, mud, and thatch, building them in the traditional round shape with conical roof that is so prominent in the countries lying across the Red Sea in Africa and that is so well adapted to the Tihamah's hot, humid climate. In the city of Saadah, mud traditionally furnishes the basic building material, and buildings appear softly shaped as a result of the superimposition of layers of mud, which the builders raise at the corners for stability. Photographer Michael Jenner wrote of Saadah, "The city has been described as halfway between sculpture and architecture." Other cities, such as Zabid in the Tihamah, also display idiosyncratic architectural styles.

The style of traditional highland houses dates from antiquity and demonstrates ingenuity, architectural skill, and a well-developed aesthetic sense. It also physically represents highland social organization and its need for defense and isolation. The houses are built as multistoried "apartment" buildings that possess stained glass, half-moon windows set above clear glass panes, and elaborate doors. The many rooms are capable of housing a large extended family; each married couple is assigned its own room. In the rural highlands the houses huddle together in little defensive clusters, exacerbating the isolation produced by the rugged terrain and presenting an impressive, easily defended fortification to outsiders. Houses in Sanaa are of this apartment style.

Social Class and Tribe

Rigid social status groups existed throughout the society in the mid-1980s, although the manner in which the status system operated varied regionally. Anthropologists have likened these status groups to Indian castes in their rigidity, ascriptive status, occupational specialization, and presence of hypergamy (the norm that a woman may marry an equal or higher-status man but is prohibited from marrying a lower-status mate). The concept of tribe is associated with the phenomenon of caste-like status groups. Tribes demonstrated great regional variation both in importance and in structure. In general, tribal affiliation remained tremendously important to those groups living in highland areas, often but not always Zaydi, and to the largely Shafii beduin groups in the eastern region. In the Tihamah, Shafii tribal affiliation varied in importance from one locality to another; one of the most important tribes, the Zaraniq, inhabited the Tihamah. In the predominantly Shafii south, tribal affiliation occupied a less important place than it did in other areas of the country.

The traditional status groups consist of sayyids, qadis (see Glossary), *qabayl* (sing., *qabili*; tribesmen), and Bani Khums (or Khadam), low-status individuals who rely on *qabayl* for protection and who usually perform some sort of service or craft. (The Arabic plural for sayyids is *sada* and for qadis is *quda*. Although many authors use the Arabic forms, the English versions are used herein.) Additional categories exist between and within these groups. It was difficult in 1985 to assess accurately the salience of this social status system to the lives of Yemenis, but scholarly observers generally agreed on the continued presence of these status groups in the 1970s and 1980s. Although the approximate rankings of status groups were generally constant throughout the country, the status groups demonstrated great local variation in their behavior. Some of the variation in reports of the caste system in North Yemen apparently resulted from the complexity of this social structural phenomenon; scholars with divergent perspectives often arrived at different understandings of the status groups.

Sayyids

In his historical description of North Yemeni sayyids, Swedish anthropologist Gerholm comments on the antiquity of the sayyid's social role. Before the advent of Islam, tribal Arabian groups had instituted the custom of sacred sanctuaries presided over by a religious elite protected by tribesmen. The sanctuaries were politically neutral and provided feuding tribes with a safe place to meet and to resolve their differences, possibly aided by the religious functionaries. Gerholm argues that the Prophet Muhammad and his family assumed the role of the old religious elite in mediating disputes and in providing sanctuary. But Muhammad's family added another trait—Muslims believed them to be imbued with a special spiritual power (*baraka*). Their decisions in mediation were especially respected, and they could use their power to cure illness (see Education and Health, this ch.). It was in this special role of mediator that the first imam of Yemen entered the country (see Early Islamic Rule in Yemen, ch. 1; table A, Preface). The sanctuary provided by the sayyids, the hijra (see Glossary), retained its importance in modern Yemen. Throughout the period of the imamate, sayyids formed the basis of the ruling elite and were better educated and often better off financially than other Yemenis; in addition, the sayyids selected the imam from among their own ranks. Although they were often associated in the minds of Yemenis with urbanized culture, sayyids were dispersed throughout Yemen fulfilling the functions of mediation and healing, and they were often wealthy landowners.

The disestablishment of the imamate deprived the sayyids of their right to rule, but the collapse of the imamate did not greatly revolutionize the traditional social order. Sayyids retained the imputation of spiritual power and were still, in the mid-1980s, among the best educated and wealthiest members of society. In the late 1970s and the 1980s ethnological accounts of the sayyids differed according to where in North Yemen the studies had been carried out. In the Harazi town of Manakhah, Gerholm found that sayyids did not serve as mediators, although Manakhans were well aware of that traditional sayyid role; sayyids still performed as healers, but the importance of this role was diminishing. The majority engaged in occupations connected with learning, a traditional sayyid specialty, although some sayyids followed occupations traditionally associated with lower-status groups, such as merchants. The sayyids viewed themselves as a separate group and adhered to traditional marriage patterns. Their self-imposed autonomy and their past role in the imam's repressive regimes led Manakhans to regard sayyids with ambivalence, simultaneously revering them, as of old, and disliking them.

In a study of the southern town of Ibb, anthropologist Brinkley Messick pointed out that many key administrative posts were still held by sayyids because of their education and large landholdings. In 1981 Swanson reported the similar advantageous position of sayyids in the northwest highlands. Adra, who studied tribes in the Central Highlands, observed in a 1982 report that Central Highlanders believed that three ranked social classes existed, but in her observation the people behaved in a much more egalitarian way than their stated ideology would indicate that they should. The sayyids in the Central Highlands still performed many of their traditional duties in 1982: they mediated disputes, acted as Quranic teachers and religious experts, taught in secular schools, served as healers, and maintained hijras. They were still believed to possess special spiritual power. Adra, like Gerholm, reported that tribesmen felt ambivalent toward sayyids for reasons similar to those of Gerholm's town residents.

Qadis

Qadis, also known in some regions of the country as *fuqaha*, were traditionally an educated elite with lower status than sayyids and with no claims to descent from the Prophet's lineage. Sayyid men may marry qadi women, but a sayyid woman may not marry a qadi. In much of the Arabic-speaking world the word *qadi* denotes a traditional judge, but in North Yemen the qadis also engage in occupations that are not linked to the practice of traditional Islamic law. Today many qadis, like sayyids, occupy administrative and teaching positions because of their superior education.

Reports of qadis vary; in some parts of the Tihamah the social status group appears to be entirely absent, while in the Central Highlands a *qabili* or a Bani Khums may become educated and enter the qadi class, transmitting membership in the class to his or her descendants. In addition to their educational and administrative roles, qadis have traditionally served as mediators who might maintain a hijra, and some accounts indicate that highland qadis continued to fulfill this role in the late 1970s and early 1980s.

Qabayl

Any description of this group must begin with a definition of the concept of tribe. In theory tribes view themselves as consisting of the descendants of a common ancestor, whose name often provides the name of the group. The internal divisions of the tribe are seen as consisting of the descendants of intermediate descendants of the founder. Thus an entire tribe may see itself as descended from a man 10 or more generations in the past. Smaller segments composed, for example, of the grandsons of the same grandfather or the great-grandsons of the same great-grandfather form the units of residence and strongest personal loyalty. Despite the theoretical importance of genealogy as an organizing principle, however, authorities believe that tribal genealogies reflect the reality of politics rather than of history. And, although they endorse the principle of genealogy, tribesmen also recognize this fact.

Tribesmen may rally to the aid of ever more distant relatives, forming ever larger segments of the tribe at higher and higher levels of organization. Thus the grandsons of the same grandfather might oppose one another on a certain issue but join together if necessary to oppose the descendants of the brother of their common great-grandfather. In practice, however, this rarely if ever occurs. Tribesmen tend to be spatially distributed with little regard for their supposed genealogical ties and may even be interspersed with members of other tribes; kinship segments not expressed in residential arrangements appear to find very little expression in reality.

In North Yemen geographical territory is the most important tribal marker. Great variation exists among tribes of the Central, Northern, and Eastern Highlands. Even within the Central Highlands some tribal ideology follows the ideal segmentary lineage principle, while other tribes have no myth of common descent. Adra traces the "major economic differences between tribes" in the Central Highlands to geographical differences in topography and water supply. Everyone in North Yemen is conscious of what tribe she or he belongs to. Even the sayyids, for example, are members of a tribe—they belong to the same tribe as the Prophet (the Quraysh). The significance of tribal affiliation, however, varies by geographical location.

The connotations of *qabili* in Yemen are rich and complex. Although beduin are tribesmen who often practice pastoralism, most people among whom tribal identification is most important are sedentary farmers, and thus land is very important to them. British anthropologist Paul Dresch writes that "one can reasonably say that [tribes] men are united in a section by their land as they are united in a family by their mothers and sisters." In the Central Highlands, territory and tribes are so closely linked that if a member of one tribe moves to the territory of another, he becomes a member of that tribe by virtue of residence. Tribes, remarks Adra, are synonymous with territory. Tribesmen are bound to protect the honor of female relatives and corporate tribal honor, often expressed as defense of tribal territory. The tribes have occupied their territories for centuries; a tenth-century record associates most of today's tribes with the territories that they continued to occupy in 1985.

Tribesmen regard themselves as noble; they accord higher status to sayyids, but often grudgingly. Their traditional role is to protect the sayyids and the qadis in association with their tribe as well as to protect their clients, the Bani Khums. In the Central Highlands crucial items of

President Ali Abdallah Salih
Courtesy Embassy of the Yemen Arab Republic, Washington

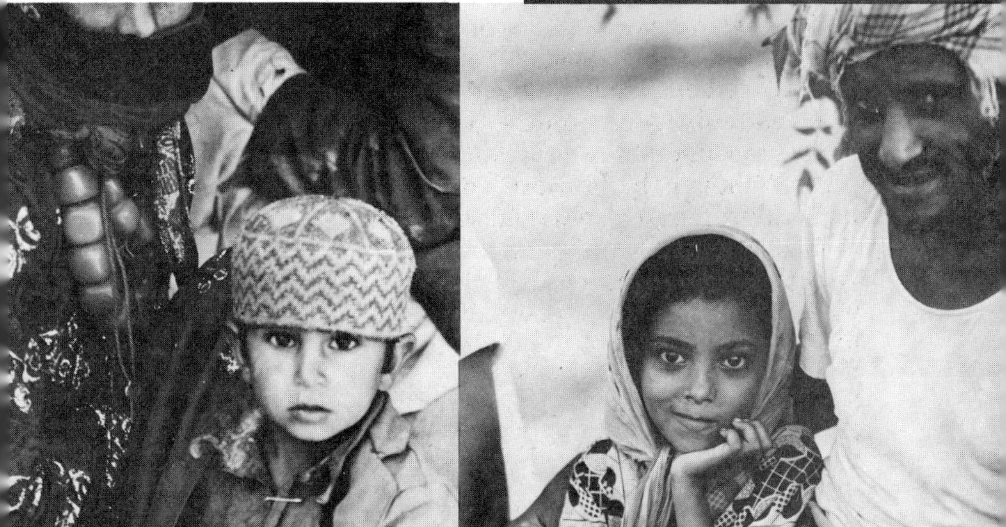

Children with their parents, Sanaa
Courtesy World Bank/Sennett

Woman chewing qat while drumming and singing at a wedding

Women baking bread in a traditional kitchen

Veiled women at work
Photos courtesy Cynthia Myntti, Women and Development in Yemen Arab Republic

Plowing and planting

Water channel from a tubewell

Photos above courtesy World Bank/Sennett

Rural woman and her camels in Tihama area
Courtesy
Embassy of the Yemen Arab Republic, Washington

Male resident of Sanaa

Man repairing his boat, Mocha

Unloading bags of cement from a dhow in Mocha

Photos courtesy World Bank/Sennet

qabili behavior are honor, meeting obligations, and generosity. Tribal values stress equality of tribal members as well as autonomy and cooperation.

Politically, tribes often form confederations; the Bakil and Hashid form the largest tribal confederation and are located in the Northern Highlands. Confederations are loose political alliances that often have more ideological than behavioral significance; tribes act as a confederation when it is advantageous to do so and act alone when conditions favor tribal autonomy. *Qabayl* often perceive confederations as genealogically linked tribes.

In 1985 authors disagreed about the role of tribal leaders, *mashaykh* (sing., shaykh), and their place in the caste structure. All agreed that the shaykh is elevated above other tribal members and that tribal leaders must come from families whose members have traditionally been *mashaykh.* A shaykh fulfills the role of mediator, as well as leader, and may provide hijra. A *shaykh mashaykh* administers a confederacy of several tribal sections and is chosen by the *qabayl* and other *mashaykh.* A *shaykh mashaykh,* if he is skilled politically, may maneuver himself into a position of national political prominence. Any male member of a shaykhly family may become a tribal leader if he demonstrates the requisite leadership qualities, has enough wealth to entertain guests on the tribe's behalf, and has a history of just mediations. Mediation is one of the shaykh's most important functions, and his mediation is not confined to his own lineage or segment; a respected shaykh may be called upon to adjudicate disputes from many segments.

A shaykh must also schedule and supervise cooperative efforts, care for those under tribal protection, such as guests or Bani Khums, and protect tribal records of land transactions or tribal disputes. In the Central Highlands the office is ideally a lifetime post and is patrilineally transmitted; however, unpopular *mashaykh* are deposed. A final duty of the shaykh is to administer *urf,* or customary tribal law.

Urf antedates Islam, and Muslim religious law has never entirely replaced customary law in tribal society. In Yemen *urf* governs public aspects of behavior, whereas sharia (Islamic law) governs most aspects of inheritance, marriage, and religious ritual. A breach of *urf* is shameful and dishonoring, but in the Central Highlands, unless the crime is of the most dishonorable category—such as the intentional murder of a woman, child, or someone a man is sworn to protect or befriend—the transgression is reparable.

The geographic diversity of North Yemen and the territorial stability of tribes have led each tribe to adapt to a specific geographical location, and consequent differences occur in customs of tribes from different areas. Some tribal customs appear to be widespread, however. *Qabili* values esteem weaponry. Traditionally, males in all castes but Bani Khums and Jews wore the *jambiyya*, a curved dagger worn in a special belt, but in 1985 Bani Khums and male city dwellers also sported the *jambiyya*. Traditionally, the kind of *jambiyya*, its sheath, kind of belt, and the position in which it was worn denoted the caste, geographical origin, and tribe of the wearer. By the mid-1980s observers reported that this specificity of *jambiyya* wear was declining, although the popularity of wearing the *jambiyya* remained unabated. In addition, tribesmen armed themselves with rifles and ammunition belts. Weaponry was easily purchased in the 1980s; rifles and more sophisticated arms could be bought in special sections of the traditional open-air Middle Eastern market (*suq*).

Traditionally, dress denoted caste, but social status differences in apparel, while still present in the mid-1980s, were less marked. Observers reported that in the mid-1980s the tribes continued to possess their own dances. Tribesmen performed these ritual men's dances, *baraa*, at weddings, religious holidays, cooperative work activities, when traveling with other male members of the tribe, and at home to honor guests. Each tribe's *baraa* differed from others in its steps and in how the performers held their *jambiyyas*. Other distinguishing features of tribal aesthetics included orally composed poetry (which each tribesman is ideally capable of fabricating in appropriate situations), dress, and cuisine. Food may have urban or tribal associations. Traditional Central Highland tribal cuisine includes porridges made from the flour of locally grown grains, lentils, and breads; urban foods include fenugreek concoctions, vegetable stews, and rice dishes. Although tribes may distinguish between urban and tribal food, the kind of food consumed by the tribe varies by region.

Bani Khums

The final social category includes several groups, and observers' reports of the various status groups often disagreed; scholars, for example, disputed the names and relative status of the groups composing the lowest class. All agreed that members were traditionally under the protection of the *qabayl*. Genealogy is extremely important in North Yemen, and this status group is believed to have "no genealogy," i.e., its members maintain very shallow lineages. Many scholars include in this status group the Akhdam, people of African ancestry who often live in the highlands and who perform the most culturally devalued tasks. The Bani Khums traditionally specialized in such despised occupations as barber, musician, butcher, cupper and bloodletter, and innkeeper. In the past Bani Khums did not farm in the Highlands; the tribes under whose protection they resided provided a portion of the harvest as well as cash and other payments for their services. This was still largely the case in the mid-1980s, but migrants came from all social classes so that the families of Bani Khums migrants have profited from remittances and have been able to buy land, which they were previously prohibited from doing.

North Yemen contains another lowly social group—the *abid* (sing., *abd*); African in ancestry and descended from slaves, they live scattered throughout the country. The imamate countenanced slavery, and slavery was not abolished until 1967, five years after the republic was established. In the past slaves were used by owners to cultivate farms in the Tihamah. In 1985 *abid* continued to perform the most despised, lowly occupations and often lived segregated from other members of society.

By the mid-1980s the traditional social status system was obviously changing, but the extent of change could not be assessed, nor were there many accounts of urban status groups available. In one of the few accounts of urban status, Messick describes status in urban Ibb in the late 1970s as a complex interaction of descent, education, honor, occupation, material circumstances, political power, and marriage rules. Some occupations were still despised, e.g., barber, butcher, and bath worker, and traditionally honored professions retained their high status, e.g., legal, bureaucratic, and religious specialties. Although members of status groups did not always follow their traditional occupations, they continued to follow endogamous marriage rules.

Akhdam in Ibb were Muslims, but they functioned as they had in the past and were excluded from most interactions with non-Akhdam, performing the most dishonorable occupations and being prohibited from entering the public bath and the mosque. In 1985 many North Yemenis wished to deny the importance of traditional status groups, but most continued to contract marriages along status lines, and nowhere were despised occupations performed by any but members of the lowest-status groups.

Local Development Associations

Local Development Associations (LDAs) were self-help organizations financed through local tax revenues and collections from local household heads who were assessed equally (although in practice wealthier families were often assessed more, while poor families sometimes were omitted from some of the collections). LDAs existed before they were incorporated into the Confederation of Yemeni Development Associations (CYDA), a government organization (see Agriculture; Regional and Local Government, this ch.). The object of LDAs was cooperation on a local level to identify and carry out projects that satisfied local needs. Although LDAs existed primarily in rural areas, the projects initiated through them were often not directly related to agriculture, e.g., road construction, water projects to provide accessible water to a community, and erection of schools and clinics. Swanson evaluated the success of LDAs in 1981 in a Northern Highland area and found that local residents regarded the LDA with hostility because of the alleged corruption of its members and the connection between the LDA movement and the government in Sanaa. He also noted that almost all LDAs in his study area made no attempt to collect LDA dues from temporary migrants residing in nearby Saudi Arabia. Anthropologist Mary Hebert, observing LDAs in the Tihamah, noted that residents elected traditional leaders to LDA posts and then followed them confidently and apathetically.

Although LDAs were organized as a democratic movement in which all residents could participate and voice an opinion, in the mid-1980s LDAs had come to mirror the social and political structures of their districts. The success or failure of LDAs, then, has depended upon local factors. There was no doubt that many kilometers of roads were laid and public buildings constructed through LDAs; their successes, however, have been uneven.

Gender Roles

North Yemeni society, as well as other societies of the Middle East, distributes authority according to gender along patriarchal, patrilineal lines. Individuals trace descent through males and inherit property through relatives related to them through their fathers. They also recognize that they are related to their mothers' kin, but the content of these relationships tends to be more affective and less laden with connotations of property and authority. Children must accord both parents, but especially their fathers, marked respect. Observers in the mid-1980s reported that men do not smoke in front of their fathers, as this is considered disrespectful. Women are required to demonstrate respect for their husbands; a woman should speak softly and modestly, never raising her voice above that of her husband. The father, or the male head of the extended household, is the final authority and is ultimately responsible for all decisions relating to the family.

Tradition, sharia, and the 1976 Family Law govern marriages in North Yemen, tradition often overruling law. Marriages are arranged between families, and the bride and groom often have little say in their nuptials. Islam accords the bride veto power to reject a prospective groom, but in practice the girl often has no say. The legal minimum age at marriage for girls was 16, but this regulation was extremely difficult to enforce in the mid-1980s, given the lack of registration of births in much of the country. Perhaps because of the high cost of marrying, polygyny was not common in the early 1980s, although Muslim men may have four wives simultaneously; women in Islam may have no more than one husband at a time.

In 1985 the custom of a groom paying bride-price (*mahr*) to the bride's family continued; the amount of the *mahr* was greatly inflated over earlier levels. Migrants could afford to pay more for a wife so that the cost of marriage for all grooms increased, and many prospective grooms were forced to migrate to Saudi Arabia to work in order to pay for marriage costs. The bride's relatives receive the bride-price in cash and in other gifts; the bride receives from one-tenth to one-half of the total payment, her share varying by locality and family custom. The *mahr* she receives is hers alone, and she retains full control over her money even after marriage.

Historically, gender roles and women's status have tended to be tied to property relations. North Yemenis, like many Middle Easterners, have been sedentary cultivators for millennia. Property, especially land and housing, is extremely important in the society, and women and children tend to be assimilated into the concept of property and to belong to a male. Islam improved women's status somewhat and established women's right to inherit half of what their brothers receive. In reality, however, it is often difficult for a women to assert her inheritance rights in North Yemen. Divorce is common and is primarily the prerogative of the husband. A woman must maintain good relations with her father and brothers so that if divorced or widowed she will have a place to go and a male to protect her. Observers report that women often did not assert their claim to their inheritance until they were the mothers of adult sons and thus assured of male protection through their male offspring. A mother would then ask her sons to demand her property from her brothers.

Islam enjoins believers to maintain as much difference as possible between the sexes; Muslims must not, for example, don clothing typically worn by members of the opposite sex. In North Yemen the genders are not only differentiated but also separated; seclusion of women, including the practice of veiling, is a feature of North Yemeni culture. Scholars agree that the practice of seclusion rests both on the conception of women as property and the belief, long current in the Middle East, of the inherent danger and irresistibility of sex. Women are thought to have less moral control and capability for physical restraint than men and must therefore be placed out of harm's way. The extent of seclusion of women varies according to region, social status group, and wealth and between urban and rural areas. Urban women and wealthy rural women tend to experience the strictest seclusion, but all women are secluded to some extent. Myntti commented in the late 1970s that even unveiled rural women "are restricted to work in the fields and visiting other women within a certain distance. They do not go to markets to buy goods, and many are restricted from going to town hospitals and clinics." Akhdam women do not veil their faces, even in town, and educated urban women often do not veil their faces. Rural women veil when traveling to a market town. Urban women's experience with seclusion varies; some attend schools and work in offices, while others rarely leave their houses. Women may stay home either to protect their reputations or because they have many children to care for and much work to do.

Many different forms of veiling coexisted in 1985. A type of long coat, the *balto* (derived from the Turkish and Russian word for coat), was beginning to become popular in urban areas as an alternative to the traditional *sharshaf*, *sitara*, or *shaydor*, which covered the women completely.

All Yemeni boys are circumcised; Islam enjoins male circumcision but does not specify at what age the operation must be performed. In 1985 some Sanawi observers commented that male infants were circumcised at seven days after birth. Islam does not mandate female circumcision (clitoridectomy), but this procedure continues to be widely practiced in the Horn of Africa, Sudan, and Egypt. Not surprisingly, because of the Tihamah's links to Africa, female circumcision has been reported in this region as well.

Women's duties encompassed cooking, which they often performed in dark, poorly ventilated, smoke-filled rooms. Urban women might cook on a stove fueled by bottled gas, but most rural women used traditional stoves that burned wood or sorghum stalk, creating billows of smoke. Rural women were also responsible for collecting firewood and fetching water, both arduous tasks frequently demanding travel over considerable distances. In 1979 it was estimated that only 8 percent of the population could easily obtain water. In the Tihamah water was trucked in and purchased by families, whereas in the highlands women were often compelled to travel long distances over treacherous paths to collect water that was frequently contaminated; the women then carried their extremely heavy water-filled cylinders on their heads up steep, rocky mountain paths.

Men were responsible for representing the family publicly, participating in politics, supporting the family financially, and protecting women and children of the family. Women might exercise considerable influence in the public sphere, but their control was generally indirect and expressed through men.

Religion

In 1985 the population was still divided among Zaydi, Shafii, and Ismaili sects of Islam; an estimated 2,000 to 9,000 Jews lived in the area around the northern city of Saadah, and there were no Yemeni Christians. Few recent accounts of religion existed in the mid-1980s, but reliable observers reported that most people sought to gloss over all religious differences within the country, particularly those between Zaydis and Shafiis (see Islam, ch. 1). Nevertheless, Zaydis continued to dominate national politics, and regional differences were reinforced by religious differences, which continued to follow a geographic distribution.

Individuals or families who migrated to an area populated by members of a different sect might become practitioners of the predominant regional sect. In the urban center of Ibb, a largely Shafii town, many families originally from the Zaydi Northern Highlands practiced Shafii Islam. They did not undergo a ritual of "conversion" but merely sent their children to schools staffed by local instructors. There the children learned Shafii precepts, which the parents also adopted. Information on intermarriage among the three sects was not available in 1985.

The Economy

It would be difficult to find a country that was less economically developed than North Yemen at the time of the revolution in 1962. The lack of a school system meant that there were few literate people and almost none with a secular, modern education. A government and public administration in the usual sense did not exist. There was no local currency or banking system and almost no health facilities, electricity, modern communications, and potable water and sewage systems. Transportation was largely on the backs of people and animals; many parts of the country were isolated from the rest. Agriculture employed more than 90 percent of the work force, and industry was confined to handicrafts. Production was small-scale, traditional, and mostly limited to family needs. People were quite poor and lived at a bare subsistence level. Aspirations for economic improvement contributed to the civil war that followed Imam Ahmad's death (see Civil War in North Yemen, ch. 1).

By 1985 North Yemen remained one of the least developed countries in the world, but the economy was considerably advanced after the early 1960s. In 1983 gross national product (GNP—see Glossary) amounted to US$4.2 billion—US$510 on a per capital basis, according to the methodology used in World Bank *Atlas*, and substantially higher than in some other developing countries, such as India and Pakistan. This represented substantial real economic growth since the early 1970s, but it was the result of special factors that might not prevail during the last half of the 1980s. Oil was discovered in 1984, however, and that could provide an important spur to continued economic development if the discovery proves large enough to permit significant exports (see Industry, this ch.).

Profile of the Economy

North Yemen's break with its centuries-old economic ways and self-imposed isolation began when the last imam signed aid agreements with the Soviet Union and China for those countries to construct roads and port facilities. Before the 1960s only tracks existed, making motorized transport impossible or extremely costly. Cargo from abroad had to be transported by nonmotorized boats to the beach from freighters offshore; cargo was then waded ashore by laborers. Modernization had to begin at the most elementary level.

Economic development began in the 1960s, despite the civil war. China completed a paved road between the port of Hodeida and Sanaa in 1961. The United States constructed a gravel road between the port of Mocha and Sanaa via Taizz in the 1960s. The Soviet Union completed major facilities for berthing, cargo handling, and storage at Hodeida in 1962 and a paved road from the port to Taizz in 1969. Hodeida became the country's major port, although only small vessels of shallow draft could enter; the shallow draft forced North Yemen to import its petroleum products in small, expensive shipments. The port at As Salif has deeper water but up to the mid-1980s had been used mostly for export of salt mined nearby. Mocha was a minor port capable of berthing only very small vessels. China completed an integrated cotton textile mill—the country's first large industrial plant—at Sanaa in 1967.

As the economy changed, measuring the change was difficult because almost no statistics were kept in the 1960s. In the early 1970s a statistical program was instituted to facilitate planning and formulation of policy. Over the years the collection and processing of statistics improved, but by the mid-1980s there still were weaknesses and gaps, for a reliable statistical reporting system takes time to develop. Like those of many other developing countries, North Yemen's economic statistics should be viewed as approximations without ascribing a high degree of reliability or precision to them.

National accounts data have been published since the early 1970s. Between fiscal year (FY—see Glossary) 1970 and FY 1980, gross domestic product (GDP—see Glossary), in constant prices, rose by an average 9.6 percent a year, according to estimates by the Central Planning Organization (CPO). This was a high rate of growth, reflecting in part the small base from which most sectors started the decade. The high rate of growth was stimulated by the inflow of foreign aid and remittances from workers abroad. All sectors grew more rapidly than GDP, except agriculture, which expanded at an average of 5.3 percent a year (in constant prices). Industry grew at 13.1 percent a year and construction at 14.7 percent annually. Trade, transportation, and public administration each rose between 10 and 11 percent a year, and business services at over 16 percent annually, largely because of real estate activity.

In the early 1980s the economy continued to expand at a high rate. Because of the change in the fiscal year in 1980 to coincide with the Gregorian calendar year and a shift to constant prices of 1981, a new time series for GDP was published. Between 1981 and 1983 real GDP expanded an average of 9.7 percent a year, despite a decline in the value added by agriculture of 11 percent between 1982 and 1983 caused by the drought in the latter year. CPO estimated that real growth of government services (29 percent a year) and industrial value added (19.7 percent a year), plus much smaller growth in other sectors, more than compensated for the agricultural decline and sustained the economy's high growth rate.

The high rate of economic growth for most sectors other than agriculture produced a pronounced shift in the structure of the economy. Agriculture contributed 52 percent of GDP (in current prices) in FY 1970 but only 21.2 percent in 1983, marginally less than the 21.6 percent contributed by government services (see fig. 7). In the intervening years between FY 1970 and 1983, all kinds of services increased from about 38 percent of GDP to 62 percent. The economy, which had formerly been oriented toward the production of commodities, became service oriented. Although many services increased their contribution to GDP somewhat, government services in the form of public administration, defense, education, health, and other services rose from 7 percent of GDP in FY 1970 to almost 22 percent by 1983.

A substantial part of the economic growth that occurred between 1970 and 1983 was the result of the inflow of foreign economic aid and remittances from workers abroad. Foreign aid financed budget deficits, including increasing current expenditures for teachers and health care personnel, as well as most of the public investment. Workers' remittances financed both domestic consumption in various forms and investment by the private sector in such things as houses, real estate, taxis and trucks, pumps, and businesses, including manufacturing. Investment averaged around one-third of GNP between FY 1977 and 1981, an impressive achievement. Worker's remittances, which amounted to about US$65 million in the early 1970s, rose to around US$1.2 billion annually between 1977 and 1983 and financed a tremendous growth of imports. Part of the growth of services was the import, distribution, and sale of a flood of foreign goods.

By the early 1980s the economy began to encounter difficulties. Budget deficits were growing at an alarming rate, caused in part by declining grants from abroad. Inflation was kept in check by increasing imports until the balance of payments pressures became too great. The country's healthy foreign exchange reserves of the late 1970s were largely depleted by 1983. In December 1982 a severe earthquake caused considerable damage in the Dhamar area. A drought in 1983, which continued in 1984, sharply reduced farm output.

In 1983 and 1984 the government began to work on these problems. Government spending was slowed, and revenues increased, which reduced the size of the budget deficits. The currency was devalued by about 25 percent, and controls were established to limit imports. The prospect for 1985 and the immediate future was for continued austerity and slower economic growth unless foreign aid and remittances from workers abroad picked up. Exports of crude oil could ease the financial constraints by 1987 or 1988 if the discovery proved large enough.

Role of Government

Before the 1962 revolution, the imam and a few family members wielded virtually absolute power; there was no public administration in the modern sense. The administration that existed—including appointments—was looked after personally by the imam. The system of government aimed to fortify his personal power and to help collect taxes. The basic tax was the *zakat*, sanctioned by Islamic law and levied on wealth. Assessment was not uniform, but collection was rigorous. The public treasury was nearly identical to the imam's purse. Without a base or tradition of public administration, economic institutions and administration had to be started from scratch.

Following the revolution, efforts were made to establish an administrative structure. The efforts in the 1960s were less than adequate because of a succession of governments and a prolonged civil war, but the first steps toward economic ministries, a tax system, and economic planning were taken. Greater progress was made in the 1970s; a central bank was established in 1971, a central budget bureau was formed in 1972, and the CPO was created in 1972, for example. The country's first comprehensive budget was drafted in 1973. Many additional economic institutions, programs, and public enterprises were established in the 1970s and in the first half of the 1980s, including in 1985 a supreme council to supervise oil and gas development following the discovery of oil.

Creating an administrative structure was easier than making it effective. The extreme shortage of educated, qualified, and experienced personnel in the country that persisted in the mid-1980s will be remedied only over time. The shortage existed throughout the economy and not only in the public sector; trained personnel were often lured away from government by the private sector and employment abroad. Although government employment had grown tremendously since the early 1970s, many vacancies

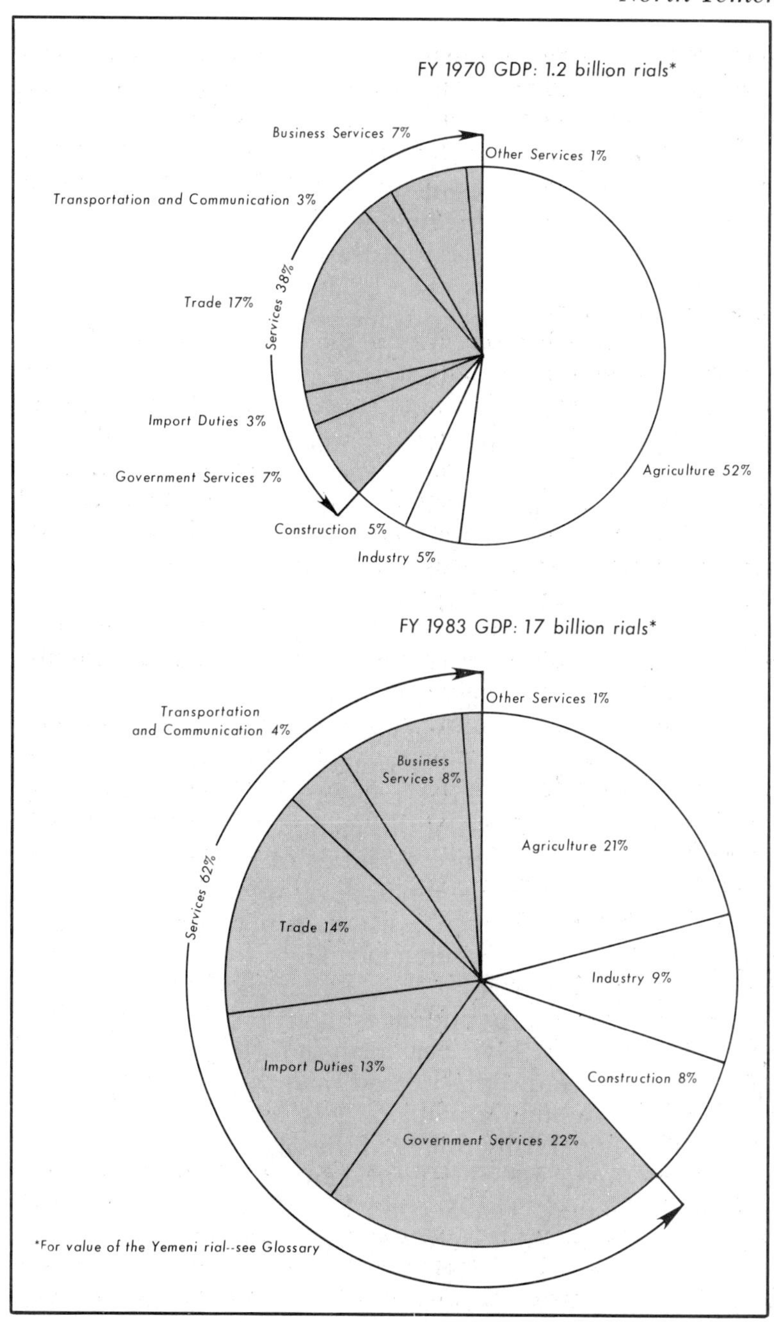

Source: Based on information from Yemen Arab Republic, Central Planning Organization, *Statistical Year Book, 1983*, Sanaa, 1984, 357, 392.

Figure 7. North Yemen: Gross Domestic Product by Sector, FY 1970 and FY 1983

existed in technical positions in economic organizations in the early 1980s. Foreign experts sent to provide technical assistance often found that there were no qualified counterparts to train, and North Yemenis who received training frequently left government service for higher-paying jobs elsewhere. Although the foundations of a modern nation had been laid quickly, administration and economic management remained weak even by standards of other developing countries, although most had had some administrative base before independence. North Yemen's absorptive capacity for investment and its potential for development would continue to hinge on improvements in the government's economic organizations.

Perhaps because of administrative difficulties and perhaps because of ideological leanings, North Yemen's government has kept regulation of the economy and interference with market forces to a minimum. In general, the government sought to create an infrastructure and a climate that would promote initiative and investment by the private sector whether the investors were domestic or foreign. In 1983 licensing of imports and other measures were instituted to ease balance of payments strains, but observers believed that these were temporary measures.

Since the early 1970s government policy has been aimed largely at improving the country's human resources and physical infrastructure. A series of plans were drafted by the CPO to guide economic development toward these goals. The CPO has been assisted in planning by foreign experts financed from foreign aid. The CPO's first plan was for three years (FY 1974-77). The first endeavor was largely a partial listing of public investment projects considered essential. The First Five-Year Plan (FY 1977-81) was more comprehensive and sophisticated than the first. Although a number of economic growth targets were met, public investment only partially followed the plan and fell considerably below the target; agricultural output, in particular, was less than planned. The Second Five-Year Plan (1982-86) called for an annual 7-percent growth of GDP and a total investment of about US$6.5 billion (in 1981 prices). By 1983, as the government sought to deal with mounting economic problems, the second plan goals were revised downward.

Growing budget deficits were causing increasing concern. Between FY 1978 and FY 1982 revenues rose only half as fast as expenditures and by the latter year represented only 40 percent of expenditures. The main source (47 percent in 1983) of the government's current revenues came from duties on imports (see table 2, Appendix). Most of the remaining revenues came from indirect taxes on goods and services. Direct taxes, mostly from individual income taxes, supplied only 14 percent of current revenues in 1983. In addition, the government received large but unknown amounts of foreign loans and grants to finance expenditures. Saudi Arabia, for example, supplied substantial grants as budget support, but this aid began to decline in the first half of the 1980s. There was an abrupt fall in foreign assistance in 1982, and economists expected the flow of external aid to remain smaller for a few years than it had been in the late 1970s and early 1980s.

Rapidly increasing expenditures were a major contributor to the growing deficits. Current expenditures in particular mounted quickly in the late 1970s and early 1980s. One reason was an insurgency that required growing expenditures on defense and security forces; these expenditures amounted to 53 percent of total current spending in 1983 (see table 3, Appendix). In addition, the government's staffing and maintenance costs rose as projects were completed, such as schools and roads. Moreover, the government had to increase salaries and wages of employees as wage rates in the country rose. Thus the bulk of current expenditures went for security, public administration, and education. The government also spent additional sums on development projects (YR 4.3 billion in 1982). Foreign aid financed a large but uncertain portion of development expenditures, but the government also contributed, particularly after 1982.

The fiscal crisis became severe in 1982, the total financial deficit amounting to about YR 5.3 billion, or 33 percent of GDP. Foreign financing dropped sharply, and the government had to borrow from the banking system, primarily from the central bank, to cover the deficit. In 1983 the rise of current expenditures was halted, development expenditures were reduced by 12 percent to about YR 3.8 billion, and current revenues were increased by 44 percent. The budget deficit declined 9 percent but was still an unhealthy 28 percent of GDP. The government continued austerity measures in 1984 and 1985, which along with increases in revenues slowly reduced the size of the deficits, although they remained substantial and threatened a return of inflation. Austerity in government spending would likely be necessary for a few more years unless additional revenues were found.

Foreign aid has been a crucial ingredient in the government's development effort. Financial assistance is believed to have exceeded US$3 billion between 1962 and 1984. Probably about half was in the form of grants requiring no repayment. The grants included food aid, technical assistance to train citizens, and budget support. The other half of the grants were loans, nearly all having concessionary terms and many of them financing specific projects. Aid came from a variety of sources, including Saudi Arabia, Kuwait, the United Arab Emirates (UAE), Iraq, the United States, the Federal Republic of Germany (West Germany), China, and the Soviet Union, as well as such international agencies as the World Bank group and Arab development funds.

The outstanding external public debt at the beginning of 1984 was believed to be about US$1.6 billion. Debt service in 1983 was US$42 million, only about 3 percent of gross foreign exchange earnings, which included workers' remittances. Debt servicing was expected to be more burdensome in the last half of the 1980s. The Iran-Iraq War and the sharp fall of oil revenues of the oil exporters on the Arabian Peninsula caused a drastic decline of foreign aid commitments in 1983 that was expected to persist beyond the mid-1980s. By early 1984 aid commitments that North Yemen could still draw on appeared to amount to about US$700 million. If substantially more aid were not forthcoming, officials would have to increase considerably the mobilization of domestic resources to finance the country's economic development.

Labor Force

Data on the labor force were sparse and of uncertain reliability. The 1975 census reported a work force of 1.1 million when relatively few North Yemenis were working abroad. About 74 percent of the domestically employed were engaged in agriculture, 3 percent in industry, 5 percent in construction, and the remainder in services—largely social services and trade. In 1981 the domestic labor force was believed to number about 1.2 million, of which

830,000 were engaged in agriculture, 54,000 in industry, and 318,000 in services.

The number of citizens working abroad was not known with any certainty. It was known that the number increased rapidly after oil prices shot up in 1974. The large development programs in the Arab oil-exporting states of the Gulf attracted most of the Yemenis working abroad. The 1981 census listed nearly 1.4 million North Yemenis residing abroad, but many observers placed those working in other countries in the neighborhood of 1 million (see Emigration, this ch.). As revenues of the peninsula oil exporters declined and as construction activity slowed in the early 1980s, the total number of North Yemenis working there may have declined somewhat by 1985. The amount of remittances home from workers abroad, although not known precisely, appeared to fluctuate after 1979 but had exhibited no definite trend by 1985. These remittances were in the neighborhood of US$1.2 billion annually between 1977 and 1983, and they contributed significantly to disposable income, investment, and the growth of imports.

The exodus of workers had a substantial impact on the domestic economy in other ways. Because there were nearly as many males working abroad as there were workers in the domestic labor force, an acute labor shortage developed in North Yemen. This was partially compensated for by increased participation of women in the work force, particularly in farming. Wage rates shot up after the mid-1970s as domestic employers were in effect having to pay nearly the same wages as those in Saudi Arabia. North Yemen's wage costs were much higher than those in other developing countries, such as Pakistan and India, which, along with the shortages of trained personnel and inadequate infrastructure, made the country unattractive to many foreign investors. The exodus of workers, however, eliminated unemployment and probably any unwanted underemployment.

North Yemen's labor force was critically short of almost every conceivable skill. The country's long isolation lasted almost to the 1970s. Education also was a recent development (see Education and Health, this ch.). In 1985 literacy was still appallingly low. Although schooling and specific training had expanded substantially by the mid-1980s, it will take many more years before the work force can be upgraded and can begin to meet the needs of the economy.

Progress so far has been hampered by the lack of administrators and managers capable of implementing programs and projects. This too can only be corrected over time.

Agriculture

Farming has long been the main activity of the people. Even into the 1960s farming composed nearly all of GDP and furnished almost all of the employment. By 1983 agriculture's share of GDP had fallen to 21 percent, for other sectors had developed rapidly, but farming still employed about 70 percent of the labor force. Agriculture also provided much of the country's exports, but such earnings dropped sharply in the 1970s, falling from US$ 14 million in FY1974 to US$5 million in 1983 because of declining cotton production. Planners were aware of the importance of increasing agricultural productivity in order to raise living standards among the population.

Lack of basic data hampered policy and planning in all parts of the economy, but it was particularly acute in agriculture, the sector that affected the most people. Soil and hydrological surveys, for example, did not exist. The CPO and the Ministry of Agriculture and Fisheries had agreed on a time series for area, production, and yields of major farm products, but land-use statistics had not been published for several years because of large discrepancies between various data collected, such as sample censuses and the published figures on area, production, and yields. North Yemen's agricultural statistics were best viewed as orders of magnitude and indicators of trends.

Until better data become available, observers concluded that the cultivated area accounted for about 1.5 million hectares out of a total land area of approximately 19.4 million hectares. A further 2 million hectares were usually considered marginal agricultural land; when rainfall was favorable, some of it was cultivated, but otherwise it was largely forage area for livestock. Coarse, sparse vegetation on much of the rest of the land provided some additional forage. The country had no forests in the usual sense, but woody vegetation existed in many places. Some of it was large enough to provide poles and other materials for construction purposes, but the woody vegetation primarily provided fuel, some of which was marketed at escalating prices for rural household cooking. In recent decades cutting greatly exceeded growth, and woody vegetation was rapidly disappearing. The growing shortage and high price for fuelwood caused farmers to plant trees, a process the government endeavored to accelerate because it lessened growing erosion problems and contributed a renewable energy source.

Climatic conditions varied widely even within small areas because of the mountainous terrain, affecting the crops that could be produced (see The Physical Environment, this ch.). Although North Yemen received the most rainfall of any area on the Arabian Peninsula, it varied widely between parts of the country and from year to year. Rainfall was the primary determinant of good harvests and farmers' prosperity. The country experienced prolonged droughts at times, such as during the 1968-73 period; subnormal rainfall reduced harvests in 1983 and 1984, the last years for which data were available in mid-1985. The major rains usually fell in July, August, and September, and minor rains in April and May.

Nearly 85 percent of the cultivated area depended on rainfall; in 1984 about 250,000 hectares were believed irrigated, roughly half by pumps year-round. The rest was irrigated by spate flood flows, wells, and intermittent streams that might afford moisture for a single crop a year. The rapid expansion of drilled wells and pumps (for urban drinking water and crop irrigation) since the mid-1970s had caused serious drops in the water table, particularly in the vicinity of Sanaa, where it fell five to six meters a year in the early 1980s. Some areas, mostly on the coastal plain, had salinity problems from the increased irrigation. In 1982 the government established the High Council for Water Resources, chaired by the prime minister, to study and exert greater control over water resources. In practice, however, the council has not exerted much control and probably cannot, given the lack of government control in rural areas.

Five distinct agricultural areas based on temperature and rainfall existed. The Tihamah—the coastal lowlands along the Red Sea—has a hot and humid climate but receives low rainfall. Most cropping occurs close to the mountains and depends mainly on the flood discharge of the five major and 12 small wadis, plus pumping from groundwater in recent years. The area cultivated was probably about 235,000 hectares. The main crops were sorghum, millet, and cotton, but tobacco, corn, sesame, vegetables, and fruits were also grown.

The landscape of the southern uplands—the Southern Highlands and Southern Midlands—is rugged with deep gorges containing alluvial bottomland and terraces up the mountainsides. The cultivable area was about 550,000 hectares. In the foothills, where humidity was higher, sorghum, corn, bananas, papaya, citrus fruits, and vegetables were grown; at the higher elevations, sorghum, qat, coffee, fruit, and vegetables were important crops. Livestock were important in the area, which had about 30 percent of the country's cattle, sheep, and goats.

The Central Highlands constitute the most important crop and livestock area of the country, containing about 600,000 hectares of cultivable land and 35 percent of the cattle, sheep, and goat population. The main crops were wheat, barley, alfalfa, sorghum, grapes, qat, coffee, figs, vegetables, and stone fruits.

The Northern Highlands contain the higher mountains of the central mountain chain. Annual rainfall was considerably less than in the more southern highland, usually ranging from 20 to 40 centimeters. The area had about 130,000 hectares of cultivable land, which were used mainly for sorghum, wheat, and grazing. The area had perhaps 15 percent of the country's livestock.

The eastern region is the large area where the mountains taper off to the desert of Rub al Khali. Rainfall is low, temperatures are high, and soils are poor. Cultivation on perhaps 25,000 hectares was mainly along the wadis draining from the mountains toward the desert. Sorghum and millet were the main crops. Raising livestock was a minor activity.

In antiquity the eastern slopes were an important agricultural area. The ruins of a dam near Marib show a highly developed irrigation system. The dam, first built in the seventh century B.C., was in use for about 1,200 years. In late 1984 the cornerstone of a new dam was laid, located some three kilometers from the old dam. The UAE was financing the US$75 million construction cost of the dam, which is to be built by a Turkish contractor and is to be completed in about three years. It will be 39 meters high—more than twice the height of the old dam—and will eventually irrigate some 20,000 hectares.

Landownership patterns and the tenure system were complex and varied considerably in different regions. Statistics on landholdings were almost nonexistent. Most farms were believed small, although holdings in the Tihamah and in the Southern Highlands could be quite large. A substantial amount of tenancy and sharecropping existed, largely based on verbal agreement and on a year-to-year basis. The prevailing system in the early 1980s contributed to excessive fragmentation of plots, which greatly lessened the possibilities of mechanization, and to reduced incentives for the cultivator to care for the soil and to adopt modern practices involving costly inputs. By the mid-1980s major reforms of ownership and tenure patterns were not under consideration, but a need for more secure tenure and for a means of providing agricultural credit that did not require mortgaging land was apparent.

Many observers described the farmers as industrious and ingenious in the way they recycled everything to produce crops and raise livestock from the scarce water and available land. A striking feature of the mountainous area was the numerous contoured terraces—the accumulated effort of generations of farmers—stretching high up the mountainsides. The terraces were well designed and solidly built, using carefully laid stones to retain rich, deep soil that caught a maximum of the water runoff; the terraces also controlled erosion. Foreign agronomists found the soils in these terraced plots amazingly fertile after centuries of continuous cultivation, the result of careful care. Animal manure and ashes from cooking fires—fueled partly by roots and lower stalks of the previous year's crop—were worked into the fields annually. Animal fodder consisted largely of the leaves and upper stalks of the grain crops. But these were centuries-old practices that provided a bare subsistance.

By the early 1980s the terrace system was endangered by a lack of maintenance. Part of the problem resulted from road construction; displaced earth and rock, along with inadequate drainage from roads, weakened rock walls. Use of too-large tractors on the small plots also weakened the walls. Abandonment of marginal terraced plots and failure to maintain the walls threatened the terraces below. Once terraces became eroded because of collapsing rock walls, they became prohibitively expensive to restore because of the labor shortage and high wage rates.

The traditional farming practices evolved over centuries when most households farmed. Each household tended to be largely self-sufficient. Cropping and the raising of livestock were meant primarily to supply the household. Exchange of some commodities and services within a local area provided most of the household's remaining needs. There was little commercial activity and little use of money. Development of trade in the 1930s between the Southern Highlands and the British-controlled port of Aden in what is now South Yemen began a swing toward more commercial farming. Road construction, beginning in the 1960s, opened additional commercial opportunities. By 1985 probably most villages were accessible by trucks, although earthen roads remained common. Circumstances changed more rapidly in the 1970s with the large emigration of workers abroad, their substantial remittances home, and development of a labor shortage and high wage rates throughout the economy. By the early 1980s farmers faced a far different situation than the one they had grown up with and had been prepared to meet.

Crop statistics, although weak, provided an indicator of farmers' responses to emerging opportunities in commercial farming. The estimated increase of agricultural production in the decade up to 1981 was about 4 percent a year. This growth was the result of shifts in cultivation to such higher-value produce as legumes, vegetables, fruits, and potatoes in response to consumer demand for a more varied diet—a demand resulting from higher incomes. Production of higher-value crops more than compensated for a decline in production of traditional, low-value crops. Production and acreage of export crops, essentially cotton, fell sharply.

Crop production has always been heavily concentrated in food grains—particularly sorghum and millet—but with minor amounts of wheat, barley, and corn. These crops historically accounted for about 95 percent of cultivated acreage, but by 1985 they probably accounted for somewhat less than 90 percent because of the diversification of cropping. Sorghum and millet were planted on 689,000 hectares in 1982 (down from a peak of 1.1 million hectares in FY 1976), and production amounted to 580,000 tons (down from a peak of 921,000 tons in FY 1975). The drought in 1983 reduced production to 268,000 tons from the same amount of acreage as in 1982 (see table 4, Appendix). Although wheat was rapidly supplanting sorghum as the basic food grain in the diet, it was largely imported. Domestic production averaged around 65,000 tons a year in the mid-1970s, and yields remained static at about 1 ton per hectare, except in drought years such as 1983. Corn acreage increased modestly after the mid-1970s; production was 67,000 tons in 1982 and 34,000 tons in 1983. Fruits, vegetables (including potatoes), and legumes were the other food crops, and production increased from about 323,000 tons in FY 1972 to 691,000 tons in 1983.

Cotton and coffee were the main export crops. Cotton production dropped from a peak of 27,000 tons in FY 1975 to 2,800 tons in FY 1980 because of increasing labor costs. In the late 1970s the government increased purchase prices and provided subsidized inputs to increase supplies to local gins and mills. By 1983 production had risen to 6,500 tons. Coffee has long been produced in North Yemen, and its port of Mocha provided one of the names used for coffee. Production was reportedly about 12,000 tons in the 1930s when it was a major source of foreign exchange. Production stagnated in the 1970s and early 1980s, amounting to 3,300 tons in 1983. Qat and coffee grew in the same areas.

Qat is a plant that is widely consumed by the population for its stimulating and relaxing properties (see Qat, this ch.). An extremely efficient marketing system, perhaps the most effective in the country, moved the fresh-cut qat sprigs from producers to consumers. Low production costs and increasing prices in the 1970s made qat the most profitable crop that could be grown; production and sales expanded rapidly as incomes rose. Data on qat production were unavailable, but most observers believed that its market value far exceeded that of any other cash crop. Because qat production was excluded from national accounts, the value added in agriculture presumably was understated. Official government policy frowned on qat production and consumption, but neither was rigorously proscribed. Some private industrial firms, however, prohibited qat chewing on the job. Many observers noted that qat consumption was frequent, often daily, and costly, requiring a large proportion of expenditures by those of average means.

Farmers traditionally raised some livestock. Cattle, camels, and donkeys furnished draft power and in the past were frequently used to transport produce, although by 1985 trucks had largely taken over this function where roads were available. Sheep and goats were raised for milk, fiber, and meat. Hides of slaughtered animals were mostly exported. Stalks and leaves of crops provided much of the fodder, but sheep and goats were also grazed on the available natural vegetation. Feed was a major constraint, and overgrazing had degraded much of the rangeland. The livestock population, other than poultry, had stagnated since the early 1970s. In 1983 there were nearly 4 million sheep and goats, 942,000 cattle, and 58,400 camels. Draft animals will probably continue to be needed on small terraced plots, and the population's demand for meat presumably will continue to rise. But the future of livestock activity was problematical, given the feed constraints and the changing structure of farming.

Commercial chicken farms presented a different trend. Farmers have long kept a few chickens, and the number of such local varieties rose slowly into the early 1980s. But commercial poultry raising, relying on modern techniques and imported feed, increased rapidly. The number of poultry rose from 500,000 in 1978 to nearly 4.4 million by 1983. The supply of chicken meat to consumers increased more than sixfold after 1977 to reach nearly 22,900 tons in 1983, surpassing the amount of meat available from cattle and sheep.

The fish catch also rose, albeit more slowly, as a protein source in the diet, reaching 17,600 tons in 1983. Fishing was handicapped by its operation out of small ports lacking adequate roads and marketing facilities and generally relying on small boats and rafts. Fishing provided a meager income and was done mostly on an individual basis.

Although traditional farming practices still prevailed, more modern techniques were gaining acceptance in the 1980s. In little more than a decade, tractors had increased from a negligible number to about 20,000 in 1983. Wells and pumps had expanded irrigation substantially. Use of pesticides, fertilizers, and improved varieties of seeds increased, particularly near development projects and demonstration plots that were usually funded as aid projects by foreign governments and institutions, but the use of fertilizers was still quite low. Highland farmers, however, readily adopted improved varieties of seeds for wheat and potatoes where they were available. Nonetheless, the transition from the traditional, nearly subsistence farming to commercial cropping involving the risky use of costly inputs was bound to be slow, however necessary. In addition, the lack of trained extension agents to introduce the new agricultural techniques and inputs to the farmers will continue to hamper the adoption and proper use of the new procedures. The country had little additional land that was cultivable, and a growing agricultural sector meant that the land and water available had to be used more productively.

The government was committed to increasing the productivity of farmers. Since the early 1970s institutions have been formed and projects started to aid agriculture. Much of the government's research, training, and extension services have come from aid and technical assistance provided by foreign governments and institutions. In 1982 the government consolidated other financial agencies to form the Cooperative and Agricultural Credit Bank (CACB) as the single institution to provide credit to agriculture and for rural development. The aim was to provide credit, at subsidized rates, if necessary, to stimulate higher productivity. By 1985 the government's activities had had only slight direct effect on agriculture because most of the activities were related to institution building, which would take time to have an impact. Moreover, the government's efforts were hampered by funding constraints and the extreme shortage of North Yemenis possessing education and training. Additionally, the government's pay scales made it difficult to attract or hold those citizens who had skills.

Two local organizations also fostered rural development. By the early 1980s there were about 35 farm cooperatives, largely for marketing, but little information was available about their activities. The other organizations were the Local Development Associations (LDAs). LDAs started in 1963 in response to a government decree for local groups to form self-help organizations to build the basic infrastructure rather than wait until the government could do so. The number of LDAs grew slowly until the Confederation of Yemeni Development Associations (CYDA) was formed in 1973, which standardized the organization of LDAs and provided an intermediary between the government and LDAs. LDAs were not government agencies but communal organizations, the CYDA being their medium for influencing, and being influenced by, the government. In 1975 these arrangements were formalized by the government. By the early 1980s there were over 200 LDAs.

LDA projects were financed from various sources but primarily from voluntary labor contributed by an LDA's members. LDAs also received 75 percent of the revenues from the tax on the value of agricultural production in their areas, 2.5 percent of net import duties from the government via CYDA, foreign grants channeled via CYDA, portions of other funds collected by the national and local governments, and nominal membership dues. In the early 1980s yearly revenues were around YR200 million, and the bulk of these resources financed construction of roads, water projects, schools, and health clinics. LDAs were an important instrument in the rapid expansion of infrastructure in rural areas, but critics charged that they were often dominated by the rural elite and that the projects reflected their goals and not necessarily those of most members.

The government's interest in promoting increased productivity from farming was twofold. As long as the bulk of the population was engaged in agriculture, rising standards of living had to come mostly from increased farm output. Moreover, during the 1970s imports of agricultural products, mostly food, rose sharply and increased pressure on the balance of payments. Imports of food rose from US$80 million in FY 1974 to over US$450 million in 1982; they accounted for about 40 percent of domestic consumption in 1980. Imports of wheat between FY 1974 and FY 1980, for example, rose from 130,000 tons to about 400,000 tons. Imports of high-valued meats, dairy products, fruits, and vegetables rose even more in percentage terms because of increasing incomes and dietary preferences. But changing the traditional practices that evolved over centuries, developing the institutions and structures needed for commercial farming, and overcoming the severe constraints of limited agricultural land, water, and trained personnel would not come easily or quickly.

Industry

Important progress was made in industralizing the economy during the 1970s, despite serious constraints. In the 1970s value added (in constant prices) by industry—including mining, manufacturing, and public utilities—increased by over 12 percent a year and by nearly 20 percent a year between 1981 and 1983. Industry's contribution to GDP rose from 5.4 percent in FY 1970 to 9.5 percent in

1983. This was a remarkable shift in the structure of the economy.

Energy

In 1984 the country's economic and energy prospects took a dramatic upturn. The Yemen Hunt Oil Company, consisting of Yemeni, American, and South Korean firms, announced discovery of the country's first oil about 70 kilometers northeast of Marib. Delineation of the fields and their contents was not expected before late 1985 at the earliest, and by mid-1985 recoverable reserves of oil and gas and the probable production level were only speculative. North Yemeni officials, possessing more information than was publicly available, indicated that production would likely be 100,000 to 200,000 barrels per day (bpd) and possibly 300,000 bpd (about 14 million tons a year) of very light crude oil. A discovery of this magnitude would not be large by world standards, but it would be significant to North Yemen's economy as an energy source, supplier of government revenues, and contributor of foreign exchange earnings. In early 1985 the Yemen Hunt Oil Company agreed to construct a small refinery to supply petroleum products to the domestic market and a crude oil pipeline to the coast with a sea terminal for exports. The refinery will have an initial capacity of 10,000 bpd of gasoline, kerosene, and diesel fuel. Exports probably could not begin until about 1988. The fields, when finally defined, might extend across the border into South Yemen or Saudi Arabia. The discovery spurred other foreign oil companies to arrange exploration concessions with the North Yemeni government.

The discovery of oil was timely, for in 1985 the country had two sources of primary energy—imported petroleum products and firewood—the latter including minor amounts of animal and agricultural wastes. In the early 1980s firewood supplied about 60 percent of the total energy consumed, primarily by households in rural areas. For several decades firewood cutting had greatly exceeded regrowth. By the mid-1980s the country had lost much of its sparse cover of trees and shrubs, causing increasing erosion problems and increasing the likelihood of a complete loss of woody vegetation before the turn of the century if the current rate of depletion persisted. Although firewood was considered a noncommercial energy source because many rural residents collected their own, it was, in fact, also sold in villages and towns. The price of firewood increased sharply after the early 1970s. Increasingly, households were using kerosene and bottled gas (liquid petroleum gas-LPG) where available. This was a desirable development in view of the country's rapid loss of its sparse vegetation. Economists argued that in the second half of the 1980s and later, government policy should control cutting to a greater degree and promote limited afforestation so that a renewable energy source could continue to supplement supplies of LPG and kerosene.

In 1985 commercial primary energy was supplied completely by imported petroleum products because the country had no refinery. Consumption of petroleum products increased sharply after the early 1970s as the economy—particularly road transport—developed. Precise figures for petroleum imports were unavailable because perhaps nearly one-third of total consumption was unofficially trucked in from Saudi Arabia in response to the large differential between Saudi and North Yemeni prices, the latter reflecting world prices and distribution costs. Total petroleum imports were estimated at nearly 950,000 tons in 1982 and were projected to increase to nearly 1.5 million tons by 1986. The government imported and distributed official petroleum imports through the Yemen Petroleum Company (YPC). In 1978 YPC became a subsidiary of the newly formed and government-owned Yemen Oil and Mineral Resources Corporation (YOMINCO). YOMINCO held the government's interest in the newly discovered oil fields.

Highway transport consumed about 57 percent of imported petroleum products—539,000 tons in 1982—most of which was gasoline. The rapid expansion of the road network after the early 1970s was accompanied after the mid-1970s by an even more rapid increase in the vehicle fleet as North Yemeni workers abroad used earnings to purchase trucks and taxis. By the early 1980s the commercial vehicle fleet exceeded cargo and passenger demand by perhaps threefold. Freight rates were quite high because of the excessive number of vehicles and because of high operating costs caused by the mountainous terrain and poorly maintained roads. Nonetheless, vehicles were the only modern means of transport available. In 1982 the other major consumers of imported petroleum products were electrical generation, 100,000 tons; agriculture (mostly diesel tractors and pumps), 98,000 tons; households (LPG and kerosene), 93,000 tons; and industry, 37,000 tons. The remainder was believed to be mostly diesel fuel used in small generators supplying a single rural family or possibly a few families.

In 1985 imported petroleum products were landed at the port of Hodeida and trucked to retail outlets by YOMINCO, the only company operating a fleet of trucks. The shallow waters at Hodeida permitted entry of only extremely small tankers. In mid-1985 it became known that As Salif, which has much deeper water, would be developed as the major port even though Kamaran Island, just offshore, belonged to South Yemen. In 1984 there was discussion of a white-products (gasoline, kerosene, and diesel fuel) pipeline from As Salif to Sanaa to facilitate distribution of imported petroleum products; it was not clear whether the discovery of oil would preclude construction of this pipeline.

Consumption of commercial energy in the form of electricity grew rapidly after the end of the civil war—well above 25 percent a year between 1975 and 1982. The rapid growth partly reflected the small base. In the 1950s only the imam and a few other individuals and institutions had electricity from their own generators. In 1960 there was an estimated total of only two megawatts of generating capacity in the country and by 1975 possibly 45 megawatts. In 1982 capacity was at least 420 megawatts, and electricity generated probably was about 640 million kilowatt-hours.

The generation of electricity began as small individual diesel generators owned by government agencies or individuals. In the 1960s larger systems evolved for the main cities of Sanaa, Taizz, and Hodeida, but they did not have standardized voltages and could not meet the demand for electricity. In 1975 the government-owned Yemen General Electricity Company (YGEC) was formed to develop a national system, taking over the companies in the three main cities. By 1982 YGEC had about 120 megawatts of capacity (all diesel) compared with at least 300 megawatts of capacity (all diesel) belonging to individuals, villages, and companies, such as industrial plants. YGEC units tended to be larger and more efficient than those outside the system, but the public system suffered from outages and voltage drops.

Losses in the system represented about 30 percent of the electricity generated.

In 1983 the first oil-fired steam generator (165-megawatt capacity) was completed just up the coast from Hodeida, and a second was scheduled for completion in about 1987 at the port of Mocha. By 1985 transmission lines linked the first steam generator to many of the larger towns and cities, providing an interconnected system for part of the country. The latest additions were expected to improve the supply and reliability of public electricity, resulting in gradual phaseout of separate generators where the public system was available. But the YGEC system would be limited largely to urban areas for several years. Rural areas would have to rely for some time on small private diesel generators, as they were doing in 1985.

In 1985 investigations of geothermal sources for power generation were underway. Preliminary surveys in the Dhamar-Ridaa area indicated that sufficient steam might be available for a 55-megawatt power station. If additional surveys showed the site to be feasible, production could begin in the early 1990s. Electricity from geothermal sources would provide significant savings if fuel oil had to be imported for power generation.

Mining and Manufacturing

Industrialization has been limited by the scarcity of natural resources. Until oil was discovered in 1984 after an extended search, important exportable minerals had not been found. Deposits of coal, copper, cobalt, iron ore, gold, nickel, and zinc were believed to exist, although the deposits found by 1985 had not proved to be economically exploitable. Surveys were under way to find metallic minerals. Nonmetallic minerals suitable for building materials, such as limestone, clays for bricks and tiles, kaolin for ceramics, sand for glass, and marble were more plentiful, supplying expanding building materials industries. A government-owned salt company, a subsidiary of YOMINCO, mined rock salt near the port of As Salif for export; 151,000 tons of salt were extracted in 1983, although capacity was considerably higher. Construction of a plant to use salt to produce soda ash had been under consideration since the early 1980s.

Manufacturing faced several additional constraints besides the scarcity of natural resources and problems with the supply of energy. The domestic market was small and dispersed; economies of scale were difficult to achieve. The few trained managers or skilled workers available frequently necessitated the hiring of foreign personnel at considerable cost. The rapid increase of wages since the mid-1970s made the use of domestic workers, even the unskilled, very expensive—roughly comparable with southern Europe and much higher than the cost of labor in Turkey, India, and other developing Asian countries. Inadequate infrastructure in much of the country often meant that an industrialist had to develop a site from the ground up, including access roads, power generators, and a water supply (or haul water by tank trucks from a distant location as an alternative). Land prices were also high by the 1980s. Moreover, the open economy and its generally low import duties offered little protection from established foreign manufactures.

In spite of the numerous constraints, manufacturing expanded rapidly after the early 1970s when there was a handful of modern enterprises in textiles, soft drink bottling, presses for cottonseed oil, and stamping of aluminum household items. Aided by the flow of remittances from workers abroad, both investment in manufacturing and the industrial value added increased in real terms by more than 12 percent a year in the second half of the 1970s; fixed assets in industry (in constant prices) rose by 24 percent a year. Rapid growth continued in the early 1980s, when there were about 70 large (for North Yemen) industrial establishments—each with 10 or more employees—which employed a total of over 5,300 workers and accounted for about two-thirds of gross manufacturing output.

In the early 1980s there were about 3,000 registered manufacturing establishments. Most were small shops and artisans. About 90 percent employed fewer than five workers, and 3 percent had 10 or more workers; about 7 percent employed between five and nine people. Manufacturing was dominated by food processing, which accounted for 44 percent of the value added in manufacturing. Building materials accounted for 21 percent of the value added, chemicals, e.g., plastic footwear, paint, detergents, polyurethane foam, and PVC pipes, 10 percent; light engineering (metal doors, water tanks, steel cabinets, and aluminum utensils and window frames), 10 percent; textiles, 5 percent; and woodworking, 5 percent. Manufacturing tended to concentrate around Sanaa, Taizz, and Hodeida, particularly near the capital. The private sector owned and operated most manufacturing enterprises. Large trading companies were responsible for much of the manufacturing investment after the mid-1970s, although some returning workers set up metal fabrication plants using skills acquired abroad. The government owned a handful of large enterprises (usually completed foreign aid projects) producing textiles, cement, tobacco products, drugs, and milled flour.

Government policy encouraged industrialization. Fiscal incentives included exemption of import duties on equipment and spare parts, a 25-percent reduction for five years on import duties for raw materials and intermediate goods, and a five-year tax holiday. Licensing procedures were minimal, and import restrictions and price controls were few. Subsidized credit was available, fees for sites at the government's industrial park were nominal, foreign investors were welcome, and repatriation of profits was guaranteed. Import of foreign technicians and skilled workers was permitted when necessary.

Manufacturing was based almost exclusively on import substitution—most frequently products that because of bulk or other factors pertaining to transportation costs were afforded some advantage over imports. In the early 1980s exports of manufactured articles were limited to bakery products to South Yemen and to textiles, perhaps as a form of loan repayment, to China. Much of manufacturing was the final processing and packaging of products; the import content was usually high, and the value added in North Yemen was often small. Because of the high cost of labor, capital-intensive technology was used. Building materials were the major exception where local materials were processed. By 1985 two public sector cement plants had the capacity to meet most or all of North Yemen's demand for cement; the Soviet aid plant at Bajil was expanded to a capacity of about 350,000 tons a year, with further enlargement to 500,000 tons a year planned; and a new plant with a capacity of 500,000 tons a year was completed by the Japanese at Amran in 1982 (see fig. 6). Production increased from 85,000 tons in 1981 to 623,400 tons in 1983 as the new capacity came onstream.

By the early 1980s difficulties confronted many manufacturing establishments, both public and private. Despite the heavy investment in machinery to compensate for the shortage of labor and its high cost, capacity use was frequently low, even on a one-shift basis. Inadequate maintenance and technical problems contributed to underutilization of machinery. Quality control was inadequate, and the quality of many domestically produced articles was inferior to imports. Management was usually weak. As a consequence, production costs were high, and profitability was often low. Some of the public sector plants required subsidies. The integrated public sector textile mill at Sanaa, a Chinese aid project, was an example. The mill operated near designed capacity of about 1,200 tons of yarn and 10 million meters of cloth a year in the early 1970s. By the mid-1970s rising wage costs, departure of skilled North Yemenis trained by the Chinese, and rising textile imports cut back production and profits. In 1977 cloth production amounted to about 2 million meters, and in 1979 a rehabilitation of the mill was begun by the Chinese to return it to profitability. The status of profits was not available, but by 1983 cloth production had climbed back to nearly 6.5 million meters.

Although manufacturing expanded significantly in less than two decades, the country was still at an early stage of industrialization in the mid-1980s. Moreover, prospects for further industrialization were limited for the next decade or so. The country faced the same constraints as those faced by other developing nations, but few confronted the combination and severity of constraints as those in North Yemen. It would take time to remedy the shortage of skills and managerial ability in the work force and to develop the infrastructure.

Banking and Monetary Policy

In 1985 North Yemen's financial system was at an early stage of development, having started little more than two decades earlier. Foreign coins long served the country's small monetary needs. Before 1964 the Maria Theresa thaler, an Austrian silver coin that was widely used in the Red Sea area, was the only legal tender. In 1964 the Yemen Currency Board was established and began issuing paper notes called the rial (YR), the new national currency. In 1962 the Yemen Bank for Reconstruction and Development (YBRD) was established with majority government ownership (49 percent private Yemeni shareholders) after the government took over a bank previously owned by Saudis. The YBRD engaged in commercial banking while also acting as the government agent for deposits and monetary policy. The YBRD and the currency board were the country's financial institutions, serving both the government and the private sector.

In 1971 the government established, with assistance from the International Monetary Fund (IMF), the Central Bank of Yemen (CBY) to take over the central bank functions of the currency board and the YBRD. The Central Bank was assigned normal responsibilities: it issued the currency and managed reserves, acted as banker to the government, regulated other banks and credit, and set interest rates. In 1972 four foreign banks were licensed to operate in the country, breaking the monopoly of commercial banking then held by the YBRD.

From these humble beginnings the banking system gradually expanded. By 1984 there were 10 commercial banks with 60 branches. The government-controlled YBRD was by far the largest, accounting for 62 percent of commercial assets and 22 branches, the most widely spread system in the country. The remaining nine commercial banks were at least partly foreign owned. About 90 percent of commercial bank lending was short-term, largely financing trade, including imports. The focus of commercial banks varied considerably. The YBRD was reaching out to depositors and extending some long-term credit. Some other commercial banks were primarily concerned with lending to large private businesses or to the government and its corporations, using funds generated from its corporate system abroad. In 1985 the commercial banking system was still largely urban based and did not extend throughout the country. Moreover, after 1979 lending grew much more slowly than deposits, leaving the banks in a highly liquid position. It will take time for banking services to reach the countryside and for the system to play its part in the country's economic development.

Predating the banking system and continuing to survive because of the weakness of the banking system were many individuals, including licensed money changers, who informally served some of the rural population's banking needs. Statistical data on this informal sector were not available, but it handled an important part of remittances home from workers abroad, for example. This informal sector also extended credit to farmers and to households that were outside the government's credit supervision.

Partly to enlarge banking's services, in the 1970s the government established specialized banks (majority government ownership) to provide long-term funding to priority sectors that received little credit from commercial banks. In 1976 the Industrial Bank of Yemen was formed, and by 1983 it was the major source of industrial financing and played a key role in mobilizing private resources in industrial investment. In 1977 the Housing Credit Bank was established, but by 1983 it was mostly confined to financing houses for government employees. In the 1970s institutions were formed to provide agricultural and rural development credit; by 1983 they had been merged into the Cooperative and Agricultural Credit Bank (CACB) to provide a single source for rural credit. By 1983 the CACB had a limited number of branches and suffered from staffing problems, especially an insufficient number of experienced managers. Its role will probably grow, but the informal financial network will probably supply much of the rural credit for several years. In 1981 the YBRD formed the Yemen Company for Investment and Finance to handle its portfolio of long-term investments and to go into term financing to industry.

Since the 1960s the country's money supply has been growing rapidly, partly reflecting monetization of the economy. Monetary officials had little control over the causes for the increases in the money supply. The principal cause was the growth of workers' remittances in the 1970s and more recently the rise in budget deficits financed by the Central Bank. Expansion of bank credit to the private sector in the mid-1970s, partly for speculation in real estate and commodities, was curbed by the monetary authorities by late in the decade. Growth of the money supply contributed to periods of high inflation in the 1970s, averaging over 25 percent a year between 1972 and 1978. Because reliable and comprehensive price indices were lacking, the consumer price index for Sanaa had to serve as an indicator of inflation.

Unable to control the main cause of a rapidly expanding money supply, officials allowed almost unrestricted imports to ease inflationary pressures. The foreign exchange provided by workers' remittances permitted such a policy. The rapid increase of world prices in the 1972-74 period resulted in some imported inflation. Physical bottlenecks in the landing and distribution of imports in the mid-1970s limited the effectiveness of the policy at first. By the late 1970s, however, inflation had been brought down to a manageable level. Between 1979 and 1983 the Sanaa consumer price index rose an average 5.3 percent a year. The large budget deficits after 1981, however, greatly increased the money supply, which reportedly rose an average of about 30 percent a year in 1983 and 1984. Prices began to rise also—by about 10 percent in 1983 and by perhaps between 15 and 20 percent in 1984. Because the government tried to limit the growth of imports in 1984 and 1985 while still incurring substantial deficits, escalating inflation was a serious threat in the mid-1980s.

Foreign Trade

The country's lack of natural resources and its early stage of development afforded few exportable commodities. In 1982 (the latest year for which data were available in mid-1985) total exports amounted to YR113.2 million (US$24.8 million), of which at least 59 percent were reexports of imported goods. Exports of North Yemen products were about US$10 million—largely agricultural products. Cotton and hides plus a little coffee accounted for US$4.6 million of exports. Live animals, vegetables, and fruits were exported to Saudi Arabia. Bakery and confectionary products were exported to South Yemen. Some salt and cottonseed cake were also exported. South Yemen accounted for 76 percent of exports (including reexports) in 1982.

Imports exhibited remarkable growth, increasing from US$87 million in FY 1972 to US$1.85 billion in 1980. By 1982 imports had declined to US$1.5 billion. Until 1983 the country exercised almost no control over imports or foreign exchange, and import duties were low. In fact, imports were substantially higher—by more than one-third, according to observers—than those recorded by customs officials. Most of this unrecorded trade consisted of goods smuggled or unofficially allowed entry from Saudi Arabia. Visitors remarked on the wide array of goods exhibited by North Yemeni merchants and noted that markets were comparable to those in oil-rich Saudi Arabia.

In 1982 imports of food and live animals constituted the largest category of official imports, amounting to about US$450 million, or 29 percent of recorded imports. About 525,000 tons of wheat and flour were imported. A variety of manufactured goods amounted to 22 percent of recorded imports; machinery and transport equipment (including automobiles and trucks), 19 percent; petroleum products, 12 percent; and chemicals, 7 percent. Imports were supplied by many countries. In 1982 Japan supplied 13 percent; Saudi Arabia, 10 percent; France, 7 percent; and West Germany, Britain, Italy, and the Netherlands, 5 percent each. The United States supplied 2 percent. About 20 percent of imports were supplied in such small amounts that the individual countries were not listed. Imports supplied by Saudi Arabia included goods transshipped at Saudi ports to smaller vessels with a draft suitable for North Yemen's ports.

Balance of Payments

North Yemen was largely free of balance of payments constraints in the decade preceding 1983. In fact, the country built up substantial foreign currency reserves in the second half of the 1970s, despite a rapidly growing imbalance between imports and exports. The growth of workers' remittances financed the bulk of the trade imbalance, but also contributing to it was increasing foreign aid. By the late 1970s, however, workers' remittances stopped growing and hovered around US$1.2 billion, while the trade imbalance continued to grow. The Central Bank began drawing on foreign exchange reserves to sustain imports. In the early 1980s declining oil revenues of the Arab oil-exporting nations and the Iran-Iraq War caused these countries to reduce their aid, particularly in 1983. Official grants declined from US$445 million in 1982 to US$186 million in 1983 (see table 5, Appendix). In 1983 the country faced a serious balance of payments problem; foreign exchange reserves had been drawn to about the minimum level, sufficient to cover about three months of imports, and foreign aid had been sharply reduced.

By early 1983 officials had implemented a number of measures to deal with the balance of payments difficulties. Tariffs on imports were increased, import licenses were delayed or rejected for goods considered luxuries, and other controls on imports were instituted, including a prohibition of imports of fresh fruit. In addition, the Central Bank halted the automatic supply of foreign exchange to commercial banks, except for imports deemed essential. The intent was to force banks to seek foreign exchange from the private economy by paying a premium based on the assumption that a large amount of foreign currency had been physically carried back by workers returning from abroad and held in private caches. In October 1983 the rial was unpegged from the dollar, and a series of devaluations followed as the official rate attempted to catch up with the rate in local markets; the devaluation amounted to 25 percent by August and was expected to decline further. The measures reduced imports and the deteriorating trade balance in 1983.

By 1985 officials confronted difficult decisions. Continued reduction of imports threatened high inflation unless budget deficits were also curtailed. Reducing deficits by increasing taxes and making the existing economic assets more productive to finance a larger share of the country's economic development would require declining real incomes and a lower standard of living than the population had been enjoying. Decisions could also be postponed in hopes that workers' remittances might again increase, that foreign aid would return to former levels, and/or that the oil discovery would be large enough and exports early enough to provide the financial relief needed.

Political Developments, 1967-78

The Last Years of the Civil War

The presidency of Abdallah al Sallal did not survive the departure of Egyptian troops, agreed upon in August 1967 between President Gamal Abdul Nasser of Egypt and King Faisal of Saudi Arabia at the Khartoum summit of the League of Arab States (Arab League) (see Foreign Troops Leave the Yemens, ch. 1). Even before the last Egyptian soldiers left Sanaa on October 12, Sallal had already received an ultimatum from army officers demanding an end to authoritarian rule, corruption, and inefficiency. On November 3 Sallal left Sanaa for a visit to Moscow, but Yemen specialist Robert Stookey notes that Sallal privately told Abd al Rahman al Iryani that he was going to exile in Iraq and would not return. On November 4 the Sallal government was deposed without violence and replaced with the Republican Council made up of Iryani, Shaykh Muhammad Ali Uthman (a Shafii), and Ahmad Muhammad Numan (of the old Free Yemenis group). Muhsin Ahmad al Ayni, a moderate leftist, was appointed prime minister. The departure of Sallal occasioned no regrets in any quarter. The combination of his ineffective leadership and his subservience to Egypt had eroded what legitimacy he had once enjoyed. The departure of the Egyptians and the accession to power of the moderate Iryani was the beginning of a struggle for power that was mostly ideological but with strong overtones of Zaydi-Shafii factionalism.

Both the royalist and republican camps included several factions by the end of 1967. The war lasted more than two more years, but many of the elements of reconciliation were already in place, and moderate factions in both camps soon were in the ascendancy.

The royalists had obvious strength. If nothing else, they had withstood the assault of Egyptian troops for five years and had prevented republican and Egyptian forces from ever holding over half of the national territory. The military strength of the royalists, however, lay in the same element that had been the military backbone of the imamate—the Zaydi tribes of the Northern Highlands. Not all the tribes were royalist (many of the Hashid tribes had followed their paramount shaykh, Abdallah ibn Husayn al Ahmar, into the republican camp), but many of the imam's most effective forces were tribal groups.

The rallying point of the royalist camp was the inadequate Imam Badr, who lacked the traditional qualifications of an imam (see The Zaydis, ch. 1). He had alienated most of the traditional support for the imamate without having attracted the support of those whose approval he sought: Nasser of Egypt and Yemeni reformists. Those tribal shaykhs who supported the royalists did so without much attachment to the imam but as a result of traditional tribal goals, i.e., to increase an individual shaykh's power within his tribe or to obtain the money and arms that the royalists or their Saudi backers provided. As soon as the Egyptians had gone, one of the strongest motivations for tribal support of the royalist side was gone. Traditional Zaydi xenophobia lost its target with the departure of the foreign troops. Most of the tribes continued, as they done throughout Yemeni history, to change sides whenever it was convenient to do so.

The royalist camp was beset with serious divisions within the ruling Hamid al Din family, between age-groups, and between hard-liners (like the ruling family) who were determined to fight to the end and moderates who were prepared to compromise with the republicans if only the Egyptians were removed from North Yemen. At the end of 1967 the hard-liners won acceptance for a major offensive against the republicans because the Egyptians were no longer there to support them. The failure of this offensive resulted in the ascendancy of the moderates, including royalist Foreign Minister Ahmad al Shami (once one of the Free Yemenis), who would lead the way to reconciliation.

The republican camp was also divided. Although there still lay ahead ideologically oriented power struggles in Sanaa, less radical elements were encouraged by the accession of the moderate Iryani to the chairmanship of the Republican Council. Iryani was not only acceptable to most factions among republicans (and increasingly to royalists as well), but he was also popular with the people in general. He was a member of the qadi class and thus not strongly associated with Zaydi-Shafii differences (see Qadis, this ch.). His record of public service was one of integrity, and his long opposition to imamic rule gave him the appropriate republican credentials, but his imprisonment in Cairo with other republican moderates and his participation in the abortive reconciliation conferences of 1964 and 1965 showed the extent to which he was both moderate and keen on reconciliation.

There were leftist elements in the heterogeneous collection that constituted the republican camp. Many, perhaps most, of the Shafiis in the republican camp were leftists. The high watermark of this faction came with the 1968 siege of Sanaa—the royalist offensive following the October 1967 withdrawal of Egyptian troops.

The vacuum left by the Egyptian withdrawal had prompted new infusions of assistance for the republic from the Soviet Union and Syria. Domestically, the elements most determined to hold the capital and prevent a royalist victory at any cost were leftists, and for the Shafiis of the left traditional resentment of Zaydi domination under the imams added fuel to the flames of their republican sentiments.

The Saudis were still providing financial aid to the royalists, but the failure of the siege of Sanaa, which began in December 1967 and ended in February 1968, provided convincing evidence that the royalists would never achieve a military victory. Although the royalists came close to victory—cutting off all roads to the capital for most of January and February 1968—the republicans, under the personal leadership of the military strongman, General Hassan al Amri, and with substantial aid from the Soviet Union and Syria, finally broke the siege in March. Only four months after the Egyptian withdrawal the republic had proved that it could stand on its own. The failure of the siege also accelerated the disintegration of the royalist camp. By the end of the siege a number of changes had taken place in the situation as a whole, and the impetus to reconciliation began to increase.

The first major change was that the British in late 1967 left South Yemen, leaving in power the National Liberation Front (NLF). The new government of South Yemen was keen to establish union with North Yemen and was ready to provide aid to the republicans, just as the republicans had aided anti-British elements in South Yemen since 1963. The accession of radicals to power in Aden, the departure of Egyptian troops from North Yemen, the defeat of the royalists at the siege of Sanaa, and the new moderate leadership of Iryani in Sanaa in turn brought about another important change, this one in the policy of the government of Saudi Arabia. The Saudis had been willing to finance the struggle of a traditional monarch against an Egyptian-supported military coup, but the situation was now quite different. The regime in Riyadh was extremely dismayed at the turn of events in Aden, and although pleased with the Egyptian withdrawal from North Yemen, they were worried about the aid coming into Sanaa from the Soviet Union and radical Arab states. From the Saudi point of view, the Yemeni royalists were now a strategic liability. If they could not prevail against the republicans after the Egyptian withdrawal, they were unlikely ever to do so. In addition, from the Saudi perspective the Iryani government was sufficiently moderate to deal with and might be weaned from Soviet and radical Arab aid if the Saudi connection with the royalists ended. Furthermore, Faisal was now far more concerned with the NLF radicals in Aden and hoped to co-opt a moderate government in Sanaa in an effort to contain

South Yemeni radicalism. All aspects of the situation inclined the Saudis to drop their support of the Hamid al Din family and to push for compromise with the republicans.

After the end of the siege of Sanaa, Saudi policy moved in this direction. In September 1968 Faisal reportedly gave the imam a three-month subsidy but warned that no more money would be provided unless a substantial victory were achieved before the end of the year. The imam began to make economies and, in doing so, reduced some of the tribal subsidies. This precipitated a defection by angry tribal leaders, and with their withdrawal the possibility of royalist victory—already very slim—disappeared completely. Although there were some military engagements in 1969 and 1970, there was little hope in the royalist camp.

Throughout 1968 the moderates and radicals within the republican government struggled for control. Although the left had played a major role in the defeat of the royalists at the siege of Sanaa, the moderates began to establish greater control in the army and throughout the government. The conflict resulted in open violence between the two sides in Hodeida in March and in Sanaa in August 1968. Nearly 2,000 men were killed in the August battle in Sanaa, and victory over the radicals, who were supported by the NLF across the border in South Yemen, was achieved only with the help of tribal forces within the republican camp. For the republican leadership, as for the royalists and, indeed, for governments reaching far back in Yemeni history, the Zaydi tribesmen were critical. As Stookey notes, "the victors were all Zaydis, while the vanquished [leftists] were Shafiis."

Within the royalist camp moderates had also begun to take hold. Royalist Foreign Minister Shami, a sayyid who was one of the foremost royalist moderates, had held secret talks with his old colleague from Free Yemeni days, Qadi Muhammad Mahmud al Zubayri (of the republican side) at the 1964 Erkowit conference. The outlines of a compromise had been discussed, which included the removal both of the imamate and of the Egyptians. By 1968 the Egyptians were gone, and hopes for the future of the imamate were dim even among the most devout royalists.

With moderates in the ascendancy on both sides, a peace conference in Jiddah in March 1970 succeeded in bringing a reconciliation between the two sides in the seven-and-a-half-year civil conflict. An agreement was reached whereby the republican government would remain in place but would incorporate some royalist leaders. The imam, faced with no other choice, told the Zaydi tribes that they were free to make their own decision. Shami and other royalists flew to Sanaa in May; Shami joined the Republican Council, other former royalists joined the cabinet, and still others were incorporated into the government at lower levels.

The wounds of the civil war took a long time to heal. Political scientist J.E. Peterson suggests that the reconciliation, which brought together the moderates of both sides, provided neither a reconstruction of the traditional legitimacy of the Yemeni government nor a new and different alternative to the old forms. He notes further that the seven years of Iryani's leadership showed the weakness and lack of legitimacy of the new government of North Yemen; it could neither provide the basic services that are expected of national governments nor attract the support of either the general population or the various political factions. The Iryani government remained plagued by factional conflict, ambitious power struggles, inability to develop the fragile infrastructure, and continuing tribal power in the highlands.

Postwar Reconciliation under Iryani

The first three years of Iryani's leadership as chairman of the Republican Council occurred before the civil war ended, and so it was not until the 1970-74 period that his government was able to begin an attempt to lay the foundations for political and economic development as a unified nation. As early as 1962 the framework of the modern government had been legally established in Sanaa, but the public administration remained "form without substance" until well into the 1970s. These were years characterized by an absence of agreement on basic political principles. Although unity had been achieved on a formal level, North Yemen remained fragmented, its weak leadership beset by internal political factions and interfering neighbors. After years of turmoil and under such conditions, it is not surprising that many North Yemenis were content with a return to traditional values.

The constitution enacted in December 1970 embodied traditional religious and political values, but it was also an attempt to prevent domination of the government by a single man. Accepted after a year of political discussions and debate, the 1970 constitution stated that Yemen was an Islamic and Arab nation, declared that sharia would be the source of all legislation, and stipulated that members of the Consultative Council (parliament) had to be practicing Muslims. (Most members were, in effect, tribal leaders.) The ruling Republican Council members were required to be well versed in sharia. Judges could only be selected from among scholars of sharia, and the leading role of the ulama was formally acknowledged. Political parties were forbidden, and although individual rights were guaranteed in a bill of rights, the provisions were even less comprehensive than was a 1956 Free Yemeni manifesto (see Growing Opposition and the Assassination of Imam Yahya, ch. 1).

The provision for a collective head of state, the Republican Council, was meant to prevent authoritarian rule, such as that of the much resented Sallal. The concept of group leadership was supported by prominent *mashaykh* who were invited to play a role in the Iryani government. Peterson suggests, in fact, that the strong role played by the traditionalists and the tribal shaykhs in the Iryani government not only resulted in conflicts with the less traditional politicians but also eventually obstructed the efforts of the technocrats to create a national infrastructure and pursue economic development.

Although the Iryani government provided a necessary breathing spell after the protracted civil war, the years between the end of the war in 1970 and Iryani's removal from office in 1974 saw little progress in economic and political development. Political infighting and repeated attempts to reconcile ambitious political figures and factions led to pronounced cabinet instability. Prime Minister Ayni was replaced by the former Free Yemeni, Numan, who served only two months in office before resigning because of what he said was the inability of the government to meet its financial obligations. He was replaced by General Amri, whose government lasted only 10 days before he had to leave office following a bizarre incident. Amri reached a wrong telephone number and was connected to a drunken Sanaa photographer. The photographer, thinking the general's call was a joke, made facetious comments that enraged Amri. The prime minister had the unfortunate man arrested and killed. The Republican Council then forced

Amri into exile and renamed Muhsin al Ayni prime minister. Such incidents, reminiscent of the capricious rule of the imams, did little to instill confidence in the government. The Iryani regime did not provide institutional, political, and economic development, but according to Ayni (prime minister during much of the regime), this period was fruitful in some ways. The North Yemenis were governing themselves for the first time since the fall of the imamate in 1962, and during this period factions were sorting themselves out and expressing a wide diversity of points of view on the political future of the country.

The government did not control all of the territory under its presumed authority. Some of the major tribal shaykhs had been co-opted by the government in Sanaa, most notably the Hashid shaykh, Ahmar, whose father had been so treacherously killed by Imam Ahmad and who, as a result, had fought for the republicans during the civil war (see The 1962 Coup d'État in Yemen, ch. 1). He cooperated with the government when it suited him but, like other tribal leaders, retained virtual autonomy in his own domain. Not all of the tribal leaders were cooperative; many were dismayed at the loss of subsidies they had received from one or both sides during the civil war. Although the government continued direct subsidies to some of the highland Zaydi tribes until 1973, there were serious tribal uprisings in 1970 and 1971. By 1971 the government had begun to rely on a policy followed by Yemeni governments for centuries: exercising direct control in the cities and in the Shafii areas but leaving the tribes in charge of local government in the areas they controlled. Even some of the shaykhs who participated in the central government, such as Ahmar, received Saudi subsidies and were therefore viewed with suspicion by other political figures. In 1985 such Saudi payments to northern tribal leaders continued to give the government in Sanaa reason to doubt the loyalty of some of the northern shaykhs.

The weak Iryani government was buffeted not only by domestic factions but also by the actions and policies of its two neighbors, each having a strong interest in North Yemen but with radically different ideologies. Although they had backed the royalists in the war, Saudi influence over politics in North Yemen increased after the reconciliation of 1970. Saudi Arabia's influence was felt not only through its direct subsidies to northern shaykhs but also because of its essential financial aid to the central government in Sanaa.

After its independence in 1967, South Yemen proclaimed its interest in Yemeni unity but on terms unacceptable to the government in Sanaa. The prospects for at least friendly relations (if not the unity that both states presumably wanted) seemed bright in early 1968. By late 1970, however, relations had begun to deteriorate. The two political systems were growing further apart, as their respective 1970 constitutions showed. The government in Sanaa was coming increasingly under Saudi influence while the government in Aden was forging stronger links with the Soviet Union. The new governments formed in each country in 1971 no longer had cabinet ministers charged with Yemeni unity. Moreover, the new government in Sanaa included a native of the north who had played an important role in the independence struggle in Aden but who had lost to—and was hated by—the NLF: Foreign Minister Abdallah Al Asnaj (see Violence in Aden, ch. 1).

Skirmishes between the armies of the two Yemens began to occur regularly as opposition groups on both sides of the border (which is unmarked for some distance) prompted retaliation from each side. The still unstable situation in South Yemen may have prompted the Sanaa government, under strong Saudi influence at this time, to seek out conflict with the South Yemenis. By late 1972 these engagements had become a serious border war. Mediation by the Arab League brought the border war to a surprising conclusion. In October 1972 Prime Minister Ayni and Prime Minister Ali Nasir Muhammad al Hasani of South Yemen met in Cairo and signed an agreement that called for a united Yemen with a single capital and government.

Despite this proclamation of intended unity, however, the agreement was effective only in halting the border war. Although both nations claimed to be eager for union, the two systems were fundamentally different, and a major power center in North Yemen—the tribal shaykhs (strongly supported by Saudi Arabia)—was unalterably opposed to union with the pro-Soviet republic to the south. Numerous tribal shaykhs in South Yemen had lost their lives following South Yemeni independence in 1967, and the northern tribesmen were not likely to acquiesce to any kind of union. Tribal opposition took the form of disagreement between the Consultative Council (of which the shaykhs were the predominant element and Ahmar the leader) and the prime minister over the issue of the unity agreement. When Ayni, architect of the unity proposal on the Sanaa side, resigned, the shaykhs, backed by the Saudis, refused to allow the unity agreement to be implemented. Iryani named as prime minister Qadi Abdallah al Hajjri, a conservative who had been a royalist minister. Public confidence in Iryani's leadership suffered as a result of this kind of vacillation.

The government in Sanaa felt compelled to exercise direct control over its southern areas because of a combination of factors that made them a great deal more threatening than the autonomy of the northern tribes. One familiar problem was the Zaydi-Shafii split. The imamate had been toppled and the republican side of the civil war fought by Zaydis and Shafiis together and, as Peterson's analysis of cabinet personnel shows, cabinets always included Shafiis—never fewer than one-quarter of the posts and never more than one-half. Nonetheless, Zaydis still controlled the government, and Zaydi-Shafii differences had been exacerbated by purge of leftists (many of whom were Shafiis) that started in 1968. After centuries of domination by Zaydis, the Shafiis were quick to take offense and were susceptible to campaigns against the Sanaa government by their fellow Shafiis across the border. Economic conditions in the southern part of North Yemen deteriorated in the early 1970s, and the quality of local leadership was not high. The vast majority of the thousands of émigrés from South Yemen crossed the border into the southern part of North Yemen, creating both economic and political pressures. Rainfall was low as well, which reduced crop yields at a time when there were increased demands on the food supply.

The Iryani government was caught among these domestic and foreign pressures and, attempting to cope with all of them, made little progress in political and economic development. Attempting to follow a path of reconciliation among conflicting domestic elements, to appease Saudi Arabia, and yet not to be too provocative vis-à-vis South Yemen, successive governments in Sanaa were unable to adopt consistent long-term policies. Successful programs—or the roots of projects that would later succeed—were mostly foreign development programs or schemes undertaken by one of the LDAs.

Although the Iryani regime laid the foundation for much of the progress that took place during succeeding governments, high-level politics stagnated during the remainder of the Iryani government, which had all it could to try to balance the tensions between conservatives and progressives and between traditionalists (like the shaykhs) and the modernists (like the North Yemenis returning home with foreign technical educations). Iryani's willingness to compromise—and his efforts to balance different factions—were welcome during efforts to end the civil war and in the early days after the reconciliation, but as time passed such policies began to be perceived as weakness. Cabinet reshuffles and Iryani's vacillation between progressive and conservative prime ministers earned him the mistrust of most elements of society, as well as of the Saudis and the South Yemenis. In August 1973 Iryani went briefly into voluntary exile in Syria, but he returned when asked to do so. Upon his return he felt strong enough politically to replace the conservative prime minister, Hajjri, with a Shafii technocrat, Hassan Makki.

By 1974 dissatisfaction was rising within the government, and the loss of public confidence in the government was spreading. The incident that precipitated the downfall of the Iryani government was the discovery in June 1974 of a plot allegedly financed by the Iraqi government. Iryani's mild-mannered reaction (sending a delegation to Baghdad for discussion of the matter) prompted an angry reaction from Shaykh Ahmar, although some observers suggested that Ahmar was probably using the plot as an excuse to withdraw from a government that he no longer favored. He rallied his Hashid tribesmen, succeeded in obtaining the resignation of the prime minister and the Republican Council, and declared that he would occupy Sanaa. With both the commander in chief and the chief of staff out of the country, the deputy commander in chief, Colonel Ibrahim al Hamdi, took power. Foreign observers point out that the decisive measures quickly enacted by the new seven-member Military Command Council (MCC) suggest that a move against the government had been anticipated in the upper levels of the military for some time. As had occurred in so many developing nations, the traditional institutions had been destroyed, new forms had not taken root sufficiently to provide stable government, and so the army intervened. Peterson suggests that the Iryani regime had attempted to create an imamate without an imam and thus had run afoul of many of the same problems that had beset the traditional Zaydi governments.

The Government of Ibrahim al Hamdi

Hamdi was a compromise choice among the officers who had planned and carried out the coup, which had been in preparation for some time. Other candidates might have faced opposition from one or another of the major tribes or have been mistrusted for being of the sayyid class. As with Iryani before him, Hamdi was a member of the qadi class, a group whose members could not, as a result of Zaydi beliefs, become imams but who had, because of their high social and educational status, participated frequently in government under the imams. In fact, because they could be trusted not to aspire to become imams, members of qadi families had predominated in the civil service of the imams, serving frequently as provincial governors and other high officials. Whereas the status of the sayyid class diminished following the end of the imamate, the status of the qadis was less impaired, although some had feared persecution in the early years of the civil war. There were other reasons for Hamdi's selection as well: he was acceptable to the Saudis, he was a competent and efficient officer who was acceptable to the army, he had been elected leader of the federation of LDAs, and he was at the time of the 1974 coup the highest-ranking officer physically in the country.

The first months of his nearly three-and-one-half-year rule showed Hamdi's skill in domestic power balancing. He suspended the 1970 constitution, quickly created a system that provided access to government for all major domestic factions, and mollified both Riyadh and Aden, at least temporarily. Hamdi co-opted the left and mollified South Yemen by reappointing Ayni as prime minister. He placated the tribal shaykhs by calling back into session the Consultative Assembly, of which Ahmar remained leader and in which tribal elements predominated.

Some of Hamdi's closest lieutenants were also of tribal background. His military chief of staff, Colonel Ahmad al Ghashmi, was a relative of a major tribal shaykh. The MCC also included two other officers with strong tribal connections. Shafii elements from the southern regions of the country were pleased by the appointment of a Shafii protégé of Hamdi, Colonel Abdallah Abd al Alim, to the key post of commander of the paratroopers as well as to membership in the MCC. Possible Saudi objections to the presence of leftists in the government were mollified by a visit to Saudi Arabia by Hamdi and the minister of interior (who was also deputy chairman of the MCC), Yahya al Mutawakkil, who was both an officer and a sayyid. The Saudis must also have been comforted to see the important post of national security chief given to a pro-Saudi figure. The reappointment of Asnaj to the cabinet also may have been designed to please Saudi Arabia, which favored the former radical because of his animosity toward the regime in Aden.

Hamdi's leadership was also boosted by the fact that he came to power at a time of deep popular discontent with the government. The period of reconciliation following the civil war was over, and more progress was expected than had been achieved under Iryani. Hamdi was able to capitalize on this situation to build a reputation for dynamism.

After the first few months of power balancing, Hamdi ceased to be content with merely consolidating his position by placating other centers of power. Analysts note that Hamdi sought to create an unassailable position of power from which he not only could guarantee his political survival but also could achieve enough freedom of action to work on his long-term objectives of modernization and political centralization. To create such a position of power, Hamdi began to remove from power possible rivals and political figures having strong tribal links. He accompanied these moves with an unsuccessful attempt to set up political institutions to support economic development and to root out corruption in government.

In January 1975 Hamdi replaced Ayni as prime minister with an apolitical technocrat, former Central Bank governor Abd al Aziz Abd al Ghani. During the summer he removed from the ruling MCC tribal figures who he did not believe had their first loyalty to him. In October he dismissed the Consultative Council in which the shaykhs played a leading role. By the end of 1975 Hamdi had no rival in government, and the handpicked MCC was composed entirely of officers who were his allies.

Hamdi's efforts at political institutionalization were less fruitful. He had been elected leader of the national association of LDAs in 1973, even before the coup. Any plans he had, however, of transforming this movement into a mass political organization were stymied by LDA elections in which Hamdi supporters were relatively unsuccessful. His other effort to create a supportive political organization, the Supreme Corrective Council (designed to end corruption and promote government efficiency), was not well received.

Other than his successful manipulations of power, Hamdi's greatest achievements lay in development planning and in the strengthening of the economy. He encouraged development assessment and planning through the new Central Planning Organization (see Role of Government, this ch.). He persuaded the Saudis to divert some of their tribal subsidies to the central government and adopted economic measures that allowed the country to enlarge its foreign exchange reserves and to increase its income.

By mid-1977 Hamdi's relations with the tribal shaykhs had become strained. Analyst Robin Bidwell suggests that Hamdi's qadi background gave him no special sympathy for the highland tribes, and he seemed determined to end their autonomous status not only in order to consolidate his own power but also because he was moving quietly toward better relations with Aden and knew that the shaykhs would never accept such a policy if they had any choice in the matter. To counterbalance the opposition he faced from the shaykhs, Hamdi began to cultivate the Shafiis of the southern part of the country, doing so with the assistance of Abd al Alim, his Shafii protégé on the MCC. In addition, Hamdi permitted parties (some with links to Aden) to form in the southern part of the country and to coalesce into the National Democratic Front (NDF), an organization that supported the Hamdi regime in a general way but that felt free to criticize it. Hamdi's efforts to subdue the northern tribes in mid-1977 went as far as deploying aircraft against them. Hamdi appeared to have achieved some success, and Bidwell notes reports of a reconciliation between the head of state and the shaykhs.

Although it may never be known what faction or individuals were responsible for Hamdi's assassination, it appears to have been triggered by his growing relationship with leftists in the southern part of the country and his rapprochement with South Yemen, which was itself going through a relatively accommodationist phase. The Saudis—as well as the North Yemeni shaykhs—were dismayed by these trends. An attempt early in 1977 by the indefatigable

Ahmar to rally the tribes against the regime failed, but Hamdi appeared to be under increasing strain. He became isolated and came to depend more and more on his closest aides, especially his brother, Abdallah (commander of one of the most important brigades), and Ghashmi, the deputy commander in chief. Observers note, however, that as Hamdi continued to isolate himself from the political groups whose cooperation he needed, Ghashmi was moving his own supporters into key positions.

On October 11, 1977, the violence that had plagued North Yemeni politics for so much of its modern history claimed another victim. Hamdi and his brother were killed in Sanaa under mysterious circumstances. It was widely believed that the assassination had been engineered by Ghashmi, who quickly took over the reins of government, or by the Saudis, who were unhappy that Hamdi had slipped away from their control and worried about Hamdi's upcoming visit to Aden, the first visit by a North Yemeni chief of state. The timing of the assassination was suggestive: Hamdi was killed the day before he was to leave for Aden.

The Government of Ahmad al Ghashmi

The allegations of Ghashmi's—and perhaps Saudi—involvement in the assassination were supported by the ease and speed with which the new ruler took control, by the conservatism of Ghashmi's eight months in power, and by the obvious intimacy between the new regime and Saudi Arabia. Hamdi's growing reconciliation with Aden and his popularity among the inhabitants of the southern region meant that his successor, who was widely suspected of involvement with the assassination, was particularly unpopular with citizens of the southern area and with the government in Aden. Ghashmi's greatest efforts during his tenure of office were expended in purging leftists and Hamdi followers from the government and in cementing a loyal following in key military positions. He devoted little or no attention to development projects, and political institutionalization appeared to be no more than a means of providing an aura of legitimacy to his rule. Although the new head of state announced vague plans for democracy, in February 1978 he appointed a 99-member People's Constituent Assembly (PCA), which consisted mostly of urban merchants, with Qadi Abd al Karim Abdallah Arashi as speaker. This carefully selected group obediently asked Ghashmi to assume the office of president.

There were only two other members of the MCC in the early days of Ghashmi's rule: Abd al Alim, the leftist Shafii commander of the paratroopers, and the more or less apolitical prime minister, Abd al Ghani. The threat represented by Abd al Alim lay not only in his being a Hamdi supporter who might pose a leftist alternative to Ghashmi but also in his role as leader of an army unit that was made up largely of Shafiis from the southern region. Shafii leftists had been defeated in the power struggles of 1968, and in the wake of the assassination of Hamdi, whom they liked, Ghashmi had reason to fear them. Rather than move against Abd al Alim directly, Ghashmi simply dissolved the MCC as soon as the PCA had been established.

Abd al Alim rebelled against this diminution of his power and deserted to his home in the southern part of North Yemen, taking with him many of his paratroopers. When mediation attempts failed, Ghashmi sent troops under the command of his proégé, Major Ali Abdallah Salih, to capture the rebels. Abd al Alim and many of his men, defeated in combat, simply moved across the border into South Yemen and joined the NDF, which was now firmly opposed to the government in Sanaa and was operating out of South Yemen. The NDF had cautiously supported Hamdi, but now that he was dead and they had no legitimate means of political opposition available, the NDF became a potent dissident force that posed an increasingly dangerous threat to Ghashmi's rule.

Although the Saudis had been incensed by Hamdi's incipient rapprochement with the radical government in Aden, they permitted Ghashmi more leeway. Some analysts suggest that the Saudis quietly encouraged Ghashmi in this direction because they felt that he had not—and perhaps could not—slip out of their control. The nature and timing of Ghashmi's contacts with Salim Rubay Ali, the chairman of the Presidential Council in South Yemen, are unknown, but discussions had certainly taken place by the middle of 1978. The eight months of Ghashmi's presidency came to a violent end in an incident closely tied to events in Aden.

On June 24, 1978, Ghashmi received in his office an envoy who ostensibly was from Rubay Ali. The messenger's briefcase exploded, killing both men. Observers have suggested that hard-liners in Aden had been aware of the envoy being sent and had forcibly switched messengers in order to further their own ends in Aden, where only two days after the explosion, Rubay Ali lost a fierce battle against hard-line opponents within the NLF and was executed.

Unlike the murder of Hamdi, there was no evidence to suggest that the assassination of Ghashmi was connected with domestic political elements, and no one stepped forward quickly to take his place. It was assumed that the assassination had been planned in Aden, and diplomatic relations were broken. By general consensus at the upper levels of government, Ghashmi was succeeded by Assembly Chairman and Vice President Arashi as acting president for a period not to exceed 60 days, during which time the PCA was to choose a new leader. Although Arashi and other candidates were suggested, a Ghashmi protégé, deputy chief of staff Ali Abdallah Salih, aggressively sought the post. Unlike Arashi, Salih had no obvious qualifications for the presidency and was neither highly educated nor widely experienced in government. He showed himself to be skilled in political maneuvering, however, by his success in obtaining army support for his selection by the Assembly.

Contemporary Government and Politics

Political Institutions

On September 26, 1962, the day of the military coup that ended the millennium-long rule of the Zaydi imams, the Revolutionary Command Council (RCC) proclaimed itself the country's executive organ, and two days later the RCC established the country's first council of ministers. On October 31, 1962, the RCC proclaimed a transitional constitution to be the legal basis of the new republic for a maximum five-year period while a permanent constitution was being drafted; this 1962 document has become known as the country's first constitution. It defined the legislative functions of an independent national congress, in practice amounting to joint meeting of the RCC and the cabinet.

Under Egyptian guidance, the RCC prepared a permanent constitution well ahead of the five-year deadline, but its publication on April 28, 1964, was greeted with resistance. On May 8, 1965, another transitional constitution was proclaimed; it changed the RCC to the three-member Republican Council and provided for an expanded ministerial system and an advisory body, the Consultative Assembly. After the Egyptian withdrawal and overthrow of President Sallal in late 1967, this 1965 document continued to be the primary legal basis of the new regime established by Iryani. Many of the framers of the 1965 transitional constitution were members of the new government. It is notable because it was the first constitution drawn up solely by North Yemenis.

President Iryani promised that a permanent constitution would be drafted as soon as possible, but it was not until after the end of the civil war that a new draft was made public. In his role as chairman of the Republican Council, Iryani proclaimed the new constitution on December 28, 1970 (see Postwar Reconciliation under Iryani, this ch.). But it had been in effect for only two and one-half years—and few laws had been formulated to implement its proposals for new institutions—when on June 13, 1974, Iryani was deposed by Hamdi. The constitution was suspended, and the MCC assumed all legislative and executive functions. On June 19, 1974, another provisional constitution was decreed that asserted a legal basis for Hamdi's coup d'état. Hamdi promised a new permanent constitution within a year, but by mid-1985 neither he nor his successors had fulfilled this promise, and the 1974 provisional constitution apparently remained in effect.

Like the 1970 constitution, the 1974 document asserts the Arab and Islamic character of the nation and proclaims sharia as the source of all laws. The fundamental rights and duties of citizens are defined in some detail. It places the MCC at the apex of the governmental system but defines the judiciary as independent, there being "no authority over it except for the law." Article 19 asserts that "during the transitional period action shall be taken to restore constitutional and democratic life on sound bases in view of the need to provide the Yemeni people with a dignified life and a bright future."

Hamdi had dissolved the Consultative Assembly in October 1975. His successor, President Ghashmi, formed a new advisory organ, the PCA, in February 1978. This 99-member body was appointed by the MCC. With the dissolution of the latter in April 1978, the PCA named Ghashmi president for a five-year term. In May 1979 its membership, all appointed, was expanded to 159 persons.

In mid-1985 the president stood at the apex of the governmental system, advised by a consultative council and assisted by a president's office, which was established in 1983 (see Political Institutions, this ch.). Formally designated by the PCA, Salih served a five-year term as president between 1978 and 1983. The president appointed the prime minister, who headed a council of ministers that in mid-1985 consisted of 23 cabinet-level members (see fig. 8; table B). There was a vice president, who in mid-1985 was Arashi.

Aside from formally nominating the president, the PCA had the function of reviewing and conferring its approval on legislation drawn up by the president and the council of ministers. Observers noted that as of mid-1985 it had never attempted to assert its independence by opposing government measures. Its apparent purpose was to serve as a transitional institution to be replaced eventually by an elected parliament; although Salih had promised PCA elections on several occasions after coming to office as part of the "completion of the democratic process in the Yemeni arena," these had not been held by mid-1985, and the PCA membership remained entirely appointed by presidential decree. Municipal elections were held, however, in 1979.

There were no legal political parties in the mid-1980s, and thus opportunities for the populace at large to take part in the political process were extremely limited. On October 24, 1982, however, Salih convened the People's General Congress (PGC) to serve as an instrument for popular political mobilization. In the words of a correspondent writing for the *Financial Times* of London in November 1984, the PGC is "like a mass political party, but officially not one; the president says he believes in 'no party government'."

The PGC's membership when organized in 1982 was 1,000 persons, 300 of whom were appointed by the government and 700 of whom were chosen in a nationwide election that was carried out in two stages. In the first stage 2,100 persons were chosen from local constituencies, and in the second, 700 representatives to the PGC were chosen from among the successful first-stage candidates. It is unclear how candidates were nominated or whether voters had a choice of more than one candidate. Members were

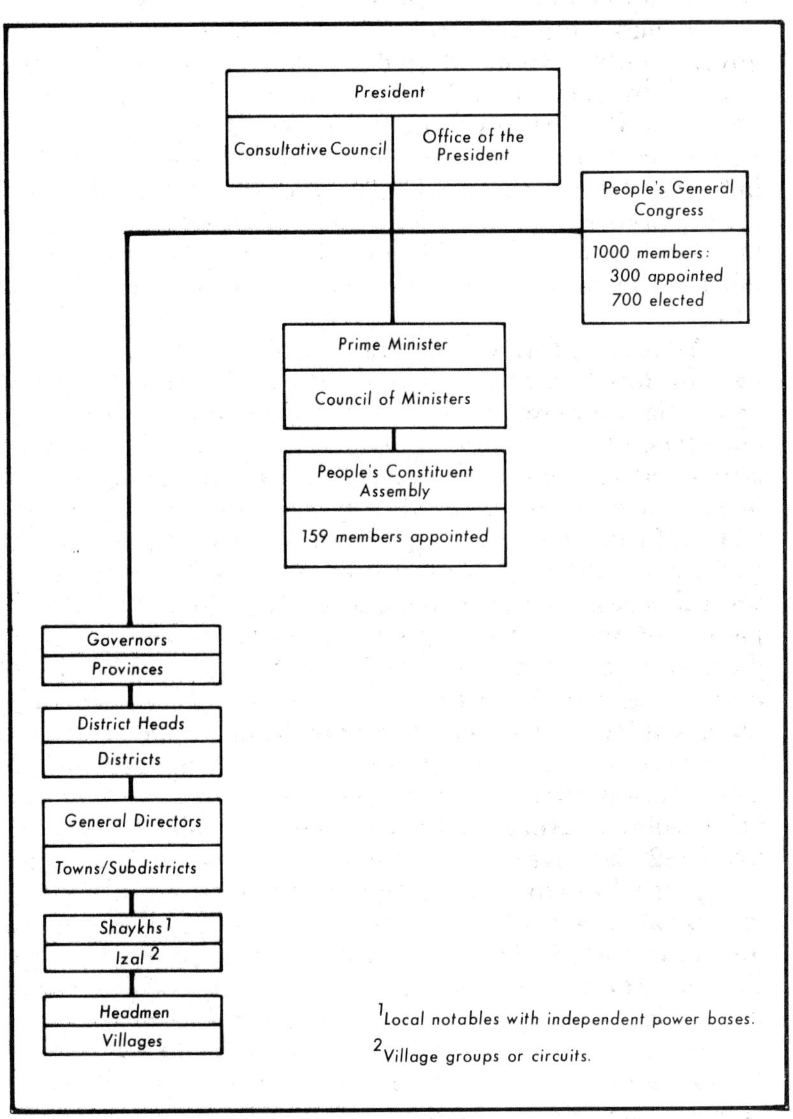

Figure 8. North Yemen: Government Structure, 1985

Table B. North Yemen: President and Council of Ministers, April 1985

Office	Incumbent
President	Salih, Ali Abdallah, Colonel
Vice President	Arashi, Abd al Karim Abdallah
Prime Minister	Abd al Ghani, Abd al Aziz
Deputy Prime Minister	Iryani, Abd al Karim al
Deputy Prime Minister for Domestic Affairs	Abu Shawarib, Mujahid Yahya, Lieutenant Colonel
Minister of Agriculture and Fisheries	Hamdani, Ahmad Muhammad al
Minister of Awqaf and Guidance	Samman, Ali ibn Ali, Qadi
Minister of Civil Service and Administrative Reform	Wazir, Ismail Ahmad al
Minister of Communications and Transport	Ansi, Ahmad Muhammad al
Minister of Development	Junayd, Muhammad Ahmad al
Minister of Economy and Industry	Barakat, Ahmad Qaid
Minister of Education	Amri, Husayn Abdallah al
Minister of Electricity, Water, and Sewage Works	Sabra, Muhammad Hasan
Minister of Finance	Wajih, Muhammad al Khadam al
Minister of Foreign Affairs	Iryani, Abd al Karim al
Minister of Health	Kabab, Muhammad Ahmad al, Dr.
Minister of Information and Culture	Lawzi, Hasan Ahmad al
Minister of Interior	Ulufi, Muhsin Muhammad al, Lieutenant Colonel
Minister of Justice	Jubi, Ahmad Muhammad al
Minister of Labor, Social Affairs, and Youth	Asbahi, Muhammad Ahmad al
Minister of Local Government	Jaifi, Muhammad Abdallah al
Minister of Municipalities and Housing	Luqman, Ahmad Muhammad
Minister of Public Works	Kurshumi, Abdallah Husayn al
Minister of Supply and Trade	Muhammad, Fuad Qayd
Minister of State	Hubayshi, Husayn Ali al
Minister of State for the Affairs of Yemeni Unity	Arshi, Yahya Husayn al
Minister of State for Cabinet Affairs	Ruayni, Ahmad Salih al
Minister of State for People's Constituent Assembly Affairs	Bahr, Ali Abd al Rahman al
Minister of State for Petroleum and Mineral Affairs	-do-
Minister of State for Youth and Sports	Darafi, Abdallah Nasir al

described in local accounts as coming from all significant social groups, and they included a small number of women.

Salih assumed the title of secretary general of the PGC. At its first meeting in late August 1982, the PGC elected 50 of the 75 members of its Permanent Committee (the rest were appointed by Salih) and ratified the National Charter of the Yemen Arab Republic, a document embodying Salih's political priorities and goals. To publicize the charter, PGC committees held meetings throughout the country. In August 1984 the organization held its second national convention.

The National Charter, popularly known as the "blue book," is a 120-page document that expresses the president's viewpoint on a range of topics related to the nature and purpose of the North Yemeni state. It is divided into five chapters: the first deals with ideology and Islamic law; the second with the duties of the citizen, democracy, freedom, and "national unity as the basis for Arab Yemeni unity"; the third with public administration, social justice, and economic development; the fourth with national defense; and the fifth with foreign policy. The National Charter appeared to be an instrument through which Salih sought to give his regime legitimacy and ideological coherence at a time when the country was deeply divided after the fighting with the NDF and when unification talks were initiated with the more tightly organized and disciplined South Yemeni regime.

Public administration in the modern sense did not exist in North Yemen before the September 26 Revolution. Although Imam Yahya had set up a cabinet in 1931, it had only one ministry, the Ministry of Foreign Affairs, with a total staff of six persons, including the foreign minister (see Independent Yemen, ch. 1). Beginning in early 1963, the setting up of modern forms of public administration proceeded at a rapid pace under Egyptian auspices: 11 ministries were established, the National Institute of Public Administration (NIPA) was organized to train civil servants (between 1970 and 1982 some 13,000 government employees took NIPA courses), and the Civil Service Commission (CSC) was set up to oversee the emerging national administration. In 1982 the number of civil servants working in national government ministries and agencies was estimated at 35,000.

Regional and Local Government

Hegemony of the central government over local authorities, especially tribal leaders, remained indirect and in most cases nominal and was exercised through traditional or military leaders according to the dictates of the region. As of mid-1985 cohesiveness between the local levels of administration and the government in Sanaa had not been achieved, although numerous attempts had been made to increase the central government's authority throughout the country. The procedures of local government, however, have remained largely unchanged since the period of Ottoman rule.

In the mid-1980s regional and local governments were divided into five levels. There were 11 provincial (*muhafaza*) governments, called governorates, which were headed by governors appointed by the president. The remaining four levels of local administration, in descending order, were the *qadawat* (sing., *qada*), or districts; the *nawahi* (sing., *nahiyya*), towns or subdistricts; the *izal* (sing., *uzla*), groups of villages; and individual villages.

At the *nahiyya* level the principal official was the general director of the *nahiyya*, who was appointed by the Sanaa government. According to Swanson, the official usually was an outsider and rarely served for more than a two-year term. On the *uzla* level the shaykhs were the most important leaders, having local power bases. They were key figures in the resolution of disputes between individuals in the *uzla*, negotiations with outsiders (including the central government), and the maintenance of peace and order. According to Swanson, the shaykh's position was "semi-hereditary with a strong element of consent on the part of the people and the government." Although shaykhs frequently received subsidies from Sanaa, it was apparent that their prestige depended in large measure on maintaining independent power bases. Swanson notes that the authority of a shaykh was usually greater when he and his followers lived in an area remote from the central government. In localities close to *nahiyya* centers, individuals sometimes bypassed the shaykh and made appeals to government officials. On the village level, the *aqil*, or headman, performed many of the same functions as the shaykh but on a reduced scale.

Beginning in 1971 LDAs were established on the *nahiyya* level to harness local energies for development projects such as roads, wells, hospitals, and schools. These cooperatives, supported in part by government subsidies and in part by local contributions, were managed by LDA general committees with 50 to 100 members; day-to-day administrative responsibilities were in the hands of a seven- to nine-member administrative committee chosen from among the membership of the general committee. These committees were popularly elected, at least in principle, and local leaders played the most prominent role. Each governorate had a Local Development Association Coordinating Council (LDACC), and on the national level the Confederation of Yemeni Development Associations (CYDA) had been established in 1973.

The Judicial System

In the mid-1980s sharia remained the principal source of public and private law, though the legal system in its totality reflected the various divisions of the population. There were several legal systems operating at various levels of administration and, although proposals had been advanced for a systematic codification, procedures, and a hierarchical court structure including a supreme court, there had been at best limited progress in the direction of establishing a unified judicial system.

After the 1962 revolution, sharia remained the designated legal system of the republican government. An older system of law that still affects a large portion of the population, however, is called *urf*, or customary law. *Urf* and other forms of customary law remain in the tribal communities; the most common means of redressing grievances under this system is through revenge and reparation (see Qabayl, this ch.).

The legal system was primarily based on the interpretations of the Shafii school of Islamic law but has also been heavily colored by the simultaneous development of Zaydi law (see The Zaydis; The Shafiis, ch. 1). Zaydi law incorporates an important concept called *ijtihad* (independent reasoning). This principle permits the judge or ruler to make decisions concerning cases not explicitly covered by sharia and in practice has itself become a source of law. This attitude of flexibility in dealing with matters outside the scope of sharia, such as commercial and labor disputes, usually permits change to occur with less resistance than in countries applying a legal system strictly derived from sharia.

Although the 1974 provisional constitution states that the judiciary is independent, the lack of autonomous, well-developed judicial institutions meant that in fact courts were under government control. Sharia courts had been under the jurisdiction of the Ministry of Justice since 1964. Their organization, however, was not uniform throughout the country, and administrative details varied from one governorate to another. The Sharia Court of Sanaa, established in 1964, was the highest court in the country.

In 1977 the government created the *niyaba al amma* (office of the public prosecutor) as an agency of the Ministry of Justice. The *niyaba al amma*, modeled on French and Egyptian precedents, placed a wide range of public officials performing judicial functions—extending from provincial governors to village heads—under its jurisdiction insofar as they exercised those functions. The office also supervised prisons. Its most important responsibility, however, was the investigation and prosecution of criminal cases. According to Messick, the most significant aspect of the office was its definition of a clearly public sphere of law and the fact that its jurisdiction extended to cases that traditionally were settled through private vengeance. It was not clear, however, how viable the institution was because of the strength of tribal traditions and the lack of central government control over rural areas.

Sharia judges were appointed by the minister of justice, and their decisions were usually held to be final, although appeal to the Sharia Court of Sanaa was possible. Because sharia is not case law, a judge does not have to follow precedent and is not bound by decisions of other judges or a higher court. In the mid-1980s the State Security Court, outside the sharia framework, heard all political cases.

The Presidency of Ali Abdallah Salih

When Colonel Salih was designated president by the PCA in July 1978, observers thought it unlikely that he would escape the fate of his unfortunate predecessors, presidents Hamdi and Ghashmi. Tensions were building with South Yemen, intertribal rivalries were intense, and an ethos that encouraged wronged parties to pursue a course of violent self-help in a land where rifles were said to outnumber the inhabitants two-to-one ensured that the president would be the target of frequent coup attempts. Although military governor of Taizz Province at the time of Ghashmi's assassination, Salih had limited education and experience. His membership in the Sanhan, a Zaydi tribe whose territory is located to the southwest of Sanaa, was a disadvantage politically because of the tribe's small size and relatively low status. His survival skills proved remarkable during his precarious first years in office. Commentators noted that he quickly learned how to balance different political forces both inside and outside North Yemen and that this contributed to his success in staying in power and garnering a moderate degree of popular support.

Salih protected himself by appointing members of the Sanhan tribe to sensitive positions in the army, police, military intelligence, and government, and in mid-1985 he still maintained a personal bodyguard of several hundred fellow tribesmen. Nevertheless, the president was described in the mid-1980s as taking considerable risk by traveling throughout the country to hold majlises (personal audiences) with local tribal and religious leaders and ordinary citizens. Through institutional development and the moderate ideology espoused in the National Charter, he sought to invest the regime with a sense of legitimacy and continuity. He also sought to build up a modest "cult of personality"; his picture, for example, was a prominent feature of government publications, including the National Charter.

In May 1979 Salih established a 15-member advisory council composed of representatives of various elements of political life, including the sayyid and qadi classes, former royalists, old-line republicans, and all varieties of moderates and conservatives. Both leftists and conservatives were given government posts, and even the shaykhs were placated by being given positions of at least symbolic importance. By the time of the October 15, 1980, cabinet reshuffle in which Abd al Ghani was moved to second vice president and Abd al Karim al Iryani (nephew of the deposed leader) became prime minister, technocrats had begun to play a growing role in government. Salih's internal balancing act was mirrored by his foreign policy, which maintained ties to both east and west and balanced links to Saudi Arabia with ties to other Arab states. Through the rest of 1978 and into 1979 unrest in the southern area of the country continued, and this, coupled with a serious abortive coup three months after his accession to power, pushed the new president to depend more than he wished on the armed northern tribes (see National Security, this ch.).

During the 1978-82 period, Salih was preoccupied with the challenge posed by South Yemen and the South Yemen-backed NDF. The period after early 1982, when reunification talks with Aden were resumed and confrontation subsided, was one of consolidation as the president sought to promote national unity through the medium of the PGC and economic development as envisioned in the Second Five-Year Plan. On May 22, 1983, the PCA unanimously elected Salih for a second four-year term as president. Although many observers commended him for giving North Yemen the most stable government since the establishment of the republic in 1962, the country remained deeply divided. The lack of strong institutions and a sense of legitimacy—as well as the country's violent traditions—left Salih's regime precariously exposed. There was no want of opponents ready and willing to seek his removal, and there were coup attempts in the mid-1980s.

The Northern Tribes in the Mid-1980s

The Zaydi tribes of the north, whose territory extends from the region south of Sanaa to the Saudi Arabian border in the north, have never fully accepted the authority of the Sanaa government. They considered the imams as legitimate rulers not only because of religious sanctions but also because they provided the tribes as a whole with unified leadership in times of crisis. The passing of the imamate left a vacuum that the succession of regimes in Sanaa has been unable to fill. In the mid-1980s large areas of tribal territory remained outside effective central control. This reflected not only the people's strong sense of independence but also the highly diffuse nature of traditional tribal authority, itself largely a product of a rugged and mountainous terrain (see The Physical Environment, this ch.).

Although intertribal relations have often been described, to borrow Mao Zedong's phrase, as "coming out of the barrel of a gun," tribal identity has been highly stable. The two major tribal confederations, the Hashid and the Bakil, have existed since pre-Islamic times. According to anthropologist Paul Dresch, each tribe maintains its own distinct territory, and the seizure of one tribe's land by another is relatively rare. Within the context of seemingly endless violence, as tribal groups sought restitution for wrongs suffered at the hands of others, there was an underlying stability as tribal leaders—the shaykhs—maintained order within their territories in compliance with customary law. Dresch notes, for example, that although tribes have customarily had the right to deny outsiders passage through their territory and to detain trespassers, they must make an announcement of their intention beforehand.

The tribal political system has traditionally been highly decentralized; authority was vested in the shaykhs who were not rulers in the conventional sense but were respected arbitrators of intratribal or intertribal disputes and leaders in time of war (see Social Class and Tribe, this ch.). On their shoulders rested the responsibility for interpreting and putting into practice the large body of customary law as it related to property rights and matters of personal and family honor. When honor was violated and shame or injury incurred, the role of the shaykh was to restore peace through the offer of proper restitution to the injured party. The widely accepted myth of tribal life, expressed by tribals themselves, was that "the nation is free because each of her sons disdains a base submission to the will of a master." This ideology of rigorous individualism was basically inimical to the imposition of any sort of vigorous central control, both before and after 1962.

The diffuseness of tribal political authority has aided the central government insofar as tribes have been unable to find a single issue or leader around which to unite and a lack of numbers and weapons necessary to challenge the armed forces. On the national level, tribal influence has tended to be highly conservative, a counterweight to pro-Soviet influences centered in South Yemen. Tribal volunteers played the key role in halting the South Yemeni and NDF advance into North Yemen in 1979. Observers in the mid-1980s believed that they posed a formidable obstacle to genuine progress in the direction of Yemeni unity.

The National Democratic Front

The NDF—a leftist movement formed in March 1976 by diverse groups of socialists, Marxists, Nasserites, and others disaffected with the Hamdi regime—sought to overthrow Salih in January 1979 with the support of South Yemeni forces. In the early 1980s the NDF, headed by secretary general Sultan Ahmad Umar, carried out an active insurgency in the southern part of the country. Guerrilla activity intensified through 1982, when several hundred rebels and government soldiers were killed. By 1985 the movement was described as largely inactive owing to the successes of the Sanaa forces.

The NDF's principal domestic support came from Shafiis living in the southern region of the country, bordering South Yemen and from some Zaydi tribes at odds with the government; although the NDF's ideology was leftist, much of its appeal was the result of sectarian sentiment and southern resentment of the alleged privileged social and political position of Zaydis. The NDF supported Yemeni unification on Aden's terms, was hostile to alleged Saudi Arabian influence in North Yemen, and combined anti-imperialist rhetoric with appeals to Islamic concepts of social justice and equity.

Islamic Fundamentalists

Islamic fundamentalism had significant support among lower-middle class and middle-class people, including university students and graduates, in the urban areas of North Yemen during the mid-1980s. The Islamic Front, the group led by Shaykh Ahmar, head of the Hashid tribal confederation in the northern tribal areas, gained importance elsewhere because of the influence of many of the 23,000 Egyptian teachers employed in North Yemeni schools. The Front had affinities with the Muslim Brotherhood (Al Ikhwan al Muslimun), a fundamentalist movement founded in Egypt in 1928, and was hostile to South Yemen and its sympathizers in the North. A number of cabinet ministers were known to be close to the Front, including at least two in mid-1985: the minister of foreign affairs, Abd al Karim al Iryani, and the minister of local government, Muhammad Abdallah al Jaifi. Many observers believed, however, that Islamic fundamentalism was not, in the mid-1980s, a cohesive or decisive factor in domestic politics.

Foreign Relations

The maintenance of a careful balance in foreign relations was an issue of the highest priority for the survival of any North Yemeni regime in a highly unstable regional environment. The country's most sensitive relations were with its northern and southern neighbors, Saudi Arabia and South Yemen. Both states, mutually antagonistic, had extensive influence within the borders of North Yemen. Many of the most influential shaykhs of the Zaydi northern tribes had close ties with Riyadh, and the porousness of the border between the two Yemens and traditional disaffection of some elements of the Shafii population in the southern part of the country provided Aden with considerable leverage in its dealings with Sanaa. In the mid-1980s Salih continued his predecessors' nonaligned foreign policy, striving to maintain amicable relations with as many states as possible and avoiding entangling alliances that could compromise the country's small measure of independence. Given the weakness of his regime in comparison with his affluent northern and highly disciplined and organized southern neighbors, Salih walked a tightrope where there was little room for error or folly. Outside the region he sought the aid and support of the Soviet Union, as manifested in the 20-year Treaty of Friendship signed in October 1984 in large measure as a counterweight to Saudi influence. Though a vocal supporter of Pan-Arab issues, particularly the Palestinian cause, North Yemen played a minimal role in the region other than the pursuit of its own immediate interests and survival.

Relations with South Yemen

In mid-1985 official statements emanating from both Sanaa and Aden stressed the theme of the unity of a single Yemeni people and outlined concrete steps for the achievement of an economic, social, cultural, and ultimately political union. The two heads of state, Salih and South Yemen's Ali Nasir Muhammad al Hasani, met on a regular basis in their capacities as heads of the Yemen Council. Within a few short years armed confrontation had given way to effusive declarations of Yemeni brotherhood. The prospects for genuine union were, however, very unclear. Mutual suspicions and divergencies in interests persisted, and within

North Yemen conservative groups, particularly the leadership of the northern tribes having close ties to Saudi Arabia, remained firmly in opposition to any Sanaa-Aden union that could result in the creation of a leftist state. From time to time in the mid-1980s small border skirmishes occurred, expressive of continuing uneasiness in the relationship.

When Salih came to power in July 1978, he was obliged to deal with rapidly deteriorating relations with Aden. The latter perceived the government in Sanaa to be moving to the right. Both nations harbored each other's dissidents, and each purge in Sanaa and Aden provided new recruits for these groups. Armed clashes between the two states became more frequent toward the end of 1978 and the beginning of 1979. Fred Halliday, a specialist on the Yemens and a self-described Marxist, suggests that although North Yemen had started the 1972 conflict, the border war of 1979 was set in motion by the government in Aden. By February 1979 border clashes had become outright war, and South Yemeni forces were fighting alongside North Yemeni dissidents in the NDF. After several weeks of fighting, the forces of South Yemen and the NDF gained the upper hand, reaching a point only 15 kilometers from the Sanaa-Taizz road. Their advance was stopped at that point not by the regular Yemeni army but by the potent force that North Yemeni leaders had relied upon for centuries—the armed tribesmen of the north, mostly members of the Hashid confederation.

A truce was arranged through the mediation of other Arab states. Although the terms of the agreement were not published, observers believed that it required Salih to bring some NDF figures into the government. It is unclear whether Salih really intended to give them a political role, however, and the Saudis opposed such a move. The March 1979 agreement ending the war between the two Yemens, signed in Kuwait, included a provision calling for Yemeni unity.

That same month Salih signaled his support for unification by removing two conservative opponents from his cabinet: the foreign minister, Asnaj, and the minister of information and culture, Muhammad Salim Basindwa. (Asnaj, although condemned to death on charges of espionage for Saudi Arabia, was later released.) Their pro-unification successors, however, were also removed from power a few months later as a conciliatory gesture toward Saudi Arabia. The cabinet changes indicated the delicacy of Salih's policy:

to move, in principle at least, toward unification with Aden while downplaying as much as possible Aden's support of the still aggressive NDF and simultaneously striving to placate Sanaa's conservative northern neighbor.

Meetings were held between Salih and Ali Nasir through 1980 and 1981 to resolve the issue of the NDF and to formulate a plan for unification. At a summit held in Kuwait on November 26, 1981, they agreed to a cease-fire between NDF and government forces. The following month a "non-interference agreement" between the two states was published. Intense fighting continued, however, into 1982 in violation of the cease-fire, and elements in the South Yemeni leadership continued to favor support of the guerrillas.

Days after the Kuwait summit, the two presidents held a second meeting in Aden and announced concrete measures to implement unification. These included the formation of the Yemen Council (also known as the Yemeni Supreme Council), comprising the two heads of state, to oversee the unification process. The Council was charged with appointing the Joint Ministerial Committee, consisting of the two states' prime ministers and foreign, interior, supply and planning, and education ministers, as well as the chiefs of staff of their armed forces. It was agreed that the committee would meet at least once every three months. A secretariat was also established to handle the administrative details of the Yemen Council and the Joint Ministerial Committee. Substantive goals included coordination and integration of social and economic development programs and the formulation of a common foreign policy line based on Arab unity and opposition to the interference of foreign powers in the region. Commitments were made to facilitate the movement of citizens between the territories of the two Yemens, to integrate school curricula, and to promote the cooperation of the two countries' media.

A 136-page draft constitution for a united Yemen, to be known as the "Yemeni Republic," was approved by a joint constitutional committee in January 1982. The document designated Sanaa the capital of the new state, Islam the state religion, and Islamic principles the basis for its ideology. An elected parliament and a judicial system based on sharia and headed by an elected attorney general were promised. The constitution was to be approved by the legislatures of the two states and then submitted to the people in a referendum. These measures had not been accomplished as of mid-1985. In the case of Sanaa, this suggested the weight of Saudi and domestic conservative opposition and perhaps Salih's own fears that North Yemen might be absorbed in a single Marxist state, despite the constitutional commitment to Islam. The Yemen Council and other binational organizations continued to meet on a regular basis through the 1982-85 period, but no practical steps toward unification were taken, and few observers viewed unity as likely in the near to mid term.

Relations with Saudi Arabia

Relations with Saudi Arabia were crucial in the mid-1980s because of Sanaa's dependence on subsidies from its oil-rich northern neighbor. Direct aid was estimated by some observers to be as high as US$1 billion annually, although economic data did not reflect aid that great. Remittances of Yemeni workers in Saudi Arabia approached another US$1.2 billion (see Balance of Payments, this ch.). By bringing its poor and populous southern neighbor into a relationship of virtually permanent economic dependence, Riyadh sought leverage to block the much heralded merger with South Yemen and the possible creation of a hostile, leftist state on its border. Although Saudi oil revenues declined significantly after 1981 and a large volume of funds was diverted to Iraq in its war with Iran, the Saudi leadership apparently regarded the costly tying down of the Salih regime with financial strings as a vital national security priority. It was unclear in mid-1985 how the discovery of oil in North Yemen would affect this arrangement.

The Saudi government also granted direct subsidies to the conservative leaders of the northern Zaydi tribes in order to encourage their independence of central authority and to ensure that a friendly buffer zone would exist along the border if a leftist regime came to power in Sanaa. The Islamic Front, headed by Shaykh Ahmar—leader of the Hashid tribal confederation, Consultative Council member, and pro-Saudi figure—had been organized in the tribal area to oppose any rapprochement with Aden. According to a 1982 report in a Beirut newspaper, a senior member of the Saudi royal family had financially encouraged the shaykhs to form an armed group under the slogan of "defending Islam against the communist threat coming from

Aden." Rumors of tribal unrest in areas where oil had been discovered in North Yemen were vigorously denied by Salih in January 1985, but tribal intransigence severely limited his options at a time when he sought friendlier relations, if not a merger, with Aden.

After the 1934 border war, Imam Yahya had been obliged to sign the Treaty of Taif, ceding the fertile Asir region to Saudi Arabia. In 1974 Riyadh pressured North Yemeni prime minister Hajjri into signing a second treaty reaffirming the original agreement and renouncing territorial claims. Domestic opposition, however, prevented its ratification, and successive Yemeni leaders have been unwilling to give their approval because of the depth of Yemeni sentiment on the issue. Border skirmishes between North Yemeni and Saudi troops were reported in the early 1980s, in some cases the result of attempts to stop smugglers from crossing the border.

Relations with the Soviet Union

Relations with the Soviet Union have displayed remarkable continuity over the years, despite chronic political instability and the frequent change of regimes in Sanaa. A trade agreement between Moscow and the imamate was concluded in 1928, and in 1956 and 1957 the Soviets provided Imam Ahmad with Yemen's first modern weapons. When the republic was established after the September 26 Revolution, the Soviets promptly offered recognition, and in March 1964 the 20-year Treaty of Friendship was concluded. During the civil war, Soviet military aid was channeled primarily through Egypt. When royalist tribesmen encircled Sanaa in December 1967 and threatened to extinguish the republic, however, a Soviet airlift supplied the republicans until the siege was broken in February 1968.

Relations through the 1970s were adversely affected by Moscow's support of an aggressive South Yemen, particularly during the 1972 border war, and the activities of the NDF toward the end of the decade. Friendly ties were maintained, however, because of the difficulties of getting military aid from Western countries and the need to have an effective counterweight to Saudi Arabia. On October 9, 1984, President Salih and Soviet president Konstantin Chernenko signed in Moscow a second 20-year accord, the Treaty of Friendship and Cooperation between the Union of Soviet Socialist Republics and the Yemen Arab Republic. This was a 10-article statement of general principles guiding amicable relations, such as mutual respect for North Yemen's "policy of nonalignment" and the Soviet Union's "peace-loving foreign policy" and avowals to "continue the struggle against colonialism, neo-colonialism, and racism in all its forms and manifestations." Although the treaty was to remain in force until 2004, either party could give notice of its suspension at the end of any of four periods of five years. It did not contain a military section—such as was included in the friendship treaties concluded by Moscow with South Yemen and Ethiopia—and thus was considered by observers to be of relatively limited significance in terms of the regional military balance.

Relations with Other Countries

Through the medium of a nonaligned foreign policy, North Yemen sought to maintain friendly relations with a wide variety of other states, both within and outside the region. Observers noted that military advisers and development aid teams came from a diverse group of foreign states, including both the Democratic People's Republic of Korea (North Korea) and the Republic of Korea (South Korea), China and Taiwan, and the Soviet Union and the United States. A foreign correspondent noted in December 1984 that Soviet and United States pilots trained Yemeni air force personnel side by side on the same airfield. The United States was also a source of aid. Over the 1962-84 period this totaled about US$244 million, of which US$28 million was in military aid.

Sanaa cultivated amicable relations with the small but oil-rich Gulf states—Kuwait, Bahrain, Qatar, the United Arab Emirates, and Oman—that joined with Saudi Arabia in May 1981 to form the Gulf Cooperation Council (GCC). These states provided the main source of aid that observers believed totaled approximately US$1 billion in the early 1980s. North Yemen supported the Palestinian cause, and in early 1985 as many as 3,000 Palestinian fighters lived in the country after their expulsion from Lebanon in 1982-83. Salih originally was silent on the Camp David Agreements between Egypt and Israel, concluded in September 1978, but Arab pressure obliged him to be outspokenly critical and to sever diplomatic relations with Cairo. Ties with Iraq were close. Baghdad had served as an intermediary with South Yemen during the 1979 border war. In turn, Sanaa has supported Iraq in its war with Iran. In December 1981 the Iranian chargé d'affaires was expelled from the country after distributing literature in Sanaa on the Islamic revolution.

National Security

North Yemen occupies a strategic location at the southwestern tip of the Arabian Peninsula between conservative, monarchical Saudi Arabia and pro-Soviet South Yemen. The central government in North Yemen has always been relatively weak and has had to contend with strong internal opposition and tribal unrest. Because of its strategic location, North Yemen has been important to both superpowers and at times has become involved in superpower rivalry. This makes the North Yemeni armed forces a crucial factor in the stability of the country.

In 1962 the religiously based monarchical system was overthrown in a coup led by Colonel Abdallah al Sallal. To sustain the shaky coup, Sallal called on his hero, President Gamal Abdul Nasser of Egypt, to send aid to the new republican regime, which was about to collapse. Between 1962 and 1967 Egypt was deeply involved in the civil war, which resulted in an estimated 200,000 casualties and provided harsh testing and training of manpower on both sides. According to President Anwar al Sadat of Egypt, at one time during the war there were about 30,000 men under arms on each side, and "the republican forces were assisted by up to 70,000 Egyptian troops." This prolonged struggle resulted in considerable practical military training for a large number of men of military age, usually considered to be 18 to 45 but greatly exceeded at both ends of the spectrum.

The second period of the military developments in North Yemen began with the coup of June 13, 1974. The leader of the junta was Hamdi, who was backed by the commanding officers of the major units stationed in the capital. Hamdi exercised power as chairman of the Military Command Council (MCC), which included the chief of staff, Colonel Ghashmi, a leading member of the Hashid tribe, and a left-leaning Shafii officer, Major Abdallah Abd al Alim, who commanded the Parachute Brigade. After two years in power Hamdi concluded that his goal of modernizing and strengthening the armed forces could not be achieved as long as much of the country continued to be dominated by conservative tribal shaykhs supported by their armed followers. In an effort to curb the tribes, he abolished the use of titles and banned the carrying of weapons in towns.

Relations between Hamdi and the tribal leaders (particularly the Hashib confederation) continued to deteriorate in the summer of 1977, and Hamdi ordered the air force to bomb several tribal strongholds. In the autumn there were reports of a reconciliation, but before this could be effected, Hamdi was murdered. Within hours the MCC, now consisting of Ghashmi, Abd al Alim, and Abd al Ghani, announced that Ghashmi would be its new chairman.

Ghashmi had little opportunity to bring about any changes. On June 24, 1978, he was assassinated by a bomb carried by a "special emissary" of the South Yemeni government, and on July 17 Salih was named president of the republic. Attempts to overthrow Salih were reported in July and October 1978, and a prolonged delay in reaching agreement on constitutional issues was attributed to continuing unrest and conflict within the army as well as between the republicans and traditionalist groups.

Attempted coups against Salih seemed to suggest that his base of support within the army was weak. A coup attempt in October 1978 involved four army units in Sanaa, but the rebels failed to obtain the support of other army officers. Following this the Salih regime undertook the bloodiest purge since the civil war. Nine army officers, the ministers of labor and social affairs, and numerous other collaborators were arrested. Something approaching 100 individuals were executed during the next two months, and thousands were imprisoned.

These purges weakened Salih's political support, and the South Yemeni president, Abd al Fatah Ismail, seems to have calculated that the NDF—thought to number a central core of around 700, reinforced by disgruntled politicians and soldiers from Sanaa and by South Yemeni irregulars to a total number of 5,000—could overthrow Salih or at least seize control of North Yemen's southern provinces. Although the initial attack by the NDF faltered, South Yemen provided air cover to counter the North

Yemeni air force, and the former's artillery gave the NDF enough assistance to move some 40 kilometers across the border and to seize the towns of Qatabah, Al Bayda, and Harib (see fig. 6).

The result was the February 1979 border war that received regional as well as international attention. Up to 7,000 deaths were reported, but the actual figure was probably much lower, and most casualties seem to have been civilians or tribal irregulars. Ismail quickly learned that he had over-estimated the strength of the NDF forces; although the support of South Yemen's forces allowed the rebels to occupy territory near North Yemen's border, they lacked significant popular support. Salih was able to mobilize tribal levies to assist his regular forces, and the combined forces defeated the NDF insurgency, leading to a cease-fire on March 4, 1979.

Salih used this South Yemeni invasion to convince Saudi Arabia and the United States that he faced a major direct threat from Soviet-backed South Yemen. As a result, the United States agreed to speed the military aid to North Yemen that it had first promised in 1976. The new arms package provided a limited number of major weapons: 12 F-5E and four F-5F fighters, 64 M-60 tanks, 100 M-113 armored personnel carriers (APCs), and a small number of artillery weapons, representing a total of US$400 million worth of arms. Although the deal also included Vulcan antiaircraft guns and modern antitank guided missiles (ATGMs), it fell short of giving North Yemen's armed forces independence. Salih and key army officers concluded that North Yemen was being made permanently dependent on Saudi Arabia.

As a result, Salih took advantage of the terms of the peace agreement with South Yemen to tilt back to the Soviets. In November 1979 he concluded a military and economic aid package with the Soviets without consulting either the United States or Saudi Arabia. The pact provided for some US$700 million dollars worth of Soviet arms only months after Saudi Arabia had agreed to fund US$400 million of American-made weapons to counter Soviet influence.

The Soviet package included MI-8 attack helicopters, some 70 fighter aircraft—including at least 36 late-model MiG-21s and 24 Sukhoi attack fighters—and enough T-54 and T-55 tanks to raise North Yemen's active strength to over 700 tanks. Despite Saudi opposition, Salih continued to seek arms from the Soviets and at the same time engaged in seemingly fruitless unification talks with the South Yemenis (see Relations with South Yemen, this ch.). In an interview Salih said that the Soviet arms "are not for the purpose of committing aggression or imposing our will on others nor for one-up-manship or to take advantage of international conflict. We can achieve security by having good relations and obtaining the arms we need by available means and according to our financial capabilities."

During early 1981 Salih procrastinated on the unification talks with South Yemen. This led the South Yemenis to stir up the NDF insurgency again. The NDF forces began to raid military bases in the southern cities of Ibb, Dhamar, and Harib. Salih responded by appealing to Moscow. He flew there and held talks with President Leonid Brezhnev, who promised to provide more than US$1 billion worth of arms. Furthermore, Salih began surrounding himself with military advisers to draw up an offensive against the NDF. Most of these advisers came from Salih's own tribe, and they were assigned positions in the national security apparatus, intelligence, air force, and the army. In addition, Salih appointed one full brother a brigade commander, another deputy minister of interior with command of the Central Security Forces, and a half brother as deputy commander of the F-5 squadron. Some observers were impressed by Salih's political astuteness and the way he managed to balance various forces and factions in his government during difficult military crises.

North Yemeni armed forces had managed to go through rapid transformations to improve their organization, communications, and command structure. With the assistance of tribal forces, they had also fulfilled two primary missions: protecting the country against foreign invasions and maintaining the country's territorial integrity. A secondary mission, considered by some observers to be of equal importance, has been to ensure internal security and public order.

Organization of the Armed Forces

In mid-1985 the armed forces totaled about 36,500 officers and men, of which about 35,000 were in the army. (Women were not recruited in any of the services.) The small air force and even smaller navy possessed some limited autonomy, and their commanders report directly to Salih. There was no defense ministry, and foreign observers were unable to determine with any precision the overall organization of the armed forces.

Army

The major unit of the army was the brigade; there were no divisions or equivalent larger units. On paper the strength of each brigade was around 3,000, but some were under complement. In late 1983 the army was expanding to a force of six armored brigades (one a training brigade), one mechanized brigade, and nine infantry brigades (one of which was a reserve unit). Twelve of these brigades were designated as active, but several were little more than reinforced battalions by United States standards.

Brigades were commanded by a brigade commander, who was assisted by a deputy commander, a brigade major (who performed most staff functions), and a brigade supply officer. Organization within the brigades was conventional: squads, platoons, companies, and battalions. In the mid-1980s 11 of the brigades had Soviet advisers, and one had both United States and Saudi advisers. The armored and mechanized brigades were relatively well equipped and had been improving steadily, but they had serious manpower shortages and suffered from inadequate training, organization, and command. Observers rated the parachute force, the guard force, and the two commando units as relatively efficient.

As of late 1983 most army equipment had been obtained from the Soviet Union, either directly or indirectly from Egypt or East European countries (see table 6, Appendix). The army's staff procedures were heavily influenced by the Soviets at the top but had retained a more traditional character at the lower echelons. Some observers reported that unit commanders often acted more like feudal warlords than conventional army commanders. The societal values tend not to encourage feelings of nationalism but rather support tribal loyalties and factionalism.

Logistic support systems in 1980 were inadequate. Accountability for property was not effective, and corruption, including the misuse or unauthorized disposal of army property for individual profit, was widespread. Press reports and comments by many officials were frequently quoted in the official *Al Thawra* paper, criticizing widespread corruption and private ownership of AK-47 rifles. The newspaper also criticized certain army officers who had sold government military equipment to the tribes.

In January 1982 Salih decided to seek a military victory over the NDF forces. The performance of the North Yemeni army surprised many observers. One observer went so far as to assert that a "new army emerged out of this experience." The NDF forces were reportedly well equipped and included more than 500 career officers who had defected from the North Yemeni army. Although there were still a few pockets of resistance in mid-1985, NDF influence had been virtually eliminated from their former strongholds in the southern and southeastern parts of the country.

Air Force

Until major Soviet aid resumed in late 1979, the air force was even less effective than the army. Maintenance problems continued to be so acute that in the mid-1980s few aircraft were fully operational. Pilots reportedly received little flight time and experience with their machines. Ongoing Soviet and United States training was correcting this situation, but the air force still lacked the ability to act as a coherent fighting force.

Since the cease-fire with South Yemen in 1979, the Soviet Union has stepped up its shipments to North Yemen. As of early 1984 North Yemen's air force consisted of 1,000 to 1,500 officers and other ranks and was limited in its capability to carry out the conventional tasks of ground support, bombing, and air-to-air combat. It was organized into five fighter squadrons, which were based largely at Sanaa, Hodeida, and Taizz. Two squadrons had a total of 40 recently supplied MiG-21s, and another had 11 American-made F-5Es and four F-5Fs. The F-5 planes were part of the US $400 million, Saudi-funded arms purchases from the United States in 1979, and they lacked the advanced avionics and munitions, such as the Maverick missiles, possessed by the Saudis. Other squadrons were equipped with 10 MiG-17s, which were barely flyable, and 15 Su-22s (see table 7, Appendix). Its relatively small transport and helicopter squadrons were hampered by constant shortages in equipment and parts. There were no modern air defense systems except for a low-quality air defense regiment equipped with 12 SA-2 SAM launchers. Climatic conditions also caused serious problems in handling complex equipment, particularly at the main base at Hodeida and at the smaller bases at Harib, Taizz, and Saadah.

It was unclear how the air force would cope with the anticipated acquisition of additional MiG-21s and Su-22s. The Soviet advisory efforts have been reasonably effective in making most of North Yemen's first-line fighters flyable and in improving basic training. In the opinion of most Western observers, however, the air force had little capacity to expand.

Navy

The navy was small and inadequately equipped for its missions of coastal defense, harbor patrol, and antismuggling operations along the long coastline. Based primarily in Hodeida, but with a small complement in Mocha, it numbered around 550 men. Few navy personnel actually went to sea; a majority were shore-based naval infantry or security personnel. Equipment was mostly Soviet, except for three United States patrol boats that were armed with Soviet weapons. The Soviets have transferred the following ships to the North Yemeni navy: 12 frigates, four FAC-Torpedo boats, four patrol craft, two mine warfare vessels, and two amphibious ships. On order in 1984 were two Osa fast-attack craft.

Harbor facilities and equipment were limited, and observers doubted that the navy would experience much improvement in the 1980s. In late summer 1984 there were many incidences of "mine" explosions in the Red Sea. The North Yemeni navy, possibly with Soviet help, deployed minesweepers to search for the mines. The North Yemenis did not participate in the multinational force composed of units of the British, Egyptian, Italian, Dutch, and United States navies. Although concrete evidence was not produced, most observers held the Libyan government responsible for the mines. On December 16, 1984, the Yemen Council issued a communiqué referring to the developments in the Red Sea as "endangering international navigation" and asserting that the North Yemeni government's "stand toward these developments is to oppose any interference by other powers." The communiqué affirmed the need to keep the "Red Sea region of peace, free of foreign military bases and far removed from international competition and struggle."

Manpower and Conditions of Service

Manpower continued to be adequate to meet military requirements without resorting to conscription. Announcements that recruits were needed have produced enough volunteers. This has been also true for officer cadet volunteers. The relatively adequate pay, prestige, uniform, weapons, transportation, and other military perquisites have proved sufficiently attractive to meet peacetime military manpower requirements. Nevertheless, some reports indicated that as many as 15,000 soldiers deserted or left the army for jobs in Saudi Arabia during the 1980-82 period. The army had also experienced a high turnover of senior officers for a variety of political reasons. According to a foreign military observer, there was roughly a 50-percent rate of absenteeism in meetings of high-ranking officers.

There were no clear enlistment standards; acceptance of illiterates was common, and boys of 12 and men over 50 have been accepted. A member of the United States House of Representatives who visited North Yemen in 1979 asserted that fewer "than 1,000 Yemeni military personnel can read and write." Although enlistments were usually for three years, many people served for longer periods. This could only partially be accounted for by the tangible benefits of service life; also significant was North Yemeni respect for the military profession and the traditional inclination to bear arms.

Recruitment has been by unit. Because recruits were naturally attracted to units containing fellow tribal members, there was a tendency for the tribal orientation to be perpetuated. Furthermore, because most North Yemenis retain a high regard for the military, the tendency to join on the basis of prestige has also been a factor. The negative side of this tendency centered on the prevailing problem of corruption. Some recruits joined the army, received training, and then disappeared, taking their guns, munitions, and other light weapons with them.

In 1985 Zaydi tribesmen continued to constitute a significant majority in the services. This has caused the Salih government to encourage Shafii enlistment in order to balance the percentage. In addition to seeking a more representative mix in the services, the government was also striving to foster unity and national loyalty other than tribal loyalty and to emphasize that military service was an honor and that defense of the homeland was a sacred duty. The third section of the National Charter asserts that "national unity is the force that makes us confront every threat against our existence, stability, and national independence. Our country is going through an important phase, a matter which makes it necessary to unite the internal front."

Ranks, Insignia, Uniforms, and Pay

In the mid-1980s military ranks for the armed forces included only five enlisted ranks and no warrant officer or equivalent ranks. There were provisions for 11 officer ranks in the army, eight in the air force, and six in the navy. Since the military coup of June 13, 1974, however, only five officer ranks have been authorized: the equivalents of second lieutenant, first lieutenant, captain, major, and lieutenant colonel. Insignia for these ranks followed the British pattern: pips and crowns for the officers in the army and air force and inverted chevrons for enlisted personnel in these services. Navy insignia were sleeve stripes for officers and inverted chevrons for enlisted men (see fig. 9; fig. 10; table C).

The basic uniform color was khaki except in the navy, where white was used for the dress uniform. Uniforms included three kinds: fatigues, a modified bush jacket of khaki, and a tailored tropical worsted winter uniform worn with a tie. The tailored uniform was rarely worn. Enhanced morale was sought by issuing camouflage uniforms to some units and by using colored berets to designate branch—maroon for paratrooper; black for armor; blue for artillery; light blue for air force; red for military police; and green for some infantry units.

Pay in the armed services was competitive with that in the civilian economy. As of late 1984 there were apparently no awards giving additional pay or allowances for specialist skills. Consequently, there was no way of rewarding increased technical skills except through promotion.

ARMY AIR FORCE AND NAVY	Mulazim Thani	Mulazim Awwal	Naqib	Ra'id	Muqaddam	'Aqid	'Amid	Liwa'	Fariq	Fariq Awwal	Mushir
UNITED STATES ARMY AND AIR FORCE EQUIVALENT	Second Lieutenant	First Lieutenant	Captain	Major	Lieutenant Colonel	Colonel	Brigadier General	Major General	Lieutenant General	General	General of the Army or the Air Force
UNITED STATES NAVY EQUIVALENT	Ensign	Lieutenant Junior Grade	Lieutenant	Lieutenant Commander	Commander	Captain	Commodore	Rear Admiral	Vice Admiral	Admiral	Fleet Admiral

Figure 9. North Yemen: Insignia of Officer Ranks, 1985

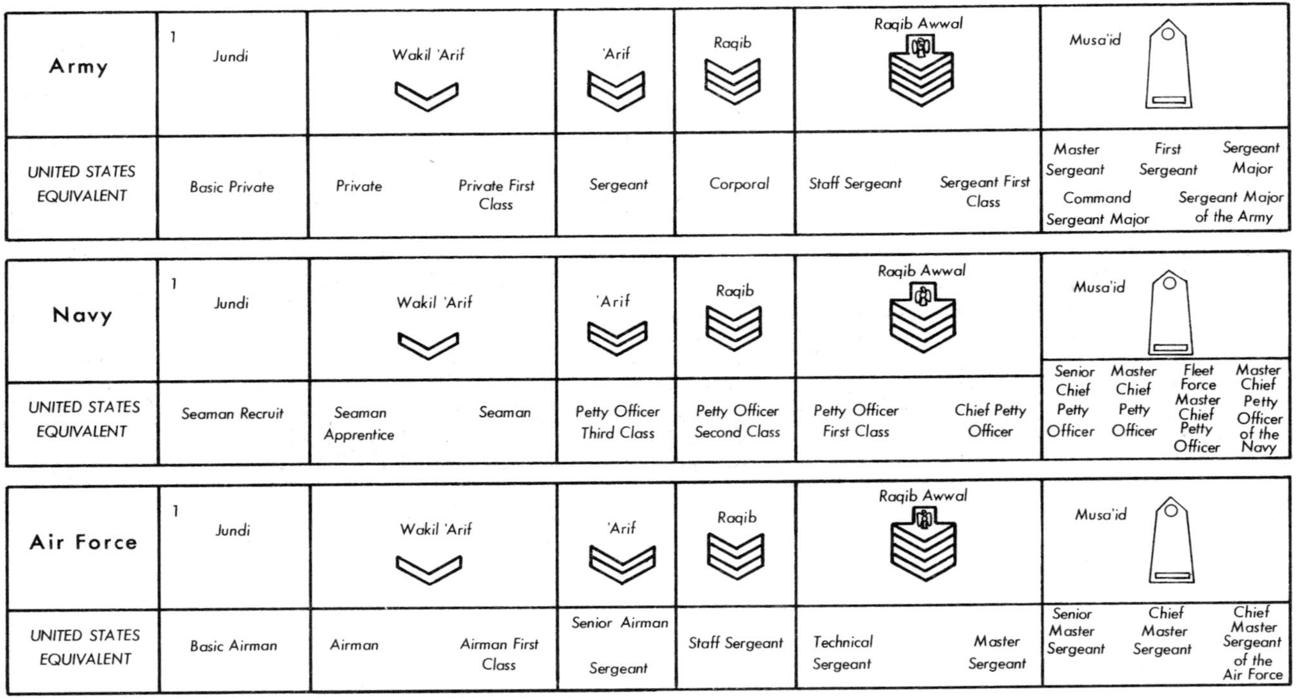

Army	Jundi[1]	Wakil 'Arif	'Arif	Raqib	Raqib Awwal	Musa'id
UNITED STATES EQUIVALENT	Basic Private	Private; Private First Class	Sergeant	Corporal	Staff Sergeant; Sergeant First Class	Master Sergeant; First Sergeant; Sergeant Major; Command Sergeant Major; Sergeant Major of the Army

Navy	Jundi[1]	Wakil 'Arif	'Arif	Raqib	Raqib Awwal	Musa'id
UNITED STATES EQUIVALENT	Seaman Recruit	Seaman Apprentice; Seaman	Petty Officer Third Class	Petty Officer Second Class	Petty Officer First Class; Chief Petty Officer	Senior Chief Petty Officer; Master Chief Petty Officer; Fleet Force Master Chief Petty Officer; Master Chief Petty Officer of the Navy

Air Force	Jundi[1]	Wakil 'Arif	'Arif	Raqib	Raqib Awwal	Musa'id
UNITED STATES EQUIVALENT	Basic Airman	Airman; Airman First Class	Senior Airman; Sergeant	Staff Sergeant	Technical Sergeant; Master Sergeant	Senior Master Sergeant; Chief Master Sergeant; Chief Master Sergeant of the Air Force

[1] No insignia

Figure 10. North Yemen: Insignia of Enlisted Ranks, 1982

Table C. North Yemen: Titles of Miltiary Rank, 1985

Rank	United States Equivalent		
	Army	Navy[1]	Air Force[2]
Officers			
Mushir[3]	General of the army	---	---
Fariq awwal[3]	General	---	---
Fariq[3]	Lieutenant general	---	---
Liwa'[3]	Major general	---	---
'Amid[3]	Brigadier general	---	Major general
'Aqid	Colonel		Brigadier general
Muqaddam	Lieutenant colonel	Captain	Colonel
Ra'id	Major	Commander[4]	Lieutenant colonel[4]
Naqib	Captain	Lieutenant commander	Major
Mulazim awwal	First lieutenant	Lieutenant	Captain
Mulazim thani	Second lieutenant	Lieutenant junior grade	First lieutenant
		Ensign	Second lieutenant
Enlisted men			
Raqib awwal	Master sergeant	Senior chief petty officer	Senior master sergeant
Raqib	Sergeant	Petty officer second class	Staff sergeant
'Arif	Corporal	Petty officer third class	Sergeant
Jundi awwal	Private first class	Seaman	Airman first class
Jundi	Private	Seaman recruit	Airman

[1]Captain is highest rank in the navy.
[2]Major general is highest rank in the air force.
[3]No persons in these ranks as of mid-1985.
[4]Commander and lieutenant colonel are the highest ranks in the navy and air force, respectively.

Military Justice

Military justice reportedly was harsh and swift. Like civilian justice, it was retributive as well as rehabilitative. Commanders were given latitude in the conduct of military justice with few apparent restrictions. Justice was tinged with practicality, however; the commanders of units largely consisting of tribal members were loath to inflict punishments that went beyond tribal norms or that might involve the commander—a tribal member himself—in a serious confrontation with the tribe of the offender.

Military Aid and Assistance

North Yemen has traditionally called on various sources for military advice and training. In the days of the imamate, this meant using Syrian or Iraqi officers to train the forces. In the 1930s and 1940s a limited number of officers were sent to nearby Arab countries, chiefly Egypt and Iraq, for training in military schools, although this was in the mid-1950s, before foreign military aid and assistance became significant. This aid came from the United States, the Soviet Union, France, Britain, Egypt, India, and Jordan. In the early 1980s the deputy prime minister for domestic affairs clarified North Yemen's arms policies: "We must obtain arms in the quantities we need. It is better to diversify sources of arms, where they come from is not important. What is important is the hand that holds the weapons and safeguards them." But as of early 1985 the largest provider remained the Soviet Union.

Soviet supply of arms commenced in 1956. Amounts supplied were not large, however, until the civil war in 1962, when shipments were substantially increased. From that time until 1978 and 1979 the government relied primarily on Soviet arms supply. During the time of the Egyptian withdrawal from Yemen in 1967, most of the Soviet arms used by the Egyptians were left for the North Yemenis. After 1967 the Soviets resumed direct arms shipments to North Yemen. There were particularly large shipments in 1968, but in 1970, after the end of the civil war and with the rise of a more leftist government in Aden, shipments were sharply reduced. Even replacement parts and training were not furnished in adequate quantities.

It was not until 1979 that the Soviets stepped in and provided direct aid. On February 24, 1979, when fighting erupted along the border between the Yemens, President Jimmy Carter's administration became so concerned about the situation that on March 9, 1979, it was announced that Carter had invoked emergency procedures to send US$400 million in arms to Sanaa without congressional approval. For the Salih regime, the problem with this aid was that it was going to be delivered through the Saudis, who were to pay for it. At first the Saudis were relieved and impressed by the United States show of force, but the border war was short-lived, and once a cease-fire was arranged (before the American-made equipment reached North Yemen) the Saudis were ambivalent about building up the North Yemeni military. The Saudis resorted to delaying tactics and withheld the delivery of some of the military equipment. United States official figures for arms sales in 1980 show that the total received by North Yemen was only US$316.4 million.

According to one military observer, as the principal financiers and planners, the Saudis were "understandably anxious to maintain full control of the program; consequently, from the beginning Saudi officials . . . sought to limit US-Yemeni contacts except on very low-level, specific operational details [such as discharging military equipment arriving at the Yemeni port of Hodeida]. United States officials on their part . . . agreed to work primarily through their Saudi counterparts inasmuch as the program was designed to meet a Saudi security problem." The North Yemenis were disappointed with Saudi Arabia's attitude toward extending military aid and, realizing that it was not possible for them to deal directly with the United States, the leadership in Sanaa became convinced of the soundness of the earlier North Yemeni policy over the past two decades of relying on the Soviets.

Figures on the number of Soviet military advisers were not precise. An estimated 35 Soviet instructors and about 50 technicians from the Soviet Union and East European countries accompanied the first shipments of arms in 1956 and 1957. During the civil war several hundred Soviet advisers helped both the Egyptian and North Yemeni forces; the Soviets reportedly sent their pilots to fly MiGs during the siege of Sanaa. By 1975 the number of advisers had dropped from a high of some 500 to about 100. They stayed at that level through 1979, but their numbers rose rapidly back to about 500 by 1983, and about the same number were believed to be in the country in 1985.

Nevertheless, North Yemen continued its attempts to diversify its arms sources. The greatest obstacle to direct United States-North Yemeni arms transfer appeared to be economic; the United States wanted Sanaa to pay full price. Although the Soviets also asked for payment, the terms were apparently more generous. Moreover, the Soviets, far from forcing North Yemen to begin paying its US$630 million arms debt, reportedly agreed to cancel US$265 million of that figure.

Despite such Soviet largess, North Yemen apparently did not intend to allow military cooperation with the Soviets to extend to granting them military facilities or an expansion of the Soviet presence, as had occurred in South Yemen. For example, in May 1983 Prime Minister Iryani said that "although the 1964 treaty with the Soviets would probably be renewed in 1984, it was certain that the parties would not introduce any articles pertaining to security matters." The 1984 treaty states that the Soviet Union respects North Yemen's policy of nonalignment, and North Yemen respects Soviet foreign policy.

The Soviet-North Yemen military relations were also conditioned by Soviet-South Yemen military relations. North Yemen kept a wary eye on the relative dimensions of the military support that Moscow gave to each of the two Yemens. There was, however, a limit to how much the Soviets would militarily assist North Yemen because, as of early 1985, it continued to refuse to become closely aligned with Moscow but also maintained a "detente" with Moscow's ally in Aden. North Yemen's reliance on Soviet military aid also meant that Sanaa was not likely to lose this assistance by attacking South Yemen. Indeed, part of the reason Moscow maintained friendly ties with North Yemen was that these served to protect Soviet interests in Aden.

Other military powers, such as France, have provided North Yemen with advanced radar systems, light tanks, and APCs. According to French and Arab sources, Saudi Arabia, which already contributed substantially to North Yemen's budget, would pick up the bill (see Role of Government, this ch.). France also agreed to provide microwave installations to modernize North Yemen's telecommunications network, electricity, and energy installations.

In mid-1985 the military goals of North Yemen were conventional: to build and maintain military forces adequate for internal and external security. To achieve these goals Salih's regime had indicated a willingness to accept military assistance from any source, but it had also shown a strong determination not to accept military assistance with strings attached. In 1980 it was clear that the government had become dissatisfied with United States military support that had strings attached, i.e., Saudi Arabia's supervision.

Public Order and Internal Security

Possible sources of dissension and disaffection in 1985 were the power and independence of tribes (particularly the northern tribes that retained strong links with Saudi Arabia), the large number of immigrants from the south, the large number of weapons in the hands of the population, the constant rivalry among the nation's military commanders, and the continuing authoritarian nature of military rule. As of early 1985 none of these threats to internal security, public order, or the regime was considered by the government to be dangerous.

According to one observer, Salih's regime continued to be the most "stable" government North Yemenis had had since the 1962 revolution, and the government exhibited a definite sense of dedication and a strong commitment to nation building. At the beginning, some North Yemenis stated, Salih viewed his job as a soldier would, i.e., he decided his policies and gave orders, but he subsequently demonstrated a strong belief in rule through consultation.

In early 1985 there were reports of occasional tribal disturbances in the north, which the government denied. There was no doubt that the regime had taken a conciliatory attitude toward the conservative tribes, however, and had allowed them some degree of "autonomy" in their activity. The army was already numerous and powerful and able to withstand an attack by the tribes. It was not, though, a question of adding up numbers on two distinct sides; a great many men were both tribesmen and regular soldiers and could therefore be counted as either.

The very distinction between government and tribes, which underlies that between tribes and army, is in some way misleading. It is true that on occasion certain tribes have been at odds with the government of the day; for instance, in 1977 a dispute existed between the government and an alliance of mainly Hashid tribes. But those who dissented from a particular administration did not consider themselves outside the republic. They were as much Yemenis and republicans as anyone else. One observer concluded that relations between tribes and state were not a matter of national security or of two forces facing each other across a common border. Many tribal leaders continued to hold high governmental or military posts. Observers describe seeing men changing from their tribal regalia and into army uniform for occasions that were deemed governmental or out of their uniforms into tribal gear for occasions deemed tribal. Furthermore, the northern tribes had sent large numbers of men to work in Saudi Arabia and the Gulf in the 1970s and early 1980s; if this trend continued, the tribes would be deprived of their much needed manpower (see Emigration, this ch.).

Another source of threat to national security had been the forces of the NDF. The NDF insurgents battled the government troops until the spring of 1982. The North Yemeni army mounted a major offensive that resulted in a seemingly definitive cease-fire. Until that time there had been numerous cease-fires and apparent negotiating breakthroughs, none of which took hold. There were negotiated attempts in February 1980, August 1980, and November 1981, all of which failed to bring about security agreements. Finally, in January 1982 Salih decided to seek a full military victory over the NDF by first dismissing several high-ranking officers who reportedly advocated a less forceful approach in order not to provoke South Yemen's retaliation. In mid-March the NDF general secretary, Sultan Ahmad Umar, stated that the NDF would give up regions in the center and south of the country if North Yemen would free 4,000 political prisoners and guarantee political and labor freedom. During this time Salih and his military advisers surprised the NDF by promising political concessions but not any military or security arrangements. This produced major splits within the ranks of the NDF. Finally, in May 1982 the North Yemeni army, aided by 6,000 northern tribesmen, attacked the NDF strongholds. In the clash some 1,000 of the 5,000 NDF fighters defected to North Yemen. A final cease-fire was signed a few weeks later by Salih and Ali Nasir. On this occasion, President Salih agreed to proclaim an amnesty for NDF members, and

Ali Nasir agreed to carry out his promise to end South Yemeni support for the NDF.

Aside from the NDF's diminished role, there have been occasional "subversive" activities by a small group of Muslim fundamentalists. These groups have had a difficult time mobilizing support for their cause. According to one observer, in the early 1980s they numbered around 300 to 500 and were mostly active in the universities. Their influence in the armed forces seemed to be minimal. Moreover, the experience of the Ayatolah Ruhollah Khomeini regime in Iran did not seem to be a good political model for the North Yemenis. Most of the people in North Yemen reportedly viewed Khomeini as too "radical" and thought that his philosophy encouraged sectarianism in Islam. The North Yemeni government has occasionally expelled Iranian diplomats, charging them with "espionage," and has claimed to have discovered a "sabotage network" under the supervision of the Iranian chargé d'affaires in Sanaa (see Islamic Fundamentalists, this ch.).

The large number of weapons in the hands of the people is not a problem in itself but a means of greatly increasing the magnitude of any dissidence that might arise. In early 1982 there were an estimated two rifles per person, and several million small arms, several hundred thousand machine-guns, mines, hand grenades, and several thousand indirect-fire weapons (mortars and artillery) had been introduced into the country during the civil war. Less than 5 percent had been accounted for, and a large amount was believed to be in the hands of the tribes in the north and northwest. The government instituted a repurchase program in order to retrieve some of these weapons. Although it had not been successful in gathering small weapons, it had been able to retrieve some of the heavy weapons for which the holders had no use.

Public Security Forces

Public security was based on three forces: the police, the tribes, and the Central Security Forces (CSF). Of these the latter were used when "domestic tranquility" could not be maintained by the tribes or police. The society remained essentially tribal, particularly in the northern and central Zaydi areas, and the central government, lacking the resources to assume close and direct police control of the tribal areas, had no alternative but to place the responsibility for internal order and security on the tribes themselves. Traditionally, the police were not welcome in the tribal region in the north. But in the southern region, police control was universally accepted. The police cooperated closely with the other branches of the armed forces, particularly the army, and with local tribal forces.

The CSF were under the Ministry of Interior. They were separate from the police and operated under an open mandate to search homes, monitor telephone conversations, read personal correspondence, or otherwise intrude into private lives when they believed that the security of the state was jeopardized. The CFS had armored personnel carriers, machine guns, and some antitank capability. According to one observer, they numbered about a brigade in strength and were trained in street-fighting techniques. They wear a blue military uniform like the police. According to the United States Department of State's *Country Reports on Human Rights Practices for 1984*, there had been credible reports that the CSF occasionally resorted to secret arrests and clandestine detention. There was no indication that the CSF had been guilty of political killings in 1984.

The police were a national organization also directly under the Ministry of Interior. Control was centralized at the national level with provision for dual operational control and administration at the governorate level. To ensure and facilitate this control, separate police radio networks have been established to link all police stations and government security forces headquarters. Limitations of the existing civilian radio and telephone communications made such networks mandatory for efficient centralized control.

The most recent data available in 1985 showed that in 1976 police strength was 13,000, a figure that included not only uniformed police but also nonuniformed civilians in the Ministry of Interior. Financial support for this organization was included under the "security services" classification, and as of June 30, 1981, it was YR1,333,400, or approximately 16 percent of government expenditures for that year. Defense expenditures for the same year accounted for about 40 percent of government expenditures; together security and defense amounted to more than 50 percent of national government expenditures.

Unlike the army, the police had specific enlistment standards; among other things, an ability to read and write was a condition of enlistment for new policemen. Their training had been given special emphasis since Hamdi seized power in June 1974. Officers and senior enlisted personnel were sent to police schools in Saudi Arabia, Kuwait, and Egypt. The police academy for officers, located in Sanaa, and other training units for enlisted personnel in the capital and in Hodeida and Taizz have gradually been strengthened and improved. The advice of police officials in Egypt, Britain, and Jordan has been sought and followed in an effort to develop a more professional police force.

Public attitude toward the police reflects the ambivalence prevalent in many other countries. With the exception of those who are in charge of traffic or social services, the North Yemenis viewed the police force as being linked with the security forces that in turn were linked with the military. In the mid-1980s the government was attempting to improve the image of the police. For example, they had been given the tasks of responding to medical emergencies and providing other social services.

* * *

The late 1970s and 1980s witnessed the production of an impressive congeries of fine scholarly research on various aspects of the society. Jon Swanson's lucid, insightful book, *Emigration and Economic Development*, supplies an overview of the culture as well as much information on labor migration in the late 1970s. Cynthia Myntti details women's role in the society in her readable book designed for development workers, *Women and Development in the Yemen Arab Republic*. In *Transactions in Ibb: Economy and Society in a Yemeni Highland Town*, Brinkley Messick provides a fascinating look at daily economic life and its relation to other elements of town life. *Market, Mosque and Mafraj* by Tomas Gerholm describes the interaction of three components of men's social world in a town in the Ismaili Haraz area. Although a dissertation and consequently more difficult to find than a book, Najwa Adra's *Qaybala:*

The Tribal Concept in the Central Highlands of the Yemen Arab Republic is well worth the effort. Adra presents an overview of tribal life, an elaboration of the meaning of tribe in North Yemen, a clear exegesis of social status groups, and a wealth of information on tribal aesthetics.

The most comprehensive study of the economy, although dated, is the World Bank's Country Study, *Yemen Arab Republic: Development of a Traditional Economy*. The *Financial Times*' Survey of November 26, 1984, provides several articles on current economic issues and problems. North Yemen's Central Planning Organization annually publishes (about April) a *Statistical Year Book* containing the latest data available on many aspects of the economy.

As for earlier periods, J.E. Peterson's *Yemen: The Search for a Modern State* and Robert Stookey's *The Politics of the Yemen Arab Republic* are indispensable, although the latter is now a bit dated. A more recent book edited by B.R. Pridham, *Contemporary Yemen: Politics and Historical Background*, comprises 17 chapters by different authors. Some of these provide an excellent background on current North Yemeni politics, especially those by Leigh Douglas, J.E. Peterson, and Paul Dresch. (For further information and complete citations, see Bibliography.)

Chapter 3. South Yemen

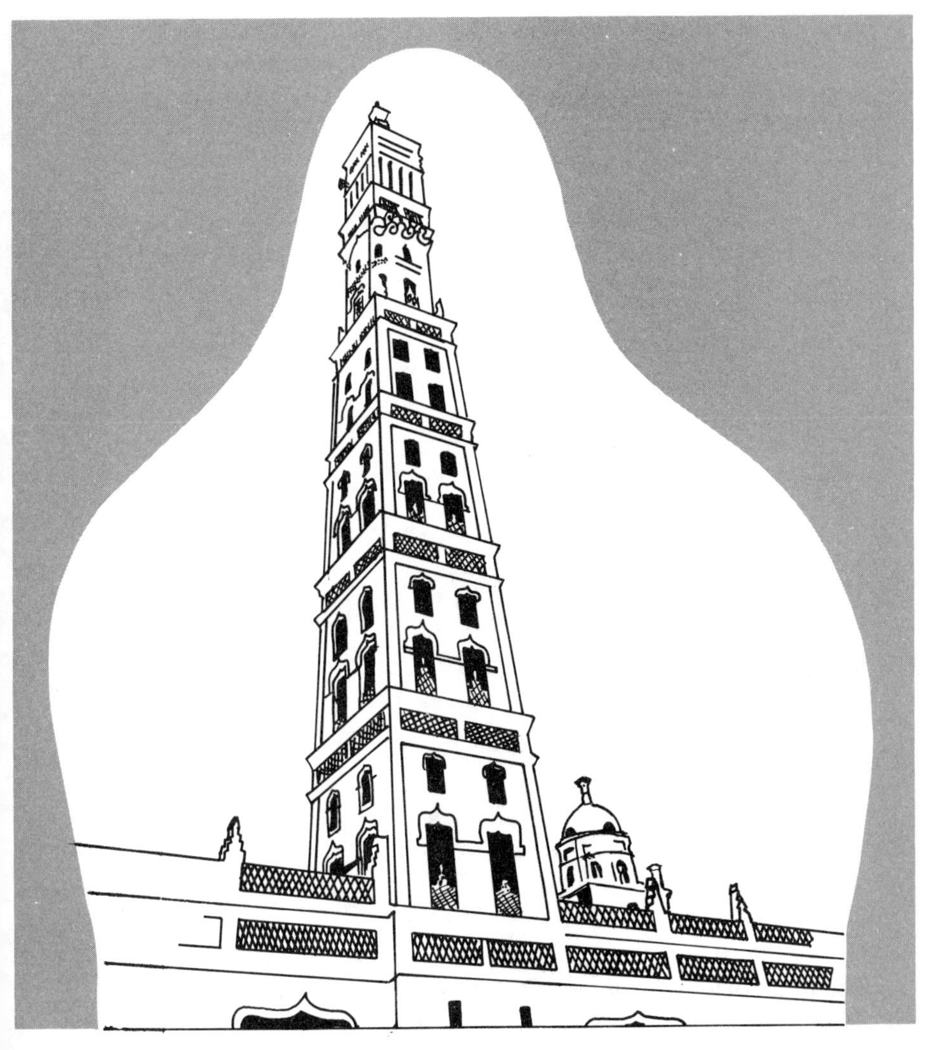

The mud-brick mosque in Tarim in the Hadhramaut, South Yemen

Country

Formal Name: People's Democratic Republic of Yemen; Jumhuriyat al Yaman ad Dimuqratiyah ash Shabiyah.

Short Forms: South Yemen; Yemen (Aden); PDRY.

Term for Citizens: South Yemeni(s).

Capital: Aden.

Flag: Red, white, and black horizontally striped banner with red star on blue triangular field on staff side.

Geography

Size: About 287,849 square kilometers.

Topography: Mountainous interior with coastal plain and eastern desert.

Climate: Varies by region but generally extremely arid and hot; high humidity in coastal regions during summer.

Boundaries: Most of border with North Yemen demarcated but some not; border with Saudi Arabia not defined; border with Oman not demarcated.

Society

Population: Estimated 2.1 million in 1985; annual rate of growth estimated at 2.6 to 2.9 percent.

Education: Free through university; eight years of Unity (elementary) school available to all children; access to secondary schools and university restricted. General literacy rate estimated at 53 percent, but figure may be inflated.

Health: Government clinics, dispensaries, and hospitals not yet evenly distributed; infectious diseases endemic.

Ethnic Groups: All native South Yemenis are Arabs; an estimated 5,000 foreign workers (Asians, Sub-Saharan Africans, and East Europeans).

Religion: Almost all South Yemenis are Shafii Sunni Muslims; small enclaves of Zaydi Shia Muslims.

Economy

Gross National Product (GNP): US$950 million in 1982- US$470 per capita (World Bank *Atlas* methodology). Economy modeled on Soviet pattern.

Agriculture: 12 percent of gross domestic product (GDP) in 1982, employing 44 percent of work force. Main crops sorghum, some other grains, fodder, vegetables, fruits, and cotton. Cropping mainly by irrigation. Fish most important natural resource but catch well below potential.

Industry: 11 percent of GDP in 1982, employing 11 percent of work force. Main industries oil refining from imported crude, textiles, food processing, and electric power.

Exports: US$18.8 million in 1981 (excluding reexports). Mostly fish but some cotton, hides, and tobacco.

Imports: US$673 million in 1981, of which 29 percent food and live animals, 23 percent petroleum products, and 22 percent machinery and transport equipment. Completely dependent on imported oil for commercial energy.

Exchange Rate: US$2.90 per YD 1 (March 1985).

Railroads: None.

Roads: About 5,600 kilometers, of which 1,650 kilometers paved (1982), 630 kilometers of crushed stone and gravel, and remainder motorable (under some conditions) tracks.

Ports: Aden main port and Khalf near Al Mukalla other important port.

Government and Politics

Government: Government structure defined by November 30, 1970, Constitution, amended in 1978 after formation of Yemen Socialist Party (YSP). Supreme People's Assembly (SPA) national legislature; chooses Presidium, whose chairman becomes president and head of state. Highest executive body Council of Ministers, headed by chairman who functions as prime minister. Regional and local government exists on three levels: governorates (six in 1985), directorates, and districts.

Politics: YSP sole political party. Formally established in October 1978 as Marxist-Leninist "vanguard" party based on Soviet model, its mission is revolutionary transformation of society. Political Bureau (Politburo), chosen by Central Committee, comprises party and national leadership. Affiliated mass organizations include General Union of Yemeni Workers, General Union of Yemeni Women, and Democratic Yemeni Youth. YSP membership estimated at 19,000 in 1983. Armed forces—in mid-1985 not under complete party control—remained significant political actor.

Foreign Relations: Designated "state of socialist orientation," South Yemen has close ties with Soviet Union and its allies through extensive state- and party-level relations. In mid-1980s unification talks proceeding with North Yemen. Because of insufficiency of aid from the Soviet Union and its allies and desire to end isolation within Arab world, regime sought to improve relations with Saudi Arabia and other oil-exporting Arab states. No diplomatic relations with United States as of mid-1985.

National Security

Armed Forces: Popular Defense Forces consisted of army (about 24,000), air force (about 2,500), and navy (about 1,000) in late 1984. About 18,000 were conscripts serving two-year tour of duty. All four headquartered in Aden.

Military Units: Army included 14 brigades—10 infantry and one each armored, artillery, mechanized, and missile. Air force included four fighter-ground attack squadrons, three interceptor squadrons; total 103 combat aircraft in late 1984. Navy possessed few patrol and various attack craft and boats.

Equipment: Almost all equipment Soviet made. Included about 450 medium battle tanks, estimated 30 MiG-17Fs, 12 MiG-21s, and 36 MiG-21Fs.

Paramilitary Force: People's Militia, under direct control of YSP, estimated 15,000 in 1984. Units dispersed in towns and villages throughout country; close relations with Popular Defense Committees.

Foreign Military Relations: Reported 3,000 Soviet, East German, and Cuban advisers in country in 1984. Attached to armed forces units, People's Militia, and Public Security Force (police).

Police: Public Security Force estimated at about 30,000 in 1985 and growing. Performs some paramilitary functions. Ministry of State Security includes secret police. In addition, Rural Police and Armed (or Civil) Police. Little known about police forces in 1985.

IN THE MID-1980s the People's Democratic Republic of Yemen (South Yemen) was the most radical state in the Arab world; its ruling party, the Yemen Socialist Party, defined its mission in terms of the total revolutionary transformation of society in conformity with orthodox Soviet concepts of Marxism-Leninism. South Yemen was not a model totalitarian state, however. The regime's ambitions were frustrated by an extreme shortage of material resources, popular indifference or hostility, and sometimes violent divisions within the leadership itself. The regime regarded the aid and guidance of the Soviet Union and its allies as indispensable, and Soviet, East European, and Cuban advisers directed the establishment of new economic, political, social, and military institutions. Although Soviet influence was paramount, Ali Nasir Muhammad al Hasani, the country's chief of state since April 1980, sought to promote amicable relations with the more conservative Arab states to the north and continued a dialogue with the Yemen Arab Republic (North Yemen) on the issue of Yemeni unity (see Introduction).

The radical government confronted enormous problems as it sought not only to revolutionize the society but also to raise the population's standard of living. In the mid-1980s the economy was one of the poorest of the developing nations. Except for rich offshore fishing grounds, the country possessed few natural resources. Less than 1 percent of the land was cultivable, and prospects for discovering significant deposits of commercially exploitable minerals—particularly hydrocarbons—were generally rated as modest. And despite important gains in literacy, the economy continued to suffer from a lack of skilled workers as well as managerial and administrative personnel.

The effect of government policy on the country's society and culture was difficult to gauge in 1985 owing to the paucity of available information, but it appeared that institutions were more amenable to change than were social structure and relationships. Health care and education were far more widespread than before 1967, when independence from Britain was secured. Other areas such as sewerage and housing appeared, according to the available data, to have changed little. New laws affecting women were introduced; women assumed a much larger role in the wage labor force, and many received an education they were previously denied. But fundamentally women's status did not appear greatly altered in most of the country.

Other cultural components changed less. Although atheism is an element in Marxist theory, the government failed to abolish religion. Much of the animal husbandry in the country rested in the hands of traditionally organized beduin tribes. The historical pattern of recourse to labor migration also continued despite government efforts to quash the practice and then to curtail or control it. In the mid-1980s, then, South Yemen displayed many traditional social features that were similar to elements in neighboring Arab countries that had non-Marxist governments. Part of the explanation for this lies in the problems the government has had to face in developing the country, and part, some scholars have noted, in the fact that the rulers of South Yemen share the culture of the country.

Geography and Population

South Yemen encompasses an estimated 287,849 square kilometers. In addition, it possesses Kamaran Island in the Red Sea, the island of Perim in the Bab al Mandab, and the 36,400-square-kilometer island of Socotra in the Gulf of Aden, as well as some smaller islands in the Arabian Sea. The political status of Perim was decided by a plebiscite. Socotra had been ruled by the sultan of Qishn, and at independence possession of Socotra passed to the new national government.

Physically, South Yemen encompasses the irregular southern end of the Arabian Plateau, which is formed by ancient granites and is partly covered by sedimentary limestones and sands. The coastal area is flat and sandy and varies from about eight to 16 kilometers in width. Farther inland the country is mountainous; the hills reach some 2,438 meters in the extreme west and gradually taper off to the east. The tableland is interspersed with deep valleys and wadis, beds of episodically flowing rivers that are usually quite dry and without any vegetation. The topography remains largely the same until it reaches the sands of the Rub al Khali, or Empty Quarter, in Saudi Arabia (see fig. 1).

A distinct topographic feature in the eastern part of the country is the Wadi Hadhramaut (which means "death is present"), a narrow valley located in the central part of the country and extending eastward to the Gulf of Aden from the area north of the desert of Ramlat as Sabatayn. The wadi runs parallel to the coast some 161 to 193 kilometers inland. Surrounded by desolate hills and desert, the broad upper and middle parts of the Hadhramaut, which possess alluvial soil and floodwaters, are relatively fertile and are inhabited by a farming population; the lower eastern part of the valley, which turns southward to the sea, is barren and largely uninhabited.

Rainfall is limited. The overall average is less than eight centimeters, but there are marked regional variations. Aden has an average annual rainfall of 12.7 centimeters, whereas the higher parts of the mountains receive from 50.8 to 76.2 centimeters a year. It is not uncommon, however, for the northern and eastern sections of the country to receive no rain for five years or more. In the Wadi Hadhramaut short, heavy showers fall unpredictably—usually during April, July, August, and September—leaving an average rainfall of five centimeters a year.

Temperatures are high throughout the country, particularly in the coastal regions. In Aden the mean temperatures range from 24.4°C in January to 31.7°C in June. Temperatures of over 37.8°C, however, are common. The summers, which run from April to October, are especially hot and humid, and only limited relief is afforded by the monsoons in July and September.

The climate of the Wadi Hadhramaut is arid and hot. Mean maximum temperatures range from 40°C in summer to 30°C in winter, the mean minimum varying from about 22°C to 12°C. The humidity varies from 35 percent in June to 64 percent in January. During April and May severe dust storms frequently damage the crops.

As of mid-1985 the only full census ever taken in South Yemen had been conducted in 1973. Unfortunately, demographers report that the census was marred by grave, nonsystematic underreporting; therefore statistical tests cannot be used to compensate for the inaccuracies. The census takers apparently missed entire villages, and estimates of underreporting ranged as high as 20 percent of the population. In 1985 all population projections nevertheless used the 1973 census data because no other full census existed.

The Population Reference Bureau, a respected source for worldwide population information, using a natural population growth rate of 2.9 percent, estimated that in mid-1985 the country's population was 2.1 million. In 1984, however, South Yemen's Central Statistical Organization (CSO) estimated the annual growth rate to be 2.6 percent. The Population Reference Bureau projected the population in the year 2000 to be 3.3 million, whereas the assistant general director of the South Yemen population survey estimated a population of 3.18 million in that year. Still other sources projected a population of 3.4 million.

By 1985 South Yemen had made impressive progress in increasing life expectancy and decreasing infant mortality. In 1960 the estimated average life expectancy at birth was only 36 years, whereas in 1985 the various estimates of the average life expectancy at birth ranged from 45 to 47 years; virtually all the progress in extending life expectancy was made after independence in 1967. The total fertility rate—the number of children a woman who lived to complete her fertile years would be expected to bear—was estimated in mid-1985 to be 6.9 by the Population Reference Bureau. Sources agreed that the crude birth rate was about 48 and the crude death rate 19—still fairly high in comparison with many other countries.

The small population nevertheless demonstrated a comparatively high growth rate, and the agriculturally based country has very little arable land on which to support the population. The government, however, did not regard the country's population growth as cause for concern in 1985. Countries usually predicate family-planning policy with a slant toward one of two hypotheses: economic development and women's employment in the wage labor force results in decreases in population growth, or development in itself is insufficient unless culturally and psychologically acceptable fertility-regulating methods are made easily accessible. South Yemen, although providing family-planning methods through maternal and child health centers, in 1985 favored the first hypothesis, i.e., it emphasized the role of development.

In 1985 the characteristics of the population were also partly determined by the role of large-scale male labor migration. A majority of migrants in the mid-1980s were young men between the ages of 15 and 34. The government tended to discourage labor migration and until late in the mid-1980s outlawed it entirely; it then reversed its policy but required the prospective migrant to obtain a permit. No accurate counts of migrants existed in 1985, but some observers estimated that in 1981 about 76,000 South Yemenis were employed in Saudi Arabia, Kuwait, and the United Arab Emirates (UAE); 4,000 worked in other Persian Gulf states; and 10,000 to 20,000 were employed in North Yemen and elsewhere in the world, yielding a total migrant population of about 100,000. Because the population was quite small, the men working abroad represented one-fifth of the total labor force, resulting in severe labor shortages. Massive emigration from South Yemen in the first years after the 1967 revolution—when an estimated 25 percent of the population fled, usually to North Yemen—also contributed to the scarcity of workers. Most of these people never returned to their country.

Labor migration is not new to South Yemen; the country has a long history of out-migration. Abdalla S. Bujra, in his classic anthropological study of the Hadhramaut, reported that the British colonial administrator of the Hadhramaut in 1938 "estimated that at least half as many Hadramis lived outside Hadhramaut as did inside. Important colonies are to be found in Saudi Arabia, . . . the East African coast, India, Indonesia, Singapore, and Malaysia." Early migrants tended to become merchants or were religious specialists. In the past, migrant remittances enabled Hadhramis to farm and to sustain the frequent drought years; migrants also returned with new political ideas.

In the 1980s the effect of migration was to produce labor shortages, shifting a greater work burden onto the shoulders of women and children and also necessitating the importation of labor. In 1984 scholars calculated that about 5,000 foreign laborers worked in South Yemen; these workers were usually from Asian or nearby African countries. South Yemeni migrants' remittances also raised the gross national product (GNP) and greatly increased construction of new houses, as housing was one of the few opportunities for private investment that the government allowed. The housing boom in turn resulted in inflated wages for skilled builders and the concomitant withdrawal of these workers from less lucrative public sector employment. It appeared that in the mid-1980s the government could do little to end the tradition of reliance on labor migration (see Labor Force, this ch.).

Social Development

The revolution had produced much change in health and education by 1985. In other areas, however, such as housing, sewerage, water supply, and agriculture, little progress had been made.

Health

Infectious diseases constituted a major threat to the health of the population in the mid-1980s. In 1978 the United Nations Fund for Population Activities (UNFPA) reported the country's leading causes of morbidity as enteritis and other diarrheal diseases, influenza and pneumonia, dysentery, amebiasis (intestinal infestation by amoebas), malaria, streptococcal sore throat, scarlet fever, tuberculosis, leprosy, communicable eye diseases, and schistosomiasis (see Education and Health, ch. 2). In the mid-1980s these diseases showed continued prevalence (see table 9 Appendix 3.). Water sources were often infested with schistosome-carrying snails and were breeding grounds for the anopheles mosquitoes that transmit malaria. In the mid-1980s chronic malnutrition still caused problems; the diet was unusually low in fruits and vegetables and lacked sufficient animal proteins and amounts of vitamins A and E, sometimes resulting in nutritional anemia. A low life expectancy and high infant mortality were the predictable results of these disease patterns.

Water sources were also often contaminated by latrines and other sources of disease-producing organisms. In 1985 reliable observers estimated that only 24 percent of the total population—30 percent of the urban and 5 percent of the rural population—had access to safe drinking water. The figures were based on the most recent available data, unfortunately from 1976. Foreign experts found water in the Greater Aden and Al Mukalla areas to be acceptable in the mid-1980s. In many rural areas, however, people drew their water from contaminated open wells. As in North Yemen, women were responsible for obtaining water, an often onerous and difficult task.

To cope with health problems of such magnitude, the government developed a health care delivery system that emphasized primary care. In the mid-1980s the system was hierarchically arranged, comprising three levels. The first level consisted of dispensaries or rural health units where paramedics provided care to residents of small villages. At the second level health centers staffed by a physician and medical assistants ministered to local populations of up to 15,000 people, supervised first-level health units, and acted as referrals for secondary care. The third level consisted of a network of hospitals—31 in 1980. Thus, access to health care would ideally be distributed equally throughout the country (see table 10, Appendix). Although international agencies have commended South Yemen on health care policy and delivery, in the mid-1980s the government was dependent on outside funding for policy implementation. Donor countries often had more say than the South Yemeni government in determining what aspects of health care would be funded. In addition, the country's meager financial resources hampered policy implementation. Therefore, South Yemeni health planners tended to concentrate on cost-efficient delivery of primary health care in order to ensure at least minimal health care to as many people as possible.

In 1985 donor agencies estimated that the physician ratio was 1 to 7,200 people. The government attempted to rely on its own citizens to staff health units and hospitals, but it had relatively few trained personnel; therefore, the country sought funding for training local people in the medical profession. In March 1985 the government invited bids to equip a US $7.1 million health-training institute financed in part by loans from Kuwaiti and Swedish organizations. Health care in the country improved greatly after 1967, but observers judged it inadequate at all levels in the mid-1980s while recognizing the problems the government confronted in attempting to provide adequate care.

Education

By 1985 the government had accomplished a great deal in raising the educational level of the population. Adult literacy during the period shortly after the 1967 revolution was about 15 percent. Saeed Abd al Khair Al Noban, a South Yemeni education specialist and former minister of education, argues that Britain's purpose in educating Adenis and other South Yemenis was to further its own colonial interests, not the good of the South Yemenis; quality mass education was not in Britain's interests. Education was therefore a high priority for the new independent government, whose objective was total adult literacy. The government encountered many obstacles in reaching the goal, and in 1985 total literacy had yet to be achieved. Still, literacy had become widespread by the 1980s, when an estimated 53 percent of the adult population was literate. This figure may have been inflated somewhat, yet clearly tremendous gains in education had been made.

The remarkable increase in literacy resulted from a number of programs aimed at eradicating illiteracy. The government first faced the necessity of building schools; in 1962 South Yemen possessed only two secondary schools—one located in Aden and one in the Hadhramaut. In the mid-1980s, however, the Hadhramaut alone contained 15 secondary vocational and general secondary schools. Between 1966 and 1981 almost 700 new schools were built. Monies allocated for education increased dramatically as well; in the mid-1980s education constituted an average 18 percent of the total budget. South Yemen, like many other Middle Eastern countries, including North Yemen, had a school system based on six years of primary, three years of preparatory, and three years of high school. In the late 1970s South Yemen converted this system to a two-part arrangement with eight years of Unity (elementary) school education guaranteed to all children, followed by restricted access to secondary education. The number of years of secondary education varied by the specialty pursued. Noban writes that secondary education in 1984 was a tripartite system including "secondary academic which prepares students to pursue studies in the University; technical which leads to technician level; and the craft course to prepare a skilled worker. The duration of study varies: four years for secondary and teachers' training, five years for technician level, and two years for the trade school."

Since 1967 the government has conducted campaigns to achieve adult literacy but without great success. In December 1984 foreign journalists reported a new literacy offensive whose target population included females aged 12 to 35 and males aged 12 to 40. The teachers in the campaign consisted of all secondary-school students and 1984

Unity-school graduates, all faculty at Unity and secondary schools, and student teachers. The campaign staff was trained in evening and weekend classes and organized hierarchically: each secondary student was responsible for teaching seven people, Unity-school teachers supervised groups of five secondary students, and secondary-school teachers supervised the Unity-school teachers. Teaching materials were provided to the students free of charge. In mid-1985 the effect of the campaign on illiteracy was not yet evident. In addition to the campaign, however, South Yemeni law mandated attendance at literacy classes for all illiterate employees in the public sector and those working for private institutions. The classes had to be held at the work site during working hours.

Another kind of school that existed in 1985 had a somewhat different purpose. The military ran boarding schools for beduin children, and their purpose appeared to be the integration of tribal children into the national culture and the destruction of the children's own culture. In late 1984 an estimated 34,000 beduin children were enrolled in such schools.

Many South Yemenis received their education abroad in the mid-1980s. Observers noted that probably several thousand children attended schools in neighboring Arab states. Norman Cigar, an analyst of South Yemeni affairs, estimated the number of South Yemeni students attending classes in the Soviet Union in 1984 to have been over 1,000. As of June 1984 South Yemeni university students were able to attend the University of Havana pursuant to an exchange agreement with Cuba. South Yemen had tried to staff educational institutions primarily with its own citizens, yet in the mid-1980s 40 percent of the law faculty at Aden University was composed of East Europeans.

Despite important gains in the general educational level of the country's population, in the mid-1980s the government continued to experience difficulties with education and was unable to meet its own goals. In 1981, for example, the number of new students entering Unity schools was 4,300 fewer and the number of graduates 7,000 fewer than the stated objectives. The 1981 goal was to decrease the number of entering secondary students to 7,800 while increasing the number of graduates. The number of entering secondary students did decrease but still exceeded the goal by 1,100 students; however, 900 fewer students than planned graduated from secondary schools. It would appear that many students dropped out of secondary school in the late 1970s and early 1980s. In 1981 the same situation pertained at the university level: more students enrolled than had been planned, but fewer than planned graduated. In addition, the military's beduin schools suffered from many problems, including insufficient teaching staff, shortages in funding and materials, and a lack of communication between administrators and students.

Sewerage

South Yemen attempted to develop other components of the infrastructure but met with less success than in the health and education sectors. Sewerage, for example, was limited in 1985. Five out of the eight towns forming the two largest metropolitan areas—Aden and Al Mukalla—had sewers in the mid-1980s. Wastewater from Al Mukalla and Aden was dumped directly into the harbors. In 1982 the government initiated a major sewerage project in Aden, but three years later no information was available on the outcome. In the Aden and Al Mukalla metropolitan area, towns that lacked sewerage facilities, septic tanks, dry pits, and night soil collection substituted for a sewerage system. In rural areas no sewerage facilities existed, and latrines not uncommonly contaminated shallow wells, which were often the only source of drinking water.

Housing

In the mid-1980s housing lagged far behind government goals. The only housing survey available in 1985 was conducted in 1979. The total number of enumerated buildings was 375,000, of which 23 percent were located in Aden. Within Aden an estimated three-quarters of the housing fell within the public sector controlled by the Ministry of Housing; outside of Aden little public housing had been built. Plans were under way in the mid-1980s for more public housing because the 1979 survey results demonstrated that less than 20 percent of the housing was in the public sector. Approximately 30 percent of all housing was temporary in 1979; this included both public and private housing and reflected the country's severe housing shortage. The highest proportion of temporary housing—

well over 30 percent—was situated in Lahij, the Hadhramaut, or Al Mahrah. The private building boom resulting from migrant remittances helped to ease the situation somewhat—particularly in the Hadhramaut—in the mid-1980s.

Architecture, even buildings erected during the 1980s, tended to display traditional regional styles. Aden, once a colonial city, does not evince traditional Arabian architectural styles. The pattern of Aden's streets and styles and materials of the buildings display characteristic European conventions. By contrast, photojournalist Michael Jenner commented in 1983 that "mud is still used in Hadramaut for a modern building such as an airport or hotel . . . The wedding cake effect is a characteristic feature of Hadramaut architecture." Shibam, a Hadhramaut town founded in the third century, has been labeled "the town with the first skyscrapers of the world." The oldest houses still standing in the mid-1980s were built in the fifteenth century. In the early 1980s the mosques, often built in traditional styles and of some antiquity, appeared to be well maintained.

Women

Since the revolution the government has attempted to change women's roles and status on several fronts with varying and often limited success. Government efforts to raise the status of women and improve the quality of their lives included passage of the 1974 family law, formation of the General Union of Yemeni Women (GUYW), special literacy campaigns aimed at women, the opening of all educational institutions to women, establishment of women's technical training centers, adoption of policies encouraging employment of women, provision of some child care in children's centers, and the establishment of maternal and child health centers. Socialist-feminist scholar Maxine Molyneux observes that "The [South Yemeni] state places greatest emphasis on two processes which it considers fundamental for bringing about women's emancipation: education and the entry into social production."

The 1974 family law embraced several areas of women's lives and appeared to reinterpret sharia (Islamic law) rather than challenge its assumptions about women and men. With respect to marriage and divorce, the law prohibited arranged marriages, requiring consultation with the bride-to-be, who must be at least 16 years old at the time of the marriage. The groom must be at least 18 years old but not more than 20 years older than the bride. The law also required registration of marriages, limited the *mahr* (bride-price) to YD100 (for value of the Yemeni dinar—see Glossary), and restricted but did not abolish polygyny. A man may marry polygynously if, for example, his first wife is infertile or disabled. *Kafaa*, a traditional rule that prohibits a woman from marrying into a social status group lower than her own, was also outlawed. The husband's right to divorce his wife by repudiation was abolished, and grounds for divorce were equalized for wives and husbands. Legislation made it difficult for either spouse to obtain a divorce. Divorced mothers received the right to retain custody of their children until the son is at least 10 years old and the daughter is at least 15 years old, at which time the courts may ascertain the child's wishes in the matter. The law also specified how property acquired during the marriage should be shared. In addition, it entitled women whose husbands had not communicated with them or supported them for three years to divorce.

As Molyneux notes, the GUYW was incorporated into the country's party and state structures in the 1970s and early 1980s. A party official, the secretary for Mass Organizations, was responsible for the GUYW and other mass organizations, such as the peasants' union and the trade unions. According to Molyneux, "there is at least one member of the Women's Union at every level of the party structure. Similarly, the Women's Union has the right to nominate a quota of members to the legislative bodies. . . ." The GUYW aided the government by implementing its policies relating to women and organizing and conducting women's training and craft projects.

The literacy campaigns directed at women provided flexibility for secluded women to learn; female high school students who served as teachers might visit individual women in their homes to instruct them privately. The response of secluded women as of the mid-1980s had not been great, however; many women—and/or their husbands—saw little use in women learning to read. In addition to basic literacy campaigns, new, higher educational opportunities opened for women. Observers reported that in 1984 half the medical-school graduates were women.

Both the government and the GUYW have successfully encouraged women's participation in the labor force. In the mid-1980s women were estimated to compose 20 percent of the labor force, whereas in 1973 only 9 percent of wage laborers were women. The government has attempted to attract women to culturally devalued or prohibited activities through training and incentives. Many Middle Easterners, including South Yemenis, consider nursing both menial and suspect because female nurses come into contact with the bodies of male strangers. In the mid-1980s the government offered a monetary incentive to women who agreed to complete their two years of national service in the field of health. The GUYW trained women in sewing, but it also taught women to be mechanics.

Almost 80 percent of the women who were economically active in the mid-1980s worked in agriculture, composing 50 to 60 percent of the workers on state farms. Only members of cooperatives, however, could own land on the farms, and although women worked in the cooperatives, they were seldom members. Observers in 1984 reported that women participated in cultivating almost every crop grown, but in-kind wages for their labor were only half those of men. Foreign observers in the mid-1980s commented that the staff of agricultural extension services was almost always male and that these services were seldom provided to women. As in North Yemen, the care and feeding of animals was considered women's work. Men usually bought and sold the animals and their products, but women retained the profits for family use.

In one case, workers in a traditional feminine occupation were reassigned to a different location and trade. Female prostitutes constituted less than 1 percent of the female population in 1967 and were concentrated in the two major port cities of Aden and Al Mukalla. The government transferred most of the women and retrained them to staff a tomato-paste factory in Al Fayush, outside of Aden, while others have joined cooperative farms.

Several scholars writing in the late 1970s to mid-1980s have criticized some of the policies affecting women on a number of grounds. The GUYW, they argue, was an arm of the party and state and not an autonomous and truly representative organization. Although women had one of the highest crude activity rates in the Arab world, not all of this could be attributed to intentional change; the mass labor migration of men also contributed to women's larger participation in the work force in the mid-1980s. Furthermore, the women's jobs tended to require less skill, and consequently women received lower pay than men. Working women were saddled with child care and household tasks in addition to their wage labor, for domestic duties continued to be regarded as a feminine province. In addition, rules allowing working mothers to enroll their children at earlier ages in child care centers did not provide much assistance because in the early 1980s the centers closed in the afternoons.

Other factors affecting women's lives—such as living arrangements, the practice of seclusion, veiling, and clitoridectomy—showed some change by the mid-1980s, particularly in urban areas, but most of the country appeared to resemble prerevolutionary conditions (see Gender Roles, ch. 2). Many women resided in multigenerational extended families; such a residential unit provided built-in babysitters, for mothers-in-law and other female relatives often were available to care for the working mother's children. Molyneux has pointed out that such arrangements are traditional and do not meet the government's goal of changing women's status; they merely follow traditional patterns in shifting responsibility for child care from one woman to another. Data on the kind and extent of seclusion of women were unavailable in 1985. The government discouraged restriction of women to the home because the custom deprived the country of women's social production.

South Yemeni women traditionally have worn a face veil and an all-encompassing overgarment, the *shaydor*. Veiling began to decline, especially in cities, by the mid-1970s. Some who did not wish to relinquish the practice of veiling completely began to substitute the *balto*, or overcoat, for the more enveloping garment. By the late 1970s and early 1980s ideas associated with Muslim revitalization movements, such as the Iranian movement, had penetrated South Yemen, and in the mid-1980s women displayed renewed interest in wearing the more traditional overgarments and head coverings. In 1985 the government had not outlawed veiling, nor had the GUYW by 1979 strongly condemned the *shaydor*. The GUYW reportedly adhered to the belief that with development women would voluntarily abandon the garment.

Information on clitoridectomy in South Yemen was difficult to obtain in 1985. It was impossible to establish the prevalence of the custom or the kind of circumcision practiced. One source reports that female circumcision was "widespread" in the mid-1980s. As of 1979 clitoridectomy was certainly legal but not encouraged. Clitoridectomy is not prescribed by Islam, whereas male circumcision is mandated by the Quran and appeared to be virtually universal in South Yemen in the early 1980s.

Using the data available in the mid-1980s, it was difficult to assess the depth or prevalence of change in the lives of South Yemeni women. Most women appeared to continue playing traditional roles and, although the 1974 family law ameliorated their situation, it neither challenged their traditional roles nor significantly raised their status.

Social Life

Recent accounts of life in South Yemen were unavailable to United States researchers in 1985, although Soviet anthropologists were conducting ethnographic research in the country in the mid-1980s. Furthermore, only a few scholars had published ethnographic accounts of the prerevolutionary society. It was therefore not easy to understand the culture and to evaluate the effect of the revolution on religion, family life, social class, and other components of the social structure.

Religion

Almost all South Yemenis are Sunni Muslims of the Shafii sect, although some sources report small enclaves of Zaydi Shias located primarily in the northern portions of the country (see The Shafiis, ch. 1). Information on the religious affiliation of foreign workers in the country was lacking in 1985. In the mid-1980s religion seemed to retain its importance for South Yemenis. The Constitution specifies Islam as the country's official religion, and Muslim holidays are observed officially. British scholar Fred Halliday notes that "on the *eid* [two Muslim feasts, one of which commemorates the intended sacrifice by Abraham of his son Ishmael and the other of which marks the end of Ramadan, the Muslim month of fasting] the President leads the prayers in the main mosque and imams officiate at certain state functions, such as honoring the dead of the revolutionary struggle on independence day." In the mid-1980s lay teachers instructed schoolchildren in Islam, emphasizing themes in Islam that are congenial to Marxist thought.

The government also took steps to decrease some of the power of religious institutions by abolishing sharia courts and confiscating waqf (religious trust) lands in 1970. Waqf ownership of land allotted the profits from the land to a religious or charitable purpose, such as the maintenance of a mosque or the provision of food and clothing to the poor. Waqf land was normally held in trust by a caretaker or caretakers, who received part of the income from the land for their pains. Before 1967 many abuses of waqf land occurred, caretakers expropriating far more income than their legal due. Nationalization of waqf land and abolition of sharia courts notwithstanding, in the mid-1980s the government recognized the strength of the citizenry's allegiance to Islam and were loath to impose an atheistic doctrine on the people, especially, as some scholars have slyly observed, because the leaders were privately devout Muslims.

Social Class

Information on social class in the mid-1980s was entirely lacking, although before independence the society had been highly stratified. Bujra's important study of social stratification in the Hadhramaut is based on ethnographic work completed in the early 1960s. He described three traditional Hadhramauti ranked social strata. At the top were the sayyids (sing., *sada*)—those claiming descent from the Prophet Muhammad and who are believed to possess special spiritual qualities. Next came the Mashaykh (sing., shaykh) and the *qabayl* (tribesmen—sing., *qabili*; pronounced and often transliterated as *gabayl* and *gabili*). The Mashaykh traced their descent from famous scholars and holy men of the Hadhramaut and ultimately to Qahtan, from whom all southern Arabs claim descent. Mashaykh derived religious status from their ancestry, but their status was lower than that of the sayyids (see Social Class and Tribe, ch. 2). The *qabayl* were divided into often feuding tribes named after their founding ancestors. They too traced their ancestry back further to Qahtan (see South

Arabia in Pre-Islamic Times, ch. 1). Tribesmen did not have a special religious status and were therefore ranked lower than the Mashaykh. The appellation of the lowest ranked group, Masakin, literally translates as poor people. The group was further subdivided into at least three ranked status classes. Occupations were generally inherited along status-group lines, and many Masakin performed despised occupations. The Masakin had no special religious status.

Scholars postulate that the sayyids, frightened of the revolutionary government's probable actions against them for their traditional financial and religious privileges, fled the country after the revolution. It is possible that remnants of the class system may have continued to exist in the mid-1980s.

Aden presented a different class structure before the revolution. Halliday argues that under British influence a true class of urban industrial workers arose with a sense of class consciousness. Many Adeni workers received some Western education, and the port city of Aden was far more cosmopolitan than the rest of the country. During the colonial period, then, Aden was more susceptible to Western cultural influence. Knowledgeable observers report that even in the mid-1980s Aden retained its cosmopolitan character.

Tribes

Information on tribes was extremely scanty for the contemporary society, but there were indications that despite government attempts to "detribalize" the country, tribes were very much a part of the social life in the mid-1980s. Tribal affiliation had played a tremendously important role before 1967. The government launched antitribal, pronationalist campaigns soon after assuming power. Notwithstanding the efforts to rid tribes of their importance to the society and of their very identity, even members of the government tended to follow old tribal loyalties in the mid-1980s. The president's tribe, the Dathina, for example, were more than amply represented in the government and the military in 1985, as they had been before independence. The government attempted to settle the beduin and to replace their unrestricted pastoral existence with a settled agricultural life. Beduin strongly resisted these moves and, because they controlled about 35 percent of the country's livestock production and represented about 10 percent of the population, the government decided to concentrate on converting beduin tribal loyalty to national patriotism by educating beduin children in boarding schools.

Qat

Mastication of mood-altering qat (*catha edulis*) leaves is a feature of South Yemeni culture, as it is of North Yemen (see Qat, ch. 2). The government of South Yemen viewed qat chewing as harmful and restricted its use. In 1985 sources disagreed as to whether legal qat chewing was limited to Thursdays and Fridays or to Fridays only. Friday is the Muslim sabbath, and South Yemeni employees, like their counterparts in many other Muslim countries, have the day off. Qat-chewing sessions were apparently formalized to some extent and probably resembled those found in North Yemen, but no descriptions of the qat-chewing gatherings were available.

The Economy

Over millennia the people who inhabited the area that is now South Yemen evolved techniques to sustain existence in the harsh environment. From a mixture of farming, fishing, and raising livestock—partly by nomads moving animals between limited forage areas—the people were able to live on the arid land but for most at a level close to bare subsistence. When the British took over the natural port of Aden in 1839, a more modern economy evolved in the immediate vicinity of the port that provided many of those favored inhabitants with a higher level of living. When the British left in 1967, the country's new leaders set about modernizing all of the economy and raising living standards of the population. Progress was made, although in 1985 South Yemen remained among the least developed countries in the World Bank (see Glossary) ranking; the economy expanded to a GNP of US$950 million in 1982—US$470 on a per capita basis, according to World Bank *Atlas* methodology. Special factors, however, contributed to the rising incomes and improved standard of living that might not prevail in the rest of the 1980s, which could result in greater austerity than the population had experienced in the preceding decade.

Profile of the Economy

At independence in 1967 South Yemen had a dual economy. More than half of the population was engaged in farming and fishing in rural and coastal areas mostly isolated from Aden and often from one another. The centuries-old techniques that they employed provided a largely subsistence economy. Superimposed on and separated from the traditional backcountry was a bustling, prosperous service economy centered on the port of Aden. Those employed in the service economy usually had much higher incomes than those employed in traditional pursuits, and they enjoyed such modern amenities as electricity, potable water, and health care that were not available in rural areas.

The service economy developed under British control of Aden. The number of ships calling at the port for fresh water and stores increased substantially when the Suez Canal was opened in 1859. Aden became an important coaling port upon the shift to steamships, and it became an even more important fueling stop as seagoing vessels switched to petroleum fuels. In 1954 a refinery was constructed at Little Aden across the bay from the port of Aden, and by 1964 only London, Liverpool, and New York surpassed Aden as bunkering ports.

The free-port status accorded Aden as a crown colony in the 1930s further stimulated the service economy. Passenger ships stopped over in Aden while tourists shopped for duty-free goods from all over the world. A sizable entrepôt trade was also developed by Aden merchants. In its last full year of operation before the Suez Canal was damaged and closed during the June 1967 War, Aden refueled, serviced, and unloaded over 6,000 ships that brought with them numerous visitors and the equivalent of US$22 million in revenue. A large British garrison established after World War II generated additional employment and markets for local products and by the mid-1960s provided more than US$30 million annually in foreign exchange to the economy. The British government also contributed nearly US$34 million in budget support in 1966.

Large foreign firms dominated much of the activity in Aden. They controlled banking, insurance, tourism, trade, shipping, bunkering, dockyards, harbor transportation, the refinery—the only important manufacturing activity in the country—and the local distribution of petroleum products. A number of merchants, both foreign (particularly Indian and Pakistani) and domestic, also engaged in substantial commercial activity. A few of the merchant houses were quite large.

The country's stormy political beginning was accompanied by equally tumultuous economic developments (see Background to Postindependence Politics, this ch.). The closure of the Suez Canal sharply reduced the ship and tourist activity at Aden in subsequent years. The postindependence closing of the British military base, which directly and indirectly may have contributed more than one-quarter of GNP, and the cessation of British budget support, which had accounted for about two-thirds of government spending, left the new government with huge economic problems. GNP probably declined by more than one-fifth between 1966 and 1968 and left about 20,000 to 25,000 workers unemployed. The problems were concentrated in the Aden area, however, and the subsistence economy elsewhere was largely unaffected.

The economy was depressed for several years following independence, particularly around Aden. Ship arrivals and the tourist trade remained low, and ship bunkering and petroleum refining declined to a fraction of former levels. Government expenditures were sharply curtailed—by as much as 60 percent for some government personnel—and taxes were increased substantially. By 1969 the government began taking over ownership and control of most of the economy (see Role of Government, this ch.). Thousands of expatriate and local merchants, businessmen, landowners, and skilled workers fled the country with an accompanying flight of capital in the early 1970s. Private investment nearly ceased, and unemployment around Aden increased. Statistics do not exist to measure the effects of the depression, but observers suggest that it took nearly a decade for the economy to recover to its preindependence level, although the Aden area was the one primarily affected.

The imposition of an economic system based on central planning and control required statistics. By the late 1960s a statistical collection and processing organization was established with foreign technical assistance. Its size and competence increased over the years, but by 1985 many problems remained. The scope and reliability of much of the statistical data were limited, and the timeliness of published statistics was poor. The Central Statistical Organisation's (CSO) *Statistical Year Book, 1983* (published in late 1984), for example, contained economic data collected no later than 1982 and some data collected earlier; the latest foreign trade statistics covered 1981. South Yemen's statistics should be viewed as orders of magnitude and indicators of trends, but in some instances contradictory figures make even directions of trends uncertain.

The CSO began compiling national accounts data with a series beginning in 1973. Between 1973 and 1980 gross domestic product (GDP, in constant prices—see Glossary) rose at an average rate of 2.7 percent a year. This low rate of growth of GDP occurred in spite of increasing investments that rose an average of over 12 percent a year in real terms; obviously little output resulted from the investments. The high rate of investment did stimulate the construction industry, the only sector of the economy that exhibited much dynamism, showing an average growth of 7.4 percent a year. Minor growth sectors were transportation and communications (3.3 percent a year) and a variety of other services, including government (2.9 percent a year). Agriculture, where much of the labor force was employed, stagnated at zero growth, and the value added by fishing actually declined marginally. Industry (including utilities, mining, and manufacturing) rose only 2 percent a year, largely because of declining oil refining through much of the 1970s. The growth of GDP and its component sectors was substantially less than planned.

According to some data, growth of the economy in the early 1980s was even less favorable. Real GDP apparently rose by 3 percent in 1981 but fell by 5 percent in 1982. Devastating floods in 1982 caused substantial crop and livestock losses, resulting in declining agricultural output. Industry rose in 1981 but fell back in 1982 to show only a slight gain over the level in 1980. An increase in refining largely accounted for the rise in 1981, but the combination of slightly lower petroleum refining in 1982 and the decreased processing of agricultural products resulted in the diminished value added in industry. Other data, however, suggested industry may have risen more significantly (see Industry, this ch.). Construction was the only sector to show substantial growth between 1980 and 1982, rising nearly 7.5 percent a year. Other sectors of the economy exhibited little growth, the real value added of some services declining slightly. Preliminary indicators suggested that real GDP would increase by about 2 percent in 1983.

The apparent slow growth of the domestic economy was compensated for by the inflow of remittances from South Yemenis working abroad and by foreign aid. The increased oil revenues of the Middle East oil-exporting nations after 1973 and their large domestic development programs, which required imported labor, particularly in Saudi Arabia, attracted many workers from both North Yemen and South Yemen (see Labor Force, this ch.). South Yemen's receipt of remittances from workers abroad increased from about US$40 million in 1974 to perhaps US$467 million by 1982, when remittances represented about half of GNP and were by far the most important source of foreign exchange. Foreign aid inflows were smaller but still substantial, financing the bulk of development expenditures (see Role of Government; Balance of Payments, this ch.). Remittances and aid financed an increasing amount of the imports that went into consumption and investment. GNP, in contrast to GDP, increased on a per capita basis by an average of 4.7 percent a year between 1973 and 1980. Remittances and aid allowed South Yemenis to consume and invest far beyond what the domestic economy produced.

When a radical, leftist government took control after independence, it set out to alter the structure of the economy and to direct it away from services so that the output of commodity-producing sectors (agriculture, industry, and construction) would predominate. South Yemen's statistical system is patterned after the Soviet model in which most services are considered nonproductive in terms of GDP. The commodity-producing sectors' share of GDP declined by 1 percent between 1973 and 1982, however, to 39 percent in the latter year (see fig. 11). The fall of agriculture's share of GDP from 22 percent to 12 percent was compensated for by construction's increased share. Industry declined marginally while most services gained a little; trade (including hotels and catering) declined, however. The slow growth of agricultural and industrial output kept the structure of the economy from changing as planned.

The hoped-for recovery of Aden port activities after the reopening of the Suez Canal in 1975 was only partly

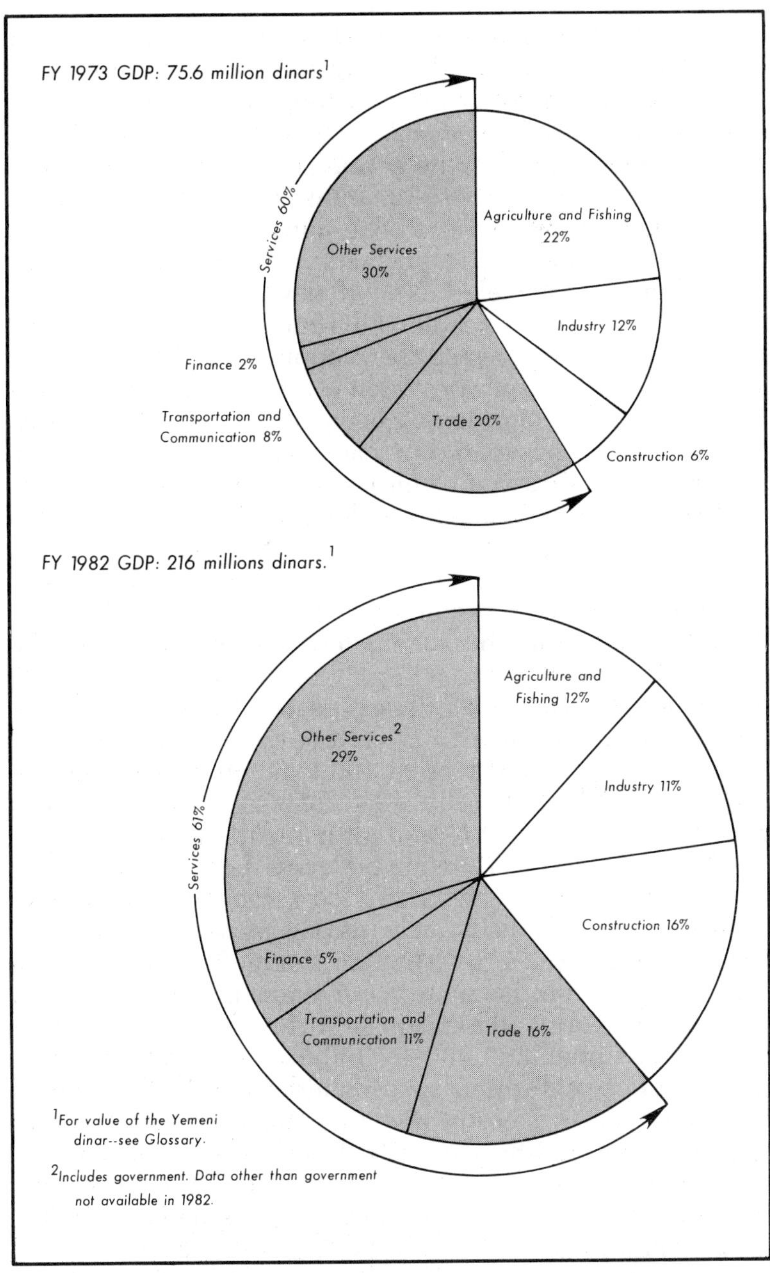

Figure 11. South Yemen: Gross Domestic Product by Sector, FY 1973 and FY 1982

realized. The number of ships calling dropped from nearly 6,000 before the canal closed to a low of 1,200 in 1974. The port was improved prior to reopening of the canal in order to provide efficient servicing. In 1977 the number of ships calling reached 2,600, but activity then stagnated, amounting to 2,360 in 1982. Bunkering remained low at about 800,000 tons in 1982, one-fourth of its former level, because of changes by shipowners in the pattern of where and when ships refueled. Nonetheless, in the early 1980s several foreign oil companies still retained their storage and bunkering facilities, which they supplied with their own oil instead of buying from the Aden refinery. The government had allowed these foreign oil companies to continue to operate through the years but had competed in bunkering services through a joint venture company with Kuwait's national petroleum company. Aden port also lost most of its formerly important transit trade to other Red Sea ports. Total dry cargo handled by the port (831,000 tons in 1982), however, had essentially regained preindependence levels as a result of South Yemen's growing volume of imports.

At independence a primary goal was to integrate the country economically. Considerable improvements were achieved. Paved roads totaled 400 kilometers around Aden under the British, but by 1982 about 1,650 kilometers linked Aden with most important population and economic centers, and more were being built (see fig. 12). Most parts of the country were accessible by vehicle, but often the more remote only had tracks usable by trucks and four-wheel-drive vehicles. By 1985 two cargofishing ports had been completed to facilitate the movements of goods more cheaply. The port of Khalf near Al Mukalla, which had a capacity of about 200,000 to 300,000 tons a year, could receive imports for the hinterlands directly rather than through the more costly and time-consuming trans-shipment from Aden. The port at Nishtun at the eastern end of the country, which had a capacity of 20,000 to 30,000 tons a year of dry cargo, should facilitate development of that area, including the marketing of fish.

Role of Government

The first government after independence proceeded slowly with economic changes because of the staggering

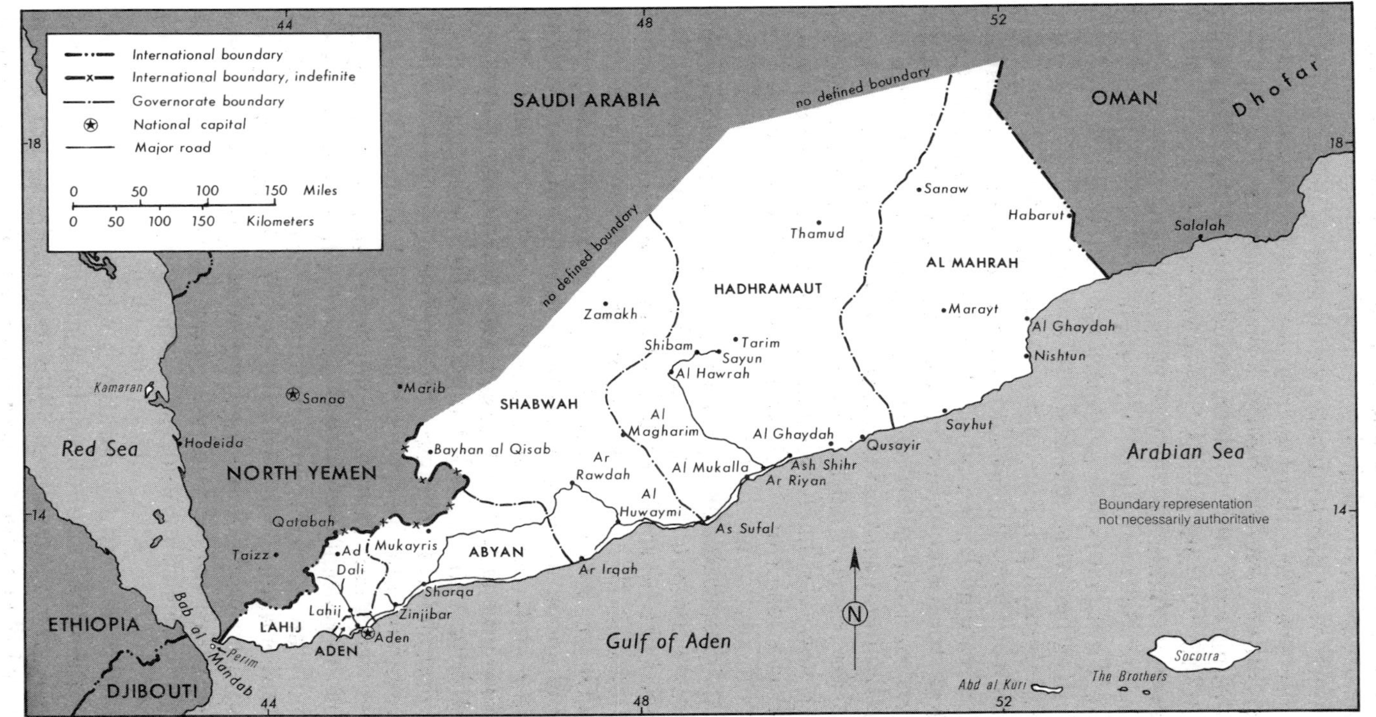

Figure 12. South Yemen: Governorates, Major Cities, and Major Roads, 1984

problems it faced and because of a concern not to disrupt further the already shattered economy of Aden. New leaders in 1969 began imposing a centrally planned and controlled economy. The Law for Economic Organization of the Public Sector and National Planning of 1969 was used to bring much of the modern foreign business under public ownership. The eight banks operating in the country, seven of which were foreign owned, were merged into the publicly owned National Bank of Yemen, the only commercial bank. The insurance companies, which were foreign owned, either were merged into a single national company or were liquidated. Five major foreign-owned trading companies were nationalized and formed into two companies—one for foreign trade and one for domestic trade. Port services at Aden except bunkering were brought under public authority. Local distribution of petroleum products was placed under a national company. Compensation for nationalized assets was paid for with long-term bonds, but a few claims under nationalization were still unsettled in the early 1980s.

Not all foreign-owned companies were nationalized. The government took over the Aden refinery in 1977 and the international communications facilities in 1978 by mutual consent. Bunkering facilities of major oil companies were allowed to continue to operate, and several remained in 1985. In 1971 and 1981 laws were promulgated to permit and encourage various forms of foreign investment, including that of South Yemenis working abroad. The response was far from overwhelming. The Soviets entered a joint fishing venture with the government. Kuwait's national oil company and the government formed a joint bunkering company. A Japanese company fished South Yemen's waters under a royalty agreement, and several foreign oil companies searched for oil under production-sharing agreements. Some foreign companies participated in hotel management and other tourist activities.

By the early 1970s governmental control was extending into all phases of economic activity. Land reform was imposed, and most farming came under cooperatives or state farms (see Agriculture, this ch.). Traditional fishing was organized into cooperatives, which owned the boats, nets, and other capital equipment. Housing, except for owner-occupied dwellings, was nationalized, but public housing did not keep pace with population growth and needs, resulting in an acute shortage of housing by the mid-1980s (see Housing, this ch.). The government set prices for nearly everything at all levels, from the initial producer to final consumer. Public companies controlled most trade, distribution, and transportation. By the 1980s the government exerted considerable control over private economic activity and directly accounted for a substantial part of production. In 1982 the public sector's share of gross output of goods and services was 42 percent, plus part of the 11 percent from cooperatives and the mixed sector (where private investors could own up to 49 percent of some companies in which the government was the majority owner). The private sector remained surprisingly active, however—especially in construction, agriculture, and trade—accounting for 47 percent of the gross production of goods and services.

From the outset the public sector suffered from staffing problems. The acute shortage of skills in the largely illiterate labor force and particularly the lack of able managers and administrators made the move into large and complex economic organizations difficult. Moreover, the emphasis on political reliability often superseded technical qualifications in choosing managers and administrators. Weak management contributed to the low productivity and inadequate return on investments in many public sector enterprises.

South Yemen's political framework required comprehensive planning for economic and social development. The first efforts to establish planning institutions were made in 1968. By 1973 a succession of organizations ended with the creation of the Ministry of Planning. Extensive foreign technical assistance contributed to developing the planning staff and formulating plans. In the mid-1980s the Council of Ministers formally issued the plans, and the High Council for National Planning, chaired by the prime minister, reviewed them. The ultimate decision making body for plans and other important economic matters, including price changes, remained outside the governmental structure, however, and consisted of the Political Bureau (Politburo) of the Yemen Socialist Party (see The Yemen Socialist Party, this ch.). The Politburo provided guidance and goals for formulation of plans by the Ministry of Planning. The ministry was assisted by, and coordinated activities of planning units in, ministries, economic agencies, and governorates.

Although there was a real commitment to planning, in 1985 serious statistical deficiencies and shortages of professional personnel continued to hamper planning.

The country's first formal plan, the Three-Year Development Plan, covered the period April 1971 to March 1974 and relied heavily on technical assistance from China, the Soviet Union, and the latter's allies. It was essentially a public investment program, financed primarily by foreign aid. The initial investment target was YD40 million but was reduced later to YD32 million (in 1970-71 prices). Actual plan expenditures amounted to YD25 million, an implementation rate of 78 percent of the lowered target. Investments were reasonably balanced to develop the country economically and socially. Implementation was remarkable in view of the low state of development and the shortages of skilled man-power.

The First Five-Year Plan (FFYP) covered the period April 1974 through December 1978. It actually covered 4.75 years because of a change in the fiscal year (FY—see Glossary) in 1976. The plan was prepared with foreign technical assistance and was much more comprehensive than its predecessor, including macroeconomic goals, sector analyses, and production targets for sectors and major commodities. The planners set the initial investment target at YD75 million, but they revised the target upward several times to YD276 million. Actual investment was YD196 million, 71 percent of the revised goal. Major actual investments were 35 percent to agriculture and fishing, 19 percent to industry, and 27 percent to transport and communications. Foreign aid provided 74 percent of the plan expenditures. The plan achieved substantial results in strengthening the economic and social infrastructure and laying a base for expanded production, but the output of the economy was not commensurate with the investments made.

The Second Five-Year Plan (SFYP), in effect from 1981 to 1985, was originally drafted to run from 1979 to 1983. It was revised to 1981-85 in response to an appeal by the Council of Arab Economic Unity to Arab countries to synchronize their planning periods. The years 1979 and 1980 had annual plans that were used largely to complete projects under the FFYP.

The SFYP contained ambitious goals. The investment target was YD508 million (US$1.5 billion), representing a substantial increase of annual investments in real terms compared with the considerable investments made since 1974. Foreign aid was scheduled to finance about 70 percent of planned investments. The rate of implementation in 1981 and 1982 was 76 percent of that planned. The SFYP shifted investment priorities from the FFYP. The shares of planned investments in the SFYP were agriculture and fishing, 17 percent; industry, 26 percent; transport and communications, 18 percent; and such social services as housing (18 percent), education, health, and water and sewerage, 35 percent. The floods in 1982 caused revisions of investment allocations toward agriculture and transportation.

The SFYP had even more ambitious growth targets; some economists regarded the goals as unrealistic, based on past experience. Real GDP was to grow by an average of 10.5 percent a year, agriculture by 9 percent a year, industry by nearly 14 percent a year, and exports by over 13 percent a year, as examples. These were far higher than had been achieved in the past. Estimates of the financing that was expected to be provided from profits of public sector enterprises appeared overly optimistic. Moreover, foreign economists questioned whether the construction industry, particularly that in the public sector, could meet the demands of the large investment program. Economists expected results to be more modest than those planned.

Low productivity of the economy, particularly in the public and cooperative sectors, was one of the most important problems confronting the country's leaders. Low productivity had many causes, including shortages of trained manpower, poor maintenance of equipment, lack of spare parts, and inexperienced and inadequate managers. The limited data available indicated that the private sector performed better in this regard than did the public sector. In addition, an inadequate incentive system lowered productivity. In the early 1980s prices and wages were adjusted in attempts to reward greater production. These constraints were often compounded by excessive government controls that created distortions and stifled initiative. The economy had a potential for a substantially greater output, particularly after the large investments of more than a decade; by 1985 the management of the economy had not found the way to realize the potential. Until the leaders did, improvements in the population's standard of living would likely be modest at best.

Since independence budget officials have struggled continuously to obtain revenues to finance growing expenditures. The task was difficult because of the country's early stage of development and the low income of the population, but the tax base was broadened, and collection improved. Between 1977 and 1981 budget revenues rose at an annual rate of 26 percent. In 1982 tax revenues amounted to 32 percent of GNP, a high level of taxation in a country so poor (see table 11, Appendix). Taxes on foreign trade were the largest producer of revenues; excise taxes, particularly on cigarettes and petroleum products, contributed to the dominance of indirect taxes in total tax revenues. South Yemen had no general sales tax. Direct taxes were primarily on corporations and were largely from public enterprises, even though some made no profits to tax. Individual income tax revenues were minor.

Nontax revenues amounted to 43 percent in 1981, a substantial part of government's fiscal income. Foreign grants were a welcome but undependable form of budget support; grants supplementing current domestic revenues were the equivalent of US$50 million in 1982. Public enterprises paid the 37.5-percent corporate tax on profits; 25 percent of the after-tax surplus was transferred to current budget nontax revenues and 50 percent of the surplus to a development fund to finance plan expenditures. In 1982 transfers from public corporations amounted to YD18 million and came mostly from financial institutions. Surpluses from other public enterprises were small and had exhibited little growth. Increased productivity and profitability of public sector business was imperative to meet financing requirements for the plan.

Budget expenditures rose by an average of 22 percent a year between 1977 and 1982 and amounted to 93 percent of GNP in the latter year. Current expenditures rose faster than development investments because of the growth of recurring costs, such as salaries of teachers and maintenance of completed projects. In 1981 current expenditures rose an unusual 46 percent because of increased defense spending and consumption subsidies. Development expenditures have been financed largely by foreign aid, and most development projects were not started until the external financing was arranged. Development investments represented an unusually high share of government expenditures (46 percent in 1982), reflecting the government's effort to enlarge the economy and improve the population's standard of living.

The inability of revenues to catch up to expenditures resulted in budget deficits that became alarming in the early 1980s. In 1982 the budget deficit amounted to nearly the equivalent of US$306 million, or 41 percent of GNP; the actual deficit may have been somewhat smaller because revenue figures were incomplete. Part of the increased deficit was caused by unusual spending following the 1982 floods. Officials were aware of the inflationary pressures caused by the government's turning to the central bank for financing budget deficits, but it remained to be seen if expenditures could be contained or public sector productivity and profits increased.

Most of South Yemen's foreign borrowing for development has been on highly concessional terms. The public external debt in mid-1984 amounted to a little over US$1 billion, mostly owed to the Soviet Union and other communist countries. Debt service payments were US$8 million in 1981 and US$15 million in 1982, only 4.5 percent of total foreign exchange earnings from the export of goods and services (including workers' remittances) in the latter year. Debt service was projected to increase in the 1980s. South Yemen, however, had to request debt rescheduling in the early 1980s, which posed questions about the country's use of borrowed funds and its ability to repay.

Foreign aid has been crucial to South Yemen's development. Between 1974 and 1982 grants—mostly from Arab countries—totaled at least US$524 million. Between 1967 and 1984 foreign credits amounted to about US$1.7 billion, most of which had already been used. The Soviet Union was by far the largest source of aid credits, accounting for probably over two-fifths. China and East European countries supplied perhaps another one-fifth. Arab countries, including their development fund agencies, provided another one-fifth. The remainder was supplied by a number of bilateral and multilateral sources, including the World Bank group. South Yemen officials expected external aid to finance about 70 percent of SFYP development expenditures, of which about half would come from communist countries, one-third from Arab countries, and the remainder from various noncommunist nations and international institutions. In 1981 and 1982 the inflow of aid was less than the planners expected, forcing the government to increase domestic borrowing from the banking system. In 1982 the amount of foreign aid declined, and early indications suggested that it declined again in 1983. Should foreign aid stagnate or continue to decline, South Yemen's development effort would confront critical difficulties.

Labor Force

Labor force data were largely estimates by the CSO and were based on assumptions and projections. Little reliable survey or census evidence existed to provide a base or means of checking labor force estimates. The lack of accurate data hampered the planning process.

The estimated domestic labor force expanded from 323,000 in 1973 to 468,000 in 1982, an average increase of 4.2 percent a year (see table 12, Appendix). Farming was by far the largest source of employment, supporting 42 percent of the population in 1982. CSO estimated a continuous growth of the farm work force in spite of substantial migration of workers from rural areas to towns and abroad. Construction showed the most rapid growth of employment, 11.8 percent a year, which was considerably higher than the increase in its value added. Construction absorbed many of the farm workers who migrated to urban areas. The private sector employed nearly 60 percent of the labor force, while the public and cooperative sectors employed about 40 percent.

Women were a small proportion, probably about one-fifth, of the work force, but their share was increasing. Part of the reason for the greater employment of women was their increased farming activities, for women filled in for men who temporarily sought higher-paying work elsewhere. Another factor was that the government provided legal equality to women and encouraged their participation in the work force, particularly in nontraditional jobs. In the early 1980s women represented about one-third of the industrial labor force, and nearly half of the new employees of the Ministry of Industry were women. But tradition dies slowly, and South Yemen's heritage would probably permit only gradual growth of the number of women in nontraditional workplaces (see Women, this ch.).

In the mid-1980s some general characteristics of the work force were known. Literacy remained low, and shortages existed for almost every skill. The government established adult literacy classes, vocational schools, and training programs at home and abroad to upgrade the labor force, but a fundamental change would take time. The migration of workers abroad eliminated unemployment and probably unwanted underemployment. There was, in fact, a labor shortage, and in the early 1980s South Yemen was importing labor. In 1982 the number of expatriate workers probably was around 5,000, largely in construction. The Ministry of Construction employed over 2,800 expatriates in 1982 out of its total of about 10,000 workers.

Little was known for certain about South Yemenis working abroad. The total number of migrant workers abroad was thought to be close to 100,000 in 1982, more than one-fifth of the domestic labor force. Most were young men who were primarily employed on the Arabian Peninsula, particularly in Saudi Arabia. The net outflow of workers appeared to peak in the late 1970s. In the early 1980s the number of workers abroad was probably diminishing slowly, but remittances home continued to climb, perhaps amounting to US$467 million in 1982. Workers' remittances were largely used to build family dwellings because of the scarcity of other investment and consumption possibilities. Moreover, some recipients of remittances appeared to opt for not working while the money lasted. Government controls appeared to have largely suppressed the effect on domestic wage scales of the large inflow of remittances, unlike North Yemen (see Labor Force, ch. 2). The remittances used in housing, however, produced a shortage of building workers and an increase of wages in the private sector, which attracted construction workers away from public sector firms.

Agriculture

By the mid-1980s farming and fishing had failed to produce as expected or commensurate with the investments made in the sector. In 1982 agriculture, including fishing, employed 44 percent of the labor force but contributed only 12 percent of GDP. Stagnation in farm output since the early 1970s required increasing imports of food for the rapidly expanding population. The country produced nearly all of the vegetables consumed but only about 30 to 40 percent of the food grains. The main food imports were wheat and flour, rice, sugar, and milk powder. By 1983 food imports alone amounted to about 40 percent of GDP. In 1982 the total value of farm output (in 1980 prices) was less than one-third of the value of food imports.

Farming was difficult. The rugged terrain received very little rainfall; precipitation was usually so meager that rain-fed cropping was almost precluded. Nearly all cultivation was based on irrigation in some 12 scattered wadis. In the early 1980s the potentially cultivable land amounted to about 200,000 hectares, less than 1 percent of the country's area. The acreage actually cropped, however, was usually in the neighborhood of 70,000 hectares annually. Between 40,000 and 70,000 hectares could be irrigated by the runoff from the precipitation that fell on the mountains, the acreage depending on the amount of runoff. The western part of the country depended primarily on this spate irrigation. The country had no rivers with continuous flows and few perennial streams. Well irrigation watered about 20,000 hectares, largely in the eastern part of the country. A shallow aquifer under the Wadi Hadhramaut has provided water for cultivation for thousands of years, but the water has a high salt content. A large, deeper aquifer contains better water and will allow for substantially greater extraction in the future but at higher costs because of the greater depths of drilling and pumping.

During most of the 1970s the government allocated more than one-fifth of development expenditure to agriculture, primarily to irrigation projects. Some new land was brought under cultivation, and irrigation on fields already cultivated was improved as a result of the investments. By the mid-1980s the possibility of bringing new land under cultivation was extremely limited except for a small amount in the Wadi Hadhramaut. Irrigation projects in the 1980s largely improved the irrigation on fields already cultivated. About half of the water was lost between the source and the fields, for example. Moreover, disastrous floods in March 1982 caused considerable damage to existing irrigation works and caused severe crop and livestock losses. In 1985 work was continuing on rehabilitation of damaged irrigation facilities. The need to improve the operation of the irrigation systems, particularly those dependent on the runoff of rainfall, was underscored by droughts in 1983 and 1984.

Soon after independence the new country's leaders began to reorganize the agricultural setting. An agrarian reform law enacted in 1968 was not implemented, but in

1970 a second agrarian reform was proclaimed that was quickly implemented. This law confiscated the lands of former rulers and former government officials and limited individual holdings to eight hectares of irrigated land and 16 hectares of rain-fed land and double these limits for a family. Land in family and religious trusts (waqf land) was included. The government took over land in excess of the limits plus so-called deadland, i.e., marginal land that had not been cultivated for a specified period. Party-encouraged uprisings by tenants caused some landowners to flee. By 1972 large holdings by individuals were essentially gone.

The government retained title to lands acquired under the land reform. Part of the land was made into state farms. Use of the remainder that was cultivable was assigned to cooperatives. In 1972 the cooperative law laid down rules for various kinds of cooperatives. Farming cooperatives encompassed both the beneficiaries of land reform, who had to join cooperatives in order to be able to farm the land, and many of the small farmer-owners who were brought into the cooperatives, using their land as shares. Some of the latter continued to farm their land individually, paying for inputs and services from the cooperatives and selling their output to the cooperatives. Individual private farms became few and were located largely in remote areas. During the 1970s government policy attempted to have farmers cultivate their land collectively in the cooperatives and to share the income.

In the early 1980s about 60 percent of the value added by farming came from 61 cooperatives, about 20 percent from 47 state farms, and about 20 percent from private farms. Cooperatives had become the main form of farming. In 1981 the 61 cooperative farms, with nearly 44,000 members, had a total of 159,000 hectares of land, 103,000 hectares of which were cultivable, and about 46,000 hectares actually under cultivation. In 1981 there were 47 state farms, 24 of which raised crops. Seven state farms raised poultry by modern commercial practices, and four were dairy farms. The remaining state farms were devoted to special purposes, such as seed production, research, and trial production (bananas, for example). In 1981 the 47 state farms had a total of 16,000 hectares, of which nearly 11,000 hectares were cultivable, and almost 6,000 hectares were actually cultivated. State farms paid wages to employees, including full-time and seasonal workers. More than two-thirds of the water for cooperative farms came from spate irrigation; wells supplied 72 percent of the irrigation for state farms. In order to benefit from drilled wells and pumps, farmers were required to belong to a cooperative farm.

A number of additional measures were instituted during the 1970s to bring farming within the centrally planned and controlled economy. All inputs were supplied by public sector organizations at government-set prices. In the early 1980s fertilizer prices to farmers were high compared with import prices, and the use of commercial fertilizers was quite low; the sale of insecticides or weed killers appeared nonexistent in the data available. Inputs or credit for their purchase was not always available at the time required. Farm output also was sold to public sector organizations at government-set prices for distribution and sale by these organizations to consumers at controlled prices. In addition, production decisions were mostly made at levels substantially removed from those who farmed.

Machine rental stations were established in agricultural areas essentially to supply machinery to cooperatives. State farms usually had their own equipment. The rental stations supplied equipment mostly for land preparation and threshing and also maintained the equipment and pumps owned by cooperative farms. Rental prices were insufficient to cover the stations' costs. Farmers complained of delays in the arrival of equipment, which could be critical on land watered by spate irrigation. By the early 1980s some economists opined that the rental stations did not appear to be the most efficient or effective way to make equipment available to farmers.

Many factors contributed to the slow expansion of farm output in the 1970s besides occasional periods of adverse weather. Rising wage rates and poor management reduced production and profits of state farms. Collective farming and rigid cropping quotas adversely affected cooperative farms. Low state purchase prices for farm produce diminished incentives for most farmers. The supply of inputs and marketing of farm produce encountered various difficulties. Various taxes and levies produced disincentives to the farmers affected.

By the late 1970s officials recognized that a more flexible approach was needed in agriculture. Starting in 1979 the prices paid for farm produce were adjusted upward. By 1982 most farm prices were above import prices; the main exceptions were cotton, bananas, dates, and tobacco. In addition, after 1980 private and cooperative farmers could sell up to 40 percent of certain basic vegetables on the open market for up to 50 percent above the official prices. Some state farms were converted to cooperatives. Collective farming in cooperatives was relaxed; by 1982 nearly half of the cooperatives had no group farming, and only two cooperatives relied completely on collective farming. Cooperative farmers using pumps were usually organized in small groups, such as two to four families. Cooperatives were beginning to have their own equipment instead of relying on machinery rental stations. In 1983 the government commissioned a study by foreign Arab experts of the operations of state farms, which presumably would guide future policy toward state farms. Changes in the taxation of farm output were being tried experimentally in some localities to determine their effect on production. Efforts were also under way to improve agricultural research and the extension services, which had been inadequate in the 1970s.

The effect of the liberalizing measures was unclear in mid-1985. The value of crop production jumped 64 percent between 1980 and 1981 as a result of favorable weather and the government's effort to stimulate production, although the effect of either was unmeasurable. The value of crop production dropped sharply, however, in 1982 because of severe floods that left the value of crop production only 7 percent above the level in 1980. More recent statistical data were unavailable in mid-1985 to determine if the government's policy changes had induced a more favorable upward trend in crop production, but Western economists viewed the liberalizing measures as a step in the right direction. The question was whether the policy changes went far enough to ease the constraints on farming.

Changes in cropping patterns accompanied shifts in policy. In 1982 sorghum remained the main crop, but for reasons unknown the acreage devoted to it increased sharply in 1981, although falling back in 1982, presumably because of the floods (see table 13, Appendix). In contrast, wheat, the cultivation of which was completely mechanized, declined after the mid-1970s, although production declined more slowly than acreage because of the improvement of yields. The area devoted to fodder increased sharply in the late 1970s, largely because it was exempt from the production tax. The government encouraged meat production, and fodder was a primary input; the policy was successful but at the expense of lower production of food grains. Cotton acreage and production declined after 1975 in response to the government's low purchase price. A shift toward production of high-value fruits and vegetables developed as consumer incomes and tastes changed. Although the country was essentially self-sufficient in vegetables, the average diet was deficient in fruits and vegetables. Undoubtedly some qat, a mood-altering plant long used by Yemenis (the main cash crop in North Yemen) was grown in South Yemen, but few data were available (see Qat, this ch; Qat, ch. 2).

Raising livestock has always been an important part of agricultural activity. Most rural households maintained animals, and in the mid-1980s perhaps as much as 10 percent of the population remained beduin, herding mostly sheep and goats but also some camels to feed off the sparse natural forage. Animals provided draft power as well as meat, milk, fiber, and hides. After the agrarian reform, state farms raising dairy cattle and commercial poultry were added. Livestock raising has flourished compared with cropping, perhaps because a substantial part remained a private activity outside of collectivization. The value of animal products in total food production rose from 37 percent in 1975 to 54 percent in 1982 if the value of sharply rising fodder production was subtracted from food crop production. Between 1980 and 1982 the value of animal production increased 32 percent (crop production, 7 percent) compared with the planned increase of 27 percent anticipated by 1985. In 1981 the estimated number of livestock (with 1973 estimates in parentheses) were cattle, 93,000 (80,000); sheep and goats, 2.2 million (2 million); and camels, 93,000 (100,000). Nonetheless, of the total animals slaughtered (domestic and imported), imported live animals increased from 40 percent in 1975 to 65 percent in 1981. Clearly the supply of domestically produced meat was falling behind consumer demand.

Production of chickens on modern, commercial poultry farms rose far more rapidly than other portions of the agricultural sector. Investments in commercial poultry farms began in the early 1970s, and by 1982 there were seven state farms specializing in such production. The output of chicken meat by the Poultry Development Corporation rose from 22 tons in 1974 to 570 tons in 1982, and egg production rose from 2 million to 27 million in the same years. By 1982 poultry meat and eggs contributed more than 10 percent of the total value of animal products.

Fish are South Yemen's richest known natural resource. Studies indicated that South Yemen's coastal waters were one of the world's most important fishing areas. Strong winds at particular times of the year cause a welling up to the surface of cool, nutrient-rich waters from deep offshore, causing a growth of plants and plankton on which offshore fish feed. Yemenis for centuries have been able to catch a variety of fish close to shore in small boats. The studies indicated the potential fish catch was about 200,000 to 300,000 tons annually. The actual catch, however, had not been up to expectations or to the investment made in boats and auxiliary facilities.

Soon after independence the government set about the rapid development of the fishing industry. In 1970 a public corporation was established to promote and carry on fishing and processing; in 1977 these activities were elevated to the Ministry of Fish Wealth. By 1985 the ministry had under its jurisdiction at least four public corporations operating fishing boats and processing facilities. During the 1970s substantial investments were made in commercial fishing boats, ports, ice and refrigeration facilities, and processing plants. By 1983 the modern commercial fishing fleet consisted of 24 vessels ranging from 200 to 2,000 gross tons. There were two canning factories and two fish-meal plants (capacity 650 tons per day), while another 500-ton-per-day fish-meal plant was under construction. About 20 cold storage plants (capacity 4,250 tons) were spread around the country for storage and distribution of iced and frozen fish.

In the early 1970s the government centralized control of the fish industry. The large, modern, commercial fishing boats were owned and operated by a public sector company. Traditional fishermen, of which in the early 1980s there were about 5,000 in some 40 fishing villages along the 1,500 kilometers of coastline, were organized into cooperatives and used traditional boats, many of which had been motorized. A public corporation purchased, stored, processed, and sold all of the catch of cooperatives, private fishermen, and the commercial fleet. In addition, the government entered into joint ventures with the Soviet Union whereby Soviet fishing boats (about 26 in the early 1980s) fished South Yemeni waters, for which the latter received 32 percent of the catch. Joint ventures were formed with two private Japanese fishing companies, one of which required annual payments in foreign currency to South Yemen for the fishing rights. The government has received technical assistance and financial aid from several sources in developing the fishing industry.

Fish production rose fairly regularly until 1977 but dropped in 1978 and 1979. In 1980 the fish catch rose substantially, reaching a peak of nearly 98,000 tons. In 1981 it dropped to 80,000 tons; in 1982 it fell to 70,000 tons (the latest data available in mid-1985). In 1982 the fish catch included sardines, red snapper, mackerel, tuna, rock cod, and shark; small quantities of high-value cuttlefish, lobster, and shrimp were also caught. In 1982 the public commercial fleet accounted for only 7 percent of the total catch; cooperatives, 30 percent; private fishermen, 21 percent; mixed foreign and South Yemeni enterprises, 4 percent; and foreign firms, 38 percent. Foreign fishing boats were the only ones to record larger catches in 1981 and 1982. Data in the 1980s suggested there was overfishing in the 1970s of lobster, cuttlefish, mackerel, sardines, and some of the deep-water fish sufficient to deplete stocks of these species. Part of the overfishing was attributable to the foreign vessels. In 1980 the export of fish and fish products amounted to 6,700 tons worth about US$17 million (nearly half of total exports of South Yemeni products); the bulk of exports in terms of value were lobster, cuttlefish, and red snapper, which went to Japan and Singapore, where they were packaged for distribution and sale.

By the early 1980s the fishing industry had many problems. The attempt to add modern fishing vessels, processing plants, and marketing systems rapidly outpaced the availability of trained manpower to manage, operate, and service the new equipment and operations. The result was great underutilization of the equipment available and little or negative returns on the large investments that had been made. Poor planning also contributed to investments that were not needed at the time, and may never be needed, because the availability of inputs was not sufficiently investigated. By 1985 it was not clear what would be done with the fish-meal plants, which essentially were closed, and the canning factories, all of which had operated far below capacity.

The bulk of investments and attention went to developing the public sector fishing, processing, and distribution system; the traditional fishermen in cooperatives received little attention or assistance. The low prices paid for fish to fishermen in any sector proved a disincentive to increase production in the 1970s. By the 1980s government-controlled prices paid for fish were being raised, and private and cooperative fishermen could sell a portion of their catch in local markets at prices 50 percent above official prices. Economists suggested that the decline in the statistics for the cooperatives' fish catch in the early 1980s may have reflected a greater diversion to local markets. Moreover, the public corporation that bought fish from cooperatives was attempting to regularize pickup by truck or boat because fish spoil quickly. By the early 1980s the data suggested that more fishermen were being attracted to cooperatives than leaving, reversing the trend of the 1970s. The government was also acknowledging the importance of cooperative and private fishermen, who were responsible for over half of the fish catch in 1982, by building and improving access roads, facilitating boat and equipment repair, and providing other services to traditional fishing villages.

Since independence government officials have had high expectations for the growth of production from farming and fishing. Considerable foreign assistance, both financial and technical, was contributed to raise productivity and output, but by the early 1980s the results were disappointing, largely because of the rigidities and disincentives of the centrally controlled system. Government policy, however, exhibited a pragmatism and flexibility in the liberalizing measures introduced since the late 1970s. It remained to be seen if the measures were sufficient to raise agriculture's contribution to the national economy and the low incomes of the large part of the population engaged in farming and fishing.

Industry

South Yemen was at an early stage of industrialization. Industry, including mining, utilities, and manufacturing, contributed 11 percent of GDP and employed 11 percent of the labor force in 1982. Most industry was small and the bulk of it in the private sector, consisting of repair shops, bakeries, and artisans. Statistics were sparse and frequently contradictory. Physical output data between 1980 and 1982, for example, strongly suggested a decline in industrial production, but other data and observers reported an average 10-percent-a-year growth of industrial value added (in constant prices) in 1981 and 1982. Such discrepancies made it difficult to be certain even of trends.

Energy

In mid-1985 the country had no domestic sources of commercial energy. Firewood, agricultural wastes, and dung provided fuel for some rural inhabitants, primarily for cooking, but it was uncertain to what extent. Coal deposits and a little oil had been discovered, but by mid-1985 these finds had not been found commercially exploitable. Some geological structures looked promising for oil or gas deposits, and several foreign oil companies were searching for oil; officials were hopeful that oil and gas would be found because it would significantly affect the economy's prospects. But in 1985 the country remained completely dependent on imported oil for commercial energy.

In 1982 domestic consumption of petroleum products was slightly above 600,000 tons, accounting for nearly one-quarter of total imports. Electric power generation and other public sector industry consumed about 36 percent (mostly in the form of fuel oil); public sector transport, 24 percent (largely diesel fuel); fishing and agriculture (state farms and cooperatives), 22 percent; and private consumers, 18 percent (in a variety of products). Government-controlled activities dominated consumption. In the late 1970s and early 1980s consumption of petroleum products increased by about 5 percent a year. South Yemen's per capita consumption of energy was low—more than one-third below that of the average of developing countries.

The Ministry of Planning was responsible for overall planning and investment allocation in the energy sector. The Ministry of Industry was responsible for the technical aspects and implementation of plans for the energy sector. Under the ministry were the Petroleum and Minerals Board, which was responsible for all activities in these fields and which was assisted by several offices, e.g., mineral and petroleum exploration departments, and public corporations, such as the Aden Refinery Corporation (ARC) and a company that distributed petroleum products. The Public Corporation for Electric Power (PCEP) under the Ministry of Industry had responsibility for the generation, transmission, and distribution of electricity in the country's main population centers.

Local distribution of petroleum products was by the Yemen National Oil Company (YNOC), a public sector corporation under the Ministry of Industry. The government set prices for the various products, and after 1979 these prices were raised several times to reduce subsidy costs in the budget. Increasing the domestic fuel prices without raising charges for electricity and prices for farm produce and fish created financial difficulties for the power company, state farms, and farming and fishing cooperatives. The government had to raise prices for their products so the organizations could pay their fuel bills. By 1982 prices for gasoline and bottled gas, primarily sold to private consumers, were above international prices, which subsidized prices less than import and distribution costs for products, particularly fuel oil, mostly used by the public sector. The price structure for petroleum products still contained disguised subsidies, did not encourage economy in the use of energy, and precluded the government from obtaining substantial budget revenues by taxing consumption of petroleum products, as most other countries did.

PCEP was formed in 1969 to bring the supply of electric power under one organization and to extend the availability of electricity. By the mid-1980s considerable success had been achieved despite serious constraints and considerable unfulfilled demand. The main system, serving a large area around Aden with interconnections between generating units, grew from about 38 megawatts of capacity in 1972 to over 120 megawatts in 1984. PCEP also provided electricity to several other large towns and had 60-percent interest in some other local facilities. In 1984 the country had an estimated 166 megawatts of capacity, of which PCEP had control of about 140 megawatts. Individuals and some municipalities had small generators, and ARC had its own power supply. There was a substantial loss of electricty between generators and consumers. In 1982 about 29 percent of the population had access to public power; the goal was 44 percent by 1985, consisting of 83 percent of the urban population and 22 percent of the rural, although many of the latter had limited electricity from small private generators. By 1986 two additional electric projects were expected to be operating in the Wadi Hadhramaut and in five towns east of the port of Al Mukalla. In 1984 agreement was reportedly reached to build a 50-megawatt steam power and desalination plant near Aden, using technical and financial aid from the Soviet Union. In 1982 electric power generation was 270 million kilowatt-hours compared with 149 million kilowatt-hours in 1972 (see table 14, Appendix).

Mining and Manufacturing

Although the country had only been partially explored for resources by 1985, no significant deposits of minerals had been found except limestone and clay for cement and silica for glass. Deposits of coal, iron ore, copper, gold, and titanium had so far not proved to be economically exploitable. By 1983 quarrying of local marble had not been decided. In 1984 the government determined to build a 350,000-ton-a-year cement plant to exploit local materials and to end dependence on imports of cement. A plant to produce glass and/or ceramics from local materials was still under consideration.

Manufacturing faced serious constraints. The few natural resources available forced industrialization to focus largely on processing farm produce and fish and on substituting local production for imports where it could be done economically. The very small market, including relatively low incomes, a dispersed population, and an inadequate transportation system, prohibited economies of scale in most manufacturing processes. The low skill levels in the work force and the extreme shortage of managers made it difficult to organize new production processes or keep existing production operating. Maintenance was usually inadequate. The focus on public ownership of the means of production restricted the contribution from the general population of funds, ideas, leadership, and risk-taking. The government's shortage of funds and foreign exchange limited investments in manufacturing. A considerable amount of government investment had to be devoted to building the infrastructure of the country, such as roads, ports, water systems, communications, electric power, schools, and health facilities.

In spite of the constraints, manufacturing appeared to grow rapidly. The gross value of manufacturing output (in 1980 prices) rose from YD25.8 million in 1973 to YD58.1 million in 1982, an average increase of 9 percent a year in the 1970s and 10 percent a year in the 1980-82 period. Most of the growth occurred in the public sector, resulting in a sharp shift in the structure of manufacturing. The share of the public sector in the gross output of manufacturing increased from about 6 percent in 1973 to 59 percent in 1982 (including the government's takeover of the Aden refinery). By 1982 the private sector accounted for only 26 percent of gross output, although it comprised the bulk of the manufacturing units and employed most of the industrial workers. In addition to the public sector, there were several fair-sized plants in the mixed sector where the government owned the majority of shares but private investors held as much as 49 percent of the equity; the cigarette factory, for example, had both private and public shareholders. In June 1982 the mixed sector contributed 14 percent of gross manufacturing output.

The structure of manufacturing also changed as new industries were added. In 1982 processing of food and fish products remained the most important, contributing 24 percent of the gross output of medium- and large-scale manufacturing—the same as in 1973. Oil refining declined, however, from 21 percent in 1973 to 18 percent in 1982. The shares of textiles, leather, salt extraction, and metal products and ship repairs also declined in varying degrees between 1973 and 1982. Much of the change in structure of manufacturing was the result of plants producing what the South Yemenis called chemicals, such as paints, plastic products, and plastic foam; chemicals' share increased from 2 percent in 1973 to 15 percent in 1982. The proportion of manufacturing output from woodpaper-printing and from building materials, such as cement blocks, increased more modestly.

The country's largest manufacturing enterprise was ARC. British Petroleum (BP) built the refinery in 1954 to take advantage of the port's location relative to Middle East oil fields and partly to bunker the large number of ships stopping in Aden when using the Suez Canal. The processing capacity of the refinery was 8.5 million tons of crude oil a year, and it operated close to capacity until the canal was damaged and closed during the June 1967 War. The early design of the refinery resulted in about half of the output being fuel oil. After closure of the canal and development elsewhere of more efficient refining processes, BP shifted refining operations away from Aden. Refinery production dropped from over 6 million tons in 1969 to about 1.6 million tons in 1976.

The refinery was not nationalized in 1969 when most other large enterprises, foreign and domestic, were nationalized because of BP's payments for payroll, taxes, and local purchases. But as the operations and payments declined, the government and BP agreed to the government's taking over the refinery in 1977. Because the refinery no longer had any value on BP's books, South Yemen's compensation amounted to under US$10 million for the mobile assets. BP agreed to remain as advisers and to train South Yemenis for two years.

Under South Yemen ownership, the refinery engaged primarily in refining crude oil for a fee for foreign countries, such as Kuwait, the Soviet Union, and Iran. The crude oil and products refined for foreign countries were not entered in South Yemen's import and export statistics. The refinery also produced most of the petroleum products for the domestic market. Economists estimated that refinery operations had to be above 3.4 million tons a year to produce a profit. In 1978 and 1979 throughput at the refinery was about 1.8 million tons a year. As a result of increased refining for Iran because of damage to its refineries in the Iran-Iraq War, throughput rose to 3.9 million tons in 1980 and 3.2 million tons in 1981. In 1984 refinery throughput was expected to be about 4.2 million tons. Officials apparently expected the operating level to remain above the break-even point, for contracts reportedly were signed with an Italian firm in 1984 to undertake some of the long-postponed improvements in the refinery. The improvements reportedly would include more white products (gasoline, kerosene, and diesel fuel), some liquid petroleum gas (for bottled gas for household use), and 100,000 tons of asphalt a year.

There were several other major government-owned manufacturing plants, mostly financed and built under aid agreements. A Chinese-supplied textile mill had a capacity of about 7 million meters of cloth a year and employed about 1,300 workers at capacity. There were bottlenecks in the mill and in the early 1980s modernization measures were planned. Other public sector manufacturing included a flour mill, a factory for dairy products, a tomato-paste cannery, a fish cannery, and plants to produce fish meal (although they may have ceased operation by 1985). Most public sector plants operated at a low level of capacity utilization. Part of the reason was often insufficient raw materials, but the shortage of capable managers and trained personnel and inadequate maintenance were additional important factors.

Although the general focus of industrial development was on the public sector, officials increasingly recognized that the private sector was also needed. In 1981 an investment law was enacted that provided incentives to private investors. Critics found the law imprecise as to the benefits a project would receive and described some of the benefits as too short-term. Official approval of projects appeared to require too much time. Those criticisms, as well as perhaps skepticism of the government's interest in private investment, limited the response. By 1983 there had been little increase in private investment, and only a few projects had been proposed.

Banking and Monetary Policy

At independence the new regime inherited a currency board, which had been formed in 1964 during the period of federation and which was responsible only for the issuance of a new currency (Yemeni dinar—see Glossary). In 1968 the board's central bank functions were broadened to include managing external resources, supervising commercial banking, and discounting and selling various bills and notes. In 1971 it became the guarantor of government borrowing. In 1972 the board was renamed the Bank of Yemen and became the country's central bank.

In 1969 the eight banks operating in the country (seven of which were foreign owned) were nationalized and formed into the National Bank of Yemen. It became the sole commercial bank, providing the government with a monopoly over the credit system. Foreign trade and exchange controls effectively regulated most dealings in foreign currencies. Credit was allocated by the plan and official direction. Traders and businessmen in the private sector had access to seasonal and longer-term credit (for establishing or expanding a business), but the amount of loans to the private sector was unknown. Cooperatives maintained their accounts with the National Bank and presumably obtained loans where they could be justified. Individual members appeared to obtain their credit from the cooperative. The financial standing of individual cooperatives probably was the main determinant of the availability of rural credit.

Unexpected expansion of credit occurred primarily when plans were not fulfilled. In 1981 and 1982, for example, when foreign aid and public enterprise profits were less than expected, government development expenditures were maintained, requiring deficit financing from the central bank. The role of the central bank greatly increased while that of the National Bank was greatly reduced; the actual roles of the two banks were almost the reverse of that planned.

The money supply has been expanding rapidly since independence. Growing budget deficits and the inflow of workers' remittances were the primary causes. Part of the expansion was necessary, for the economy was increasingly monetized. Another part was inflationary.

After the early 1970s officials faced inflationary pressures. A significant part of the inflation was imported because of the rise of world prices, but budget deficits and workers' remittances also contributed. Inflation was more pronounced between 1973 and 1975. By 1976 price controls were strengthened, and substantial workers' remittances permitted expanded imports to satisfy the demand for goods. After the mid-1970s the rate of inflation was kept at moderate levels, standing at about 4 percent in 1981, 8 percent in 1982, and probably about 5 percent in 1983. These moderate rates, however, did not necessarily represent a lessening of inflationary pressures; controlled prices, shortages and, at times, rationing indicated suppressed inflation.

Foreign Trade

The harsh fact of South Yemen's existence up to 1985 was that the country had few commodities that could be sold abroad. Exports from the domestic economy showed a slow growth after 1970, much of which was attributable to rising world prices rather than an increase in quantity of

Ali Nasir Muhammad al Hasani, chief of state in 1985

Workers in a leather factory

Photos courtesy Arab Perspectives, the League of Arab States

Zarook (dhow) in Aden port

Men repairing their dhows

Photos courtesy Aramco World Magazine

Mud skyscrapers in the Hadhramaut
Courtesy P. Darles, UNESCO Features

exportable products. In 1981 (the latest data available in 1985) exports of domestic products amounted to the equivalent of US$ 18.8 million, of which 31 percent were fish products and 45 percent a variety of products too extensive to list (see table 15, Appendix). Lint cotton had been important in earlier years but was not in 1981. Other exports, in minor amounts, included tobacco, salt, and hides. In addition, the country reexported about US$3 million worth of goods (about one-fifth of the amount in 1969 and 1970), apart from those moving out of the Free Trade Zone at the port of Aden (which did not enter into trade statistics). Main markets for exports were Japan, North Yemen, and Singapore.

Balance of Payments

Another harsh fact of South Yemen's existence was that the country needed more commodities than were available from the domestic economy. The need to import included such commodities as food grains and meat, which the country produced but not in sufficient quantities to satisfy increasing demand. Imports rose by 18.5 percent a year, far faster than the economy grew, between 1973 and 1981, amounting to US$673 million in the latter year. At least some aid imports were excluded from the statistics. In 1981 food and live animals represented 29 percent of total imports; petroleum products, 23 percent; machinery and transport equipment, 22 percent; other manufactured goods, 12 percent; and chemicals, 12 percent (see table 16, Appendix). The major food imports were wheat (including flour), rice, dairy products, and sugar. Imports came predominantly from noncommunist industralized countries, of which Japan was the most important, supplying 15 percent of total imports. Western Europe accounted for at least 27 percent of imports, Britain and the Netherlands being the most important. The United States had little if any trade with South Yemen. Communist countries—primarily China and the Soviet Union—supplied 12 percent of imports. Arab countries accounted for 28 percent of imports, most of which were oil.

The large and growing imbalance between exports and imports—US$727 million in 1982—placed South Yemen in a vulnerable balance of payments position (see table 17, Appendix). The diminished earnings from the port of Aden after independence required alternative sources of foreign exchange to sustain rising imports for consumption and investment. Private transfers, primarily workers' remittances, became the major source of foreign exchange, rising from about US$34 million in 1973 to US$467 million in 1982. Foreign aid, consisting of loans and grants, was the other major source, amounting to US$303 million (net) in 1982. These two sources were sufficient for the country to balance its international payments and since 1975 gradually to add to its international reserves, which by the beginning of 1984 were about US$282 million—enough to pay for about four months of imports.

The country's prospects for economic growth and rising living standards depended in a large measure on its ability to continue paying for increasing imports. Greater exports, primarily fish, were possible, but the contribution would likely be minor. The number of citizens working abroad appeared to diminish after the late 1970s as development programs were reduced in Arab oil-exporting nations because of the glut of oil on world markets, but remittances continued to climb in the early 1980s, perhaps in response to South Yemeni incentives that liberalized remittance-financed imports, allowed construction of private dwellings from remittances, and paid higher interest rates to nonresident bank depositors. It was unclear whether remittances had peaked or would continue to increase. Expanding foreign aid was also questionable. Preliminary data indicated that foreign grants dropped by nearly 60 percent in 1983 and that disbursements on foreign loans rose but not quite enough to keep total foreign aid receipts from declining. Even a shift from grants to credits in the makeup of foreign aid could create problems, for in the early 1980s South Yemen had to request debt rescheduling with some of its major creditors because of repayment difficulties. By the mid-1980s South Yemen was at a critical point. The large investments permitted by foreign aid and workers' remittances had not resulted in the increased production expected to repay loans and to provide for rising personal incomes. Reduced levels of aid or of workers' remittances would probably require rather harsh austerity measures, including sharp cuts in subsidies and investments. The reaction of the population could be explosive if the required austerity was severe.

Background to Postindependence Politics

Several factors that influenced the course of events in Aden and the protectorates before independence were also important elements in the early years of the new nation (see Consolidation of British Control over the Protectorates and Aden, ch. 1). Among the more important were the erosion of indigenous political institutions and the British failure to implant viable new ones and the fundamental disparities between Aden and the protectorates. In addition, the vulnerable Aden economy, the link between politics in North Yemen and South Yemen, and the political struggles among and within the various nationalist groups, principally the constituents of the victorious National Liberation Front (NLF), also were contributing factors.

The degree to which British actions had eroded the indigenous political system without successfully implanting a new one was not only a significant reason for the anarchic conditions before independence but also helps to explain why and how a political and social revolution accompanied national independence in South Yemen, unlike many newly independent nations. In their desire to find governments with which they could deal directly and through which they could implement "indirect rule," the British had upset the delicate balance within ruling houses and between tribes in the protectorates, had altered the relationship between ruler and ruled, and had created groups whose rising expectations could not be met within the existing system. Assuming that local rulers were like hereditary European monarchs on a small scale, the British signed protection treaties that froze the current leaders and their direct heirs in place, thus destroying the dynamics of traditional rule. Incompetent or unpopular leaders could no longer be replaced by the consensus of the ruling family. These families were often not related to the people of the areas they ruled, and British actions widened the distance between ruler and ruled. Ruling families had often maintained balance within the family and with other prominent families through sinecures or outright payment. This technique was also upset by the British, who forced the rulers to abandon this practice because it was inconsistent with Western notions of governmental efficiency and effectiveness. At the same time, the British were not loath to remove from power intractable rulers who were hard for them to handle. Paradoxically, the British expected too much from the local rulers, placed heavier burdens of control on them than they could handle, and yet made clear their subservience to British interests. Many of the British officials who served in Aden and the protectorates subsequently expressed remorse at the way the British had set up these rulers, made it impossible for them to rule in the traditional way, made them dependent upon British support, and then deserted them when the social and political revolution became unmanageable.

Another key factor that constrained and colored British policy—the political, social, and economic differences between Aden and the protectorates—became an important element in the victory of the NLF over its rivals in the nationalist struggle: the People's Socialist Party (PSP) and its later incarnation, the Front for the Liberation of South Yemen (FLOSY). In the early part of its rule in the area, Britain had been content to leave the protectorates under indirect rule, but by the 1950s British strategic policy both worldwide and in the region had altered to fit changing conditions. Aden became considerably more important in British strategy in 1960, replacing Cyprus as the headquarters of the military command for the whole Middle East. At the same time, however, nationalist sentiment in the region was rising. To meet these apparently conflicting factors, the British began to favor the notion of uniting Aden and the hinterland. The plan that the British finally implemented—unification of Aden and the protectorates with limited self-government—brought together areas that were markedly different politically, socially, and economically. Yemen specialist Fred Halliday points out that the formula was designed to retain the British base in Aden and let Aden's prosperity support the hinterland, while the hinterland provided the conservative political influence necessary to protect British interests permanently. The shaykhs—whose "governments" were in a sense British creations—needed the British and could be counted on to resist possible Adeni radicalism. The British may have hoped that nationalist demands could be met by the limited autonomy of the shaykhdoms and the even more limited political participation granted to Adenis.

As the political situation deteriorated progressively through the 1950s and 1960s, however, British repression of politics in Aden and attempts to use the conservative weight of the shaykhdoms to balance the instability in Aden were unsuccessful. On the contrary, as Britain repressed political demands in Aden, they created the conditions for the triumph of the radical NLF over the slightly more amenable FLOSY. The British colonial government limited legitimate means to express nationalism and political grievances and in doing so gave greater credibility to the NLF, which as early as 1963 had proclaimed the need for violent measures against British rule. Furthermore, by clamping down on political and terrorist activities in Aden, the British facilitated the victory of the NLF over its rivals in FLOSY, because the NLF had strong ties to the hinterland whereas FLOSY was primarily an Adeni organization.

A third factor that was significant before independence but which became even more important to the South Yemeni leadership after 1967 was the nature and state of the national economy. Not only were there two completely different economies (Aden and the hinterland), but also the more prosperous element, Aden, was a service-oriented economy almost wholly dependent upon external sources of revenue: British financial aid, port and bunkering revenues, trade income, and other revenues stemming from the British presence (see Profile of the Economy, this ch.).

Economic changes both in Aden and in the less developed areas of the protectorate fostered economic and social dislocations that fed the revolution. The availability of work in the port of Aden attracted vast numbers of peasants from the countryside of North Yemen as well as the protectorates, creating an urban working class. At the same time, the service-oriented economy of Aden was vulnerable to sudden changes (the 1956 Suez War and the June 1967 War, for example) that threw many of these people out of work. The British kept the non-Adeni workers disenfranchised but gave the vote on a limited basis to other non-Adenis (Britons, Indians, Pakistanis, Somalis) who were able to meet the residency requirement, thus heightening political demands and helping to bring together the economic and political grievances of the workers. Even the modernizations and reforms of the British alienated elements of the population, such as the armed warriors whose work had always been the protection of travelers and the transport of goods—services now provided by motor vehicle and British guardianship over transport between the protected areas.

A fourth factor that was significant for South Yemen both before and after independence (and for North Yemen as well) was the link between politics in the two nations. In addition to the historical links between the two and the presence of North Yemeni dissidents in Aden after the mid-1940s, the political connection became very clear after the coup d'etat in Sanaa on September 26, 1962 (see table A, Preface). Only on September 26 had the Legislative Council (a profoundly unrepresentative group) reluctantly agreed to the unification of Aden with the shaykhdoms. Even the British governor of Aden was aware that the Legislative Council could not have been pushed into agreement if the coup in the north had come one day earlier. As Halliday points out, the atmosphere in Aden was already volatile because of overt British pressure on the question of unification, so that nationalists were all the more elated by news of the coup in Sanaa. On September 28 the PSP organized a demonstration supporting the republicans in North Yemen, and sentiment among nationalists favoring ultimate unification of the two Yemens was boosted by the end of imamic rule (see Repercussions of the Yemen Coup in Aden, ch. 1).

A fifth factor that proved to be an important element in the politics of the new nation was the violent power struggle within the nationalist movement as a whole and the ideological conflict within the NLF. The key to the success of the NLF in the months preceding independence was its link to the hinterland, whereas FLOSY remained primarily an Adeni organization. FLOSY's relationship with Gamal Abdul Nasser of Egypt—from whom at least one faction in the NLF was alienated—also turned out to be a liability. Once the British had given up hope of leaving the South Arabian Federation in power, they favored the NLF not only because it was steadily winning control over the protectorates but also because Nasser supported FLOSY. Abdallah al Asnaj and the relatively moderate elements that made up FLOSY steadily lost ground to the NLF during the last year of British rule, and when independence was achieved in November 1967, many FLOSY members fled—mostly to North Yemen—with as much alacrity as the shaykhs of the protectorate.

Because postindependence political developments were integrally connected with the struggles over power and ideology within the elite of the NLF, a clear understanding of the history, structure, and factions of the NLF is essential. Several of the major scholars of South Yemeni politics provide insight into the origins and early development of the NLF. Halliday notes that the NLF was formed by militants who had gone to the aid of the regime in Sanaa after the coup there in September 1962, and Yemeni specialist Robert Stookey suggests that the principal organizers were members of the Shabi clan, who were tribesmen of Lahij under the leadership of Qahtan al Shabi and his cousin, Faisal Abd al Latif al Shabi.

The NLF in its early days was loosely organized and was without strong ideological direction. Like other such organizations in the Arab world, the roots of the NLF lay in the Arab Nationalist Movement (ANM) founded in Beirut in 1954. Author Helen Lackner notes that the South Yemeni branch was the only group growing out of the ANM to achieve power. Those who founded the Aden branch of the ANM and who later played prominent roles in the struggle for independence and in the South Yemeni government included Qahtan al Shabi, Salim Rubay Ali, and Abd al

Fattah Ismail. The South Yemeni branch of the ANM began in the 1950s with the enthusiastic support of Egypt's Nasser, but by the 1960s its leaders had begun to criticize him and to move toward the break that would occur in the late 1960s. The NLF, as its name implies, was a front rather than a single organization; it included the Yafai Reform Front, the Mahrah Youth Organization, the Nasserite Front, the Adeni Revolutionary Vanguard, the Secret Organization of Free Officers and Soldiers, and other such organizations both from Aden and the protectorates.

By 1963 these groups had begun to coalesce, and in mid-June of that year they held a meeting in Sanaa under the leadership of Qahtan al Shabi, who was at that time an adviser on South Yemeni matters for the republican government in Sanaa. The formation of the NLF was announced after the meeting. By October 14, 1963—a day now celebrated as the national day in South Yemen—the NLF proclaimed its determination to lead the struggle to oust the British by force. Military action by the NLF began in Radfan. The NLF military leader in Radfan, Ali (Antar) Ahmad Nasir al Bishi, then became the leader of the military arm of the NLF.

The guerrilla tactics employed by the NLF and its allied forces were increasingly troublesome to the British and the local rulers in the federation. The conventional forces of the British, designed to establish control over a territory, were the prey of unconventional forces that aimed not at control but at making British control costly and dangerous. With their repressive response the British fell into the trap of classic guerrilla warfare: by cracking down on local supporters of the guerrillas, they succeeded only in alienating the population still more. It took the British over six months to subdue Radfan, at great cost. This was heartening to NLF branches elsewhere, and violence spread from Radfan into other areas of the protectorates.

Meanwhile, in Aden the less militant PSP, under the leadership of Asnaj, continued to advocate peaceful change and steadily lost ground to the militant NLF. Encouraged by British trade unionists and by the coming to power of the British Labour government in October 1964, Asnaj remained committed to nonviolence until late 1965. Asnaj's ambivalence on the question of violence undermined his hold on the increasingly militant workers of Aden. Some observers suggest that the Adeni workers were attracted to the violent struggle against the British not only because the concept was attractive but also because it was a modernized form of traditional, armed, tribal conflict. Asnaj's agreement to merge with the remnants of the more conservative South Arabian League in the Organization for the Liberation of the Occupied South (OLOS) in May 1965 also discredited him among many of the radicalized Adeni workers.

A split within the NLF seems to have begun almost simultaneously with the birth of the organization. Having grown out of the South Yemeni branch of the ANM, the NLF inherited the ANM's ideological divisions. The first major split in the organization grew out of disputes that were both ideological and organizational. The top NLF leadership—Qahtan al Shabi and his followers—was committed to Nasserism, while the second level of young NLF members was turning more to Marxism, encouraged by a small communist group in Aden, the Popular Democratic Union, led by Abdallah Ba Dhib (one of the founders of the Aden Trade Unions Congress). The top leaders dominated the First Congress of the NLF, held in Taizz in June 1965. The "National Charter" produced by the First Congress was clearly the product of compromise and illustrated some of the ideological divisions within the organization. It used socialist terminology and called for the building of socialism, but it did not go so far as to call for nationalization. The second-level, more radical elements of the NLF were already turning away from Nasserism to Marxism, but they did not control the NLF yet, and the charter did not challenge Nasserist ideas or Nasser's leadership in the Arab world.

By 1966, however, the second-level leaders of the NLF had begun to make clear their dissatisfaction with the NLF leadership's links to Egypt and its inattention to social revolution. Egyptian efforts to unify all nationalist groups operating in South Yemen to bring them under Egyptian control only more confused the situation. Asnaj of the PSP already had a close relationship with Nasser and also favored merging. Even the less radical members of the NLF may have found the idea of merger appealing to a certain extent. Three NLF leaders were persuaded to agree to a merger of the NLF and the PSP in Cairo in January 1966. Many NLF members—including all the radicals—were violently opposed to this. In March 1966 Nasser persuaded the NLF leaders to come to Cairo for more discussions. They were detained and missed the Second Congress of the NLF in June 1966. Unwittingly, the Egyptians aided the rise of the radicals who took charge of the meeting. The NLF radicals expelled the three NLF members who had agreed to a merger in January (plus NLF leader Qahtan al Shabi and his cousin, Faisal) and selected a new leadership dominated by radicals. The radicals included most of the men who would become the leaders of South Yemen after the first postindependence split in the NLF in 1969: Ismail, Muhammad Ali Haytham, Rubay Ali, Ali Antar, and Ali Salim al Baydh.

The Egyptians kept pressing the NLF to join FLOSY, and NLF leaders Qahtan al Shabi, Faisal al Shabi, and Ismail signed a new agreement to join FLOSY in August 1966. The NLF members, angered at Egyptian pressure and moving to the left of Nasserist thinking, simply began to operate as individual units, threatening the leadership with a split in the organization and loss of control unless they withdrew from FLOSY.

The open split in the organization was healed in November 1966 when most of the older leaders agreed to end their reluctant association with Asnaj and FLOSY. In November 1966 the Third Congress of the NLF declared a complete rupture with FLOSY, which then became nothing more than a new name for the armed units of the PSP. From this point on the NLF was as much at war with FLOSY as with the British authorities.

The reunited NLF, now in a strong position throughout the protectorates as well as in Aden, was on the verge of victory over both the British and its FLOSY rivals, but the fundamental ideological differences within the organization remained and erupted again shortly after independence. Under NLF rule, political differences in South Yemen took the form of intraparty conflict.

Independence and the Qahtan al Shabi Regime

In 1967 the federation and British rule collapsed rapidly. By the end of summer most of the states of the federation were under NLF control. When the federation army showed itself clearly on the side of the NLF, the British gave in and began negotiations with the NLF in Geneva on November 21. On November 29 the last patch of South Yemen fell to NLF forces when they landed on Socotra

Island; on the same day the last British troops left Aden. At midnight the People's Republic of South Yemen was declared.

The new nation was not in a promising position in any respect. Its leadership was already divided, and its impoverished economy was a shambles. The British-trained army was of questionable loyalty to the new leadership, and the defeated rump of the nationalist movement (the right-wing South Arabian League and the moderate, left-wing FLOSY) was poised on its borders and supported by neighboring North Yemen and Saudi Arabia.

Qahtan al Shabi, who was the only NLF leader over 40 years of age, became chairman of the presidential council (head of state), prime minister, and commander of the armed forces. His cousin Faisal became secretary general of the party, and others of the NLF "right wing" were in important positions in the hierarchy.

Some of the trappings of sovereignty were easily assumed by the new government. The NLF, which after independence became the National Front (NF), took on legislative powers in the absence of any government institutions. Power rested in the hands of the NF elite. Diplomatic relations were established with many of the Arab states and even with the British (despite their failure to provide the postindependence aid they had once promised). By the end of 1967 Yemen had joined the League of Arab States (Arab League) and the United Nations (UN). The old shaykhdoms were abolished, and the country was divided into six governorates. Some areas of the country had actually been administered by the NLF for some months before independence through "popular committees," "popular guards," and other administrative groups made up of NLF members. At the same time, some vestiges of the colonial administration still existed, such as the civil service and the army.

The first months of the new government were far from easy. In addition to its severe economic and social problems, the year and a half of Qahtan's presidency was marked by his struggles with both the NF leftists and the remnants of the moderate FLOSY and with the deposed shaykhs from beyond South Yemen's borders.

Dissent from the left wing of the NF proved difficult for the government to handle. There was a serious ideological dispute between the moderates of the NF (Qahtan and his group, who controlled the new government) and the more radical group (the second-level NF leaders who had so vehemently opposed cooperation with FLOSY and Nasser). This conflict had been pushed aside within the movement in the year before independence because full attention had to be given to the twin goals of driving out the British and defeating FLOSY. The ideological splits came to light again upon independence and took shape in disagreements over the form the state should take. Qahtan and his group favored gradual change made on the basis of the existing system at the time of independence. The radicals wanted to remove every vestige of the old structure, including the civil service and the old federation army. Both had been set up and recruited by the British and were profoundly mistrusted by the NF radicals, who wanted a completely new, smaller civil service made up of NF partisans and a new, regular army plus a revolutionary militia. The radicals also favored the establishment of peoples' committees in each village to elect members for a supreme popular council, limits on privately owned land, nationalization of all foreign capital, and unification with North Yemen on NF terms.

There were other aspects of the ideological quarrel. Some of the more prominent radicals, such as Ismail, were North Yemenis by origin and had their strongest political ties in South Yemen to the Hadhramaut. The Shabi family was of South Yemeni origin and from an area of the former Western Protectorate near Aden, Lahij. Because of the ties of the radicals to the Hadhramaut, the homeland of such radical leaders as Minister of Defense Baydh, it was the location of the earliest manifestations of the radical rebellion.

This ideological dispute—with its regional aspects—came into the open at the Fourth Congress of the NF in March 1968. Despite the opposition of Qahtan and his cohorts, the leftists succeeded in having all their positions adopted as resolutions: collective decisionmaking; the purge of the army and civil service; a centrally planned economy; and confiscation of land owned by waqfs, wealthy peasants, or traditional landowners. A new general command of 41 members, dominated by leftists, was elected by the Fourth Congress. Qahtan, however, retained control of the army, which still included a large number of lower-level officers and soldiers trained and recruited by the British. This army—which the NF leftists mistrusted and wanted to abolish—supported the president and sought in turn the abolition of the NF's irregular militias. Before the end of March 1968 violent conflict had broken out between these NF irregulars and the forces of the army and the police in Aden. The army and police put down the uprising, and many prominent leftists were jailed, including Minister of Culture Ismail and Minister of Defense Baydh. Qahtan took an ambivalent position, assuring the army and the police that they would not be purged but portraying their crackdown on the left as a mistake. Clashes continued in other parts of the country. The resolutions of the Fourth Congress remained unimplemented, and the leftists were now more or less removed from the government. By the beginning of the summer of 1968 the government had put down opposition from the left only to find itself assaulted from the right.

Most of the important shaykhs had fled before the November 1967 victory of the NLF, and some had been tried and sentenced to death in absentia. By mid-1968 they had found support from the North Yemeni and Saudi Arabian governments and had begun to make attacks across the borders of South Yemen. Some tribes rose in rebellion with outside support. Only by the end of the summer of 1968 was the new government able to subdue these rebellions and repel the expatriate assaults.

Within a few months assaults from the exiled opposition began again, however, and Qahtan al Shabi, left with only the army behind him, allowed leftists to regroup within the government because he needed their support against opposition from the right outside the country. By early 1969 the leftists had begun to take advantage of Qahtan's precarious position and his failure to make progress on the society's serious economic and political problems. In April 1969 the left was able to force the president to give up the post of prime minister, but he insisted on giving it to his unpopular cousin, Faisal.

The issue over which Qahtan was finally ousted was the issue of control of the army. Minister of Interior Haytham was from the Dathina tribe (as was much of the army) and had enjoyed much contact with the junior officers during the struggle for independence. The president tried to stop Haytham's inroads into the army by firing him in mid-June 1969. On June 22 the president, his cousin Faisal, and the entire moderate group were outsted as the left seized control of the government. Some of the deposed leaders were imprisoned or killed; others fled.

The Presidency of Salim Rubay Ali

Having ousted the moderate, nationalist wing of the party in what was called the "Corrective Movement," the left sought to implement the radical program outlined at the Fourth Congress. The first step was the establishment of collective leadership in the form of a five-man presidium: Rubay Ali (president and chairman of the council), Haytham (prime minister), Ismail (NF secretary general), Ali Nasir (defense minister), and Muhammad Salih Awlaqi. They promulgated a new constitution in November 1970, the third anniversary of independence. The new rulers changed the country's name to the People's Democratic Republic of Yemen, implying that the NF did not foresee Yemeni unity through the merger of two states but regarded the South Yemeni government as the legitimate state, which North Yemen should join.

The transformation imposed by the new leftist leadership took many forms. The army and civil service were not abolished outright, as some leftists had originally advocated, but they were purged of all personnel who had been connected with the British. At the same time, the new regime sought to involve the army in nonmilitary projects—such as road and school construction. Commissars were appointed to undertake the political education of the armed forces.

All newspapers had been banned at independence, and by 1973 the major means of communication were the radio station in Aden and the government newspaper, *14 October*. At the same time that communications came more strictly under government control, education was expanded as rapidly as the impoverished economy could support it (see Education, this ch.). The government made determined efforts to undercut and destroy tribalism, which it regarded as a vestige of primitive life that prevented all other aspects of social transformation, especially the abolition of class differences. Despite the inroads into traditional society made by the NLF in the years preceding independence, the nationalist struggle had not been protracted, and tribalism had remained a powerful factor in the hinterland. Some steps had been taken during the presidency of

Qahtan al Shabi, such as the redivision of the country into six governorates that crossed traditional tribal boundaries. In 1968 the government had decreed a "General Truce Among the Tribes," hoping that during the five years of this truce the government could supplant tribal law by which tribal life and tribal conflict were regulated. By 1970 the government made tribal murder a capital crime and began to ban tribal associations in some areas. Although religious practices were not banned, the regime in Aden sought to eliminate elements of Islam that conflicted with their goals of social transformation.

The NF left wing as a group gained control of the state in the Corrective Movement of June 1969, but the new leadership still confronted two problems: the task of converting the NF from a guerrilla organization to a socialist party and persistent ideological differences within the leftist leadership. The first of the presidium members to leave was Haytham, who departed for a year's stay in Moscow.

The Fifth Congress of the NF in March 1972 was far more harmonious than previous congresses and confirmed the victory of the left as more orthodox, Soviet-style structures were created: a central committee and a politburo. In 1975 the NF merged with two small parties that had been permitted to survive: the Popular Democratic Union, a pro-Soviet communist party, and the Vanguard Party, a leftist-Baathist party, to form the United Political Organization of the National Front (UPONF). Under the surface, however, throughout the mid-1970s a struggle occurred between two factions within the NF. One faction was headed by President (and NF assistant secretary general) Rubay Ali, an independent-minded Marxist who seemed to favor a Chinese model of social transformation. He encouraged the popular uprisings, reminiscent of Mao Zedong's Cultural Revolution of the early 1970s, and he resisted the transformation of the NF into a vanguard party in the style of the Communist Party of the Soviet Union (CPSU). Rubay Ali was unable to obtain significant aid from China, however, and agreed on the necessity of Soviet assistance, visiting Moscow in November 1972 to sign military, economic, and cultural aid agreements. He had also been willing to open up relations with the Saudis and had used aid from this quarter to finance his own pet economic projects. The South Yemeni president moved toward closer relations with North Yemeni president Ibrahim al Hamdi, who was assassinated on the eve of a visit to Aden in 1977 (see The Government of Ibrahim al Hamdi, ch. 2).

Opposing this group was the faction headed by NF secretary general Ismail, an orthodox, pro-Soviet figure. Scholars disagree on the sequence of events that led to the downfall of Rubay Ali. Author Manfred Wenner suggests that Rubay Ali was, in fact, behind the assassination of North Yemeni president Ahmad al Ghashmi, who was killed in June 1978 when the briefcase of a messenger (allegedly from Rubay Ali) exploded in his office. Wenner believes that the South Yemeni president did this not only to warn Saudi Arabia (which was widely believed to have had Ghashmi assassinate his predecessor, Hamdi, in 1977) but also to bolster his position within the NF. According to Wenner, the rest of the NF turned on Rubay Ali as a result of this affair. Halliday suggests that Rubay Ali tried to use his personal followers from the military and the party to stage a coup to remove the other leaders from power but that this attempt failed. Stookey postulates that Rubay Ali deliberately provoked an armed confrontation with his rivals in the NF, hoping that a subsequent popular uprising would support him. Whatever the background, violent clashes between followers of the president and the rival faction erupted on June 26, 1978, and hundreds were killed. Rubay Ali was captured and executed along with some of his followers. NF secretary general Ismail became chief of state and retained his party post as well. In October 1978 the party leaders dissolved the NF and replaced it with the Yemen Socialist Party (YSP) (see The Yemen Socialist Party, this ch.).

The Presidency of Abd al Fattah Ismail

The victory of the pro-Soviet faction led the government naturally to a style of government more closely modeled on the Soviet system and to closer relations with East European countries. In 1979 South Yemen became an observer of the Soviet economic alliance—the Council for Mutual Economic Assistance (Comecon)—and in October President Ismail signed in Moscow a 20-year treaty of friendship. The rapprochements Rubay Ali had engineered with both Saudi Arabia and North Yemen were downgraded.

Several problems plagued Ismail's government, however, and he ruled for only two years. Many party members were unhappy with his heavy reliance on the Soviet Union and were displeased with the rupture of incipient relationships with North Yemen and Saudi Arabia. South Yemen's economic problems remained very serious, and some party members blamed this situation on the meager aid provided by the Soviets and the refusal of Arab states to aid a government as closely tied to the Soviets as Aden was. Another problem was the failure of the newly organized party to end partisan factionalism and of the new head of state to generate personal support. Halliday suggests that Ismail was viewed as an unrepresentative intellectual who did not understand the difficulties of the average citizen. His North Yemeni origins may not have been a factor in his downfall, but they probably did not endear him to South Yemenis.

On April 21, 1980, Ismail was ousted from the presidium of the YSP, and Prime Minister Ali Nasir took control of both the party and the government, becoming chairman of the presidium and YSP secretary general while retaining the post of prime minister. The deposed Ismail was given the honorific title of party president. The pro-Soviet faction now gave way to a new leadership that, while still Marxist, was more nationalist than orthodox in its approach to politics.

Government Structure

South Yemen's basic law is the Constitution proclaimed on November 30, 1970, by the NF and amended substantially in October 1978. This 135-article document begins with a statement citing the significance of the September 26, 1962, revolution in North Yemen that overthrew the imamate; it defines popular movements in both North and South Yemen as a common struggle against "imperialism and reactionary conspiracies" and proclaims the ultimate goal of uniting the two halves of the Yemeni nation. The Yemeni people are recognized as part of the "Arab nation," and Arabic is identified as the official language.

Composed after the 1969 Corrective Movement that firmly placed South Yemen on a leftward course, the Constitution gives the state the responsibility for "managing the society so that national democratic revolution is achieved on a basis of scientific socialism" (Article 8). Other provisions affirm the right of citizens to elect public officials, recognize other civil and human rights (including the equality of men and women, Article 36), and legitimize the establishment of a nationalized, centrally planned economy. Article 31 promises that the state will "safeguard the Arab and Islamic legacy," but it also commits the state to combat "corrupt concepts spread by imperialism and colonialism" and "backward tribal and communal tendencies." Islam is recognized as the state religion in Article 46, an anomaly in a Marxist-Leninist state but one apparently adopted to appease a still strongly conservative population (see Politics and Society, this ch.).

The National Government

The 1978 amendments to the Constitution established a Soviet-style parallel hierarchy of state and party organs supervised and directed by the YSP. The Constitution places the Supreme People's Assembly (SPA), the national legislature (also known as the Supreme People's Council), at the apex of the state hierarchy. The SPA is popularly elected, although when it was first convened by the NF leadership in March 1971 its 101 members were appointed.

From December 16 to 18, 1978, SPA elections were held for the first time, and an expanded membership of 111 persons was chosen. Candidates were nominated by the YSP and its mass organizations. One observer noted that as many as 40 SPA members were elected as independents, although this probably reflected the small size of the new ruling party rather than active dissent. According to a statement made by President Ali Nasir in June 1981, by-elections for the SPA and local elections drew 94.6 percent of a total registered electorate of 771,763 persons.

The SPA is responsible for debating and approving major policy measures and ratifying agreements with foreign states. It chooses the Presidium, containing 11 to 17 members, whose chairman becomes president and head of state. The Presidium, described by a Soviet writer as a "permanent, collegial organ of state power," nominates a Council of Ministers, the highest executive authority. In mid-1985 the chairman of the Presidium and the president was Ali Nasir. He also served as prime minister (formal title: chairman of the Council of Ministers) from August 1971 until

February 1985, when he resigned and was replaced by Haydar Abu Bakr al Attas (see table D).

Table D. South Yemen: President and Council of Ministers, April 1985

Office	Incumbent
Chairman, Supreme People's Council Presidium	Hasani, Ali Nasir Muhammad al
Chairman, Council of Ministers	Attas, Haydar Abu Bakr al
Deputy Prime Minister	Ba Dhib, Ali Abd al Razzaq
Deputy Prime Minister	Numan, Yasin Said, Dr.
Minister of Agriculture and Agrarian Reform	Nasir, Muhammad Sulayman
Minister of Culture and Tourism	Thabit, Rashid Muhammad
Minister of Defense	Qasim, Salih Muslih, Brigadier General
Minister of Education	Sallami, Hasan Ahmad al, Dr.
Minister of Energy and Minerals	Ba Jammal, Abd al Qadir
Minister of Finance	Madhi, Mahmud Said al
Minister of Fish Resources	Numan, Yasin Said, Dr.
Minister of Foreign Affairs	Dali, Abd al Aziz al, Dr.
Minister of Health	Bukayr, Abdallah Ahmad, Dr.
Minister of Housing	Abdallah Sharjabi, Muhammad Said
Minister of Industry	Aziz, Abdallah Muhammad
Minister of Information	Abd al Qawi, Muhammad
Minister of Installations	Abdallah, Fadl Muhsin
Minister of Interior	Buttani, Muhammad Abdallah, Colonel
Minister of Justice and Religious Trusts	Mansur, Khalid Fadl
Minister of Labor and Civil Service	Ali, Nasir Nasir
Minister of Local Government	Bidh, Ali Salim al
Minister of Planning	Ghanim, Faraj ibn, Dr.
Minister of State Security	Husayn, Ahmad Musaid
Minister of Trade and Supply	Fadli, Ahmad Ubayd al
Minister of Transport	Husaynun, Salih Abu Bakr ibn
Minister of State for Council of Ministers Affairs	Ghanim, Abdallah Ahmad
Minister of State for Sports Affairs	Qatabi, Ahmad Muhammad al
Minister of State for Union Affairs	Ushaysh, Mahmud Abdallah
Chairman, Higher Committee for Party People's Control	Said, Mahdi Abdallah

Source: Based on information from United States, Central Intelligence Agency, Directorate of Intelligence, *Chiefs of State and Cabinet Members of Foreign Governments*, Washington, April 1985, 105.

Regional and Local Government

During the period of British colonial rule in Aden, no attempt was made to establish a system of modern regional and local government in the patchwork of sultanates and amirates that composed the Eastern Protectorate and the Western Protectorate. In the year after independence, the South Yemeni authorities enacted a law that established a basic structure of local government on three levels: governorates, directorates, and districts. The old states and tribal groupings were formally abolished. In mid-1985 the country remained divided into six governorates. Originally these had been designated numerically, but in 1980 they were given names (see fig. 12).

Little information on the nature or function of regional and local government was available to observers outside the country. In principle, the system operated according to the Marxist-Leninist principle of "democratic centralism." In the Soviet context this has meant not only that the authorities on all levels of party and government are elected but also that they must follow the decisions of the higher levels in all important matters, leaving them little or no autonomy. In South Yemen each of the subnational units of government had a popularly elected people's council. The people's council chose an executive committee that apparently was the functional analogue of the national-level Council of Ministers. There was also a chief executive (governor at the governorate level, director at the directorate level, and district commissioner at the district level), who was appointed by the executive committee at the next higher level. All candidates for regional and local office were screened and approved by the YSP. The apparatus of subnational government was the responsibility of the minister of local government in the national-level Council of Ministers.

All evidence suggested that in the mid-1980s significant areas of the country remained outside the formal structure of local administration. Because of the lack of adequately trained administrative personnel, poor communications, and the persistence of tribal ways of life in the areas outside Aden, a system of democratic centralism remained an aspiration rather than a reality. One observer notes, for example, a 1982 comment in the government newspaper *14 October* that persons living in remote villages in Abyan had to travel for several days on foot to reach a settlement where they could register a marriage with the authorities.

The Judiciary

Until independence numerous systems of law could be found in what is now the territory of South Yemen. In Aden the British established a network of lower courts, hearing all civil and criminal cases in the crown colony; it was responsible to a single high court, the Court of Appeal for East Africa in Nairobi, Kenya. In the protectorates, traditional systems of law predominated. The oldest system of law in these regions was *urf*, customary tribal law; but the most widely observed legal code was sharia, or Islamic law.

The development of a new legal system has progressed slowly since the departure of the British in 1967. The 1970 Constitution provides that the state "shall guarantee the unity of the judiciary and shall issue gradually a democratic civil law, a law of employment, a family law, and a criminal law in accordance with the principles of the constitution" (Article 119). It also describes the responsibilities of the office of attorney general (Article 124). Unlike the constitution of North Yemen, the South Yemen Constitution does not tie the legal system to sharia.

In January 1968 the Supreme State Security Court was established in Aden. Under the authority of the minister of justice and the NF, the court was responsible for establishing guidelines for a unified judiciary. Numerous magistrate's courts were also set up in different parts of the country; they were given jurisdiction in matters of criminal law and were allowed to try former rulers and political prisoners. Beginning in the early 1970s, a legal framework was gradually erected. Important steps included the passing of a family law in 1974, a penal code in 1976, a labor law in 1978, a law pertaining to the legal profession in 1982, and an extensive civil code—composed of 1,930 sections—in 1983. In 1978 a law faculty was founded at the University of Aden.

According to Naguib Shamiry, president of the Supreme Court in Aden, South Yemen had a fully operative judicial hierarchy in the mid-1980s. This comprised the Supreme Court of the Republic at the apex, provincial courts in the governorates, and divisional magistrates in the districts. The Ministry of Justice and Religious Trusts supervised the administration of the courts. The SPA appointed a procurator general who was responsible not only for public prosecution but also for supervision of the operation of all state bodies in conformity with law. Judges on the Supreme Court and provincial courts and district magistrates were chosen by the legislative bodies on their respective levels.

In mid-1985 there was considerable evidence that the judiciary was far less developed than Shamiry claimed. Observers noted that outside Aden customary and Islamic law were still pervasive. As in the case of local administration, the secular courts had grave shortages of trained personnel, and it often took several years for criminal cases to be tried. Rather than submit their disputes over land or water rights to a slow and cumbersome bureaucracy, peasants preferred traditional means of resolving differences.

The Yemen Socialist Party

A decisive event in the development of South Yemen's political system was the establishment of the YSP in October 1978. In terms of its formal ideology, organization, and role in society, the YSP operated, and continued to operate in the mid-1980s, as a Marxist-Leninist "vanguard party" based strictly on the Soviet model. According to the amended Constitution, the YSP "determines the general prospects for the development of society and the guidelines for the internal and foreign policy of the state." From the Soviet perspective, South Yemen was one of a number of "socialist-oriented" states in the developing world in which former national liberation movements were beginning the transition to socialism under tutelage of a revolutionary party; other socialist-oriented states included Afghanistan, Angola, Mozambique, Ethiopia, and Nicaragua. At the NF's Fifth Congress in May 1972, the party leadership established a Soviet-style central committee and politburo and adopted a number of innovations from Cuba, the first "socialist-oriented" state. These included Popular Defense Committees, which were placed in charge of grass-roots security and surveillance. Ties between the YSP and the CPSU were high-level and intimate, and the process of party building continued under CPSU tutelage in the mid-1980s.

Organization and Membership

The YSP in the mid-1980s was organized hierarchically and operated according to the principles of democratic centralism. Party bodies paralleled their state counterparts on the national, governorate, directorate, and district levels. On the national level the Party Congress was convened every five years (though extraordinary sessions could be convened by the YSP Central Committee). Congress delegates, representing the subnational units, elected the Central Committee, which normally served for a five-year term. In late 1984 it had 47 members and 11 candidate members. This body in turn designated functional committees. These included an executive committee (eight members and three candidate members), a secretariat (five members), an information committee (10 members), and an appeals committee (six members). The most important grouping at the top of the party hierarchy was the Politburo, which had 11 members in the mid-1985 (see fig 13). This was the nerve center of the YSP, responsible for supervising state administration and the formulation of policy. Its membership in mid-1985 included the YSP secretary general, Ali Nasir. In 1978 the YSP had 26,000 to 28,000 members; in 1983, however, a Soviet source reported a membership of 19,000 as the result of a purge conducted in 1980.

Mass organizations played a central role in the party's strategy of building a popular base. The most important were the General Union of Yemeni Workers, which had 84,000 members; the General Union of Yemeni Women, 15,000 members; and the Democratic Yemeni Youth, 31,000 members. These groups were urban based. It was unclear in the mid-1980s to what extent rural people, the great majority of the population, were organized, although there was a Yemeni Democratic Federation of Peasants. The network of Popular Defense Committees had apparently been extended to rural areas, but there was considerable evidence that they enjoyed little popular support.

Party cadres were trained at the Aden Higher School for Scientific Socialism, an institution established and staffed by Soviet advisers. The school had given courses to as many as 20,000 persons by the mid-1980s. The YSP depended in other ways on Soviet support. Cuban advisers assisted the Popular Defense Committees and the People's Militia, and East German personnel played a central role in

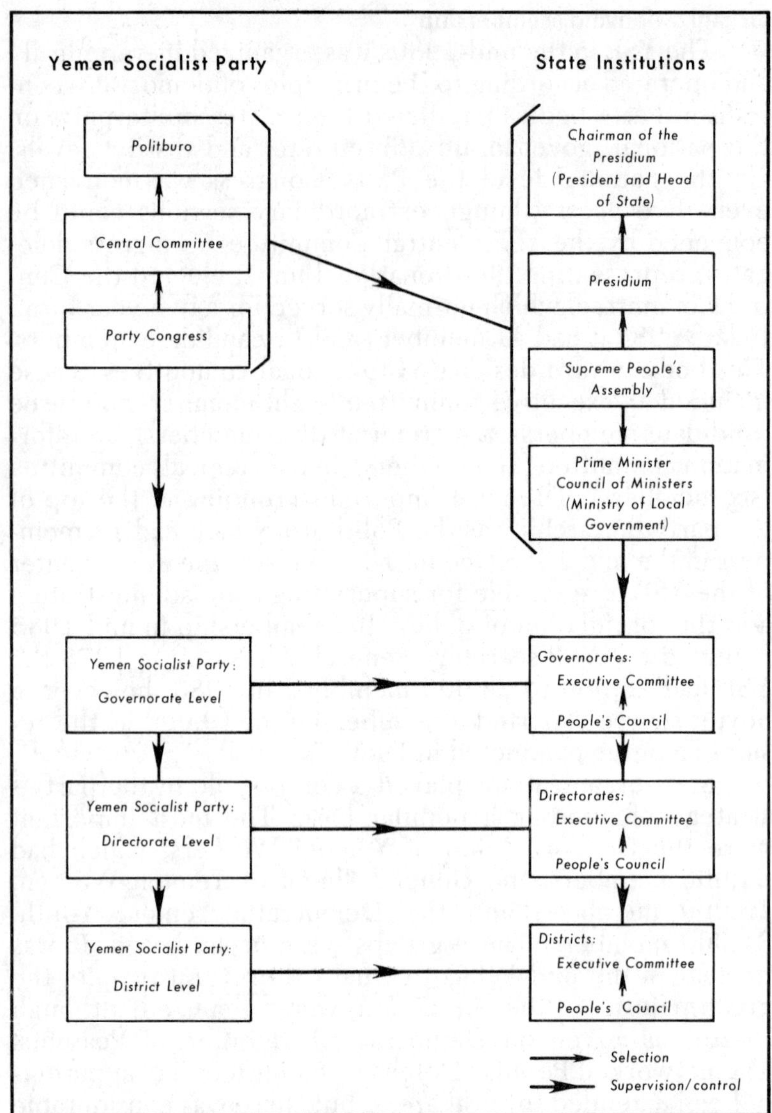

Figure 13. South Yemen: Party and Government Structure, 1985

the establishment and administration of a state security apparatus (see National Security, this ch.)

Divisions Within the Leadership

Little was known of the internal dynamics of the YSP in the mid-1980s. Sources were fragmentary and often unreliable. The paucity of non-East European foreigners in the country and the government's reluctance to allow any real contact between citizens and outsiders made it extremely difficult for observers to interpret political developments. It was known, however, that the establishment of a Marxist-Leninist ruling party, formally operating on the principle of "democratic centralism," did not preclude fierce and sometimes violent factional struggles. The fall of Ismail in April 1980 was not a conclusive victory for Ali Nasir and his moderate supporters. The armed forces maintained their own power base that after April 1980 became the focus of opposition to the president. Some analysts believed that the party congress scheduled for October 1985 might be the occasion for hard-liners or doctrinaire Marxist-Leninists to reassert control over the political system.

Although the YSP leadership was committed to Marxism-Leninism, analysts commonly defined intraparty divisions in terms of the polarity between moderates who sought flexibility in domestic and foreign policy and hard-liners who followed Soviet initiatives unquestioningly (though personal ambitions and animosities also played a formidable role). Moderate opposition to Ismail had evolved from resentment over South Yemen's subservience to the Soviet Union, isolating it from the rest of the Arab world, and the stinginess of Soviet aid. Ismail was a doctrinaire and inflexible Marxist-Leninst who had earned for himself the nickname of *faqih*, or "theoretician"; many of his associates felt that his literal application of the Soviet model of revolution was inconsistent with local conditions. They preferred a more gradual approach that took account of traditional tribal and religious values. While hard-liners sought to strengthen ties with other revolutionary regimes—such as East European countries, Ethiopia, and Libya—moderates wanted a more balanced foreign policy, which included improving relations with Saudi Arabia. The prospect of aid from the oil-rich Arab states of the Persian Gulf was clearly an element in their calculations. Another issue dividing moderates and hard-liners was the latter's support for National Democratic Front (NDF) insurgency in North Yemen. Ismail, a North Yemeni, apparently wanted to achieve union with North Yemen as quickly as possible, preferably through the establishment of a friendly, leftist regime in Sanaa. Ali Nasir also avowed the goal of Yemeni unity enshrined in the 1970 Constitution, but he preferred less confrontational means to achieve that end. He was also one of the first of a new generation of leaders born in South Yemen and had a distinctly South Yemeni perspective; unity could be postponed, he thought, until South Yemen was sufficiently developed to prevent its being absorbed by a country having four times its population.

After his resignation from the top party and state positions in April 1980, Ismail did not suffer the violent fate of his predecessor, Rubay Ali. Ali Nasir apparently felt his position was sufficiently secure to allow Ismail to live and even gave him the honorary but powerless post of chairman of the YSP. In August 1980, however, Ismail departed for the Soviet Union, where he remained in exile. At an extraordinary congress of the YSP convened by Ali Nasir two months later, Ismail's principal supporters were dropped from the Politburo. Ali Nasir now monopolized political power; he was secretary general of the YSP, chairman of the Presidium (president), and chairman of the Council of Ministers (prime minister).

He was unable, however, to gain control over the armed forces. Minister of Defense Brigadier General Ali Antar had supported him in his 1980 bid for power but turned against him when it became apparent that Ali Nasir was unwilling to share power. Ali Antar, a prominent veteran of the guerrilla struggle against the British, strengthened his power base in the armed forces by promoting 300 officers loyal to him without obtaining the president's prior approval. He proposed to the YSP Central Committee that the party's People's Militia, the armed force most loyal to Ali Nasir in his capacity as YSP secretary general, be incorporated into the regular army. Had this measure been adopted, it would have left Ali Nasir powerless. Tensions grew as the president put People's Militia units in Aden on alert to forestall a possible coup attempt by Ali Antar in January 1981. The president whittled at his position by purging several of his most powerful supporters. In May 1981 Ali Antar was obliged to resign as defense minister.

He was given the less important portfolios of deputy prime minister and minister of local administration, but in February 1985 he was removed from these posts as well. Yet his successor as defense minister, Brigardier General Salih Muslih Qasim, was equally jealous of the independence of the armed force, and on at least one occasion he placed army units on alert as a warning to the president. "Bonapartism" (in Soviet parlance, the refusal of the military to submit to party control and even to pose a threat to party rule) remained in the mid-1980s one of the most serious obstacles to the YSP's development as a full-fledged revolutionary party.

Hard-line supporters of Ismail were moving back into responsible state and party positions in the mid-1980s, and their influence may result in more radical practices. Ismail apparently continued to entertain hopes of toppling the president. In the summer of 1982 he went to Sofia to confer with Muhsin al Sharjabi, South Yemen's ambassador to Bulgaria; before Ismail's ouster he had been head of the East German-trained internal security apparatus and had earned for himself the reputation of being the "Beria of South Yemen." The Aden regime, suspecting a plot between the two men, recalled Sharjabi and then arrested and executed him. There was evidence that the Soviet Union had played some role in their intrigues (or at least had not prevented the two men from meeting by allowing Ismail to leave Moscow). At a YSP Central Committee plenary session held in 1984, hard-liners caustically described Ali Nasir as "being impotent from an ideological point of view to lead the political ideology of the party," and there apparently were demands that Ismail be allowed to return from the Soviet Union. In the cabinet reorganization of February 1985, Ali Nasir gave up his position as prime minister, and Qasim, one of the most powerful hard-liners, was reappointed defense minister. Ali Antar, however, was dropped from the cabinet. In March Ismail returned to the country, and relations among the most senior leaders remained tense.

Politics and Society

The limited data available to foreign observers in the mid-1980s suggested that traditional values and forms of social life persisted, despite the regime's efforts to transform South Yemen into a socialist society. The regime had gone further than any other in the Middle East in the direction of Marxist-Leninist revolution. Halliday notes that "whilst seeing itself as part of the Arab revolution, it has rejected any ideological compromise with the theories of a special Arab or Islamic socialism of the kind espoused by Nasserites, Qaddafi, the Ba'ath or the Algerian NLF." But it faced formidable obstacles in the continued adherence of the majority of the population, especially outside Aden, to tribal and Islamic norms. A lack of material resources and trained personnel, moreover, circumscribed its area of effective control. Halliday observes that "while much analysis of Third World revolutions has stressed the element of *will*, the South Yemeni case is a harsh reminder of the *objective*, material and cultural, preconditions for any full transition and the difficulties involved in a voluntaristic approach to revolutionary transformation."

After independence the NF regime removed the ruling class of sultans, amirs, and shaykhs that the British had fostered in their protectorates, as well as some members of the religious elite. A new social elite was composed of NF or, after 1978, YSP cadres. On the higher levels they enjoyed the privileges and prerequisites of a Soviet-style "new class." They had material benefits, such as spacious and comfortable housing, not available to the ordinary population, and they could travel overseas. Corruption was apparently widespread, and bribes were routinely expected in the performance of government services.

In the hinterland, tribes remained significant political actors, and tribal rule was often more effective on the local level than the state apparatus imposed by Aden. Even on the national level, tribal politics was a factor that could not be entirely discounted. Ali Nasir belonged to the Dathina tribe, and his most loyal followers were allegedly members of this group. Successive purges had removed two important preindependence groups from the ruling strata: Aden Arabs and Hadhramis, both of whom had had extensive overseas ties before 1967.

South Yemen is perhaps the only Marxist-Leninist state whose Constitution designates an official religion, Islam. (In 1985 Afghanistan's basic law promised the "promotion of Islam and its human values.") This unusual compromise was the result of almost universal popular opposition to the regime's initial attempts to stamp out religion and propagate atheism. In 1970 the regime nationalized the waqfs, thus making religious institutions, such as mosques and schools and the Islamic clergy, dependent on state subsidies. The government has sought since then to co-opt the clergy and harness its influence for its own ends. The role of sharia was sharply curtailed. Leaders were highly selective in their efforts to accommodate Islam and revolution in the state-run schools and media. The spiritual aspects of the religion—the Quran's exposition of humanity's relationship with God—were downplayed or ignored. According to Middle East analyst Norman Cigar, the authorities emphasized Islam's "liberation theology," i.e., its preaching against injustice and exploitation. At the same time, Ali Nasir and other leaders sought to project an image of themselves in the media as practicing Muslims by attending prayers and conferring with religious figures.

The media were all state owned and managed. These included a daily newspaper, *14 October*, which had a circulation of about 20,000, and several magazines, such as the weekly *Al-Thawra* (The Revolution), published by the YSP Central Committee. The Democratic Yemen Broadcasting Service maintained radio and television stations. There were an estimated 110,000 radios and 37,000 television receivers in South Yemen in the early 1980s. Lack of resources made it almost impossible for the regime to bring its ideological message to more remote parts of the country. Official broadcasts reached a smaller audience than the broadcasts of neighboring countries, especially those of Egypt and Saudi Arabia. The government's careful treatment of the religious question was at least in part because broadcasts from religiously ultraconservative Saudi Arabia could inflame religious sentiment.

The state was exposed in a second way. An estimated 100,000 South Yemenis, mostly young men, were employed outside the country, mostly in Saudi Arabia and other conservative, oil-rich states of the Arabian Peninsula, where they were exposed to Islamic revivalist and fundamentalist influence. In the mid-1980s it was unclear what effect this had had on internal political dynamics. There was no evidence of an organized Islamic militant movement, but observers believed that as more expatriates returned home, an Islamic challenge to Marxism-Leninism and a co-opted clergy could develop.

Foreign Relations

South Yemen's foreign relations in the mid-1980s were guided by both ideological and pragmatic considerations. The country maintained intimate diplomatic and party-level ties with the Soviet Union and its allies, particularly Cuba and the German Democratic Republic (East Germany). Moscow assisted in, and conferred legitimacy on, Aden's state- and party-building endeavors and gave a limited amount of economic aid. Soviet, East German, and Cuban advisers served in the most important political, social, and military bodies. In turn, Aden faithfully supported Moscow's international initiatives, such as the call for a "zone of peace" in the Indian Ocean. More substantially, it provided the Soviets with basing access and storage facilities for their Indian Ocean Fleet at Aden and Socotra (see National Security, this ch.).

The country's deep poverty and the inadequacy of Soviet development aid, however, contributed to the evolution of a more balanced foreign policy. During the 1970s Aden's radicalism and its active support of insurgencies in North Yemen and Oman had isolated it from the rest of the Arab world. Ali Nasir adopted a more accommodating posture in order to secure economic aid from his oil-rich northern neighbors. Closer ties with the Arab world were not meant to entail a more distant relationship with Aden's chief patron, Moscow, but the hard-line fraction within the YSP opposed them as an unjustified compromise of their state's revolutionary commitment.

In mid-1985 about 25 foreign states maintained embassies in Aden. These included not only the Soviet Union, its East European allies, and the Soviet-aligned regimes of Cuba, Ethiopia, and Vietnam, but also several Arab states, including Saudi Arabia, Kuwait, the UAE, Iraq, and Libya (although Egypt was not represented because of South Yemen's opposition to the Egypt-Israeli peace treaty). Iran, India, Pakistan, Somalia, the Democratic People's Republic of Korea (North Korea), Japan, and China also had embassy-level diplomatic representation. During the 1980s ties were established with several West European countries, including Britain, France, Italy, and the Federal Republic of Germany (West Germany). South Yemen was a member of the UN and its related organizations, such as the International Labor Organization (ILO), the World Health Organization (WHO), and the United Nations Educational, Scientific and Cultural Organization (UNESCO), the Nonaligned Movement (despite the clearly pro-Soviet orientation of its foreign policy), the Arab League, the Islamic Development Bank, the International Monetary Fund (IMF), the Group of 77, and other international organizations.

The Chinese presence had been substantial during the presidency of Rubay Ali but declined after his removal in 1978. The United States, in Aden's eyes the center of world imperialism and reaction, had not had diplomatic relations with South Yemen since 1969. The beginnings of a rapprochement between Washington and Aden were reportedly evident under Rubay Ali, but the proposed visit of a United States diplomat to South Yemen in October 1977 was canceled after the assassination of North Yemeni president Hamdi. Given the inadequacy of Soviet development aid, Aden's promotion of relations with West European countries and Japan was largely motivated by economic considerations. Trade with Japan, Britain, Australia, France, and China surpassed that with the Soviet Union in the early 1980s, and Italian, Japanese, Belgian, West German, and British firms were involved in a variety of projects ranging from oil exploration to harbor construction (see Foreign Trade, this ch.).

Relations with the Soviet Union and Its Allies

On October 25, 1979, President Ismail signed in Moscow the 20-year Treaty of Friendship and Cooperation between the Union of Soviet Socialist Republics and the People's Democratic Republic of Yemen. The 16-article document is a statement of general principles guiding future relations rather than an elaboration of specific agreements. Aden and Moscow vow to promote economic, cultural, technical, and scientific exchanges, "develop cooperation in the military field," carry on the struggle against "imperialism, colonialism, and racism in all its forms and manifestations," and safeguard world peace. The treaty also affirms that the two signatories will consult with each other on matters of mutual importance and that each will refrain from entering into agreements with other states that might jeopardize the security or interests of the other. The participants, however, can terminate the treaty before the beginning of each of four terms of five years, totaling 20 years. Similar treaties were concluded by Aden with East Germany in November 1979, Czechoslovakia in September 1981, and Hungary and Bulgaria in November 1981.

Although Ali Nasir was far more active than his predecessor in promoting relations with states outside the Soviet sphere, South Yemen remained important to the Soviet Union in the mid-1980s for ideological and strategic reasons. In the terminology of Soviet analysts, it was a "state of socialist orientation." This represented a new concept of Third World revolution and a departure from earlier Soviet thinking, which had emphasized united fronts of socialists and nationalists against foreign imperialism. Such arrangements, particularly in Egypt and other Middle Eastern countries, had failed to foster Soviet interests or (from Moscow's perspective) genuine socialist revolution. The idea of "states of socialist orientation" acknowledged the difficulty of promoting revolution in highly traditional societies such as those of the Middle East and enjoined support for tightly organized revolutionary parties rather than mass movements invoking diverse anti-imperialist forces. In the mid-1980s South Yemen, Afghanistan, Nicaragua, Ethiopia, Angola, and Mozambique were designated "socialist-oriented states." The revolutionary party in each of these countries had originally been noncommunist, but each had evolved in a Marxist-Leninist direction under Soviet tutelage. Their importance to Moscow was symbolized in the prominent place given Ali Nasir and his fellow "socialist-oriented" leaders at the funeral of Soviet president Leonid Brezhnev in November 1982. Soviet policy toward Aden, however, was complicated by the evenhanded attitude displayed toward successive regimes in North Yemen. In 1979 Moscow became North Yemen's principal supplier of arms at a time when Sanaa's forces were fighting the South Yemen-backed NDF, and in October 1984 North Yemen and the Soviet Union signed a 20-year friendship treaty very similar to the 1979 Aden-Moscow agreement, although the Sanaa-Moscow agreement did not contain a military clause (see Relations with the Soviet Union, ch. 2).

Relations with North Yemen

The unity of the Yemeni nation, comprising both North Yemen and South Yemen, is recognized in the 1970 Constitution as a vital step in the building of a single nation. Nevertheless, relations between Aden and Sanaa have alternated between protestations of brotherly solidarity and armed confrontation since the early 1970s (see Relations with South Yemen, ch. 2). In September 1972 a border war flared up, but the mediation of other Arab countries led to the signing of an agreement the following month in Cairo on the unification of the two states. Aden, however, feared the growth of Saudi Arabian influence in North Yemen after the imposition of a military regime by Colonel Hamdi in June 1974. South Yemeni troops made frequent incursions over ill-defined borders into North Yemeni territory, and in March 1976 the leftist NDF was formed in Aden. Although at first the NDF assumed the character of a movement for peaceful change, it rapidly evolved into an armed insurgency based in the southern part of North Yemen.

In February 1979 fighting between the two states broke out on a large scale. The cycle of confrontation and reconciliation, however, made a full turn with the negotiation of cease-fire agreements in March 1979 and, more conclusively, in November 1981. In December of that year, presidents Ali Nasir and Ali Abdallah Salih announced new measures to implement Yemeni unity. These included the formation of the Yemen Council (also known as the Yemeni Supreme Council) consisting of the two presidents, a joint ministerial committee, and a secretariat to coordinate the unification process. Agreements were concluded to facilitate the movement of citizens between the two states, integrate educational and cultural programs, and promote the cooperation of their media. A new constitution for a unified "Yemeni Republic" was drafted in early 1982 by a constitutional committee appointed by the two governments, though its approval by their legislatures had not been accomplished as of mid-1985. Given the political and ideological differences between the two states, it was unclear how successful these plans for unification could be; observers suggested that a reassertion of hard-line control over the political system could result in a more hostile stance and renewed attempts to topple the Sanaa regime.

Other Regional Relations

The normalization of relations between South Yemen and Oman in October 1983 promised the end of almost 15 years of tension and armed confrontation. The political ideologies and security perspectives of the two states, however, remained deeply divergent in mid-1985. Oman was a conservative, absolute monarchy. Power was concentrated in the hands of the sultan, Qaboos bin Said Al Bu Said, scion of the oldest ruling house on the Arabian Peninsula. While the NLF of South Yemen had expelled the British in 1967, Oman's armed forces were staffed by British officers. The June 4, 1980, agreement signed by Oman and the United States, giving United States forces the use of installations on Omani soil at times when it served the security interests of both states, was perceived by Aden as a hostile and threatening measure to counteract its own radicalism and the presence of Soviet military personnel within its borders (see National Security, this ch.).

From Oman's perspective, South Yemen's support of the Popular Front for the Liberation of Oman (PFLO) insurgency in the southern region of Dhofar had been its most urgent security concern. Although Omani forces had crippled the insurgency by the mid-1970s, cutting it off from sources of arms and provisions in South Yemen, the PFLO Executive Committee was still based in Aden. A more conciliatory line toward Oman in the mid-1980s was an expression of Ali Nasir's moderate foreign policy. Foreign observers, however, believed that it was unlikely that the YSP leadership had abandoned completely the goal of revolutionary overthrow of the Omani monarchy.

The 1980 security agreement between Oman and the United States, the participation of Omani forces in United States-sponsored military exercises, and intermittent border fighting strained relations, but rapprochement was achieved through the mediation of other Arab states. In 1982 the foreign ministers of Kuwait and the UAE arranged consultations between high-level South Yemeni and Omani officials. In October of that year, agreement on a "declaration of principles" was reached, including a commitment to normalize relations. Other provisions included the establishment of a "technical committee" to deliberate on border disputes, an avowal that foreign forces were not to be used by either country for aggressive acts against the other, a moratorium on hostile propaganda, and a promise to exchange diplomats.

Formal diplomatic relations between South Yemen and Saudi Arabia were established in 1976, but Aden's support of insurgency in North Yemen and growing ties with the Soviet Union deepened longstanding Saudi suspicion and hostility. Economic and security factors each played a role in the substantial improvement in relations after the fall of President Ismail in April 1980. South Yemen desperately needed economic assistance, and a devastating flood that occurred in March 1982 left it greatly dependent on donations from oil-producing Arab states. Saudi Arabia, in turn, sought improved ties with South Yemen as a means of encouraging moderation among YSP leaders.

Within the regional context, however, South Yemen continued to support radical causes. In the mid-1980s it was a member of the Pan-Arab Front of Steadfastness and Resistance (Steadfastness Front), which opposed Egypt's peace treaty with Israel (other members were Libya, Syria, Algeria, and the Palestine Liberation Organization—PLO). Close ties were maintained between Aden and radical Palestinian groups, such as the Popular Front for the Liberation of Palestine (PFLP) and the Palestinian Communist Party, though Aden supported Yasir Arafat's leadership of the PLO. South Yemen gave moral support to Iran in its war with Iraq, perceived as a common enemy. Relations with Baghdad had become hostile in 1979 when a "hit squad" based in Iraq's embassy in Aden assassinated an Iraqi Marxist professor lecturing at the University of Aden. In addition, Baghdad offered refuge to antiregime exiles. Although both South Yemen and Iran publicly committed themselves to eliminating "alien hegemony" from the region, their concepts of revolution—Marxist-Leninist and Islamic—were not compatible ideologically, and there was limited basis for future joint action.

Ties with the fellow "socialist-oriented" regime of Lieutenant Colonel Mengistu Haile-Mariam in Ethiopia were close. Aden supported Ethiopia in its war with Somalia over Ogaden and its suppression of the separatist movement in its northern region of Eritrea. In December 1979 the two states signed a 15-year pact, the Treaty of Friendship and Cooperation between the People's Democratic Republic of Yemen and Ethiopia; like the October 1979 South Yemen-Soviet agreement, it was a statement of general principles governing bilateral relations. In August 1981 the two states, along with Libya, signed a trilateral treaty of friendship and cooperation affirming opposition to the United States military presence in the Indian Ocean,

Persian Gulf, Red Sea, and Mediterranean regions and establishing a mutual security arrangement. By mid-1985, however, the treaty had not led to closer ties with Libya, but relations with Ethiopia were good.

National Security

In mid-1985 the nation's regular armed forces, known as the Popular Defense Forces, maintained a level of about 27,500 officers and men, of whom about 18,000 were conscripts. A paramilitary force, the People's Militia, had an estimated strength of about 15,000. Not part of the military but performing quasi-military functions was the Public Security Force (police), which observers estimated as being approximately twice as large as the People's Militia.

At independence in 1967 the armed forces in the area that became South Yemen were believed to total 10,000. The lack of an external threat and the protection afforded by isolation, rugged terrain, and an almost nonexistent road net leading into the country combined to make larger forces unnecessary. Since independence, however, internal conditions that at times approached civil war and external relations with the neighboring countries of Oman, Saudi Arabia, and North Yemen that at times deteriorated into active warfare have required a strengthening of the armed forces.

Before independence the indigenous security forces consisted of the South Arabian Federal Army, the Federal National Guards, the Hadrami Beduin Legion, and the Mukalla Regular Army. In addition, there were local tribal guards and constabulary forces.

The South Arabian Federal Army of some 8,000 men was formed in 1961 from elements of the Aden Protectorate Levies, a British-commanded Arab force formed long before World War II to protect Aden Colony on the landward side and maintain peace in the tribal areas (see Consolidation of British Control over the Protectorates and Aden, ch. 1). The levies, and hence the federal army, were composed mainly of Audhali and Aulaqi tribesmen, a fact that rival tribes of Dathina resented. The Federal National Guards was formed in 1959 out of the original Government Guards of the Western Protectorate, a tribal force of about 2,000 troops responsible for internal security in the Western Protectorate. The 2,000-strong Hadrami Beduin Legion had originally been established in the 1930s to keep order among the feuding tribes in the Hadhramaut. The Mukalla Regular Army was a small tribal force responsible for security in Quayti State of the former Eastern Protectorate. The Mukalla Regular Army, like the other three forces, was trained by British officers but, unlike the others, was not commanded by British officers.

Upon independence in November 1967 the four security forces became the Southern Yemen Army. The initial arrangements were that Britain would continue to help develop the new republic's armed forces. In February 1968, however, the Aden government dismissed the 28 British officers attached to the Southern Yemeni forces. All military assistance from Britain was promptly terminated. The government in Aden subsequently turned to the Soviet Union, which in the summer of 1968 agreed to provide military aid and advisers.

In the mid-1980s South Yemen's military and internal security forces remained almost totally dependent on the Soviet Union for weapons and equipment. Soviet, East German, and Cuban advisers continued to perform training and other functions with the various defense and security units. Soviet and South Yemeni officials regularly stressed the "common ideology and political and strategic interests" that linked the two countries and praised the strong bilateral cooperation over a wide range of activities. The area in which close cooperation was most obvious was undoubtedly military affairs.

Mission, Control, and Capacity

The primary mission of the Popular Defense Forces was conventional: maintenance of territorial integrity and protection from foreign invasion. A secondary mission was the maintenance of internal security and public order. In accomplishing both missions the armed forces operated in concert with the Public Security Force and the People's Militia. All forces acknowledged a third mission in support of the people and society—civic action. In May 1973 the government announced the formation of Popular Defense Committees, which were modeled on the Cuban system and were designed to combine educational and social welfare activities with security duties. In addition, a number of serving military officers have been appointed to the middle and lower ranks of the administration.

Political control of the Popular Defense Forces by the YSP was direct and absolute. As elsewhere in the bureaucracy, political loyalty and reliability were valued more highly than experience and ability. Disloyalty and deviation from accepted doctrine, actual or suspected, reportedly resulted in severe punishment of those involved. The purges of the armed forces caused by the ongoing power struggle reportedly have undermined the effectiveness as well as the leadership of the armed forces. Inexperienced personnel of unknown military abilities have consequently attained key positions. In 1984 the commanders of the navy and air force were two young majors, and some brigades of the army were commanded by captains. Since independence this growing emphasis on party membership has been consolidated in the armed forces through "ideological classes" as well as training abroad in communist countries.

In mid-1985 the YSP in principle maintained firm control of the military. Brigadier General Salih Muslih Qasim, minister of defense, and Colonel Ahmad Musaid Husayn, minister of state security, were in the YSP's decisionmaking apparatus. The Supreme Defense Council was in charge of overall national defense policy. In mid-1985 its members were the president, the minister of defense, the commanders of the army, navy, and air force, the minister for state security, the minister of interior, and the head of the People's Militia. Command and control were exercised from the Popular Defense Forces headquarters in Aden. Direct command of the largest military units, the brigades, was also exercised from this headquarters, although the governors had some limited local control.

The South Yemeni armed forces have been involved in limited military conflicts with its three land neighbors: North Yemen in the border wars of September 1972 and February 1979; Saudi Arabia in 1969 and in December 1983 and January 1984; and Oman, in whose Dhofar Province a guerrilla war was waged with South Yemeni assistance in the mid-1970s.

Army

In the mid-1980s the combat units of the 24,000-man army consisted of 14 brigades: one armored, one artillery, one mechanized, one missile, and 10 infantry. The authorized strength of each brigade was 1,500 officers and men, which would total 21,000, but in late 1983 many of the brigades reportedly were significantly under strength.

Triangular organization was usual; for example, three companies would form a battalion, and three battalions would form a brigade. A larger or smaller number of battalions, however, might be attached to a brigade, according to the stationing, mission, terrain, or other military or political factors. Other combat arms—armor and artillery—were believed to be part of an infantry brigade organization, either organically or in attachment. There were also supporting administrative and logistical elements.

Three to five Soviet advisers reportedly served with each infantry brigade, one with each battalion, and one adviser with each armor or artillery unit attached to the brigade. (In late 1985 an estimated 1,500 Soviet military advisers were serving in South Yemen.)

Army training was primarily conducted by units, although there were training battalions in Aden believed to be charged with the training of recruits. Most of the technical and advanced officer training was done in the Soviet Union, and this training involved extensive political indoctrination at all levels. Training of lower ranks reportedly was conducted in a military school in Aden. On the whole, political training was mandatory at all military echelons and received maximum emphasis under the direction of the deputy minister of defense for political guidance.

The army's organizational structure had reasonable flexibility because battalions and other elements could be interchanged, and support units and the units of other combat arms could fit into the various brigade organizations, either organically or as attachments. The army had plans to expand and to receive more modern Soviet weapons. According to some military observers, the government hoped to increase the armed forces to around 50,000 men. This expansion would include acquiring Soviet-made T-62 and T-72 tanks to replace the old T-54 and T-55 tanks and in the process to increase the tank inventory from 450 to 700.

The army was heavily dependent on the Soviet Union and the Soviet Military Mission for equipment, spare parts, and technical support in maintenance (see table 18, Appendix). The limited road network made logistic support difficult in the areas distant from the Aden base. Despite these limitations, the army had a reputation for mobility and had demonstrated its capability in supporting military operations on its border with Oman, Saudi Arabia, and North Yemen.

Air Force

The air force in 1984 had more than 2,500 personnel. Well equipped and reportedly well maintained, it was capable of accomplishing its threefold mission: control of the country's airspace, tactical support of the ground forces, and air transport of men and matérial. Its operational capabilities were somewhat limited, chiefly by personnel deficiencies, but actual operations along the country's borders in the 1979 conflict with North Yemen had provided training and demonstrated capability. As in the army, political reliability was the prime requisite for command, and because of purges the air force had not escaped the consequences of the power struggle among South Yemen's leaders. The air force commander reported to the headquarters of the Popular Defense Forces.

The air force was organized in three sections: fighter, transport, and bomber. The combat elements were organized into four fighter-ground attack squadrons, two of which were equipped with 30 MiG-17Fs, one with 12 Mig-21s, and one with 25 Su-20s and Su-22s. There were three interceptor squadrons that flew 36 MiG-21Fs; one transport with 3 An-24s; one helicopter squadron with 15 Mi-24s and 30 Mi-8s; and one squadron with 10 Beagle light bombers. There was one SAM (surface-to-air missile) regiment with 48 SA-2s, and some AA-2 Atoll air-to-air missiles (see table 19, Appendix).

South Yemen would like to phase out its Mig-17s, and as of late 1984 it was considering selling them to Nicaragua. The South Yemenis want to replace these fighters with more sophisticated Mig-21 fighters. There was one squadron of advanced aircraft (MiG-23BMs) that was located near Aden; it was believed to be flown and maintained entirely by Soviets and Cubans and was designated to the defense of Aden. Some other combat and transport aircraft were flown by Cubans. The air force was based mainly at the Khormaksar International Airport near Aden and at Bayhan al Qisab, but new bases were being built at Thamud and Al Ghaydah.

There were also small military airstrips in Al Ansab, Ad Dali, Lawdar, and Ataq (see fig. 12).

Like the army, the air force was entirely dependent on foreign support for replacement aircraft, technical advice, guidance, and logistics support. The extremely limited road network hindered the rapid movement of vehicles into the country's interior, and air ferry operations have proved invaluable for moving troops and supplies into remote regions. During the 1981-82 uprising by the NDF in North Yemen, the South Yemeni air force provided some air cover for the guerrillas and assisted in ferrying supplies to the NDF forces within South Yemen.

Some foreign military observers have suggested that the Soviets and Syrians have trained special airborne commando units for South Yemen. As of mid-1985, however, there were no reports to confirm these speculations.

Navy

The 1,000-man South Yemeni navy had undergone considerable improvement, but in 1985 it remained the least developed of the armed forces. The navy lacked the ability to patrol even a fraction of the nation's vast coastal regions. The headquarters and the main operating base were located at Aden. The commander of the navy was subordinate to the Popular Defense Forces headquarters. Little formal training was carried on in the country; officers and technicians were sent to the Soviet Union. Repairs and maintenance were accomplished under the guidance of Soviet naval personnel in two shipyards in Aden. The navy was dependent on the Soviet Union for resupply of equipment, spare parts, and technical guidance. The Soviets also actively patrolled South Yemeni waters with ships and aircraft and had access to bases and facilities in the port of Aden and in Socotra and Perim islands.

In 1984 the navy possessed one corvette (a converted T-58 minesweeper) and eight Osa-class fast-attack craft with four Styx missiles. The navy also had two SO-1 large patrol craft, two P-6 FACs with torpedoes, two Zhuk FACs for patrol, two Mol fast torpedo boats, one Ropucha LST (landing ship-tank), three Polnocny LSTs, and three T-4 assault boats. All were of Soviet manufacture.

People's Militia

The organization of a paramilitary force subordinate to the party had been advocated by the ideologists of the NLF at the time of independence. These recommendations not only were in keeping with communist tradition but also had been incorporated into the Zinjibar Resolutions, which had called for the establishment of a militia. Little was done, however, until the change of government in June 1969. At that time President Rubayi Ali, impressed by China's example and wishing to counterbalance the army, launched the formation of the People's Militia under the tutelage of Chinese advisers.

Chinese arms and military personnel arrived in early 1971. Rapid development and expansion of the People's Militia began in mid-1971. The purpose of the People's Militia was to supplement the army and the Public Security Forces, help maintain internal security, establish the authority of the party throughout the country, and provide a means for the transmission of the party's program and propaganda countrywide. Unlike the other armed forces and police, which nominally at least were under government control, the People's Militia answered only to the party. A secondary argument for the establishment of the militia was economy; in a desperately poor country that in the 1969-71 period was spending nearly half its budget to maintain the regular armed forces, the militia offered a cheaper means of securing a military force. The wisdom of arming the undisciplined tribesmen, whose tribal loyalties might transcend party and national loyalty, was argued but accepted in the party.

Training centers for the People's Militia were established in several parts of the country. The length of training was three months, and the trainees were tribesmen and peasants. Many were marginally literate or illiterate, and literacy training was part of the curriculum. The major emphasis was on political training: Marxism, political economy, organization, and leadership. There was also instruction on new methods of husbandry and farming and on using and maintaining small arms. After training, the crash-course graduates returned to their districts, where they formed the nucleus of militia units. Especially talented students were given additional training as leaders.

In their home areas the militiamen were given responsibilities for the indoctrination and education of their people and the administration and defense of their villages. They served as links between and among the government, party, and villages. In those areas where there were limited police force or army stations, the militia units were given responsibility for internal security and continued loyalty to party and state. It was planned from the outset that they should assist in economic development, national integration, consolidation, and protection of the regime. They cooperated very closely with the Popular Defense Committees and were consistently closer to the party leadership than to the army, and on the occasion of the clash between Rubayi Ali and the Central Committee, their support was critical.

In 1984 the estimated strength of the People's Militia was around 15,000. Not uniformed and equipped only with small arms, the militiamen have remained a part of the population and blend easily into it. The Chinese advisers were replaced by cadres from East Germany. Ali Nasir had sought to reduce the level of tension between the regular armed forces and the People's Militia. Despite glowing and highly publicized accounts of militia successes in the war of 1979, its efficiency as a military force has been questioned. Lack of centrally organized training, inadequate weaponry, brief political indoctrination, and lack of leadership had been cited as factors inhibiting the militia's role as a military force. It was, however, a political-military force and a significant factor in maintaining internal security and the continued existence of the YSP in power. On August 20, 1983, Minister of Defense Qasim announced the establishment of a "General Department of Civil Defense," to be organized under the command of the People's Militia. In mid-1985 the purpose of this department was not publicly known.

Manpower and Conditions of Service

A military service law established in 1977 provided for compulsory military service for males for two years. In July 1984 the minister of defense issued a recruitment decree that instructed the graduates of all specialized institutions in the country to report for national military service. When enlisting new recruits for the army, officers were instructed to examine the young men, investigate their social background, and inquire extensively about their loyalties. Officers were required to encourage those whom they considered best suited to become politically active after completing their military service.

Living conditions for military personnel were as good or better than those of the general population. Housing was adequate, rations were ample if monotonously repetitive, and health and dental care were believed acceptable. Cubans were involved in improving the health care in the military, and South Yemeni personnel had been sent to Cuba for training, although the exact number was not known.

Rank, Pay, and Insignia

Pay was considered adequate in comparison with pay in the civilian economy. At independence the South Yemen military was reportedly the second-best-paid military force on the Arabian Peninsula, following that of oil-rich Kuwait. Because of the severe economic conditions and budgetary limitations imposed on the country after the closure of the Suez Canal and the departure of British forces and their financial support after independence, the salaries of government employees were slashed by amounts ranging from 6 to 60 percent. The military was affected as well, but exact pay reductions were not known.

The armed forces had five enlisted ranks in 1985, corresponding to private, private first class, corporal, sergeant, and master sergeant. There were two warrant officer ranks in the army—the equivalents of warrant officer and chief warrant officer—but only one in the air force, that of warrant officer; there were no known warrant officer ranks in the navy (see fig. 14).

There were six officer ranks in the navy, ranging from the Yemeni equivalent of ensign to that of captain, and seven officer ranks in the air force and army. Army ranks ranged from second lieutenant to brigadier general and air force ranks from second lieutenant to colonel, the seventh rank being without equivalent in corresponding United States services, an interim rank between major and captain. There was one peculiarity of officer ranks: the titles for the equivalent ranks were exactly the same (in Arabic) for all three services, although the uniforms and insignia were different for each service (see table E).

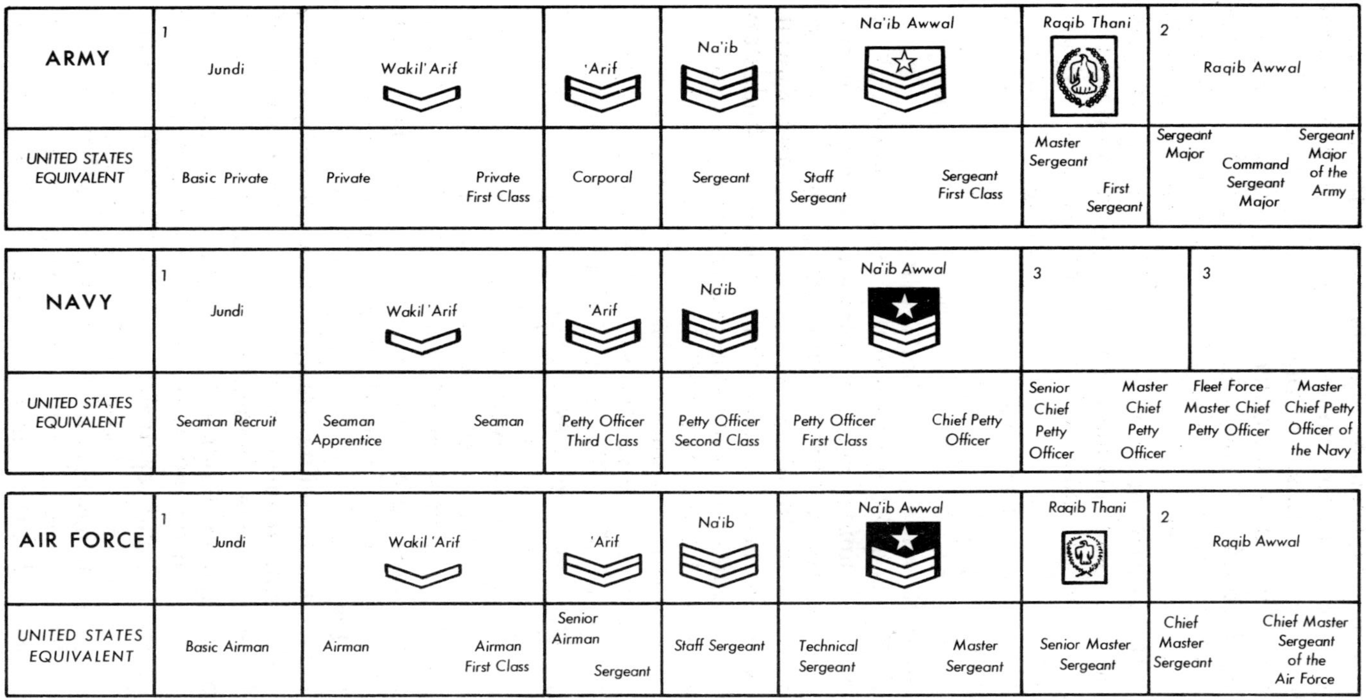

ARMY	Jundi[1]	Wakil 'Arif	'Arif	Na'ib	Na'ib Awwal	Raqib Thani	Raqib Awwal[2]
UNITED STATES EQUIVALENT	Basic Private	Private; Private First Class	Corporal	Sergeant	Staff Sergeant; Sergeant First Class	Master Sergeant; First Sergeant	Sergeant Major; Command Sergeant Major; Sergeant Major of the Army

NAVY	Jundi[1]	Wakil 'Arif	'Arif	Na'ib	Na'ib Awwal	[3]	[3]
UNITED STATES EQUIVALENT	Seaman Recruit	Seaman Apprentice; Seaman	Petty Officer Third Class	Petty Officer Second Class	Petty Officer First Class; Chief Petty Officer	Senior Chief Petty Officer; Master Chief Petty Officer	Fleet Force Master Chief Petty Officer; Master Chief Petty Officer of the Navy

AIR FORCE	Jundi[1]	Wakil 'Arif	'Arif	Na'ib	Na'ib Awwal	Raqib Thani	Raqib Awwal[2]
UNITED STATES EQUIVALENT	Basic Airman	Airman; Airman First Class	Senior Airman; Sergeant	Staff Sergeant	Technical Sergeant; Master Sergeant	Senior Master Sergeant	Chief Master Sergeant; Chief Master Sergeant of the Air Force

[1] No insignia. [2] Insignia not known. [3] No rank.

Figure 14. South Yemen: Insignia of Warrant Officers and Enlisted Ranks, 1982

Insignia of rank generally follow British example with inverted chevrons for noncommissioned personnel and modified pip and crown combinations for army officer personnel. Air force and navy officer insignia also follow British example closely (see fig. 15).

Military Aid and Assistance

The area that became South Yemen has traditionally relied on outside assistance for military aid and advice. Before 1967 this support was provided almost exclusively by Britain, and the latter was prepared to continue its support after independence. After the dismissal of the British military advisers in early 1968, however, and the pronounced shift to the political left by South Yemen, Britain terminated this assistance. Since that time military aid, assistance, and training have been provided almost exclusively by communist countries, chiefly the Soviet Union. The 1979 treaty with the Soviet Union calls on the Soviets to provide emergency assistance "in the event of the emergence of situations which constitute a threat to peace or violation of world peace."

The Soviet Union has two military interests in South Yemen: to train and equip the South Yemeni armed forces so that they are able to defend themselves and to acquire access to bases and facilities in South Yemen that can be of use for the Soviet Union's global strategy. The first military agreement between the two countries was reached in February 1968, and since then the South Yemeni armed forces have been reorganized and almost completely reequipped along Soviet lines. As of 1985 there were more than 1,500 South Yemenis in the Soviet Union. Some military sources indicated that there may be as many as 3,000 Soviet, East German, and Cuban military advisers in South Yemen.

South Yemeni government officials have consistently denied the existence of Soviet naval bases in Aden, but foreign intelligence reports have indicated that the Soviet military vessels use South Yemeni naval bases for refueling, changing crews, and repair work, an important function in the Soviet Union's military strategy and presence in the Indian Ocean. It has also used Aden as a staging post for flights to Ethiopia and other destinations in Africa. When in 1981 the tacit alignment of Libya, South Yemen, and Ethiopia was formalized into the Tripartite Military Alliance, the

Soviets called it a "defensive pact against United States imperialism" in that region. The Sudanese charged that this pro-Soviet pact was aimed at overthrowing their government, and Somalia's president Mohamed Siad Barre closed down the Libyan embassy after accusing Libya and South Yemen of providing military support for the opposition Somali Salvation Front.

Public Order and Internal Security

Various human rights reports have called South Yemen the worst police state in the Arab world, an estimated one-quarter of its population allegedly being engaged in some kind of security work. The charge, at least as far as the estimate of the population's involvement, was probably exaggerated, but it served to point up the reputation for ruthlessness, power, and efficiency that the security forces had gained since independence. Beyond all doubt the country was a police state, but because of the very ruthlessness, power, and efficiency, details of organization and operation of the Public Security Force (police) were not publicly available.

Nevertheless, the low level of available technology, the forbidding terrain, the considerable distances involved, and the lack of trained personnel have often made police enforcement a slow and haphazard process in the countryside. In some areas of Hadhramaut Governorate, for example, the police were said to learn of crimes committed in villages only long after they occurred, and officials acknowledged that they were poorly equipped to deal with lawbreakers. In the cities the establishment of the Civil Police in 1983 had helped to organize sufficient control.

Sources of possible internal dissension in 1984 were many and varied. Chief among them was the inevitable stress engendered by the imposition on a tribal population of a Marxist-Leninist state. Many of the traditional leaders either had fled or had been liquidated and replaced to a large extent by a new class constituted by the regime and composed of party officials and military officers. Family members of these officials reportedly had precedence in entry to government schools, such as the Police Academy, without any other qualifications. There were, however,

Table E. South Yemen: Titles of Military Rank, 1985

Arabic Name	United States Equivalents		
	Army[1]	Navy[2]	Air Force[2]
Officers			
Zaim	Brigadier general	---	---
Aqid	Colonel	Captain	Colonel
Qaid	Lieutenant colonel	Commander	Lieutenant colonel
Wakil qaid	Major	Lieutenant commander	Major
Wakil qaid thani[3]	---	---	---
Rais	Captain	Lieutenant	Captain
Mulazim awwal	First lieutenant	Lieutenant junior grade	First lieutenant
Mulazim thani	Second lieutenant	Ensign	Second lieutenant
Warrant Officers			
Wakil dabit awwal	Chief warrant officer	---	---
Wakil dabit thani	Warrant officer	---	---
Wakil dabit	---	---	Warrant officer
Enlisted			
Naib awwal	Master sergeant	Senior chief petty officer	Senior master sergeant
Naib	Sergeant	Petty officer second class	Staff sergeant
Arif	Corporal	Petty officer third class	Sergeant
Jundi awwal	Private first class	Seaman	Airman first class
Jundi	Private	Seaman recruit	Airman

--- means no United States equivalent.
[1]Brigadier general is highest rank in this service.
[2]Captain (colonel) is highest rank in this service.
[3]Air force rank only; there is no United States equivalent.

ARMY AIR FORCE AND NAVY	Mulazim Thani	Mulazim Awwal	Ra'is	Wakil Qa'id	Qa'id	'Aqid	'Amid				
UNITED STATES ARMY AND AIR FORCE EQUIVALENT	Second Lieutenant	First Lieutenant	Captain	Major	Lieutenant Colonel	Colonel	Brigadier General	Major General	Lieutenant General	General	General of the Army or the Air Force
UNITED STATES NAVY EQUIVALENT	Ensign	Lieutenant Junior Grade	Lieutenant	Lieutenant Commander	Commander	Captain	Rear Admiral (Lower Half)	Rear Admiral	Vice Admiral	Admiral	Fleet Admiral

Figure 15. South Yemen: Insignia of Officer Ranks

some indications that tribes still functioned and were treated as political actors in the mid-1980s (see Politics and Society, this ch.). Although those in government may be "detribalized" and depict tribal loyalties as ideologically unsound, they tended to view their own tribe as a ready-made power base to be used for personal advancement. Therefore, strong tribal loyalties have posed threats to the regime.

Other factors posing possible threats to internal security and the stability of the regime were resentments caused by the suppression of political opponents. Although thousands of political opponents have been jailed and hundreds of thousands had fled into exile since independence, there continued to be reports of the detention and house arrest of political figures out of favor with the current regime. The latest estimate available (1976) was that there might be as many as 10,000 political prisoners, but no current statistics were available in 1985.

The most serious known attempt at subversion was made during December 1981 and January 1982 by a group of 12 people who, according to the charges against them, tried to commit acts of sabotage against industrial, electrical, and oil installations. They were arrested and tried in two groups during February, March, and April 1982. All were sentenced to death and executed. Despite the prolonged trial, the South Yemeni media revealed little about the composition and origin of the group. The government asserted that the members had been trained in intelligence techniques and in the use of explosives by agents of the United States Central Intelligence Agency (CIA) stationed in Saudi Arabia and North Yemen. The group was alleged to have crossed into in South Yemen, where it was instructed to collaborate with "reactionary" elements and to carry out acts of sabotage. A Kuwaiti paper reported that the 12 were former police and army officers, some of whom had served under the British, but neither this nor other sources disclosed any further details.

There was little sign of activity by Abd al Qawwi Makkawi, leader of the National Grouping of Patriotic Forces in South Yemen. In February 1981 Makkawi announced that "military operations" were about to start, but the only sign of activity was an attack on the South Yemeni embassy in Paris a few days later. In exile in Cairo in mid-1985, he seemed to have restricted his activities to publishing an occasional article attacking the regime for its subservience to the Soviet Union and for the sufferings it inflicted on the population.

Externally, the opposition of the conservative regimes of the country's neighbors, Oman and Saudi Arabia, remained a constant threat to the regime in the mid-1980s. Occasionally there were unconfirmed reports of border clashes with Saudi Arabia (December 1983 and January 1984). Earlier, in the 1970s, a clash involving both the Saudi forces and the 5,000-man-strong Army of Deliverence, comprising South Yemeni exiles financed in Saudi Arabia, had brought the two countries to the brink of full-scale war. In Oman, South Yemen supported the guerrilla forces of the PFLO. The Oman government, however, had suppressed the rebellion before reaching a peace agreement with South Yemen in October 1982. The rebel forces outside Oman would now be little more than a token threat to Oman if South Yemen broke the peace accord. As of late 1983 they consisted of a small camp in South Yemen near Dhofar with fewer than 500 men. The training facilities of the camp shut down in 1977 because of a lack of recruits.

Omani forces did find South Yemeni forces and oil survey teams seven to 10 kilometers within Omani boundaries near Shahar in March 1981 and exchanged fire with the South Yemeni troops. These incidents were repeated in April and November 1981. However, as of 1985, relations between the two had improved, and in March 1985 Oman agreed to allow South Yemen's national airline to overfly its territory on services to Persian Gulf countries.

The Ministry of State Security

In a February 1985 cabinet reshuffle, the Committee for State Security (the secret police) was upgraded to the Ministry of State Security, with Colonel Husayn as minister. The secret police had its origins in the British-supported police forces existing in the area before independence. These forces were suspected by the leftist government that took power at independence and were heavily purged during the first months of 1968.

In 1985 the Ministry of State Security was one of three divisions of the security force, the other two being the Armed (or Civil) Police and the Rural Police. The total strength of the force was not known but was believed to rival that of the militia or the army. Furthermore, these forces were supplemented by the Popular Defense Committees. According to Halliday, however, popular social and educational activities had been largely replaced by security functions.

The mission of the secret police was internal security. Although elements had occasionally been employed across the country's borders, the force was not designed to defend the nation against external threats. Adequate to control subversion and minor threats to internal security, the secret police would probably require the assistance of the army or militia in the face of any serious threat. As part of this reinforcement, a new intelligence unit called the Military Intelligence Department was set up to assist the secret police in plot detection, antisabotage, counterespionage, and "forestalling and surprising plans and attempts by reactionary imperialist forces and the counterrevolution against the National Front organization and the state organizations."

The security forces in South Yemen have been organized and trained by East Germans and Cubans. There reportedly were about 730 Cubans in the training camps in the mid-1980s. The number of East German military advisers was not known in the mid-1980s, but it was clear that they supervised much of the internal security effort in Aden and other urban areas.

Terrorism

In a list of questions submitted in writing by the United States House of Representatives Subcommittee on Europe and the Middle East to the Department of State in May 1982, members of the subcommittee inquired whether South Yemen provided training camps for terrorist groups. The department responded that "while there have not been recent reports on the use of such camps, we believe they still exist." The YSP apparently still has a close association with the PFLP and has welcomed dissidents from a number of Gulf countries.

Independent observers have noted that South Yemen had terrorist training camps in the cities of Al Mukalla and Al Ghaydah. Among terrorist groups alleged to have received training there were West Germans, South Moluccans, members of the Irish Republican Army, the PFLP, the PLO, and an obscure Dutch terrorist group named Red

Resistance Front. Furthermore, 16 experts—seven Soviets and nine Cubans—reportedly arrived in Aden in early March 1983 to conduct three-month and five-month courses in the four main PLO training camps located north of Aden. The curriculum was said to include the handling of explosives and the preparation of improvised explosive charges, the use of infantry weapons, bridge demolition and mine-laying, and the gathering of information.

Crime and Punishment

Before independence crime had not posed a major problem. The traditional mechanisms of criminal control—tribal law and Islamic law, supplemented, in the Aden area at least, by British statutory law—had seemed adequate to control crime. Upon independence and the advent of the leftist regime, however, opposition to the party became a crime. Secular revolutionary courts were established throughout the provinces, and dissidents were classified as criminals and severely punished.

Prison populations before independence were not large; with independence and the institution of criminal penalties for political opposition, they jumped dramatically. Although prison conditions in the Al Mansura prison in Aden were thought to be relatively good, conditions elsewhere were reported to be poor. Sanitary facilities were grossly inadequate, rations were monotonous and meager, and treatment was excessively harsh. Many prisoners were held incommunicado for months and, when released, were placed under surveillance.

In addition to the jailing of thousands of political opponents, many opposition figures have simply disappeared. Exact figures were impossible to ascertain in the mid-1980s. In November 1983 the human rights organization, Amnesty International, wrote to the ambassador of South Yemen in London, enclosing a list of the names of 29 people whose cases had been investigated by the organization. These included several individuals whose whereabouts remained unknown and who were possibly no longer alive.

Arrests were not publicly announced, nor were the results of the trials except when deemed expedient by the government and party. Although torture is forbidden by the Constitution, there have been reports of the introduction of sophisticated forms of torture. Moreover, in the early

1970s there were reports of groups of political prisoners shot while attempting to escape and numerous official reports of trials for sabotage, espionage, and embezzlement and the subsequent execution or long-term imprisonment of those found guilty by the revolutionary courts. Estimates of executions ranged into the thousands. There have been several reports of actual or attempted assassinations, in and outside the country, which have been attributed to the party or factions within the party. By the 1980s lack of opposition within the country had reduced the number of trials, sentences, executions, and reported assassination attempts, although police and security force vigilance had apparently not abated.

* * *

Reliable material on the economy and the society is sparse. A dated but classic study of social stratification in the Hadhramaut is Abdalla S. Bujra's *The Politics of Stratification: A Study of Political Change in a South Arabian Town.* More recently, social scientist Maxine Molyneux visited South Yemen and subsequently wrote a series of articles on women, including "Women and Revolution in the People's Democratic Republic of Yemen" and "State Policy and the Position of Women in South Yemen." In 1985 the most comprehensive study of South Yemen's economy was the World Bank's country study, *People's Democratic Republic of Yemen: A Review of Economic and Social Development,* which was dated but still valuable. South Yemen's annual *Statistical Year Book* provides the most recent economic data available, although with considerable time lags. Other fragmentary socioeconomic information may be gleaned from such publications as the *Middle East Economic Digest* and the *Middle East Contemporary Survey,* edited by Colin Legum et al.

Little is written in Western languages on South Yemen's political system and practically nothing on the armed forces and the police. Marxist scholar Fred Halliday's essay, "The People's Democratic Republic of Yemen: The 'Cuban Path' in Arabia," published in *Revolutionary Socialist Devel-*

opment in the Third World, edited by Gordon White et al., provides a sympathetic and informative overview. A collection of short essays, *Contemporary Yemen: Politics and Historical Background*, edited by B.R. Pridham and published in 1984, includes a useful contribution by Halliday entitled "Soviet Relations with South Yemen" and one by Manfred Wenner, "South Yemen since Independence: An Arab Political Maverick." Roberto Aliboni's discussion of South Yemen's regional role in *The Red Sea Region: Local Actors and the Superpowers* is also useful. The International Institute for Strategic Studies' annual *The Military Balance* provides limited information on the armed forces and their equipment. (For further information and complete citations, see Bibliography.)

Appendix

Appendix

1 Unit Conversion Definitions
2 North Yemen: Summary of Government [illegible], 1981–85 [illegible]
3 North Yemen: Summary of [illegible], 1977–84
4 North Yemen: Area and Production of Major Crops, Crop Year 1979, 1982, and 1984
5 North Yemen: Summary of Balance of Payments, 1980 [illegible]
6 North Yemen: Major Army Equipment, 1987
7 North Yemen: Major Air Force Equipment, 1987
8 North Yemen: [illegible] Major Command [illegible], 1980s
9 South Yemen: [illegible] Cities, 1973 [illegible]
10 South Yemen: Members of [illegible] by [illegible], 1980 [illegible]
11 South Yemen: [illegible]
12 South Yemen: [illegible], Selected Years, 1973–[illegible]
13 South Yemen: [illegible] of Major [illegible], Selected Years, 1977
14 South Yemen: [illegible] Fish [illegible] Products, Selected Years, 1977–[illegible]
15 South Yemen: [illegible], 1979–84
16 South Yemen: [illegible], Selected Years, 1973–[illegible]
17 South Yemen: [illegible] of Payments, Selected Years, [illegible]
18 South Yemen: Major Army Equipment, 1987
19 South Yemen: Major Air Force Equipment, 1987

Table 1. Metric Conversion Coefficients

When you know	Multiply by	To find
Millimeters	0.04	inches
Centimeters	0.39	inches
Meters	3.3	feet
Kilometers	0.62	miles
Hectares (10,000 m^2)	2.47	acres
Square kilometers	0.39	square miles
Cubic meters	35.3	cubic feet
Liters	0.26	gallons
Kilograms	2.2	pounds
Metric tons	0.98	long tons
. . . .	1.1	short tons
. . . .	2,204	pounds
Degrees Celsius . . . . (Centigrade)	9 divide by 5 and add 32	degrees Fahrenheit

Table 2. North Yemen: Summary of Government Current Revenues, 1981-83
(in millions of rials)[1]

Current Revenues	1981	1982	1983[2]
Direct taxes			
Zakat	25	101	192
Individual income taxes	172	276	332
Business taxes	116	147	160
Other	27	37	62
Total direct taxes	340	561	746
Foreign trade taxes			
Import duties	1,159	1,301	1,580
Defense tax	301	344	605
Statistical tax	125	138	242
Other	49	57	48
Total foreign trade taxes	1,634	1,840	2,475
Taxes on goods	205	187	368
Taxes on services	130	128	204
Revenues on state properties	551	523	802
Revenues from government departments	469	453	707
TOTAL	3,329	3,692	5,302

[1]For value of the yemen rial--see Glossary.
[2]Provisional--subject to revision.

Source: Based on information from Yemen Arab Republic, Central Planning Organization, Statistics Department, *Statistical Year Book, 1983*, Sanaa, 1984, 202-204.

Table 3. North Yemen: Summary of Current Expenditures, 1981-83 (in millions of rials)[1]

Current Expenditures	1981	1982	1983[2]
Public administration	550	984	820
Security	387	541	565
Defense	1,354	2,166	2,109
Education	612	1,030	1,017
Health	103	162	192
Other social services	104	116	143
Economic services	180	162	201
Interest on the public debt	35	20	21
TOTAL	3,325	5,181	5,068

[1]For value of the Yemeni rial--see Glossary.
[2]Provisional--subject to revision.

Source: Based on information from Yemen Arab Republic, Central Planning Organization, Statistics Department, *Statistical Year Book 1983*, Sanaa, 1984, 205-206.

Table 4. North Yemen: Area and Production of Major Crops, Fiscal Years 1972, 1982, and 1983

Crop	1972		1982		1983	
	Area[1]	Production[2]	Area[1]	Production[2]	Area[1]	Production[2]
Sorghum and millet	840	573	689	580	689	268
Wheat	30	30	61	67	61	34
Corn	10	8	36	59	36	30
Barley	97	109	50	53	50	30
Vegetables	15	137	30	305	34	326
Dry legumes	60	60	70	75	70	40
Potatoes	5	58	12	150	12	163
Grapes	8	35	13	68	14	72
Other fruits	5	28	15	85	15	85
Coffee	9	4	8	3	8	3
Cotton	15	15	7	6	7	6
Tobacco	4	5	6	7	6	6
Sesame seeds	8	4	10	6	10	4

[1]In thousands of hectares.
[2]In thousands of tons.

Source: Based on information from Yemen Arab Republic, Central Planning Organization, Statistics Department, *Statistical Year Book, 1983*, Sanaa, 1984, Table 1/3.

Table 5. North Yemen: Summary of Balance of Payments, 1980-83 (in millions of United States dollars)

	1980	1981	1982	1983
Exports (f.o.b.)[1]	13	10	5	10
Imports (c.i.f.)[2]	−1,915	−1,748	−1,967	−1,796
Balance of trade	−1,902	−1,738	−1,962	−1,786
Service payments (net)	−21	−51	−37	−48
Private transfers and remittances (net)[3]	1,084	788	924	1,103
Official grants	148	337	445	186
Balance on current account	−691	−664	−630	−545
Drawings on official loans	467	262	232	224
Repayment of official loans	−15	−57	−42	−24
Other capital transactions (net)[4]	128	198	76	136
Drawings on reserves	111	261	364	209

[1]f.o.b.—freight on board.

[2]c.i.f.—cost, insurance, and freight.

[3]Includes remittances from workers abroad.

[4]Includes errors and omissions.

Source: Based on information from Yemen Arab Republic, Central Planning Organization, Statistics Department, *Statistical Year Book 1983*, Sanaa, 1984, Table 1/8.

Table 6. North Yemen: Major Army Equipment, 1984

Type Designation	Quantity	Country of Manufacture
Medium tanks T-54/-55	500	Soviet Union
Light Tanks T-34	100	-do-
Mechanized infantry combat vehicles BMP	50	-do-
Armored fighting vehicles BTR-40/-60/-152, M-113	400	Soviet Union and United States
Guns/howitzers 75mm, 76mm, 105mm, 122mm, 155mm	200	-do-
Self-propelled guns SU-100	30	Soviet Union
Multiple rocket launchers BM-21 122mm	60	Soviet Union
Mortars 82mm, 120mm	200	Soviet Union and United States
Antitank weapons LAW, M-72, TOW Recoilless, Vigilante	276	United States
Antitank guided weapons Dragon	24	-do-
Self-propelled antiaircraft guns ZSU-23/-24, Vulcan, SAM, 32mm, 37mm, 57mm, 85mm	114	Soviet Union and United States

Table 7. North Yemen: Major Air Force Equipment, 1984

Equipment Designation	Quantity	Country of Manufacture
Fighters F-5E, MiG-17F, Su-22, Mig-21	76	Soviet Union and United States
Transports C-130H, C-47, Skyvan, Ii-4, An-24, An-26	11	-do-
Helicopters Mi-8, AB-206/-212, Alouette	33	Soviet Union, United States, and France
Trainers F-5B, MiG-15UTI	8	Soviet Union and United States
Missiles SA-2 SAM, AIM-9, Sidewinder, AA-2 ATOLL	n.a.	-do-

n.a.—not available.

Table 8. North Yemen: Imports by Major Commodity Group, 1980-82 (in millions of rials)*

Commodity Group	1980	1981	1982
Food and live animals	2,213	2,182	2,033
Beverages and tobacco	104	104	120
Raw materials	43	40	34
Fuels and lubricants	609	608	828
Animal and vegetable oils	66	45	56
Chemicals	432	413	454
Machinery and transport equipment	2,348	1,866	1,342
Manufactured goods	2,140	1,633	1,499
Other	499	449	574
TOTAL	8,454	7,340	6,940

* For value of the Yemeni rial—see Glossary.

Source: Based on information from Yemen Arab Republic, Central Planning Organization, Statistics Department, *Statistical Year Book, 1983*, Sanaa, 1984, table 3/7.

Table 9. South Yemen: Incidence of Disease, 1980

Disease	Number of Cases	Disease	Number of Cases
Dysentery and amebiasis . . .	12,622	Bilharzia	199
Influenza	7,877	Chicken pox	59
Pneumonia	6,222	Poliomyelitis	55
Malaria	5,917	Diphtheria	30
Measles	3,766	Tetanus	29
Enteritis and other diarrheal diseases	2,549	Typhoid and paratyphoid . .	19
Whooping cough	1,844	Leprosy	4
Tuberculosis	710	Acute respiratory infection	n.a.
Epidemic meningitis	419	Gonorrhea	n.a.
Mumps	391	Syphilis	n.a.
Infectious hepatitis	309	TOTAL	45,001

n.a.—not available

Source: Based on information from People's Democratic Republic of Yemen, Ministry of Planning, Central Statistical Organization, *Statistical Yearbook, 1983*, Aden, September 1984, 56.

Table 10. South Yemen: Number of Medical Establishments by Governorate, 1980

Establishments	Governorate						
	Al Mahrah	Hadhramaut	Shabwah	Abyan	Lahij	Aden	Total
Hospitals	1	6	4	5	8	7	31
Medical Centers	1	9	1	3°	4°	1	19
Medical Units	11	90	41	52	60	23	277
Clinics	2	28	5	7	12	24	78
Dispensaries	n.a.	n.a.	n.a.	n.a.	n.a.	5	5
Mother and child care centers	2	7	4	3	9	9	34
Maternal centers	n.a.	n.a.	n.a.	n.a.	n.a.	1	1

n.a.—not available.

° Including a primary health care center.

Source: Based on information from People's Democratic Republic of Yemen, Ministry of Planning, Central Statistical Organization, *Statistical Yearbook 1983* Aden, September 1984, 53.

Table 11. South Yemen: Summary of Government Budget, 1979-82 (in millions of Yemeni dinars)[1]

	1979	1980	1981	1982
Revenue				
Taxes	43.1	68.9	87.9	90.0
Nontax revenues	17.2	34.4	32.2	36.3
Foreign grants	8.2	10.5	19.4	19.3
Other revenues	10.9	7.4	14.4	n.a.
Total revenue	79.4	121.2	153.9	145.6
Expenditure				
Current expenditures	75.3	94.5	138.0	142.1
Development expenditures[2]	44.7	60.9	91.2	120.7
Total expenditure	120.0	155.4	229.2	262.8
Budget deficit (financed by)				
Foreign loans (net)	18.5	27.3	47.9	52.1
Domestic banking[3]	22.1	6.9	27.4	65.1
Total budget deficit	40.6	34.2	75.3	117.2

n.a.—not available.
[1]For value of the Yemeni dinar—see Glossary.
[2]Includes only budgeted investments.
[3]Residual.

Table 12. South Yemen: Labor Force, Selected Years, 1973-82 (in thousands of workers)

	1973	1980	1981	1982
Agriculture	152	195	195	196
Fishing		9	9	9
Industry	20	45	48	50
Construction	15	33	36	41
Trade	25	39	42	44
Transportation and communications	14	27	29	29
Other services	97	92	96	99
TOTAL	323	440	455	468

Table 13. South Yemen: Area and Production of Major Crops, Selected Years, 1975-82

Crop	1975		1980		1981		1982	
	Area[1]	Production[2]	Area[1]	Production[2]	Area[1]	Production[2]	Area[1]	Production[2]
Sorghum	18.87	15.5	20.12	16.6	31.05	24.4	22.23	20.0
Wheat	7.95	8.8	5.48	7.8	5.38	7.5	4.92	7.4
Corn	1.40	1.2	3.49	3.2	3.07	2.9	2.40	2.6
Cotton	9.30	10.8	6.52	5.4	4.86	5.2	3.45	3.4
Tobacco	0.63	1.3	0.31	0.6	0.43	0.8	0.34	0.8
Sesame	3.33	2.2	3.86	1.4	4.13	1.8	4.12	1.4
Tomatoes	1.42	11.1	1.30	15.4	1.49	17.6	1.20	12.5
Onions	0.23	1.3	0.40	3.3	0.44	3.5	0.47	3.3
Melons	0.85	9.2	1.23	9.7	1.93	16.4	1.89	10.0
Potatoes	0.21	1.9	0.51	5.3	0.59	6.6	0.86	8.9
Fodder	3.23	40.5	11.63	137.7	19.27	273.9	18.38	145.4
Dates	7.15	19.9	4.89	7.9	5.90	10.4	5.91	11.2
Bananas	0.81	11.4	0.80	12.5	0.42	8.7	0.57	15.5

[1]In thousands of hectares.
[2]In thousands of tons.

Table 14. South Yemen: Production of Selected Industrial Products, Selected Years, 1978-82

Industrial Product	Unit	1978	1980	1981	1982
Textiles	millions of meters	3.3	1.9	1.8	2.7
Cement blocks	thousands of pieces	327.0	502.0	300.0	500.0
Cigarettes	millions	982.0	1248.0	1248.0	1150.0
Liquid batteries	thousands of pieces	20.4	13.0	14.5	17.7
Tomato canning	tons	1,203.0	1,228.0	900.0	800.0
Flour milling . .	thousands of tons	38.4	31.8	34.5	19.2
Dairy products	millions of liters	4.4	5.7	5.7	4.8
Soft drinks	millions of bottles	34.0	16.0	54.0	56.0
Aluminum utensils	tons	507.0	400.0	300.0	300.0
Paper bags	-do-	426.0	521.0	557.0	514.0
Plastic utensils	-do-	149.0	339.0	154.0	262.0
Foam rubber . .	-do-	501.0	619.0	526.0	545.0
Plastic shoes . .	thousands of pairs	1,378.0	122.0	n.a.	294.0
Paints	millions of liters	1.2	1.5	1.9	1.6
Perfumes	thousands of liters	26.0	9.0	6.0	16.0
Nails	tons	327.0	297.0	238.0	345.0
Tiles	thousands of pieces	869.0	1,200.0	700.0	1,300.0
Shirts	-do-	472.0	322.0	406.0	332.0
Leather	-do-	28.0	78.0	136.0	181.0
Leather shoes	thousands of pairs	134.0	94.0	105.0	157.0
Electricity	millions of kilowatt-hours	198.0	198.0	220.0	270.0

n.a.—not available

Table 15. South Yemen: Major Exports of Local Products, Selected Years, 1973-81 (in thousands of Yemeni dinars)[1]

Product	1973[2]	1978	1980	1981
Fish products[3]	1,128	2,123	6,387	2,014
Coffee	234	32	8	0
Raw tobacco	56	330	672	697
Hides	320	148	121	72
Cotton lint	2,139	1,426	3,083	450
Salt	117	358	191	279
Water (for ships)	53	104	87	88
Other local products	279	1,663	2,973	2,889
TOTAL	4,326	6,184	13,522	6,489

[1]For value of the Yemeni dinar—see Glossary.
[2]Exports by land excluded.
[3]Excludes fish products under royalty arrangement.

Source: Based on information from People's Democratic Republic of Yemen, Ministry of Planning, Central Statistical Organization, *Statistical Year Book 1983*, Aden, September 1984, 157.

Table 16. South Yemen: Imports by Major Commodity Group, Selected Years, 1973-81 (in millions of Yemeni dinars)[1]

Commodity Group[2]	1973[3]	1978	1980	1981
Food and live animals	16.7	40.7	66.1	66.4
Beverages and tobacco	1.1	3.2	5.3	2.6
Crude materials (excluding fuels)	1.4	3.9	9.5	3.6
Petroleum products	26.9	6.8	51.9	54.2
Oils and fats	0.3	7.2	5.5	4.9
Chemicals	1.6	5.2	8.1	11.1
Manufactured goods	6.1	17.9	25.7	28.5
Machinery and transport equipment	3.0	30.9	44.2	52.0
Other manufactured articles	2.6	6.4	8.8	9.2
TOTAL[4]	59.8	122.8	225.3	232.5

[1]For value of the Yemeni dinar—see Glossary.
[2]According to Standard International Trade Classification system.
[3]Includes some oil imports excluded in later years and excludes imports by land.
[4]Figures may not add to total because of rounding.

Source: Based on information from People's Democratic Republic of Yemen, Ministry of Planning, Central Statistical Organization, *Statistical Year Book, 1983*, Aden, September 1984, 158.

Table 17. South Yemen: Summary of Balance of Payments, Selected Years 1973-82
(in millions of United States dollars)

	1973	1980	1981	1982
Exports[1]	13.9	38.3	28.4	20.6
Imports[1]	−119.8	−649.9	−761.4	−747.3
Trade balance	−105.9	−611.6	−733.0	−726.7
Services (net)	6.5	13.9	10.0	−6.4
Investment income[2]	4.0	29.8	44.0	49.5
Private remittances[3]	33.7	348.1	410.0	467.3
Official transfers	0.3	82.9	144.0	125.7
Balance on current account	−61.4	−136.9	−125.0	−90.6
IMF credits allocations (net)[4]	11.3	−6.7	−3.4	23.1
Other government credits (net)[5]	24.7	76.3	171.0	177.2
Short-term capital (net)[6]	23.0	91.6	−21.9	−77.9
Balance on capital account	59.0	161.2	145.7	122.4
Change in reserves[7]	2.4	−24.3	−20.7	−31.8

[1]Net of re-exports.
[2]Primarily from international currency reserves.
[3]Largely remittances from workers abroad.
[4]IMF—International Monetary Fund.
[5]Primarily foreign aid loans.
[6]Includes errors and omissions.
[7]A minus sign indicates an increase in reserves.

Table 18. South Yemen: Major Army Equipment, 1984[1]

Equipment Designation	Quantity
Medium tanks	
T-54/-55/-62	450 (medium and light tanks combined)
Light tanks	
T-34	
Mechanized infantry combat vehicles (MICVs)	100
BRDM-2	
BMP	
Armored personnel carriers (APCs)	300
BTR-40/-60/-152	
Guns/howitzers	350
M-1945 85mm	
M-1955 100mm	
M-46 130 mm	
M-38 122 mm	
D-30 122mm	
Multiple rocket launcher (MRLs)	n.a.
BM-21 122mm	
Mortars	n.a.
160mm, 120mm	
Surface-to-surface missiles (SSMs)	12
FROG	
Scud B	6
Antitank weapons	n.a.
AT-3 (Sagger)	
Antiaircraft (AA)	200
23mm ZU-23[2]	
23mm ZU-23-2	
37mm ZSU-23-4	
57mm ZSU-23-4 (towed)	
Surface-to-air missiles (SAMs)	
SA-2	6
SA-3, SA-6/-7	3

[1]All equipment Soviet-made.

[2]Light antiaircraft gun (towed).

Source: Based on information from *The Military Balance, 1984-1985*, London, 1984, 74; and Mark Heller et al., *The Middle East Military Balance, 1984*, Boulder, 1983, n.p.

Table 19. South Yemen: Major Air Force Equipment, 1984[*]

Equipment Designation	Quantity
Fighters	
MiG-17F	30
MiG-21	12
Su-20/-22	25
MiG-21F	36
Transports	
An-24	3
Helicopters	
Mi-24	15
Mi-8	30
Trainers	
MiG-15UTI	3
Missiles	
SA-2	48

[*]All equipment Soviet-made.

Source: Based on information from *The Military Balance, 1984-1985*, London, 1984, 73.

Bibliography

Abraham, Nabeel. "Detroit's Yemeni Workers," *MERIP Reports*, 57, May 1977, 3-9.

Adra, Najwa. *Qaybala: The Tribal Concept in the Central Highlands of the Yemen Arab Republic.* (Ph.D. dissertation, Temple University, 1982.) Ann Arbor: Xerox University Microfilms, DEP83-11576.

Al-Abiadh, Ahmed. "Modernization of Government Institutions, 1962-1969." Pages 147-53 in B.R. Pridham (ed.), *Contemporary Yemen: Politics and Historical Background.* New York: St. Martin's Press, 1984.

Ali, Hussein, and Ken Whittingham. "Notes Towards an Understanding of the Revolution in South Yemen," *Race and Class* [London], 16, No. 1, July 1974, 83-100.

Aliboni, Roberto. *The Red Sea Region: Local Actors and the Superpowers.* Syracuse: Syracuse University Press, 1985.

"Ali Nasir Muhammad Views Domestic, Regional Issues," Foreign Broadcast Information Service, *Daily Report: Middle East and Africa*, 5, No. 69 (FBIS-MEA-85-069), April 9, 1985, C4-C6.

Al-Marayati, Abid A. "United Nations and the Problem of Aden," *India Quarterly* [New Delhi], 22, No. 3, July-September 1966, 257-78.

Al-Noban, Saeed Abdul Khair. "Education for Nation-Building: The Experience of the People's Democratic Republic of the Yemen." Pages 102-23 in B.R. Pridham (ed.), *Contemporary Yemen: Politics and Historical Background.* New York: St. Martin's Press, 1984.

Anderson, J.N.D. *Islamic Law in the Modern World.* New York: New York University Press, 1959.

Anderson, J.N.D. (ed.) *Changing Law in Developing Countries.* New York: Praeger, 1963.

Anthony, John Duke. "The Communist Party of the People's Democratic Republic of Yemen: An Analysis of Its Strengths and Weaknesses." Pages 232-39 in B.R. Pridham (ed.), *Contemporary Yemen: Politics and Historical Background.* New York: St. Martin's Press, 1984.

______. *The Red Sea: Control of the Southern Approach.* (Middle East Problem Paper, No. 13.) Washington: Middle East Institute, 1975.

Arab Information Center. *British Imperialism in Southern Arabia.* (Information Papers, No.6.) New York: November 1958.

Arif, Muhammad. "People's Democratic Republic of Yemen Seeks to Develop Productive Capacity of Economy," *IMF Survey*, April 1983, 119-22.

Awn, Peter J. "Faith and Practice." Pages 1-27 in Marjorie Kelly (ed.), *Islam: The Religious and Political Life of a World Community.* New York: Praeger, 1984.

Barrat, Patrice. "The Al Khaukha Camp," *Refugees* [Geneva], 14, February 1985, 17-18.

Barthoff, Douglas F. "The Soviet Dilemma in Yemen," *SAIS Review*, 12, No. 1, Autumn 1967, 15-22.

Becker, Abraham S., Bent Hansen, and Malcolm H. Kerr. *The Economics and Politics of the Middle East.* New York: American Elsevier, 1975.

Bell, J. Bowyer. "South Arabia: Violence and Revolt," *Conflict Studies* [London], No. 40, November 1973.

Bethmann, Erich W. *Yemen on the Threshold*, 3. Washington: American Friends of the Middle East, 1960.

Bibby, Geoffrey. *Looking for Dilmun.* London: Collins, 1970.

Bidwell, Robin L. *The Arab World, 1900-1972.* London: Cass, 1973.

______. *The Two Yemens.* Boulder: Westview Press, 1983.

Birks, J.S., and C.A. Sinclair. "Employment and Development in Six Poor Arab States: Syria, Jordan, Sudan, South Yemen, Egypt, and North Yemen," *International Journal of Middle East Studies*, 14, No. 1, February 1982, 35-51.

Birks, J.S., C.A. Sinclair, and J.A. Socknat, *International Migration Project Country Case Study: Yemen Arab Republic.* (Research paper.) Durham, England: Department of Economics, University of Durham, 1978.

Blaustein, Albert P., and Gisbert M. Flanz. *People's Democratic Republic of Yemen.* (Constitutions of the Countries of the World series.) Dobbs Ferry, New York: Oceana, 1972.

Boals, Kathryn D. "Modernization and Intervention: Yemen as a Theoretical Case Study." (Ph.D. dissertation.) Princeton: Department of Political Science, Princeton University, 1969.

______. *The Role of International Law in the Internal War in Yemen.* (Center of International Studies Research Monograph.) Princeton: Princeton University Press, 1968.

Braun, Ursula. "Prospects for Yemeni Unity." Pages 261-69 in B.R. Pridham (ed.), *Contemporary Yemen: Politics and Historical Background.* New York: St. Martin's Press, 1984.

Brown, William R. "The Yemeni Dilemma," *Middle East Journal*, 17, No. 4, Autumn 1963, 349-67.

Buckmaster Viscount. "The Yemen Arab Republic Today," *Asian Affairs* [London], 14, No. 3, October 1983, 287-96.

Bujra, Abdalla S. "Political Conflict and Stratification in Hadramaut—II," *Middle Eastern Studies* [London], 4, No. 1, October 1967, 2-28.

______. *The Politics of Stratification: A Study of Political Change in a South Arabian Town.* Oxford: Clarendon Press, 1971.

______. "Urban Elites and Colonialism: The Nationalist Elites of Aden and South Arabia," *Middle Eastern Studies* [London], 6, No. 2, May 1970, 189-211.

Bukair, Salem Omar. "The PORY: Three Designs for Independence." Pages 63-75 in B.R. Pridham (ed.), *Contemporary Yemen: Politics and Historical Background.* New York: St. Martin's Press, 1984.

Bulliet, Richard W. *The Camel and the Wheel.* Cambridge: Harvard University Press, 1975.

Burrowes, Robert D. "The Yemen Arab Republic and the Ali Abdallah Salih Regime: 1978-1984," *Middle East Journal*, 39, No. 3, Summer 1985, 287-316.

Carapico, Sheila, and Richard Tutwiler. *Yemeni Agriculture and Economic Change: Case Studies of Two Highland Regions.* Sanaa: American Institute for Yemeni Studies, 1981.

Chelhod, Joseph. "Les cérémonies du mariage au Yémen," *Objets et mondes* [Paris], 13, No. 1, Spring 1973, 3-34.

______. "L'organisation sociale au Yémen," *L'ethnographie* [Paris], No. 64 (New Series), 1970, 61-86.

______. "La société yémenite et le droit," *L'homme* [The Hague], 14, No. 2, June 1975, 67-68.

______. "La société yémenite et le kat," *Objets et mondes* [Paris], 12, No. 1, Spring 1972, 3-22.

Chirkin, V., and Y. Yudin. *A Socialist Oriented State: Instrument of Revolutionary Change.* Moscow: Progress, 1983.

Cigar, Norman. "Arab Radicalism: The Case of South Yemen." (Paper presented at February 27, 1985, meeting of the study group on Arab Radicalism, Council of Foreign Relations.)

———. "State and Society in South Yemen," *Problems of Communism*, 34, No. 3, May-June 1985, 41-58.

Cline, Ray S., and Yona Alexander. *Terroism: The Soviet Connection*. New York: Crane, Russak, 1984.

Cohen, John M., and David B. Lewis. "Capital-Surplus, Labor-Short Economics. Yemen as a Challenge to Rural Development," *American Journal of Agricultural Economics*, March 1979, 523-28.

Coon, Carleton S. "Southern Arabia: A Problem for the Future." Pages 187-220 in *Papers of the Peabody Museum of American Archaeology and Ethnology*. Cambridge: Harvard University, 1943.

Corbin, Henry. *Cyclical Time and Ismaili Gnosis*. London: Kegan Paul , 1983.

Cordesman, Anthony H. *The Gulf and the Search for Strategic Stability*. Boulder: Westview Press, 1984.

Coulson, Noel J. *A History of Islamic Law*. Edinburgh: Aldine, 1964.

Creekman, C. "Sino-Soviet Competition in the Yemens," *U.S. Naval War College Review*, 32, No. 1, July-August 1979, 73-82.

David, Clifford B., and Patricia Hallett David. "Bottle-Feeding and Malnutrition in a Developing Country: The 'Bottle-Starved' Baby," *Journal of Tropical Pediatrics* [Oxford], 30, No. 3, June 1984, 159-64.

Dekmejian, R. Hrair. *Islam in Revolution: Fundamentalism in the Arab World*. Syracuse: Syracuse University Press, 1985.

Delury, George E. (ed.) *World Encyclopedia of Political Systems and Parties*. 2 vols. New York: Facts on File, 1983.

Dobson, Christopher, and Ronald Payne. *The Terrorists: Their Weapons, Leaders, and Tactics*. New York: Facts on File, 1982.

Doe, Brian. *Southern Arabia*. New York: McGraw-Hill, 1971.

Douglas, Leigh. "The Free Yemeni Movement: 1935-1962." Pages 34-45 in B.R. Pridham (ed.), *Contemporary Yemen: Politics and Historical Background*. New York: St. Martin's Press, 1984.

Dresch, Paul. "The Position of Shaykhs Among the Northern Tribes of Yemen," *Man* [London], 19, No. 1, March 1984, 31-49.

———. "The Several Peaces of Yemeni Tribes," *Journal of the Anthropological Society of Oxford* [Oxford], 12, No. 2, 1981, 73-86.

———. "Tribal Relations and Political History in Upper Yemen." Pages 154-74 in B.R. Pridham (ed.), *Contemporary Yemen: Politics and Historical Background.* New York: St. Martin's Press, 1984.

Efrat, Moshe. "The People's Democratic of Republic of Yemen: Scientific Socialism on Trial in an Arab Country." Pages 165-201 in Peter Wiles (ed.), *The New Communist Third World, an Essay in Political Economy.* New York: St. Martin's Press, 1982.

El-Affendi, Abdelwahab, et al. "Yemen File," *Arabia: The Islamic World Review* [East Burnham, England], No. 30, February 1984, 37-46.

El Azhary, M.S. "Aspects of North Yemen's Relations with Saudi Arabia," *Asian Affairs* [London], 15, Part 3, October 1984, 277-86.

Elmi, Abdullahi S. "The Chewing of Khat in Somalia," *Journal of Ethnopharmacology* [Limerick], 8, No. 2, August 1983, 163-76.

Entelis, John P. "Nationalism, Nasserism, and the Arab World," *Arab Journal*, 4, No. 1, Winter 1967, 35-42.

Farnworth, John. "Focus on North Yemen, Developing Agriculture in the Highlands," *Middle East Agribusiness* [Redhill, Surrey, England], 4, No. 7, July-August 1984, 28-30.

Fayein, Claudie. *Yemen.* Paris: Éditions du Seuil, 1975.

Fergany, Nader. "The Impact of Emigration on National Development in the Arab Region: The Case of the Yemen Arab Republic," *International Migration Review*, 16, No. 4, Winter 1982, 757-80.

Fisher, W.B. *The Middle East: A Physical, Social, and Regional Geography.* London: Methuen, 1971.

"From Arabia Felix to Arabia Deserta? Conference Notebook," *The Middle East* [London], September 1983, 60-63.

Fyzee, Asaf A.A. "The Ismailis." Pages 318-29 in A.J. Arberry (ed.), *Religion in the Middle East: Three Religions in Concord and Conflict, Vol. 2: Islam.* Cambridge: Cambridge University Press, 1969.

Gable, Richard W. *Government and Administration in the Yemen Arab Republic*. Davis: University of California, 1979.

Gavin, R.J. *Aden under British Rule, 1839-1967*. London: Hurst, 1975.

Gerholm, Tomas. *Market, Mosque and Mafraj: Social Inequality in a Yemeni Town*. Stockholm: Stockholm Studies in Social Anthropology, 1977.

Gibb, H.A.R., and J.H. Kramers (eds.). *Shorter Encyclopedia of Islam*. Ithaca: Cornell University Press, 1953.

Gochenour, D. Thomas. "Towards a Sociology of the Islamisization of Yemen." Pages 1-19 in B.R. Pridham (ed.), *Contemporary Yemen: Politics and Historical Background*. New York: St. Martin's Press, 1984.

Great Britain. Admiralty. Naval Intelligence Division. *Western Arabia and the Red Sea*. (Geographical Handbook Series, No. BR-527.) Oxford: 1946.

Guskov, A. "The Sound Foundations of Soviet-Yemeni Friendship", *International Affairs* [Moscow], December 1982, 73-76.

Haddad, George M. *Revolutions and Military Rule in the Middle East. The Arab States, 3: Egypt, the Sudan, Yemen, and Libya*. New York: Speller and Sons, 1973.

Hajar, M.M., et al. "Prevalence, Incidence, and Epidemiological Features of Poliomyelitis in the Yemen Arab Republic," *Bulletin of the World Health Organization* [Geneva], 61, No. 2, 1983, 353-59.

Halliday, Fred. *Arabia Without Sultans: A Political Survey of Instability in the Arab World*. New York: Random House, 1975.

______."The People's Democratic Republic of Yemen: The 'Cuban Path' in Arabia." Pages 35-74 in Gordon White et al. (eds.), *Revolutionary Socialist Development in the Third World*. Lexington: University Press of Kentucky, 1983.

______."Soviet Relations with South Yemen." Pages 208-31 in B.R. Pridham (ed.), *Contemporary Yemen: Politics and Historical Background*. New York: St. Martin's Press, 1984.

______."The Yemens: Conflict and Co-existence," *World Today* [London], 40, Nos. 8-9, August-September 1984, 355-62

———. "Yemen's Unfinished Revolution: Socialism in the South," *MERIP Reports No. 81*, 9, No. 8, October 1979, 3-20.

Hamilton, R.A.B. "Social Organisation of the Aden Protectorate, II: The Tribesman Class," *Journal of the Royal Central Asian Society* [London], 30, Nos. 3-4, September 1943, 267-74.

———. "The Social Organisation of the Tribes of the Aden Protectorate," *Journal of the Royal Central Asian Society* [London], 30, No. 2, May 1943, 142-57.

Hart, Jane Smiley. "Basic Chronology for a History of the Yemen," *Middle East Journal*, 17, Nos. 1-2, Winter-Spring 1963, 144-53.

Hartley, John G. "The Political Organization of an Arab Tribe of the Hadhramaut." (Ph.D. dissertation.) London: London School of Economics, 1961.

Hassa, Yassin A., Fereydoun Arfaa, and Mohammed Haggar. "Studies on Schistosomiasis in Taiz Province, Yemen Arab Republic," *Tropical Medicine and Hygiene*, 32, No. 5, 1983, 1023-28.

Hebert, Mary. *Community Structure and Participation*. Ithaca: Cornell University Press, 1983.

Heller, Mark, et al. *The Middle East Military Balance, 1983.* Boulder: Westview Press, 1983.

Hermann, Jens. *Ambition and Reality: Planning for Health and Basic Health Services in the Yemen Arab Republic.* Frankfurt: Lang, 1979.

Hitti, Philip K. *Islam: A Way of Life*. Minneapolis: University of Minnesota Press, 1970.

Hodgson, Marshall C.S. *The Venture of Islam. The Classical Age of Islam*, 1. Chicago: University of Chicago Press, 1974.

Hofmann, Michael. *Development Potential and Policies in the South Arabian Countries: Yemen Arab Republic, People's Democratic Republic of Yemen, Sultanate of Oman.* Berlin: German Development Institute, 1982.

Hottinger, Arnold. "The Depth of Arab Radicalism," *Foreign Affairs*, 51, No. 3, April 1973, 491-504.

Hourani, George Tadlo. *Arab Seafaring*. Beirut: Khayats, 1963.

Ingrams, Doreen. *A Survey of Social and Economic Conditions in the Aden Protectorate.* Eritrea: Government Printer, 1949.

———. *A Time in Arabia*. London: Murray, 1970.

Ingrams, Harold. *Arabia and the Isles.* London: Murray, 1966.

______. *The Yemens, Imams, Rulers, and Revolution.* London: Murray, 1963.

International Monetary Fund. "Yemen, P.D. Rep.," *International Fiscal Statistics*, May 1985, 494-95.

Iungerich, Raphael. "USCENTOM Is Not Alone," *Armed Forces Journal International*, October 1984, 106-107.

Jafri, S. Husain M. *Origins and Early Development of Shia Islam.* London: Longman, 1979.

Jenner, Michael. *Yemen Rediscovered.* London: Longman and the Yemen Tourism Company, 1983.

Joint Publications Research Service—JPRS (Washington). The following items are from the JPRS series: *Near East/South Asia Report.*

"Ali Nasir Muhammad 'exclusive interview' with Ariel Zapata, Prensa Latina Reporter," *Granma*, Havana, October 23, 1983. (JPRS 84846, No. 2857, November 30, 1983, 127-30).

"An Attempt to Evaluate Yemen's Foreign Policy," *Al-Thawrah*, Sanaa, November 1982. (JPRS 83032, No. 2717, March 8, 1983, 151-53).

"Briefs: New Intelligence Unit," *Al-Wahdah*, Cairo, September 15, 1983. (JPRS 84887, No. 2861, December 6, 1983, 69).

"Cabinet Statement Underlines Cabinet's Abidance by Bases and Principles Contained in Brother Leader and President's Message to Chairman and Members of New Cabinet," *Al-Thawrah*, Sanaa, December 26, 1983. (JPRS 84-035, March 2, 1984, 38-62).

"Comrade Haydar Abu-Bakr al-Attas, Member of the Politburo, Prime Minister," *Al-Thawri*, Aden, February 16, 1985. (JPRS NEA 85-034, March 25, 1985, 124).

"Development of the Revolutionary Process and Leading Role of the Party in Democratic Yemen," *Partinyaya Zhizh*, Moscow, June 1983. (JPRS 84958, No. 2867, December 15, 1983, 115-19).

"The First Congress of the National Grouping is Held in a Democratic Atmosphere and Elects the Members of the National Council," *Al Wahdah*, Cairo, January 20, 1984. (JPRS NEA 84-062, April 12, 1984, 105-11).

"Foiled Coup Attempt," *Kuna*, Kuwait, November 3, 1984. (JPRS 85-002, January 7, 1985, 20).

"Friendship, Cooperation Treaty," *Al-Mustaqbal*, Paris, October 20, 1984. (JPRS 84-185, December 21, 1984, 148).

"Geological Survey Talks for Yemens Conducted," *Al-Thawrah*, Sanaa, September 7, 1983. (JPRS 84752, November 15, 1983, 113).

"Guerrilla Training Camps," *Al-Wahdah*, Cairo, September 15, 1983. (JPRS 84887, No. 2816, December 6, 1983, 70).

"Interview with Mr. Abd-al-Qawi Makkawi, Secretary General of the National Grouping of Patriotic Forces, by Muhammad Shudri," *Al-Wahdah*, Cairo, February 15, 1984. (JPRS 84-066, April 23, 1984, 47-51).

"Leader President and General Secretary Issues Decree Organizing President's Office and Defining Its Powers," *Al-Thawrah*, Sanaa, November 22, 1983. (JPRS 84-033, March 1, 1984, 133-36).

"Opposition Group Leader Interviewed," *Al-Wahdah*, Cairo, May 15, 1983. (JPRS 84298, No. 2819, September 12, 1983, 10-15).

"PDRY: New Intelligence Unit," *Al-Wahdah*, Cairo, September 15, 1983. (JPRS 83-2861, December 6, 1983).

"Republic Decree to Establish and Organize Secretariat General of General Federation of Yemeni Expatriates," *Al-Thawrah*, Sanaa, May 7, 1984. (JPRS 84-105, July 9, 1984, 123-27).

"The Second Sessions of the Yemeni Council Took Place under Many Positive National Circumstances," *Uktuhar*, Aden, February 20, 1984. (JPRS 84-061, April 11, 1984, 108-15).

"YSP Central Committee on Future Plans," *Aden Domestic Service in Arabic*, Aden, September 28, 1984. (JPRS NEA 84-157, October 14, 1984, 85-86).

Joseph, Souad. "North Yemen: Taawun Mahit: A Case Study of a Local Development Association in Highland Yemen." In Louis J. Cantori and Iliya Harik (eds.), *Local Politics and Development in the Middle East*. Boulder: Westview Press, 1984.

Katz, Mark N. "Moscow's Double-track Policy: Sanaa and the Soviets," *Problems of Communism*, 33, No. 1, January-February 1984, 21-34.

Kennedy, John G., James Teague, and Lynn Fairbanks. "Qat Use in North Yemen and the Problem of Addiction: A Study in Medical Anthropology," *Culture, Medicine, and Psychiatry* [Dortrecht, Netherlands], 4, 1980, 311-44.

Kennedy, John G., et al. "A Medical Evaluation of the Use of Qat in North Yemen," *Social Science and Medicine* [London], 17, No. 12, 1983, 783-93.

Kour, Z.H. *The History of Aden, 1839-1872*. Totowa, New Jersey: Cass, 1981.

Kruse, Hans. "Tribal Systems and Social Stratification: The Case of North Yemen," *Indian Journal of Political Science* [Delhi], 40, No. 3, September 1979, 380-94.

Kutschera, Chris. "Ali Nasser Muhammad," *The Middle East* [London], No. 93, July 1982, 28.

______. "Snags in Boosting Aden's Production," *The Middle East* [London], 96, October 1982, 70-71.

______. "South Yemen: A Slow Move Towards the West," *The Middle East* [London], No. 94, August 1982, 20-21.

Labaune, Patrick. "Administration et société en République Arabe du Yemen: Tentative d'analyse centre/périphérie," *Peuples méditerranéens* [Paris], 16, July 1981, 131-44.

______. "Democratic Tribale et Système politique en République Arabe du Yemen," *L'Afrique et l'Asie modernes* [Paris], 129, 1981, 12-32.

Lackner, Helen. "The Rise of the National Liberation Front as a Political Organization." Pages 46-62 in B.R. Pridham (ed.), *Contemporary Yemen: Politics and Historical Background*. New York: St. Martin's Press, 1984.

Legum, Colin, et al. (eds.). *Middle East Contemporary Survey, Vol. 6: 1981-1982*. New York: Holmes and Meier, 1984.

Levy, Reuben. *The Social Structure of Islam*. (2d ed.) Cambridge: Cambridge University Press, 1969.

Lewis, Bernard. *The Origins of Ismailism: A Study of the Historical Background of the Fatimid Caliphate*. New York: AMS Press, 1975.

Liebesny, Herbert J. *The Law of the Near and Middle East: Readings, Cases, and Materials*. Albany: State University of New York Press, 1975.

Little, Tom. *South Arabia, Arena of Conflict.* New York: Praeger, 1968.

Luqman and Danowski, T.S. "The Use of Khat (*Catha edulis*) in Yemen Social and Medical Observations," *Annals of Internal Medicine*, 85, No. 2, August 1976, 246-49.

Lynch, John B. "The Superpowers' Tug of War over Yemen," *Military Review*, 61, No. 3, March 1981, 10-21.

Macro, Eric. *Bibliography on Yemen and Notes on Mocha.* Miami: University of Miami Press, 1960.

———. *Yemen and the Western World since 1571.* New York: Praeger, 1968.

Madelung, W. "Ismaliyya." Pages 198-206 in E. Van Donzel, B. Lewis, and C. Pellat (eds.), *Encyclopedia of Islam* (New ed.), 4. Leiden: Brill, 1973.

Makhlouf, Carla. *Changing Veils: Women and Modernization in Yemen.* London: Croom Helm, 1979.

Makinda, Samuel. "Shifting Alliances in the Horn of Africa," *Survival*, 28, No. 1, January-February 1985, 11-19.

Messick, Brinkley. "Prosecution in Yemen: The Introduction of the *Niyaba*," *International Journal of Middle East Studies*, 15, No. 4, 1983, 507-18.

———. *Transactions in Ibb: Economy and Society in a Yemeni Highland Town.* (Ph.D. dissertation, Department of Anthropology, Princeton University, 1978.) Ann Arbor: Xerox University Microfilms, DDJ78-18379.

The Military Balance, 1984-1985. London: International Institute for Strategic Studies, 1984.

Molyneux, Maxine. "State Policy and the Position of Women in South Yemen," *Peuples méditerranéens* [Paris], No. 12, July-September 1980, 33-41.

———. "Women and Revolution in the People's Democratic Republic of Yemen," *Feminist Review*, 1, No. 1, 1979, 4-19.

Moosa, Ebrahim. "South Yemen's Five-Year Plans 'A Disaster'," *Arabia, The Islamic World Review* [London], No. 23, July 1983, 66-67.

Mundy, Martha. "Women's Inheritance of Land in Highland Yemen," *Arabian Studies*, 5, 1979, 161-87.

Mylroie, Laurie. *Politics and the Soviet Presence in the People's Democratic Republic of Yemen: Internal Vulnerabilities and Regional Challenges.* Santa Monica: Rand, 1983.

Myntti, Cynthia. "Population Processes in Rural Yemeni, Temporary Emigration, Breastfeeding, and Contraception," *Studies in Family Planning*, 10, 1979, 282-89.

______. *Women and Development in the Yemen Arab Republic*. Eschborn: German Agency for Technical Cooperation, 1979.

______. "Yemeni Workers Abroad: The Impact on Women," *MERIP Reports*, June 1984, 11-16.

"Nasir Muhammad Resigns as Prime Minister," Foreign Broadcast Information Service, *Daily Report: Middle East and Africa*, 5, No. 032 (FBIS-MEA-85-032), February 15, 1985, C2-C5.

"Nation-Building and Political Developments in the Two Yemens." Pages 85-101 in B.R. Pridham (ed.), *Contemporary Yemen: Politics and Historical Background*. New York: St. Martin's Press, 1984.

1983 World Bank Atlas. Washington: International Bank for Reconstruction and Development, World Bank, 1983.

Nini, Yehuda. "The Jews of Sheba, or the Unknown Land of Yemen." In *The Jews of San'a as Seen by the Researchers Hermann Burrhardt and Carl Rathjens*. Tel Aviv: Beth Hatefutsoth, Nahum Goldmann Museum of the Jewish Diaspora, 1982.

"North Yemen: Economic Background Report," *Middle East Currency Reports* [London], September 1984, 1-26.

Nyrop, Richard F. (ed.). *Persian Gulf States: Country Studies*. (DA Pam 550-185.) Washington: GPO for Foreign Area Studies, The American University, 1985.

______. *Saudi Arabia: A Country Study*. (DA Pam 550-51.) Washington: GPO for Foreign Area Studies, The American University, 1985.

O'Ballance, Edgar. *The War in the Yemen*. Hamden, Connecticut: Archon Books, 1971.

Obermeyer, G. "Al-Iman and al-Imam: Ideology and State in the Yemen: 1900-1948." Pages 165-80 in M. Buheiry (ed.), *Intellectual Life in the Arab East, 1890-1939*. Beirut: AUB Center for Arab and Middle East Studies, 1981.

"Offers Sought for Health Institute," *Middle East Economic Digest* [London], March 8, 1985, 38.

"PDRY 1 Libya," *Defense and Foreign Affairs Weekly*, 10, No. 41, October 21-28, 1984.

People's Democratic Republic of Yemen. Ministry of Planning Central Statistical Organization. *Statistical Year Book, 1983*. Aden: September 1984.

"The People's Democratic Republic of Yemen." Pages 759-75 in Colin Legum (ed.), *Middle East Contemporary Survey, Vol. 6: 1981-82*. New York: Holmes and Meier, 1984.

Peterson, J.E. "Legitimacy and Political Change in Yemen and Oman," *Orbis*, 28, No. 4, Winter 1984, 971-98.

______. *Yemen: The Search for a Modern State*. Baltimore: Johns Hopkins University Press, 1982.

Piepenburg, Fritz. *Traveller's Guide to Yemen*. Sanaa: Yemen Tourism Company, 1983.

Pillsbury, Barbara. *Traditional Health Care in the Near East. (Research paper.) A Report Prepared for the U.S. Agency for International Development*. Washington: A.I.D., March 1978.

Political Handbook of the World, 1982-1983. New York: McGraw-Hill, 1983.

Population Reference Bureau. *1984 World Population Data Sheet of the Population Reference Bureau, Inc.*Washington: April 1984.

______. *1985 World Population Data Sheet of the Population Reference Bureau, Inc.* Washington: April 1985.

Pradas, Alfred B. "Trilateral Military Aid in the Middle East: The Yemen Program." (Conference paper.) Washington: National Defense University, 1979.

Pridham, B.R. (ed.). *Contemporary Yemen: Politics and Historical Background*. New York: St. Martin's Press, 1984.

"Prime Minister Interviewed on Cabinet Reshuffle," Foreign Broadcast Information Service, *Daily Report: Middle East and North Africa*, 5, No. 42 (FBIS-MEA-85-042), March 4, 1985, C3-C4.

Rouleau, Eric. "Yemen Arab Republic: Corrupting Petrodollars," *Le Monde* [Paris], 126, No. 26, June 27, 1982, 12.

Schacht, Joseph. *An Introduction to Islamic Law*. Oxford: Clarendon Press, 1964.

Serjeant, R.B. "Historical Review." Pages 3-31 in A.J. Arberry (ed.), *Religions in the Middle East: Three Religions in Concord and Conflict, II: Islam*. Cambridge: Cambridge University Press, 1969.

______. *The Portuguese off the South Arabian Coast*. London: Oxford University Press, 1963.

______. *The Saiyids of Hadramawt.* London: School of Oriental and African Studies, University of London, 1957.

______. "The Two Yemens: Historical Perspectives and Present Attitudes," *Asian Affairs* [London]. 60, No. 1 (New Series), February 1973, 3-16.

______. "The Zaydis." Pages 285-301 in A.J. Arberry (ed.), *Religions in the Middle East: Three Religions in Concord and Conflict, II: Islam.* Cambridge: Cambridge University Press, 1969.

Shamiry, Naguib A.R. "The Judicial System in Democratic Yemen." Pages 175-94 in B.R. Pridham (ed.), *Contemporary Yemen: Politics and Historical Background.* New York: St. Martin's Press, 1984.

Smith, Pamela A. "PDR Yemen." Pages 307-309 in *Middle East Review, 1984.* (10th ed.). Essex, England: World of Information, 1984.

"Spreading the Word in Rural Yemen," *The Middle East* [London], No. 122, December 1984, 47-48.

Steffen, Hans. *Population Geography of the Yemen Arab Republic: The Major Findings of the Population and Housing Census of February 1975 and of Supplementary Demographic and Cartographic Surveys.* Wiesbaden. Reichert, 1979.

Steffen, Hans, and Urs Geiser. *Yemen Arab Republic—Preliminary Report No. 5: Databank of Yemen's Population and Housing Census, 1975.* Zurich: Swiss Technical Cooperation Service, May 1977.

Stookey, Robert W. *The Politics of the Yemen Arab Republic.* Boulder: Westview Press, 1978.

______. "Religion and Politics in South Arabia." Pages 349-62 in Michael Curtis (ed.), *Religion and Politics in the Middle East.* Boulder: Westview Press, 1981.

______. "Social Structure and Politics in the Yemen Arab Republic," Pt. 1, *Middle East Journal*, 28, No. 3, Summer 1974, 248-60.

______. "Social Structure and Politics in the Yemen Arab Republic," Pt. 2, *Middle East Journal*, 28, No. 4, Autumn 1974, 409-18.

______. *South Yemen: A Marxist Republic in Arabia.* Boulder: Westview Press, 1982.

______. "Yemen: Revolution Versus Tradition." Pages 79-108 in Robert W. Stookey (ed.), *The Arabian Peninsula—Zone of Ferment.* Stanford: Hoover Institution Press, 1984.

Swanson, Jon C. *Emigration and Economic Development: The Case of the Yemen Arab Republic*. Boulder: Westview Press, 1979.

Swanson, Jon C., and Mary Hebert. *Rural Society and Participatory Development: Case Studies of Two Villages in the Yemen Arab Republic*. Ithaca: Cornell University Press, 1981.

Sweet, Louise E. "The Arabian Peninsula." Pages 199-266 in Louise Sweet (ed.), *The Central Middle East*. New Haven: HRAF Press, 1971.

Tabatai, Allaman Sayyid Muhammad Husayn. *Shiite Islam*. London: George Allen and Unwin, 1975.

"10th Session of YSC Secretariat Begins in Aden," Foreign Broadcast Information Service, *Daily Report: Middle East and North Africa*, 5, No. 080 (FBIS-MEA-85-080), April 25, 1985, C5-C6.

Trevaskis, Sir Kennedy. *Shades of Amber: A South Arabian Episode*. London: Hutchinson, 1968.

United Nations. "Population Policy Briefs: Current Situation in Developing Countries, 1983." New York: February 21, 1984.

United Nations. Conference on Trade and Development. Secretariat. "Democratic Yemen." Pages 126-29 in *The Least Developed Countries 1984 Report and Annex: Basic Data*. New York: 1984.

———. "Yemen." Pages 214-16 in *The Least Developed Countries 1984 Report and Annex: Basic Data*. New York: 1984.

United Nations. Economic Commission for Western Asia. *The Population Situation in the ECWA Region, Democratic Yemen*. Beirut: 1979.

———. *The Population Situation in the ECWA Region, Democratic Yemen*. Beirut: 1980.

United Nations Fund for Population Activities. *People's Democratic Republic of Yemen Report of Mission Needs Assessment for Population Assistance: Report Number 7*. New York: November 1978.

United Nations. General Assembly Conference on the Least Developed Countries. Secretariat. "Democratic Yemen." Pages 1-9 in *United Nations Conference on the Least Developed Countries, Paris, 1 September 1981*. Paris: 1981.

United States. Agency for International Development. *Near East: Yemen Arab Republic Statistical Data by Sex.* Washington: 1981.

United States. Central Intelligence Agency. Directorate of Intelligence. *Chiefs of State and Cabinet Members of Foreign Governments.* Washington: April 1985.

United States. Congress. 96th, 1st Session. House of Representatives. Committee on Foreign Affairs. Subcommittee on Europe and the Middle East. *Proposed Arms Transfer to the Yemen Arab Republic.* Washington: GPO, 1979.

United States. Congress. 97th, 2d Session. House of Representatives. Subcommittee on Europe and the Middle East. *U.S. Policy Toward the Persian Gulf.* Washington: GPO, 1983.

United States. Department of Defense. *Soviet Military Power, 1985.* Washington: GPO, 1985.

United States. Department of State. *Country Reports on Human Rights Practices for 1984.* (Report submitted to United States Congress, 99th, 1st Session, Senate, Committee on Foreign Relations, and House of Representatives, Committee on Foreign Affairs.) Washington: GPO, February 1985.

Vaglieri, Laura Veccia. "The Patriarchal and Umayyad Caliphates." Pages 57-103 in P.M. Holt, Ann K.S. Lambton, and Bernard Lewis (eds.), *The Cambridge History of Islam, Vol. 1: The Central Islamic Lands.* London: Cambridge University Press, 1970.

Van Beek, Gus W. "The Rise and Fall of Arabia Felix," *Scientific American*, 211, No. 6, December 1969, 36-44.

Varisco, Daniel Martin. "Irrigation in an Arabian Valley: A System of Highland Terraces in the Yemen Arab Republic," *Expedition*, 25, No. 2, Winter 1983, 26-34.

Waterfield, Gordon. *Sultans of Aden.* London: Murray, 1968.

Watt, W. Montgomery. *Islamic Political Thought.* Edinburgh: Edinburgh University Press, 1968.

———. *Muhammad: Prophet and Statesman.* London: Oxford University Press, 1961.

"Weekly Update: PDRY," *Defense and Foreign Affairs Weekly*, 11, No. 7, February 25-March 3, 1985.

Wenner, Manfred W. *Modern Yemen: 1918-1966.* Baltimore: Johns Hopkins Press, 1967.

______. *North Yemen*. Boulder: Westview Press, 1981.

______. "The People's Republic of South Yemen." Pages 412-29 in Tareq Y. Ismael et al., *Governments and Politics of the Contemporary Middle East*. Homewood, Illinois: Dorsey Press, 1970.

______. "South Yemen since Independence: An Arab Political Maverick." Pages 125-46 in B.R. Pridham (ed.), *Contemporary Yemen: Politics and Historical Background*. New York: St. Martin's Press, 1984.

______. "Yemen." Pages 380-411 in Tareq Y. Ismael et al., *Governments and Politics of the Contemporary Middle East*. Homewood, Illinois: Dorsey Press, 1970.

Wenner, Manfred W., and Lealan N. Swanson. *An Introduction to Yemen for Researchers and Scholars*. (Yemen Guide Series, No. 1.) Portland: American Institute for Yemeni Studies, May 1984.

Williams, John Alden (ed.). *Islam*. New York: Braziller, 1962.

World Bank. *People's Democratic Republic of Yemen: A Review of Economic and Social Development*. Washington: 1979.

______. *Yemen Arab Republic: Development of a Traditional Economy*. Washington: 1979.

The World Factbook, 1984. Washington: United States Central Intelligence Agency, 1984.

Wrase, Michael. "South Yemen: A Soviet Outpost," *Swiss Review of World Affairs* [Zurich], July 1979, 25-27.

Yearbook on International Communist Affairs, 1984. Stanford: Hoover Institution Press, 1984.

Yemen Arab Republic. Central Planning Organization. Statistics Department. *Statistical Yearbook, 1981*. Sanaa: 1982.

______. *Statistical Year Book, 1982*. Sanaa: 1983.

______. *Statistical Yearbook, 1983*. Sanaa: 1984.

Yemen Arab Republic. Prime Minister's Office. Central Planning Organization. *The Second Five-Year Plan, 1982-86*. N. pl. n. d.

Zabarah, Mohammed Ahmad. "The Yemen Revolution of 1962—Seen as a Social Revolution." Pages 76-84 in B.R. Pridham (ed.), *Contemporary Yemen: Politics and Historical Background*. New York: St. Martin's Press, 1984.

______. *Yemen: Traditionalism vs. Modernity*. New York: Praeger, 1982.

(Various issues of the following publications were also used in the preparation of this book: *Arabia: The Islamic World Review* [London]; *Christian Science Monitor*; *Deadline Data on World Affairs*; Economist Intelligence Unit, *Quarterly Economic Review (Bahrain, Qatar, Oman, and the Yemens)* [London]; *Financial Times* [London]; Foreign Broadcast Information Service, *Daily Report: Middle East and North Africa*; *IMF Survey*; *International Financial Statistics*; Joint Publications Research Service, *Near East/South Asia Report*; *Keesing's Contemporary Archives* [London]; *Manchester Guardian Weekly* [London], *Middle East* [London]; *Middle East Economic Digest* [London]; *New York Times*; and *Washington Post*.)

Glossary

banu—Plural of *ibn* (*q.v.*); used to designate tribe or clan.

bint—Daughter of.

dinar, Yemeni (YD)—The Indian rupee was the only legal tender in Aden Colony until 1951, when the colony joined the East African Currency Board. The East African shilling replaced the rupee as legal tender in Aden and circulated widely, although metallic coins of many nations also circulated in the hinterland. In 1964 the Federation of South Arabia established its own currency board, which issued the South Arabian dinar, consisting of 1,000 fils; it was equal to one British pound sterling and to US $2.80. The dinar was devalued in 1967 in line with the British pound devaluation (one pound and one dinar equaled US $2.40). In 1968 the currency was renamed the Southern Yemen dinar, and in 1971 it was renamed the Yemeni dinar. The dinar's value in terms of dollars rose in the early 1970s as the dollar was devalued. One dinar averaged US $2.40 in 1970, US $2.407 in 1971, US $2.606 in 1972, US $2.862 in 1973, and US $2.895 in 1974 (essentially US $2.90), a value it retained at least through February 1985.

fiscal year (North Yemen)—Since January 1, 1981, the fiscal year has coincided with the Gregorian calendar year. Before 1981 the fiscal year began July 1 and ended June 30.

fiscal year (South Yemen)—Until 1975, from April 1 through March 31. The fiscal year for 1975 ended December 31, amounting to only nine months. Beginning in 1976 the fiscal year became the same as the Gregorian calendar year.

GDP (gross domestic product)—A value measure of the flow of domestic goods and services produced by an economy over a period of time, such as a year. Only output values of goods for final consumption and investment are included because the values of primary and intermediate production are assumed to be included in final prices. GDP is sometimes aggregated and shown at market prices, meaning that indirect taxes and subsidies are included; when these have been eliminated, the result is GDP at factor cost. The word *gross* indicates that deductions for depreciation of physical assets have not been made. *See also* GNP.

GNP (gross national product)—The gross domestic product (GDP—*q.v.*) plus the net income or loss stemming from transactions with foreign countries. For both North Yemen and South Yemen, GNP is usually larger than GDP because of remittances from workers abroad. GNP is the broadest measure of the output of goods and services by an economy. It can be calculated at market prices, which include indirect taxes and subsidies. Because indirect taxes and subsidies are only transfer payments, GNP is often calculated at factor cost by removing indirect taxes and subsidies.

hijra (pl., *hujar*)—Literally, to migrate, to sever relations, to leave one's tribe. Used in two senses. Throughout the Muslim world hijra refers to the migration to Medina of Muhammad and his early followers. In this sense the word has come into European languages as Hegira and is usually and misleadingly translated as "flight." In the area that is now North Yemen, a traditional process by which a holy man would accept an invitation to join a tribe or a group of tribes as judge or mediator. Also, a neutral sanctuary maintained by a mediator.

ibn (or *bin*)—Son of.

imam—A word used in several senses. In general use it means the leader of congregational prayers; as such it implies no ordination or special spiritual powers beyond sufficient education to carry out this function. It is also used figuratively by many Sunni (*q.v.*) Muslims to mean the leader of the Islamic community. Among Shia (*q.v.*) the word takes on many complex and controversial meanings; in general, however, and particularly when capitalized, it indicates that particular descendant of the House of Ali who is believed to have been God's designated repository of the spiritual authority inherent in that line. The identity of this individual and the means of ascertaining his identity have been the major issues causing divisions among Shia. Until deposed in a military coup in 1962, the Zaydi imams ruled what became North Yemen and at times parts of present-day South Yemen as absolute secular and temporal rulers.

International Monetary Fund (IMF)—Established along with the World Bank (*q.v.*) in 1945, the IMF is a specialized agency affiliated with the United Nations and is responsible for stabilizing international exchange rates and payments. The main business of the IMF is the provision of loans to its members (including industrialized and developing countries) when they experience balance of payments difficulties. These loans frequently carry conditions that require substantial internal economic adjustments by the recipients, most of which are developing countries.

jihad—The struggle to establish the law of God on earth, both within oneself and in relations with others; often interpreted to mean holy war.

qadi (Arabic pl., *quda*)—Judge of Islamic law (sharia). In North Yemen also refers to a traditional class of educated bureaucrats who might or might not be judges.

rial, Yemeni (YR)—The national currency consisting of 100 fils. The average value of rials per US $1 fluctuated from 2.79 in 1968; 4.44 in 1969; 5.50 in 1970; 5.43 in 1971; 4.69 in 1972; 4.62 in 1973; and 4.57 in 1974. From 1975 through 1982 the rial remained stable at YR4.56 per US $1. In 1983 the rial was unpegged from the dollar and began to decline, averaging YR4.58 per US $1 in 1983 and YR5.35 per US $1 in 1984.

sayyid (Arabic pl., *sada*)—Those who claim direct descent from the Prophet Muhammad.

sharif (Arabic pl., *ashraf*)—Specifically, a descendant of a member of the Prophet's family, the Hashim. In general use means noble, exalted, or having descent from illustrious ancestors. Frequently used as an honorific.

Shia (from Shiat Ali, the party of Ali)—A member of the smaller of the two great divisions of Islam. The Shia supported the claims of Ali and his line to presumptive right to the caliphate and leadership of the Muslim community, and on this issue they divided from the Sunni (*q.v.*) in the major schism within Islam. Later schisms have produced further divisions among the Shia over the identity and number of imams (*q.v.*).

Sunni (from Sunna, orthodox)—A member of the larger of the two great divisions of Islam. The Sunnis supported the traditional method of election to the caliphate and accepted the Umayyad line. On this issue they divided from the Shia (*q.v.*) in the first great schism within Islam.

Wahhabi—Name used outside Saudi Arabia to designate adherents to Wahhabism (*q.v.*).

Wahhabism—Name used outside Saudi Arabia to designate official interpretation of Islam in Saudi Arabia. The faith is an austere concept of Unitarianism (the call to the oneness or unity of God) that was preached by Muhammad bin Abd al Wahhab, whence his Muslim opponents derived the name.

World Bank—Informal name used to designate a group of three affiliated international institutions: the International Bank for Reconstruction and Development (IBRD), the International Development Association (IDA), and the International Finance Corporation (IFC). The primary purpose of the IBRD, established in 1945, is to provide loans to developing countries for productive projects. The IDA, a legally separate loan fund but administered by the staff of the IBRD, was set up in 1960 to furnish credits to the poorest developing countries on much easier terms than those of conventional IBRD loans. The IFC, founded in 1956, supplements the activities of the IBRD through loans and assistance designed specifically to encourage the growth of productive private enterprises in the less developed countries. The president and certain senior officers of the IBRD hold the same positions in the IFC. The three institutions are owned by the governments of the countries that subscribe their capital. To participate in the World Bank group, member states must first belong to the International Monetary Fund (IMF—*q.v.*).

Index

Index

Published Country Studies

(Area Handbook Series)

550-65	Afghanistan	550-151	Honduras
550-98	Albania	550-165	Hungary
550-44	Algeria	550-21	India
550-50	Angola	550-154	Indian Ocean
550-73	Argentina	550-39	Indonesia
550-169	Australia	550-68	Iran
550-176	Austria	550-31	Iraq
550-175	Bangladesh	550-25	Israel
550-170	Belgium	550-182	Italy
550-66	Bolivia	550-69	Ivory Coast
550-20	Brazil	550-177	Jamaica
550-168	Bulgaria	550-30	Japan
550-61	Burma	550-34	Jordan
550-83	Burundi	550-56	Kenya
550-50	Cambodia	550-81	Korea, North
550-177	Cameroon	550-41	Korea, South
550-159	Chad	550-58	Laos
550-77	Chile	550-24	Lebanon
550-60	China	550-38	Liberia
550-63	China, Republic of	550-85	Libya
550-26	Colombia	550-172	Malawi
550-91	Congo	550-45	Malaysia
550-90	Costa Rica	550-161	Mauritania
550-152	Cuba	550-79	Mexico
550-22	Cyprus	550-76	Mongolia
550-158	Czechoslovakia	550-49	Morocco
550-54	Dominican Republic	550-64	Mozambique
550-52	Ecuador	550-35	Nepal, Bhutan and Sikkim
550-43	Egypt	550-88	Nicaragua
550-150	El Salvador	550-157	Nigeria
550-28	Ethiopia	550-94	Oceania
550-167	Finland	550-48	Pakistan
550-155	Germany, East	550-46	Panama
550-173	Germany, Fed. Rep. of	550-156	Paraguay
550-153	Ghana	550-185	Persian Gulf States
550-87	Greece	550-42	Peru
550-78	Guatemala	550-72	Philippines
550-174	Guinea	550-162	Poland
550-82	Guyana	550-181	Portugal
550-164	Haiti	550-160	Romania

550-84	Rwanda	550-178	Trinidad and Tobago
550-51	Saudi Arabia		
550-70	Senegal	550-89	Tunisia
550-180	Sierra Leone	550-80	Turkey
550-184	Singapore	550-74	Uganda
		550-97	Uruguay
550-86	Somalia	550-71	Venezuela
550-93	South Africa		
550-95	Soviet Union	550-57	Vietnam, North
550-179	Spain	550-55	Vietnam, South
550-96	Sri Lanka (Ceylon)	550-183	Yemens, The
		550-99	Yugoslavia
550-27	Sudan	550-67	Zaire
550-47	Syria		
550-62	Tanzania	550-75	Zambia
550-53	Thailand	550-171	Zimbabwe

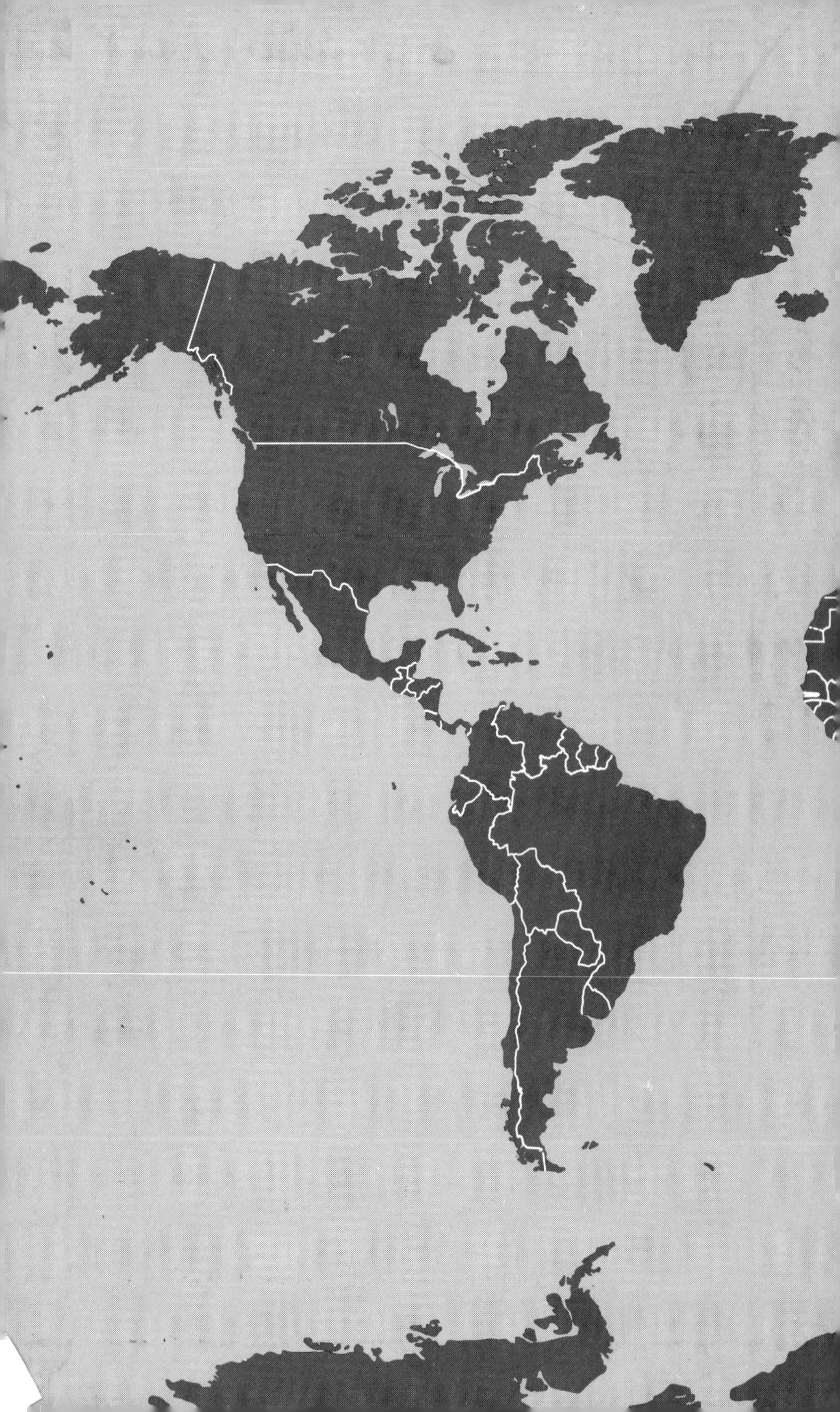